Freedom and the
Foundation

ALFRED A. KNOPF

New York 1969

Thomas C. Reeves

Freedom *and the* Foundation

The Fund for the Republic in the Era of McCarthyism

THIS IS A BORZOI BOOK
PUBLISHED BY ALFRED A. KNOPF, INC.

First Edition
Copyright ©1969 by Thomas C. Reeves
All rights reserved under International and
Pan-American Copyright Conventions. Published in the United States
by Alfred A. Knopf, Inc., New York, and simultaneously
in Canada by Random House of Canada Limited, Toronto.
Distributed by Random House, Inc., New York.
Library of Congress Catalog Card Number: 70–79315
Manufactured in the United States of America

To Irving F. Laucks

For several years, the moderate, the respectable, and serious elements in our political élite have allowed themselves to be bullied and misled by a very small minority of vociferous demagogues and their febrile popular following. The moderates, fearing that they were perhaps out of touch with the true course of opinion, accepted the leadership, the perspective, and the standards of a handful of men who claimed to speak for the populace. Nothing could have been less justified or more unwise.

The time has now come for these errors of judgment and political tactics to be rectified. Let the respectable moderates, the true liberals in both parties, take the lead in the rediscovery of the obviously sensible thing to do about security—to make secure what needs to be secure for purposes of national military strength—and let all else go free. They will be surprised to discern the calming effects this will have on American opinion and how much assent they will find for the policy. They will be remembered for years to come for their reinstatement of America's good name in the world, and they will have earned the appreciation of all who prize freedom and America's embodiment of it.

—EDWARD SHILS

There can be no education without controversy.

—H. ROWAN GAITHER

Preface

Few shafts of light have penetrated the carefully constructed façades of America's numerous, powerful, and exceedingly wealthy tax-exempt foundations. Highly sensitive to the public and political pressures inherent in their possession of billions of tax-exempt dollars, foundations have been loath to open their files to those seeking to explore dispassionately their motives, methods, and achievements. Some information is available. Since 1963 the Internal Revenue Service has made public a few pertinent facts through revised regulations of annual tax reports, currently no more than a few hundred of the more than 20,000 foundations issue reports on their expenditures, and New York's Foundation Center houses narrow data on a minority of these philanthropic bodies. Moreover, Congressman Wright Patman and his Subcommittee of the House Small Business Committee have revealed, in a series of penetrating studies, dubious financial activities to which a few foundations have been prone, while others have called attention to disturbing ties between foundations and universities and American foreign policy. There is a small formal literature on foundations, but almost all of it smacks heavily of the public-relations firm and is designed to counter charges by critics suspicious of the growing trend toward tax "avoidance." A recent volume of this nature cites as its central issue the question: "Does the positive record of the American philanthropic foundations justify the continuing existence of these tax-free institutions?" Overall, our knowledge of foundations is extremely meager.

The tradition of secretiveness was ruptured in late 1963 when the officers of the Fund for the Republic submitted to the entreaty of a rather brash young graduate student, allowing him complete access to the foundation's minutes, records, and collected papers to assist in the creation of a Ph.D. dissertation. The officials knew that they had been participants in a novel, personally exciting, and very controversial venture, and, having nothing to conceal—including a little pride—they accepted the young man's contention that the story of their efforts might be informative and instructive.

When I first saw the Fund's half-ton of collected materials, it had been reduced by a fire three years earlier to a burned and water-soaked rubble. In return for being permitted to probe this mountain of memorabilia, it was agreed that I would expend every effort toward restoration of the files for their transmission to the library of Princeton University, a two-year labor which proved to be as educational as it was toilsome.

This book, an expansion of my dissertation, is not an official history, and the author accepts full responsibility for its interpretations and whatever defects and errors it may possess. It should be added that at no time did the officers and staff of the Fund greet the author with anything other than courtesy and frankness; no attempt was made to censor or alter a line. In this, as in so many other ways, the Fund, which has gone virtually unmentioned in formal foundation literature, has set an important and admirable precedent for the world of philanthropy.

Special thanks go to Paul G. Hoffman, and Jubal R. Parten for allowing me to examine relevant portions of their private papers. I am also greatly indebted to the following for providing perceptive and often trenchant commentary on this work at various stages of its development: Harry Ashmore, H. Arnold Barton, Alexander DeConde, Sigmund Diamond, W. H. Ferry, C. Warren Hollister, Wilbur Jacobs, Frank Keegan, Robert Kelley, Frank Kelly, Eulah Laucks, Joseph Lyford, Jubal Parten, Charles B. Spaulding, and Henry A. Turner. Professor A. Russell Buchanan is a great adviser, teacher, and friend. To my wife, Kathie, I owe more than I can possibly acknowledge.

This project was assisted by the Academic Research Committee of the University of California, Santa Barbara, and by the Council on Research and Creative Work of the University of Colorado.

References to certain documents, usually internal memoranda, have been abbreviated for the purpose of clarity. Full information on the files of the Fund may be found in the bibliography of the dissertation.

T.R.

COLORADO SPRINGS

Contents

Freedom and the Foundation

Ford's Foundation

The Revenue Act of 1935, part of the New Deal's effort to outflank Huey Long, was one of the most ambitious attempts in American history to redistribute wealth. Quite predictably, by levying an excess profits tax, dramatically increasing surtax rates, stepping up gift and capital stock taxes, and creating an estate tax which climbed to 70 per cent of excess over $50,000,000, the Administration sustained an almost unprecedented uproar from those influential few who managed to remain securely aloof from the ravages of the nation's worst economic collapse. To William Randolph Hearst the Wealth Tax was a Communist plot, to Henry Ford a "new form of destruction," a plan "to get independent institutions like ours into the hands of the money lenders."[1]

The Ford Motor Company was indeed vulnerable to such legislation. Since 1919, when the last of the minority stockholders were bought out, it had become the largest family-owned business corporation in the United States. And one of its founder's deepest fears concerned the possible loss of the family's absolute authority at his death. It now appeared probable that when that day arrived diversified ownership would be necessary to meet the government's estate-tax demands. Ford firmly believed that a way out would be found somehow, by someone. "We do not intend to be destroyed," he blustered.[2]

Little was publicly known about philanthropic foundations in 1935, aside from their association with celebrities like John D.

Rockefeller and Andrew Carnegie, who had used them even before the Sixteenth Amendment to carry out their social penance in an orderly fashion. They were tax-exempt (presumably to encourage private giving), chartered by individual states, and not required to make public accountability. Their number was small, their assets relatively modest, their gifts evidently in the public interest, and their critics few. As taxes increased, however, so did the number of these corporations; more than one tax lawyer understood the correlation.[3] Foundations were created—there is no way of knowing how often—to avoid taxes, to accumulate working capital, and to retain control of business assets. Though Henry Ford had frequently and publicly disparaged large-scale philanthropy,[4] sometime after July 1935, he, his wife, and son Edsel began consultations with lawyers culminating in the creation of what would soon become the world's richest tax-exempt foundation.

Shares of the Ford Motor Company were divided in the wills of Henry and Edsel Ford so that the Foundation would receive the 95-per-cent Class A nonvoting common stock, while the family retained control of the company with the 5-per-cent Class B voting stock. Edsel, on January 15, 1936, announced soberly that the purpose of the Ford Foundation was "to receive and administer funds for scientific, educational, and charitable purposes, all for the public welfare and for no other purpse."[5]

No one knew the value of the 3,452,900 shares of company stock when Edsel died in 1943, as they had never been on the market. But four years later, at Henry's death, the government and the family agreed on $135 a share. By now the Class A and Class B stock ratio had been revised to 90–10, and when the final 286,099 shares came to the Foundation from Henry Ford's estate the book value for the Class A stock was $417,137,580.[6] Except for the existence of the Foundation, the federal tax bill would have been $321,000,000.[7]

Until this time the Foundation's income had limited philanthropic expenditures to no more than a million dollars a year, parceled out by a small group of trustees who were closely associated with the Ford family.[8] The anticipated income from the newly acquired stock meant, however, that the Foundation's pace would have to be increased sharply to quell possible charges of tax evasion. Serious consideration was given almost immediately to a revision of the corporation's original mandate, which spoke in vague language about the general advancement of human welfare. And, to the accompaniment of much fanfare, the board of trustees was expanded to include several prestigious outsiders. Old Henry's spirit was not to be disturbed, however, for in spite of the praise heaped upon the family for the technical surrender of its fortune ("a truly spectacular gesture of self-denial," wrote Robert Heilbroner), the evidence shows that it was not forgotten whose money was being spent for the public welfare.[9] The Ford Foundation in 1948 was clearly dominated by the company's young president, the Foundation's chairman of the board, Edsel's son, Henry Ford II.

Well-meaning, earnest, thirty-one-year-old Ford, as might be expected of one of America's richest and most powerful men, issued the Foundation's significant pronouncements, posed for the publicity pictures, and selected those responsible for planning and administering expenditures. One close associate later recalled that Henry II "expressed an opinion on every project that was advanced. . . . His view was generally accepted by members of the board. I can remember one or two occasions when he was over-ruled but he was the most influential single member."[10]

In the fall of 1948, deeply impressed by the cautious, efficient ways of a young San Francisco attorney named H. Rowan Gaither, Jr., Ford selected Gaither to head an independent, blue-ribbon study committee assigned to the task of formulating the broad categories of activity for the Foundation's future. "We want the best thought available in the United States," Ford wrote to Gaither on November 22, 1948, "as to how this Foundation can most effectively and intelligently put its resources to work for human welfare."[11] The committee should "block out in general terms those critical areas where problems were most serious . . ."[12]

One year later, after traveling 250,000 miles and consulting with over a thousand experts from a wide range of disciplines, Gaither's committee produced a 125-page report which Ford called "one of the most thorough, painstaking, and significant inquiries ever made into the whole broad question of public welfare and human needs."[13] It was accepted unanimously by the trustees and for well over a decade viewed as a constitution by scores of Ford Foundation officials entrusted with the responsibility of recommending channels to occupy hundreds of millions of dollars. Like most constitutions, however, the *Study Report* would be subject to broad, even extravagant, interpretation.

The admirably written document listed "five areas for action": "The Establishment of Peace," "The Strengthening of Democracy," "The Strengthening of the Economy," "Education in a Democratic Society," and "Individual Behavior and Human Relations." Without question, the least anticipated proposal lay within the second category; it advocated the Foundation's direct attention to certain complex and potentially volatile issues concerning individual freedoms. The Foundation's interest in civil liberties and civil rights was to be based on the broad language of Section A of the Second Program Area:

> The Foundation should support activities directed toward:
> A. The elimination of restrictions on freedom of thought, inquiry, and expression in the United States, and the development of policies and procedures best adapted to protect these rights in the face of persistent international tension.[14]

Cautious language buttressed the recommendation. Cited as matters of specific concern were the military sponsorship of academic research, the military interpretation of secrecy regulations, an inadequate definition of democracy, "certain aspects of 'un-American activities' investigations, and the conditions imposed on Government employment and Government-financed fellowships."[15] It was fair to assume that included for consideration were no lesser subjects than the growing federal loyalty-security program and the hotly disputed aims and methods of the House Committee on Un-American Activities.

The Gaither committee recommended inquiries and analyses, emanating possibly from special committees designed to define the issues, propose solutions, and educate the public. Above all, the report stressed, efforts should be independent, nongovernmental, nonpartisan. "A foundation may enter controversial areas boldly and with courage as long as it maintains a nonpartisan and nonpolitical attitude and aids only those persons and agencies motivated by unselfish concern for the public good."[16]

But how likely was it in 1949 that any probe even remotely involving the tactics and assumptions of HUAC (as the House Committee was popularly known) and the loyalty-security safeguards instituted by private industry and federal, state, and local governments could remain nonpartisan? Indeed, was it possible that at any time there existed objective guidelines for the preservation of constitutional guarantees which could be discovered by careful research and disseminated by fiat for the acceptance of all reasonable men?

Personal liberties have been won, more frequently than not, by fierce struggle and sacrifice. In this nation's history only a hazy consensus has appeared over specific applications of the Bill of Rights; the First Amendment has thrown us into fits. Neither a civil war, nor the latest study on what the founding fathers "really meant," nor scores of frequently contradictory Supreme Court decisions have been able to draw more than insecure, shifting outlines of personal guarantees against governmental oppression and the tyranny of popular majorities. Major readjustments of American freedoms have usually been fraught with the partisan uproar occasioned by tamperings with vested interests, fear, and prejudice.

It is true, nevertheless, that no matter how dim the chances were for a successfully nonpartisan investigation of civil liberties in 1949, they were greater then than they would be for the next several years.

By 1949 the Truman loyalty program for federal employees had caused consternation among civil libertarians for its use of guilt by association, its failure to make the important distinction between "loyalty" and "security," its casual remembrance of the due-process clauses of the Constitution, and its suppression of nonconformity.[17] Many pieces of legislation restricting freedom of thought and expression were being passed by both houses of Congress; the Defense Department was screening the political opinions and associations of over three million workers whose employment was connected with government contracts involving "classified data," and plans were afoot to enlarge the probe by almost six times; HUAC had conducted several bizarre "investigations" and appeared inclined to step up the volume of its questionably legal exposés;[18] Whittaker Chambers and Elizabeth Bentley had testified to a web of treason spun by several former government employees, including Alger Hiss (a confidante of highly placed national figures); scores of different types of loyalty oaths were beginning to penalize the honest possessors of "subversive" thoughts and to outrage many other citizens who cherished a liberal interpretation of the First Amendment; blacklisting was being utilized, notably in the entertainment industry, against "wrong thinkers" on the word of paid private "authorities."

But Joseph McCarthy, Harold Velde, and William Jenner had yet to scour the nation for evidence to substantiate charges of "twenty years of treason" against the political party McCarthy chose to label "Commiecrat"; the Korean War had not yet fanned the fears of internal subversion into the political device Richard Nixon and others would soon find it to be; Patrick A. McCarran's Subcommittee on Internal Security had yet to make its debut; America had yet to quake at the warning by J. Edgar Hoover that the nation's Communist party membership was 43,217—with six or seven "fellow travelers" for every official conspirator. Fear and suspicion, though clearly observable, had not yet become the national mood.

The Gaither committee's recommendations for the aseptic scrutiny of problems in civil liberties might have seemed naïve to a few readers of the report in the late autumn of 1949. But after the winter snows they would appear to many, including Henry Ford II, to be positively dangerous.

To convert the whole of the report into achievements, the Ford Foundation needed a president—and fast. During 1948 and 1949 the institution received dividends totaling $50,000,000, of which the trustees, try as they might, were able to spend but a tenth. In 1948 Senator Charles W. Tobey of New Hampshire began to investigate foundations as tax dodges. From a House and Senate Conference Committee report came a section of the 1950 Revenue Act forbidding foundations to accumulate "unreasonable" surpluses.[19] And as tax lawyers began advising all foundations to spend at least 70 per cent of their annual earnings, the trustees were awed by the new 1950 Ford Motor Company dividends: $87,000,000.[20] To fill the position of president, Henry Ford II turned to a fellow automotive figure.

Paul G. Hoffman first received the offer in December 1949, while serving as Economic Cooperation Administrator.[21] A more suitable candidate than the fifty-eight-year-old Hoffman could hardly be imagined; he had fulfilled the American dream, rising in the busines world through determination and diligent effort, and proceeding into public service in the fine tradition of Bernard Baruch and Herbert Hoover. A college dropout, Hoffman had worked his way up from car salesman to dealer to president of the Studebaker Corporation. By the time he was thirty-five, he had made a million dollars. He was a Rotarian, Mason, Republican, director of the Federal Reserve Bank of Chicago, former vice-president of the Automobile Manufacturers Association, member-at-large of the National Council of the Boy Scouts of America, member of the Department of Commerce's Business Advisory Council, a councilor for the National Industrial Conference Board, author of *Marketing Used Cars* (1930) and *Seven Roads to Safety* (1939), member of ten exclusive clubs, and the possessor (at the close of 1950) of no fewer than twenty-seven honorary doctorates.[22] He was known to be a middle-of-the-road conservative and a vigorous anti-Communist; was internationally recognized as an efficient and capable administrator; and was famous as the man who made the Marshall Plan the economic miracle it was. *The New York Times* aptly described Hoffman as "an admirable combination of the salesman, the executive and the idealist."[23] What was more, he could spend money: $10,000,000,000 in the two and one half years he guided the reconstruction of Western Europe.

The Ford Foundation appointment was revealed on November 6, 1950 (effective January 1, 1951), with young Ford stating ebulliently that the corporation "could not have obtained a better person in the world." Hoffman, whose new salary was reportedly $100,000 per annum, declared with equal exuberance that "the foundation has more potentiality for contributing to freedom here and in other parts of the world than any other private organization," and added, "that is why I accepted the post with great alacrity."[24]

Ford assured Hoffman of his complete support, even if certain activities drew adverse publicity.[25] The "five areas for action," a Ford spokesman had said, were only guidelines for the new president. They were deliberately broad "so as not to tie the president's hands."[26] Hoffman concluded shortly, with words which no doubt haunted him for years: "The Ford Foundation has the biggest blank check in history."[27] One report asserted that he would have a minimum of $50,000,000 a year to spend, assuming the continuation of the Ford Motor's Company bounding profits.[28]

Though it was acknowledged publicly that the Foundation's top position would command "enormous powers," the two conditions on which Hoffman accepted the post were not published. He insisted first that the institution's planning headquarters be located near his family in Pasadena, California.[29] The second condition to which Ford and the trustees acceded was that the new president would choose his own associate directors, the first among them, if available, being Robert Maynard Hutchins.[30]

The chancellor of the University of Chicago had been a controversial figure for nearly a quarter of a century. A dashing prodigy in a bizarre decade, Hutchins had been elected secretary of Yale University at twenty-four, dean of the Yale Law School at twenty-eight, and president of the University of Chicago in 1929 at the age of thirty. While teaching at Yale, Hutchins became acquainted with a Columbia psychologist named Mortimer Adler, and the two embarked upon a series of studies which provided Hutchins with a deep attachment to the classics and scholasticism.[31] From his talks with Adler over the course of several years, and his own intensive reading, Hutchins developed and vigorously propounded a theory of education which clashed directly with the empiricism and pragmatism then fashionable. For over two decades at Chicago the tall, brilliant, strikingly handsome "boy wonder" (as many detractors delighted in calling him) lashed out at vocationalism, the training of narrow specialists, the American romance with materialism.

To Hutchins, the disciplined mind, grounded in the "Great

Books," trained in the search for truth concerning the deepest issues of human existence, was the most noble achievement of a university. Liberal education at its best, vital to democracy, necessary for the wise development of human character, ought to be required for all students, he thought. The aim of education, he once wrote, "is wisdom and goodness and . . . studies which do not bring us closer to this goal have no place in a university."[32]

During his twenty-two years at the university made famous by the innovations of William Rainey Harper, Hutchins abolished more than three hundred courses; was instrumental in the university's acquisition of the *Encyclopaedia Britannica*;[33] started, taught, and encouraged Great Books courses (later contributing to the creation of an experimental college based on the program); eliminated intercollegiate football; hired as teachers such atomic scientists as Harold C. Urey and Enrico Fermi; and approved the world's first test of atomic reaction.

Furthermore, Hutchins eliminated compulsory class attendance, awarded bachelor's degrees to students who would normally have been completing their sophomore year, and told audiences around the country that colleges ought to specialize in intellectual activity and be managed by teachers and scholars rather than by their more opulent trustees. He also managed to raise $86,000,000 for the university, write eight books, and receive twelve honorary doctorates.[34]

Such a man did not shun controversy; his furious activities, his unequivocally positive stands on such subjects as civil liberties and international government, his studied sophistication and intellectual hauteur, left a long line of bleeding toes. "Bob Hutchins' natural bent," said an old friend, "is to go out and poke the other guy in the puss and see what will happen."[35] Controversy, beyond being personally pleasurable, was to Hutchins the soul of a democracy; the enlightenment of free men, he believed, could come about only as ideas were willingly and freely submitted to critical examination. As he once put it:

> The only political dogma in America is that discussion is the road to progress, that every man is entitled to his own opinions, and that we have to learn to live with those whose opinions differ from our own. After all, they may turn out to be right.[36]

Paul Hoffman had known Hutchins since the early 1930's when Hutchins persuaded him to join the board of the University of Chicago, and he believed the chancellor to be one of the most intelligent and capable men he had ever met.[37] After some persuasion, Hutchins accepted the offer to join his old friend in Pasadena, to work, as he said, "for the advancement of human welfare." Thus, on the first day of 1951, the two began a mission they thought would occupy the rest of their lives, investing in humanity for a foundation with assets of almost a half-billion dollars. The first problem facing them was organization.

Chester C. Davis, an old friend of Hoffman's and president of the Federal Reserve Bank of St. Louis, was employed as the second associate director and put in charge of budget and administrative matters. He also was to play an important role in the Foundation's overseas activities.[38] A third associate director, appointed no doubt at the insistence of Ford, was H. Rowan Gaither, Jr.[39] Working on a part-time basis, his job was to supervise Foundation activities in the behavioral sciences (critics would later question his qualifications for this function), look after the archives, and think about "The development of plans for approaching the untouched subjects in Area II."[40] In June 1951 the last associate director was named: former Marshall Plan coordinator and Harvard law professor Milton Katz. He would soon be supervising a variety of programs, from East European activities to "Projects relating to the Atlantic Community."[41]

The Foundation opened new Madison Avenue offices in New York in late February 1951, under the direction of Bernard "Bun" Gladieux, a former administrative assistant in the War Production Board and executive assistant secretary in the Department of Commerce.[42] This eastern office was to be utilized as "the initial point of contact for those submitting projects for The Foundation's consideration" and was to carry out preliminary investigations of worthy proposals.[43] The policy decisions, allocation approvals, and serious thinking were to be undertaken in Pasadena.

The first office of the first major foundation to locate a large part of itself in the West was a room in Paul Hoffman's California home. This was soon exchanged for the second floor of a large green barn on the Hoffman ranch. The Foundation then moved to a modest apartment on Wentworth Avenue, and finally was divided into an administrative and an executive branch. The former was at 918 Green Street, a modest building on a downtown street lined with small shops. The president and his associate directors inhabited an enormous beige estate in a wealthy Pasadena suburb. Gazing at the palm-lined mansion one day, motion-picture magnate Samuel Goldwyn (who had had some experience with splendor) said to Hoffman: "If you have to give away money, this is a wonderful place to do it."[44]

Hundreds of requests and proposals poured into both offices immediately. Within a few months semi-independent offshoots were created and staffed, such as the Hutchins-inspired Fund for the Advancement of Education, the Fund for Adult Education, and the East European Fund, set up to integrate refugees from European Communist countries into American life. The history of philanthropy records no period of comparable energy, determination, and far-sighted planning. By June Hoffman declared that he and his associates would be appropriating $25,000,000 a year. No small task, spending $96,000 a day! The initial programs of the Ford Foundation would be, Hoffman said, "bold and imaginative." The first Henry Ford's Peace Ship may have floundered, he noted, "but the idea behind it was good." "I figure if we send out three ships and one reaches port that's good."[45]

By August Hoffman, whose extensive world travels continued unabated, had recommended to the trustees that one third of the future resources be spent on overseas programs. Henceforth, he said to reporters, the Foundation would conduct a type of "Point Four" program of its own.[46] By the end of September Hoffman and his staff had appropriated over $23,000,000.[47] But even that pace seemed slow to lawyers who could not forget the federal government's vague "unreasonable" accumulation law. The fact was that in spite of the accelerated expenditures, the Foundation, in one year, had accumulated another $10,000,000. Trustees were calling for grants in 1952 of at least $45,000,000, "consistent with the principle of due investigation and care to avoid waste."[48]

In a speech before the Institute of Life Insurance, on December 11, 1952, Hoffman told of appropriations totaling $75,000,000 since January 1, 1951—or $52,000,000 for the preceding year. Approximately half of the monies (dividends on Ford stock plus a small reserve) went to Hutchins's educational projects. A third had gone to overseas ventures, consistent with the Gaither report's strong emphasis on projects to create and maintain world peace.[49] The Annual Report for 1952, then in preparation, was to remain a model of the possibilities of imaginative and creative foundation giving.

Within a few weeks, Robert Bendiner wrote a highly complimentary article on the Foundation for *The New York Times Magazine*. In it Hoffman was quoted as stating: "We have got another couple of years' work ahead of us . . . before we can say that we are really well organized to carry out the directives that came out of the study report."[50] Two days later, on February 3, 1953, at 2:30 P.M., Hoffman conferred privately with President Eisenhower about the possibility of future spot assignments for the government. The next day he officially and publicly resigned as president of the Ford Foundation.[51] Though few outsiders were aware of it, a storm of controversy had been brewing within the upper stratum of the Ford Motor Company and its foundation for long months before the trustees, at a meeting in New York in the last days of January 1953, consented to an official severance of corporate relations with Paul Hoffman.[52]

There were several major reasons for the break, though at the time the resignation was announced none was made public by Ford.

Hoffman's desire to return to Pasadena in 1951 was, as noted, a condition of his employment. He was there very seldom, however, preferring to oversee world-wide matters he felt required his direct attention. Reporters were told that the resignation was caused by Hoffman's desire to remain permanently in California.[53] The illness of his wife, shortly offered as Hoffman's "personal reason" for remaining at home, was a journalist's feeble attempt to confirm the official story.[54] While it is not to be doubted that the trustees complained of the constant airplane trips and perhaps, as has also been suggested, had a certain disdain for "the West," Hoffman himself might well have been delighted to run the Foundation from New York.[55] His consultations with Eisenhower and his resumption of duties as board chairman of the Studebaker Corporation, both involving the responsibility of travel, seriously weaken Ford's statement.

More to the point was the fact that the Ford Foundation had been the object of violent criticisms from the very start of its full-scale operations in 1951. The Chicago *Daily Tribune* inaugurated the attacks with the headline "LEFTIST SLANT BEGINS TO SHOW IN FORD TRUST"—the slant being, in part, the appointment of Paul G. Hoffman, a man who had "given away ten billion dollars to foreign countries."[56] Hearst columnists Westbrook Pegler, George Sokolsky, and Fulton Lewis, Jr., soon took up the banner, Pegler finally defining Hoffman as "a hoax without rival in the history of mankind" and the Marshall Plan as "the fabulous Roosevelt-Truman overseas squanderbund."[57] A right-wing hate group, the Constitutional Educational League, began selling 5-cent pamphlets a few doors from the Foundation's New York office linking the Ford Motor Company with Communism. Letters from dealers, customers, and cranks were received by the sales-conscious Ford Motor officials complaining of the transmission of American dollars (tax-exempt dollars) to foreign "socialists" and "Communists" like Nehru (a friend of Hoffman's). As early as January 1952 Ford showed some of this mail to his speech-writer, expressing deep concern.[58]

While young Ford had been most willing to support Hoffman's vision of a better world during the first year of the Foundation's accelerated activities, gradually and perceptibly the publicity and the letters helped to change his mind. "I told him [Ford] that I wanted to experiment," Hoffman later explained, "to change things, and that change always means trouble. But every time we got a dozen letters objecting to something we'd done—a radio show or an overseas program or whatnot—I'd have to spend hours reassuring the board. I got tired of wasting time that way. I felt I'd done a first-rate job and if, after two years, the trustees didn't agree, I didn't want to have to keep selling them. I'd rather leave."[59] Ford also had not anticipated the reactions of certain politicians who, like Ford dealers and cranks, expressed interest in the economic power and potential political influence of philanthropic foundations.

On April 4, 1952, the House of the Republican-dominated Eighty-second Congress created a seven-man committee which would be authorized to spend $75,000 to investigate possible "un-American" activities of foundations. Henry Ford had a confidential survey prepared on the attitude of Congress toward the Ford Foundation which concluded that opprobrium centered around the Republican Old Guard and a few congressman who feared the financing of integrationist groups, and that criticisms were not aimed at Ford himself but rather at "internationalism" and the "unorthodox" views of Hutchins and two other Foundation employees.[60] In May the same correspondent wrote Ford of a conversation with an attorney considered the likely counsel for the committee. The lawyer expressed the highest admiration for the Fords, describing the first Henry Ford, his son, and grandson worthy and consistent exponents of the free-enterprise system, but he also confessed bewilderment over the Foundation's employment of Dr. Hutchins, given the Ford family's tradition of patriotism.[61]

Under the chairmanship of ultraconservative Eugene Cox of Georgia, the committee worked for four months, filing a brief report which concluded that proportionately little foundation money had assisted Communist members and sympathizers. The Ford Foundation was cleared completely, but in the course of the public hearings, in the fall of 1952, Henry Ford II, Paul Hoffman, and Robert Hutchins appeared before the investigators.

Ford was forced to field several barbed questions and took the occasion to expound his institution's absolute and vigorous loyalty to the United States. Hoffman had to dismiss complaints that the Foundation was encouraging socialism. Dr. Hutchins, most sharply under attack by the Georgia segregationist as a "radical aide," spoke eloquently on academic freedom (to be quoted shortly by Supreme Court Justice Frankfurter in an Oklahoma loyalty oath case).[62] He contended that foundations were "one of the glories of the free enterprise system" and added for good measure (he had received copies of the two private letters to Ford): "I cannot condone grants to subversive individuals or organizations if the foundations had any reason to believe they were subversive, or who were ignorant of the fact when they should have known."[63] Though Ford did not appear shaken at the time, Hutchins recalls,[64] the young industrialist was now surely and acutely aware of a quality of public relations he had not foreseen two years earlier. The Fords, until recently, had not been in the habit of associating with objects of suspicion.

Another element in the estrangement between Ford and Hoffman concerned the internal structure of the Ford Foundation. In Paris, on March 18, 1952, sudden headlines appeared announcing that Hoffman was about to seek a three-month leave to campaign for the Presidential nomination of General Eisenhower. He explained that as co-chairman of the advisory committee counseling the Citizens for Eisenhower organization, he had been "pretty well limited to Sundays and evenings because of my duties in the Ford Foundation. From now on I am going to expand this, and starting next month I hope it will be a full-time job."[65] Back at the office, Hutchins could only say: "Mr. Hoffman hasn't discussed his political plans with us since he left for France."[66]

Hoffman's leave began officially on April 10, the day on which the trustees met in Detroit and elected Ford to be acting president. A few weeks later Ford traveled to Pasadena, where he became disturbed about the fuzzy organizational blueprints. Especially bothersome, apparently, was the degree of freedom enjoyed by the associate directors and the overlapping areas of responsibility assigned to each of them. Ford took charge immediately, holding a series of conferences with the officers on programing and administration, and presiding over a staff meeting. Dozens of what Ford considered administrative problems were called to the officers' attention by the Ford Motor Company's president. Chester Davis confessed to the trustees that Ford's visit had put everyone in Pasadena in intimate touch with the good thoughts of Ford and the members of his board.[67]

For some time certain trustees had sought the centralization of all activities and opposed the creation of separate funds. Hutchins, largely responsible for the creation of the two educational funds, was firmly convinced that this decentralization of operations provided a flexibility which resulted in a more responsible disbursement of monies. Hoffman agreed, but over the objections of several trustees who began to claim that the parent board seemed to be abdicating its responsibilities.[68]

In early May Ford held an unofficial meeting of the trustees in Hot Springs, Arkansas, without informing Hoffman. Mutual complaints were aired and, said Ford later: "We agreed that the Foundation had to be operated on a business-like basis."[69]

A few days later he returned to the West Coast and approved a tentative list of administrative changes drawn up by the associate directors.[70] On returning to Detroit, Ford wrote to Hoffman telling of the anxiety he and the trustees shared over the Foundation's present course, expressing the hope that Hoffman could disentangle himself from the Eisenhower campaign by July 12. The Foundation, Ford said firmly, needed leadership.[71] Ford later told Dwight Macdonald: "I couldn't see how the Foundation could go on the way Paul was running it without falling apart at the seams. . . . There was no teamwork."[72]

A further incident reveals the degree of tension existing between Ford and Hoffman by late 1952.

On September 22 an article was published in *The Wall Street Journal* in which the Fords appeared to be pondering, however ruefully, the revelation of their wealth and the sale of stock to the public. In an interview Hoffman had told reporter William G. Moore: "The Ford Co. is well run, is making big strides ahead, and I think we have a good investment in hand. . . . [But] some day, diversification will be desirable. When that day may arrive is a question of judgment among the trustees of the Foundation."[73] In response to that statement, inserted within the article. Henry II, in Rome, exploded with a stinging telegram to Hoffman expressing his great displeasure over the story, calling it both untimely and premature.[74]

Hoffman's return cable explained that he had been stalling Moore for weeks: "IN THE HOPE THAT I COULD PERSUADE HIM TO REFRAIN FROM PRINTING STORY THAT FORD STOCK WOULD BE PUT ON SALE IN NEAR FUTURE." He had only spoken of the possibility of diversification and had urged Moore to "HOLD UP ANY STORY WHATEVER UNTIL YOUR RETURN BECAUSE, AS I SAID, YOU ALONE COULD ANSWER MANY OF THE QUESTIONS HE ASKED."[75] But the damage had apparently been done. On Ford's return, over two months later, a press release was issued, saying in part:

> Ford Motor Company, at this time, does not care to comment exactly how accurate or inaccurate any of the figure estimates in the article may be. But it must be stated flatly that neither the Ford Motor Company nor the Ford Foundation has any plan under consideration for the public sale of Ford Motor Company stock.
>
> It is only fair to say, however, that the Wall Street Journal's "guess" that Ford is the second largest enterprise in the automotive industry is absolutely correct.[76]

Intermingled with each of the incidents leading to Ford's disenchantment with Hoffman lurks a persistent theme. If the first law of the successful organization man is the avoidance of bad publicity (and Hoffman had had little success in that), Clause A of the rule is deliberate self-effacement, especially when in the employ of a nationally prominent figure. The rules of the game had been written clearly into the *Study Report*: The officers

> must sacrifice a considerable degree of their freedom of self-expression. They cannot themselves be crusaders, or even take sides strongly in public on the issues involved in the work they support. They will have the satisfaction of making the resources of the Foundation available to persons in strategic positions to benefit society as a whole. In return they, like the Foundation itself. must give up the luxury of taking credit for their accomplishments.[77]

Hoffman was constantly in the news, making speeches, accepting awards, receiving honorary degrees, winning applause. As one observer put it: "I think Henry was appalled at the speed with which the Foundation was sliding out from under him. . . . he wasn't prepared to become emeritus in two years."[78]

A further reason for the incompatibility between the Hoffman administration and the Ford Foundation's trustees was the cerebral Dr. Hutchins. One source close to the scene noted the educator's "completely independent mind," which was a polite way of portraying wit, towering self-confidence, and a not overly convincing toleration of the men of high finance who sat on the Foundation's board. In retrospect it seems inevitable that two such disparate and strong-willed men as Ford and Hutchins would ultimately clash. Hutchins had warned Ford by telephone in late 1950 that his coming to the Foundation might mean controversy.[79] But at the time Ford had not yet smarted under one of Hutchins's raised eyebrows for a bland remark, or sensed the disdain caused by his conservative ways and his growing lack of confidence in Hoffman.

Then there were Hutchins's large and disquieting ideas on education, for which the Foundation had spent almost $33,000,000 by 1953. Said Ford: "I guess we gave it to him because he was the fastest talker. But I didn't like the idea of being a rubber stamp for his ideas."[80] Some critics even suggested a possible Hutchins slant to the grants. In 1952 the American Association of Colleges for Teacher Education issued a 1,100-word statement calling an Arkansas "Fifth Year" project for teachers (an idea long associated with Hutchins and sponsored by the Fund for the Advancement of Education) "unsound," "dangerous," and an "18th Century model for teacher preparation."[81] Others noticed that the Great Books Foundation received $826,000 from the Fund for Adult Education, and that Mortimer Adler's Institute for Philosophical Research was given $640,000 from the Fund for the Advancement of Education for a "dialectical examination of Western humanistic thought, with a view to providing assistance in the clarification of basic philosophical and educational issues in the modern world."[82] There were also educators who resented Hutchins's caustic assessments of modern education, and some who became bitter over the Foundation's reluctance to entertain many outside ideas, including their own. Hutchins was a prominent and willing target, not exactly an indispensable contributor to the placid, businesslike atmosphere Ford was determined to achieve for the Foundation by late 1952.

And all of this furor preceded the public announcement of the project Ford most closely associated with Robert Hutchins, the project most certain to bring down upon the Foundation untold quantities of public wrath. The Fund for the Republic, whose formation was revealed just days before Hoffman's resignation, had taken much effort and patience to create.

CHAPTER TWO

Reluctant Genesis

Before assuming his responsibilities with the Ford Foundation, Hoffman asked Gaither and his staff to revise the *Study Report* in the light of rapidly changing current events. A supplement was submitted on January 2, 1951, and on the basis of its still imprecise guidance, Hoffman offered the trustees a preliminary statement of intentions three weeks later. Pertaining to the Foundation's intentions toward the field of civil liberties, he stressed the importance of defending freedom and democracy during a time of international tension. He declared it to be the will of the officers that it was desirable to support a number of men of the highest public standing in a continuing critique of the effect of cold war tensions on American rights. The search was already under way, Hoffman informed the trustees, for citizens willing to serve on a commission dedicated to this task.[1] Behind this idea for a continuous commission was Hutchins, who, a few years before, had called for the creation of a similar tribunal to oversee the quality of the press.[2]

Sensing little enthusiasm for this first proposal, Hoffman then thought of offering assistance to the Nimitz Commission, a body organized by President Truman on January 23, 1951, to make a thorough study of the delicate balance between loyalty-security requirements and the rights of individual citizens.[3] The commission, however, could not survive objections raised by Senator Patrick McCarran and did not get off the ground.[4] In the meantime, the trustees were willing only to approve a $20,000 grant to the Institute of Creative Research for an examination of the mechanics and problems of a democratic society.[5]

While the Foundation began to dazzle spectators with rapid achievements in other fields, nothing emerged relating to its role regarding American freedoms. The staff minutes of April 23, 1951, revealed a great reluctance within the Foundation to step into the areas of civil liberties and civil rights without a great deal of careful planning. The consensus at this point was to employ a man of outstanding intellectual ability and national reputation to undertake a study which would tell the Foundation how it might advance better relations between the races.[6] Dr. Hutchins confided to George Kennan shortly: "We cannot allow anything to be associated with our name that seems naïve or utopian."[7]

In Pasadena during the early part of 1951, Hutchins visited frequently at the home of Paul Hoffman's son, Hallock, often thinking aloud about the entire spectrum of civil liberties to his sympathetic and admiring host.[8] At this time he met W. H. Ferry, a colorful figure who would be of great assistance in formulating and developing plans for the largest foundation-sponsored corporation ever set up to concern itself with civil liberties and civil rights.

Forty-one-year-old Wilbur Hugh "Ping" Ferry, mordant, iconoclastic, quarrelsomely outspoken son of auto executive Hugh J. Ferry, had become, following Dartmouth, a reporter, wartime OPA inspector, and, in 1944, a public relations director for the CIO Political Action Committee. Later, as a partner in Earl Newsom and Company, the Ford Motor Company's public relations firm, his job was to write speeches for Henry Ford II and, after January 1, 1951, to act as public relations adviser to the Ford Foundation. He was vitally concerned with civil liberties, and advised Hoffman and the trustees to reject or postpone action on the scores of proposals pouring in upon them in deference to something original which could be set up to cope effectively with some of the complex and risky problems of the early 1950's.[9]

Ferry was no mere sweetener of words. As early as April 29

he presented to the staff a lengthy, carefully prepared proposal for a Foundation-sponsored peace agency which "provoked numerous questions" but little else.[10] "I often gave advice, even when not called upon," he later recalled.[11] Hutchins and Ferry became close friends almost immediately, and the latter's counsel appears repeatedly in the private correspondence of this early period in the Foundation's development.

In August 1951 both attended a Seminar on Freedom and Civil Liberties which Hoffman created for the enlightenment of Henry Ford and the trustees. The speaker was Mortimer Adler, whose talk on "The Free Man and the Free Society" was followed by three discussion sessions in which all the guests at the Pasadena executive quarters were invited to participate. Adler furnished a bibliography (typical was an excerpt from Spinoza's *Ethics*) as well as an elaborately formulated, numbingly abstract philosophical disquisition on the freedom of man.

Attached was a two-page suggestion written by Hutchins for a "Fund for Democratic Freedoms," to be guided by a prestigious board and devoted "to continuing studies and reports on the ever-new and current dangers which threaten the unalienable rights of men in a democratic society." It would have the authority to contribute to established organizations of similar purpose, to defend individuals and groups directly, and to "institute or otherwise support efforts aimed at the elimination of inequalities in the treatment of individuals or minorities." It might, for example, examine the federal loyalty-security program and make suggestions, or "provide backing" for scientists and teachers entangled with problems of scientific and academic freedom. "The Fund would deal almost wholly in unpalatable causes," the memorandum stated. And it might rely less on financial strength "than on the moral authority that can be exerted by a Fund authorized and sanctioned by the Ford Foundation."[12]

Ford and the trustees at least appeared affable in the face of this call to arms and seemed to have a guarded interest in undertaking such bold responsibilities. To bolster the session with Adler, Ferry drew up an unrequested memorandum on the Foundation's duties, which he distributed in mid-September. It called for a program "committed to bold experimentation," one designed "to showing the way rather than travelling well-marked roads."

> Such a policy is not in conflict with the real interest of the Ford Motor Company, although it may sometimes prove irritating to some of its officials, and may embarrass temporarily, members of the Ford family. In the long run it will bring more credit to the Ford name than the easy and innocuous course of making impressive contributions to established activities or undertaking programs that cannot arouse criticism or opposition. Here it should be remembered that the reputation of the Ford Motor Company largely centers around Henry Ford's lifelong preoccupation with experimentation and pioneering ventures.[13]

On October 2 Hoffman wrote Gladieux of the keen interest shown by the staff in preparing the details for a "Fund for the Preservation and Advancement of Freedom."[14] Two days later he presented the trustees with a formal, cautiously worded proposal.

All of the *Study Report*'s considerations for the preservation of democracy, the memorandum noted, were to be consolidated within a single effort: a separate nonprofit corporation to be known as the Fund for the Republic.[15] As with the Foundation's other offshoots, the Fund would be directed by a board of between seven and fifteen citizens, the distinctive feature being that each would be approved by all of the Foundation's trustees before assuming office. This strong selling point, guaranteed to eliminate all but the most solid members of the Establishment from consideration, was coupled with a relatively modest request for initial assets totaling $1,000,000. It was the officers' judgment "that none of the tasks before the Foundation is more critical than this and that it is timely for the Foundation to take it."[16]

Their concern was based largely on the emergence of a national phenomenon which threatened to disrupt greatly the ever-tenuous American tradition of respect for individual freedom; a phenomenon which reminded certain thoughtful citizens, including Robert Hutchins, of the emotional jags the country suffered under John Adams and the incapacitated Woodrow Wilson, when fear welded the natural penchant for mass conformity onto guilt by association to lock up, terrify, and export "suspicious" people and "wrong thinkers" without as much as a glance at the Bill of Rights.

"McCarthyism" was the term used by the Wisconsin senator's opponents to describe a widespread series of actions designed to frighten Americans with false and highly exaggerated charges of Communist subversion for the purpose of political, economic, and psychological profit. Joseph McCarthy, the symbol—in part the cause—of the zealous outburst, had became famous, of course, in early 1950 by claiming that the State Department was "thoroughly infested with Communists." His charges refuted by a Senate investigating committee, McCarthy continued a mudslinging rampage, compounding hysterical allegations with an almost comical wonder at the epidemic grievances and passions he had tapped and set loose against enemies. Already there were apparently few limits to his abuse. Liberal, non-Communist Johns Hopkins professor Owen Lattimore became simply "Alger Hiss's boss in the espionage ring in the State Department." The Secretary of Defense, General of the Army George C. Marshall, whom Preisdent Truman described as the "greatest living American," was charged on the libel-proof floor of the Senate with being part of "a conspiracy so immense, an infamy so black, as to dwarf any in the history of man." Secretary of State Dean Acheson was portrayed, at best, as flagitious.

Hate groups, segregationists, and vote-hungry politicians leaped on the band wagon, eager to see how far the issue of anti-Communism would take them, anxious to discover if it could roll back what Eric Goldman has called the "Half Century of Revolution" in human rights.

The times seemed ripe to capitalize on public confusion and frustration. Communism seemed to be rolling up smashing victories abroad, as if to taunt war-weary Americans who thought that Hitler's death had somehow solved the major ills of the twentieth century; spy cases were suddenly exploding into headlines, featuring names like Judith Coplon, Klaus Fuchs, Harry Gold, David Greenglass, and the Rosenbergs; Russia was gloating over her possession of atomic power; the Korean War seemed useless and American fighting men strangely incapable of victory;

inflation was severe and getting worse; scandals were breaking out at high levels of the federal government. Eight of the nine Republican senators investigating the dismissal of General MacArthur hinted at the existence of a "pro-Communist State Department Group." The general himself, perhaps the most popular man in America at the time, added little to the nation's self-confidence by calling the Administration's policy of limited warfare in Korea "appeasement of Communism." The Republican theme for the elections of 1950 was the opposition's "softness" on Communism.[17]

As states hastily prepared legislation to curb all traces of local disloyalty, and aggrieved citizens intensified pressures on teachers, librarians, and ministers to remove "strange" books from their shelves and "unpatriotic" ideas from their lips, congressmen scurried over one another to write and support laws which would assure their constituents of their wholehearted devotion to the flag.

The McCarran Internal Security bill of 1950, opposed by the Justice, State, and Defense departments, and passed over a Presidential veto, contained a patchwork of antisubversive devices. Its major provision established a Subversive Activities Control Board which had the power to declare an organization subversive and require it to register with the federal government and submit membership lists and financial reports annually. Printed matter distributed by these organizations, as well as their radio and television broadcasts, had to be labeled Communist propaganda. Severe restrictions were placed on members of the American Communist Party, and persons who had ever been members of a totalitarian organization were forbidden entry into the country.[18]

Congressional committees stepped up their search for spies and their attacks upon all shades of leftist dissent. The Senate, in 1951, created the Internal Security Subcommittee of the Senate Judiciary Committee, which immediately resumed the torment of Professor Lattimore. It made startling newspaper copy (a preoccupation of its chairman, Senator McCarran), with almost simultaneous probes into: subversive aliens in the United States; subversive infiltration of radio, television, and the entertainment industry; Communist tactics in controlling youth organizations; subversive control of the Distributive, Processing and Office

Workers of America; subversive infiltration of the telegraph industry; subversive influence in the Dining Car and Railroad Food Workers Union; the unauthorized travel of subversives behind the Iron Curtain with United States passports; Communist propaganda activities in the United States; subversive control of the United Public Workers of America; and espionage activities of personnel attached to embassies and consulates in the United States under Soviet domination.

HUAC, now led by segregationist John S. Wood of Georgia (the previous chairman was in prison for defrauding the government), resumed its "exposures" of Communism in the motion-picture industry in 1951 and held hearings in Washington on loyalty in "the defense area of Baltimore."

Unstable witnesses like Harvey Matusow and Matthew Cvetic were employed repeatedly by the two committees to name hundreds of Communists and "Communist sympathizers." The mass media, eager to sensationalize the Red issue, publicized names and addresses of those merely mentioned by paid informers, and many victims suffered abuse and shame and were hounded from their communities. Liberal candidates for office, Democratic foreign policy, reform legislation, trade unions, intellectuals, the United Nations, the social gospel, all were frequently smeared Red on the witness stand and consequently by the ultraconservative press. A few former Communists were called upon to give the same testimony in several cities to heighten its impact. Witnesses known to be belligerent and likely to plead the Fifth Amendment were called repeatedly. Whether any of this was the legitimate function of congressional committees, few dared ask.[19]

Violence and hysteria swept Pittsburgh in late 1950 after HUAC, Cvetic, and two Pittsburgh newspapers completed months of lurid harangue. A convicted forger and former mental patient, in league with the Cincinnati *Enquirer,* stirred that Ohio city into a frenzy about the same time. (HUAC, and later the Ohio Un-American Activities Commission, were recruited to add credence to the shaky evidence of a local Communist menace.[20]) Possibly these were symptoms of an impending wave of terror that could affect many more communities, persecuting Americans without benefit of legal safeguards, inhibiting honest teaching and sound scholarship, stifling social progress in the name of national security.

The executive branch of the federal government had had difficulty finding the cadre of disloyal employees some politicians repeatedly pictured. None of those removed for security reasons by the Truman program were severed for committing *overt* actions (the traditional standard) inimical to the best interests of the government. All of these cases were judged on the *future likelihood* of an employee's committing a disloyal or treasonous deed, based on his past and present associations, expressed attitudes, even his "basic philosophy." Jobs were terminated and reputations blackened on the basis of one's *potential* for subversion. What exactly "loyalty" and "disloyalty" were, Executive Order 9835 did not say. Certain ideas and "sympathetic associations" were evidently safe and others were not. The relationship between the protections of the Bill of Rights and government employment were nebulous, to say the least.

And such vague and menacing precautions seemed about to expand. Critics warned of unnamed legions of spies living on the public payroll, bleeding the government of its secrets and the nation of its future. On August 26, 1950, Congress passed Public Law 733, prescribing security procedures for eleven federal departments and authorizing the President to extend the law as he thought "necessary in the best interests of national security." Early in 1951, at the request of the Loyalty Review Board, Truman modified the government's standard for dismissal to include cases where "there is a reasonable doubt as to the loyalty of the person involved" (rather than the more cautious "on all the evidence, reasonable grounds exist for belief that the person involved is disloyal").[21]

The Supreme Court of the United States was interpreting the Constitution not far from the current range of political discussion. In 1951 the Court upheld a variety of state programs requiring public employees to take loyalty oaths or to file affidavits disclaiming past or present membership in organizations deemed subversive. It denied the right of accused government employees to confront anonymous informants whose unsworn statements were the grounds of the charges against them. And in a major decision it declared constitutional the Smith Act, the first peacetime sedition law enacted since 1798. In doing so the Court abandoned Justice Holmes's "clear and present danger" requirement for the abridgment of free speech in favor of "probable danger" in some distant future. Speech alone, rather than action, even when leading to no immediate social injury, could now be seditious.

In a memorable dissent, Justice William O. Douglas (whose views on civil liberties were strikingly similar to those held by one of his oldest friends, Robert Hutchins) argued against the growing prohibitions on freedom of speech.

> When ideas compete in the market for acceptance, full and free discussion exposes the false and they gain few adherents. Full and free discussion even of ideas we hate encourages the testing of our own prejudices and preconceptions. Full and free discussion keeps a society from becoming stagnant and unprepared for the stresses and strains that work to tear all civilizations apart.
>
> Full and free discussion has indeed been the first article of our faith. We have founded our political system on it. It has been the safeguard of every religious, political, philosophical, economic, and racial group amongst us. We have counted on it to keep us from embracing what is cheap and false; we have trusted the common sense of our people to choose the doctrine true to our genius and to reject the rest. This has been the one single outstanding tenet that has made our institutions the symbol of freedom and equality.

Justice Hugo Black, in a concurring opinion, condemned the treatment of speech as the equivalent of overt acts and expressed the hope "that in calmer times, when present pressures, passions and fears subside, this or some later Court will restore the First Amendment liberties to the high preferred place where they belong in a free society."[22]

The restoration of those liberties seemed absolutely vital to Paul Hoffman, Robert Hutchins, and W. H. Ferry as they prepared the recommendation for a Fund for the Republic. No thought, of course, was advanced in the direction of hindering the government in its legitimate task of self-preservation. Hoffman wrote to a friend of the necessity for safeguarding vital positions of authority and responsibility from spies and saboteurs. But an independent, sober investigation was needed into the methods used to measure the loyalty of government employees and others in the professions. If it be found that these methods infringe upon the liberties of these people, he said, then even silence supports precedence dangerous to the freedoms of all · Americans.[23]

The stated objective of a Fund for the Republic, the Foundation trustees learned at their October meeting, would be to assist the promotion of a national security based on freedom and justice. The Fund would take into account:

(a) The persistent Communist effort to penetrate and disrupt free nations;

(b) The effects of international tensions on national security in the forms of hatred and suspicion;

(c) The effects of short-sighted or irresponsible efforts to combat domestic Communism;

(d) The need to better understand the spiritual and political significance of freedom and justice in the United States;

(e) The need to rededicate ourselves to the vision of a free, just and unafraid America.[24]

The trustees voted to accept the proposal and authorized the officers of the Foundation to establish the new corporation with an initial allocation of $1,000,000. The motion was actually a pledge of future disbursements contingent on the completion of the requisites for incorporation.

After the meeting it was unclear, however, even to the officers, what exactly the Fund could do. The Trustees had only approved a list of very high-sounding principles. For the next two weeks the officers discussed the matter and exchanged memoranda in an attempt to clarify the Fund's proper functions. Robert Hutchins had several projects firmly in mind.

The Fund should feel free to attack the problem of the freedom of the press; of migrant workers; of the immigration laws and the McCarran Act; of loyalty investigations; [of] the House un-American Activities Committee; of conscientious objectors; of academic freedom and teachers' oaths; of racial and religious discrimination in all its manifestations, from lynching to inequality of educational opportunity; of disfranchisement; of dishonesty in government; of the liberties guaranteed by the 1st and 14th amendments; of the administration of justice, etc.[25]

Unwilling to frighten the trustees with this or any similar catalogue of controversy, Hoffman told Benson Ford only that the officers had "reexamined the outline of possible terms of reference" and suggested that the directors of the Fund plot their own destiny. When their task was complete and scrutinized by the officers, the charter could be presented to the trustees, along with a request for a portion of the initial allocation.[26]

A few days after the trustees agreed to support the Fund, Hoffman asked them to propose candidates for the new board. Over 120 names were received, including those of such distinguished figures as Erwin D. Canham of the *Christian Science Monitor,* David Dubinsky of the International Ladies' Garment Workers Union, retired Admiral Chester Nimitz, and Russell Leffingwell of J. P. Morgan and Company. By early November the officers had narrowed the list to twenty "for intensive consideration."[27]

It was then agreed, no doubt at Ford's request, to back away from any precipitous involvement for a time, to do nothing further about the Fund for the Republic until a chairman ("or, preferably a chairman and president") could be found to bestow prestige on the venture. Trustee Charles E. Wilson was Hoffman's candidate, and a practical choice he was; the president of General Motors had conservative credentials even Westbrook Pegler would not care to challenge. Hoffman reported in December that Wilson seemed "intensely interested."[28]

But for months Wilson sat on the idea while Henry Ford read letters threatening boycotts of Ford products, pondered headlines in the Hearst press, listened to the speeches of his fellow Republicans, and observed three months of public hearings by HUAC on Communist subversion in Detroit's Local 600 of the United Automobile Workers of America. By April Hutchins was fuming at the disparity between mounting Foundation income and its lack of action. In a memorandum to fellow officers, he expressed impatience at the Foundation's lethargy with projects like the Fund for the Republic.[29]

By now, however, Hoffman was thinking mostly about General Eisenhower, the trustees were becoming disillusioned with the Pasadena operation, and Ford was hearing rumors of a congressional investigation into foundations. At the secret meeting of the trustees at Hot Springs in May, Wilson at last declined the offer. Moreover, Ford wrote Hutchins shortly, everyone present felt that the touchy undertaking should be dropped until after the fall elections. "I hope you will agree," he added.[30]

Several days before this letter was written, Hutchins had been to Detroit and New York for talks on the Fund with Ford, Wilson, and a third trustee, Donald K. David, presenting as many as fifty names for consideration as new board members.[31] Ford was a poor judge of men if he thought Hutchins would quietly acquiesce to a complete suspension, for he, more than anyone in the Foundation (except, perhaps, W. H. Ferry) was convinced of the Fund's immediate necessity. Each day's newspaper seemed to present to the lawyer-scholar some new outrage against the Constitution. Senator McCarthy at that very moment was inaugurating a sordid political vendetta against one of Hutchins's closest friends, Senator William Benton of Connecticut.

Henry and Benson Ford, along with Charles Wilson, visited Pasadena for four days of conferences in late June. Hoffman was away and the responsibility for getting the Fund started fell to Hutchins. Out of the meetings came a "new proposal" to be presented before the full board of trustees at their next meeting on July 15. The new corporation would have "a special status differing from that of the affiliated Funds already set up"—complete independence. The Fund's operations were not to involve officers of the Foundation, the accounting and housekeeping arrangements would be separate, even the headquarters was to be several thousand miles from Pasadena "in some eastern city."

The Fund would receive a total grant of between $10,000,000 and $15,000,000 to be used over "several years' time."[32] It was to be given a lump sum and told to go away and spend it—carefully. The *Study Report* did not prohibit disassociation.

Upon learning of the proposal, trustee Frank W. Abrams (chairman of the board, Standard Oil of New Jersey) expressed personal reluctance in a letter to Hutchins.

> Perhaps the most difficult of the programs to be certain about is the Fund for the Republic. I know of no topic that is of more fundamental importance—yet I know of none where the possibilities of inadvertently doing harm rather than good are more real. Perhaps that is one of the reasons why the staff and trustees of the Foundation have felt the need for more than the usual consideration in approaching the program.

Abrams suggested that the plan be placed before a five-man panel from outside the Foundation for study before taking further action. The whole matter, he said, "should be approached with great finesse."[33] Hutchins elected not to pursue the suggestion, choosing instead to drive straight ahead without any more distractions. He soon annoyed Milton Katz by placing the Fund within a list of his own administrative responsibilities. He explained patiently when challenged: ". . . some officer must see the Fund through organization, which may take months."[34]

Eight trustees, including Hoffman, gathered in New York on July 15 for the two-day meeting. In due course, the president presented a fairly generous outline of the Fund's prospective organizational structure, its scope of interest (including religious as well as racial discrimination), and possible methods of action. The proposal formulated in June was found acceptable, with the one reservation that further appropriations be delayed until all members of the new board and their program for the Fund were approved by the trustees.[35]

Now that the conditions for the corporation's future had at last been confirmed, nineteen months into his administration, Paul Hoffman could concentrate on the difficult search for conservative and respectable directors—distinguished men and women who would be both acceptable to the trustees and willing to become personally and seriously embroiled in the most bitter struggles of postwar domestic life. To assist him in this task Hoffman turned, predictably, to Robert Hutchins.

Though many of the nominees were personal friends, the associate director accepted recommendations and advice from all quarters. Throughout the course of the task over two hundred names were considered. "The motive was to find people of substance and standing; to find as many conservatives as possible because we wanted to show that even conservatives, or perhaps especially conservatives, should be interested in civil liberties and civil rights."[36] The officers of the Foundation and Ferry spent over two hard months seeking, discussing, and eliminating names of candidates. This process of unnatural selection was "very, very tough going," according to Ferry. "It almost guaranteed . . . that the board would be conservative, well-to-do and likely to be Republican."[37]

There were four survivors of a list prsented by Hutchins and Hoffman to the trustees by the end of the first week in August: George N. Shuster, president of New York's Hunter College; the pollster and marketing consultant Elmo Roper; Meyer Kestnbaum, president of Hart, Schaffner, and Marx; and Richard Finnegan, the elderly consulting editor of the Chicago *Sun-Times*.[38] On August 12, the trustees considered eight more names, of which six were accepted: James F. Brownlee, legal partner in the J. H. Whitney firm of New York; Charles W. Cole, president of Amherst College; Erwin N. Griswold, dean of the Harvard Law School; Jubal R. Parten, president of the Woodley Petroleum Company of Houston, Texas; Eleanor Bumstead Stevenson, wife of the president of Oberlin College; and James D. Zellerbach, president of the Crown Zellerbach Corporation of San Francisco.[39] By September 3 the trustees had approved twelve candidates and seven of them had accepted membership on the new board.[40] Within two weeks, the board of directors of the Fund for the Republic was officially, though not publicly, established. The last five to be included were Malcolm Bryan, president of the Federal Reserve Bank at Atlanta, Georgia; Huntington Cairns, a highly respected lawyer from Washington, D.C.; William Joyce, Jr., chairman of Joyce, Inc., of Pasadena; Russell Dearmont, a lawyer from St. Louis; and the president of the Provident Mutual Life Insurance Company of Philadelphia, Albert Linton.[41] In spite of Hutchins's privately expressed disregard for "representative boards," the new directors were noticeably representative of the various sections of the country, the professions, and the major faiths.[42]

James Zellerbach possessed almost ideal credentials and may be used to typify, in the broadest terms, the new board members. Like most major foundation trustees and directors in America, he was in his early sixties, a college graduate, and a prosperous businessman.[43] President and director of the enormous Crown Zellerbach Corporation, he also sat on the boards of directors of Fireboard Products, Inc., Rayonier, Inc., Wells Fargo Bank and Union Trust Company, the California Packing Corporation, the National Industrial Conference Board, the Stanford Research Institute, and the American Arbitration Association. And, like Paul Hoffman, he devoted much of his time and effort to civic affairs. Internationally, he had worked under Hoffman in the ECA and had been an officer and delegate to the International Labor Organization. At home, he was a member of the Department of Labor Advisory Committee, chairman of the National Manpower Council, trustee and regional vice-chairman of the United States Council of the International Chamber of Commerce, trustee of the Committee for Economic Development, and a director and national vice-chairman of the National Conference of Christians and Jews (North Pacific Division). In his city of residence, San Francisco, he was a director of the Chamber of Commerce, president and trustee of the World Affairs Council of Northern California, member of the board of governors of the San Francisco Bay Area Council, director and past-president of the city's Mount Zion Hospital, and the executive vice-president and chairman of the executive committee of the San Francisco Symphony Association.[44]

That the motives and methods of such men as Zellerbach could soon be seriously identified with conduct unbecoming a loyal American is symbolic of the frustration and hostility so prominent in what James Wechsler called "the Age of Suspicion." Indeed, within a few months Dean Griswold would be led to express privately the fear that the directors could become so eminent and respectable that the board might be unable to act with the necessary boldness.[45]

Hutchins sent each new director a form letter on September 19, 1952, voicing gratitude and informing him of the first board meeting, to be held in the Ford Foundation's New York office on October 16–17. Previous engagements, the Cox Committee hearings, and perhaps the national elections caused delays. But on November 26 members received a letter requesting their attendance in two weeks.

The Fund for the Republic was incorporated in New York as a membership corporation on December 9, 1952. Its board of directors (nine of the fifteen), along with several Foundation officers (and Ferry), held its first two-day meeting on December 10–11 in New York. At Hoffman's suggestion, a planning committee was elected, composed of Brownlee, Cairns, Cole, Griswold, Linton, Roper, and Shuster, with Dean Griswold serving as informal chairman. It was to formulate, in accordance with the July 1952 agreements, a tentative program which would be submitted to the Foundation in the hope of receiving a large sustaining sum of money. David Freeman, on loan from the Foundation, was elected temporary president and secretary of the corporation.[47]

On the second day, the board approved its initial allocation: $50,000 to be granted to the American Bar Association's Special Committee on Individual Rights as Affected by National Se- curity, as soon as the Fund's president, after further study, found the proposal satisfactory. The idea for such a committee had stemmed from a letter by President Truman to the ABA on September 1, 1951, expressing deep concern over repeated viola- tions of constitutional protections. The Special Committee, whose members were from the Bar Association's high official- dom, was created on February 26, 1952, to "bring about the best possible balance between the demands of national security and the exercise of the freedom of the individual citizen." The first of seven considerations contained in a request for funds sub- mitted originally to Hutchins on July 1, 1952, proposed to ex- amine "the extent to which Congress should place any limitations upon the scope of its investigations or should regulate their procedures so as to protect the rights of individuals by providing some of the safeguards of due process at trials."[48] As an "investigation of investigations" (as it would inevitably be labeled) would doubtless prove highly controversial, the directors of the Fund agreed to withhold public announcement of the allocation "for a reasonable length of time."[49] It first had itself to be announced.

The press release heralding the official parturition of the Fund for the Republic had been approved by the new directors and was worded cautiously: "It is expected that no announcement of its officers, staff, or program will be made for some time."[50] The *Study Report* was quoted briefly, the organization's independence was pronounced, and the names and selected titles of the board members were listed. Hutchins, ever-impatient with the modest progress of events, confided to Grenville Clark: "The Fund for the Republic got a few inches off the ground on December 10th and 11th. You may have seen the announcement on the front page of the section of *The New York Times* for Saturday last. It tells everything there is to tell."[51]

The nation's newspapers, almost without exception, responded affirmatively to the December 13 announcement. Typical headlines were: "FOUNDATION WILL SEEK TO PROTECT THOUGHT IN U.S." and "FORD FOUNDATION FIGHTS FOR FREEDOM."[52] The Fund was thought to be the latest in a long list of enlightened projects for which the Foundation should be praised greatly. Wrote the editors of the *Christian Science Monitor:*

> This comes as a welcome climax to the hearings of a House committee investigating whether the great tax-exempt foundations are supporting "subversive" activities. Spokesmen for these philanthropic trusts have given the committee and the American public some excellent lessons in the courage and intelligence necessary to sustain progress in the face of organized pressures toward timid conformity.[53]

Perhaps the most provocative reaction came from Colorado's little Grand Junction *Sentinel:*

. . .

The fact that one of the biggest foundations in the world . . . has felt impelled to set up an organization to work to eliminate the restrictions on the freedoms guaranteed Americans in their Bill of Rights, we fear, will not increase our prestige as a great democracy with other peoples. For here is implication that we do not enjoy the freedoms we boast.[54]

News commentator Eric Sevareid was soon telling his listeners on the CBS radio network that

a group of the most responsible, respectable and successful business and professional men in the country have banded together in a Herculean effort to roll back the creeping tide of what is called, for want of a better word, McCarthyism. . . . These are disturbed and alarmed individuals, these men who have taken over this fund . . .[55]

Readers of the St. Louis *Post-Dispatch* were given the first (unofficial) glimpse into the Fund's plans by city resident and Fund director Russell Dearmont. "He said its program eventually will encompass a broad field of subjects but that particular emphasis will be given to civil rights."[56] It was due to this latter, unpublicized purpose that the Fund lost its first board member.

Malcolm Bryan of Atlanta had been invited to serve by a fellow official in the Federal Reserve system, Chester Davis.[57] He attended but a single meeting, on December 10, and resigned a week later.[58] Bryan, who would later be described privately by an interviewer as "a very conservative, timid person," had apparently been unaware of the scope of the Fund's proposed operations and now fled the inevitable tumult.[59] Davis had told him earlier: "It will not be an easy assignment, but it certainly will not be dull."[60]

The Fund for the Republic, almost two years in the making, entered 1953 with little hope of easing or clarifying the strains and passions of a nation seething over "five percenters," the high cost of living, the "failings" of pin-striped diplomats, and all those traitors in the government the candidates had talked about. The popular President-elect showed less willingness than the incumbent to wage combat with friends of the new chairman of the Committee on Government Operations, Senator Joseph

McCarthy. Moreover, the senator's vague proposals for stepping up the loyalty-security hunt seemed likely, at least to some observers, to lead to an irresponsible purge of liberals, nonconformists, free thinkers—anyone who appeared "suspicious."

The Fund lacked a permanent president, a full complement of directors, and a firm financial underwriting. Even president Hoffman, a supporter capable of inestimable future assistance, was about to be separated from the Foundation from which it was itself legally and spiritually divorced.

The Fund for the Republic had the misfortune as well as the challenge of being born within a national atmosphere which embodied, as Eric Goldman put it, a "vast impatience, a turbulent bitterness, a rancor akin to revolt. . . . a strange rebelliousness, quite without parallel in the history of the United States."[61]

The Noblest Intentions

*T*he main preconditions for extensive activity facing the Fund for the Republic in early 1953 were the large grant from the Foundation and the selection of a chairman and a president; the first for sustenance, the second for guidance.

As Paul Hoffman, selected members of his staff, and the planning committee set out in January to create a reasonable forecast of the Fund's future, they faced the fact that in all the conferences and agreements leading to the Fund's incorporation, few specific proposals had been discussed and unanimously favored. The difficult question of appropriate undertakings had been deferred for fear of further Foundation delay, leaving those responsible for the Fund with few clear guidelines. It was one thing to wring a reluctant acquiescence from the trustees with a proposal to preserve American democracy, and quite another to lay before them plans, say, to investigate HUAC or to examine postal censorship. It was the common practice of large foundations to base later efforts on highly general charters, but the planning committee was required to provide the Foundation with a measurable degree of detail about what the Fund proposed to do with several millions of dollars before it received them. And it was probable that the trustees would balk at schemes resembling frontal attacks against prominent facets of McCarthyism and racism due to their inevitable association by the public with the Foundation and the Ford Motor Company.

Director W. H. Joyce, Jr., after a luncheon date with Hoffman and Hutchins, told president Freeman he believed that the trustees at their next meeting might "establish for the Fund for the Republic a grant of between ten and twenty million dollars for a five year period," provided that within the next few weeks an organization be constructed and "That a broad program . . . be ready for their consideration."[1] David Freeman was anxious to get started and submitted several ideas which he hoped the planning committee would explore and perhaps submit to the Fund's board. He was not in sympathy with a proposal to spend up to six months in self-education and attached to his memorandum a clipping which noted Senator Joseph McCarthy's plans to double the staff and budget of his Senate Permanent Investigating Subcommittee, with a field of study encompassing "every phase of government operation."[2]

At their third meeting, on January 16, the members of the planning committee finally agreed upon a list of areas which would be "for the time being, of primary concern to the Fund." In "general order of their importance" they were:

1   The size, nature and location of the international Communist menace.

2   Restrictions upon academic freedom.

3   Due process and equal protection of the laws.

4   The protection of the rights of minorities.

5   Censorship, boycotting, and blacklisting activities by private groups.

6   The principle of guilt by association.[3]

On request, a six-page draft of a proposal to the trustees was drawn up on January 19 by Orman "Orm" Ketcham, another temporary employee on loan from the Foundation. It made the usual oblation to the board's sober devotion to conservatism, but also elaborated generously upon the six areas into which the Fund might enter. Under the fifth area, for example, the American Legion was cited for involvement, as were two right-wing publications widely known to be active in Hollywood blacklisting. In the sixth area the following were listed as contributors

to the resurgence of guilt by association: the Hatch Act, the Smith Act, the McCarran Internal Security Act, the McCarran-Walter Immigration Act, the McCormack Act, The Voorhis Act, the United States Attorney General, HUAC, and many "state sedition laws and much local administrative action." The Ketcham memorandum concluded:

> The Board regards the theory of guilt by association as antithetical to the American principles of justice which punish only overt acts and which regard an individual innocent until proven guilty. Therefore, it wishes to study the present trend and *attempt to reverse it* [emphasis added].[4]

By the time the board concluded its second official meeting, ten days later, the more cautious hands of the directors had cut the draft to a mere page and a half, omitting specific references. Following a declaration of principles, which stressed the need to create and maintain "a climate favorable to the full development and expression of the individual," the proposed letter concluded:

> The Board feels it would be not only inadvisable at this time but impossible to spell out in detail the exact methods of operation, particularly since much reliance will be placed in the views of the chief administrative officer who is yet to be selected. Likewise, it is impossible to name any sum as being the exact sum required to implement a program. Much thought has been given to the question of the cost of one and another kind of program but we feel that the most we can say on that subject is that we believe we can intelligently and effectively spend somewhere between $3 million and $5 million a year over a period of five years. It may well be that a much larger sum would be needed to make this contribution which The Ford Foundation and The Fund for the Republic desire. We do feel that it is important that The Fund for the Republic be guaranteed a minimum existence of five years.[5]

The board chose not only to forego details in its proposal, but at the same time elected to raise its possible need to the $25,000,-000 level and beyond. Perhaps these decisions reflected the fact that at this meeting of January 29 the directors suddenly selected a rather formidable and determined chairman: Paul G. Hoffman. In early February newspapers carried the story of Hoffman's resignation from the Ford Foundation, and a few weeks later came the announcement of his association with the Fund. Rumors spread rapidly at the time, and years later the charge was made openly that the Fund for the Republic was simply "Paul Hoffman's severance pay." Several writers have misinterpreted the facts and many close to Hoffman to this day express confusion at the transition.[6]

The truth is that though the Fund was a convenient *deus ex machina* to a potentially explosive drama, it was neither created nor implemented as a vehicle for Hoffman's departure. The Fund had been in the works for well over a year, and a knowledge of the true causes of Hoffman's exit from the Foundation reveals the unlikelihood that Ford was eager to turn millions of dollars earmarked for probable controversy over to one so prone (in his judgment) to poor public relations. The key to the complex evolution of events lies in the official minutes of the January 29 meeting.

Hoffman's abrupt release by the trustees occurred on January 26. Three days later he attended the gathering of the directors, "by invitation." After a discussion of the corporation's bylaws, "There followed an extended discussion of candidates for the positions of president, chairman of the board, and honorary chairman of the board." No formal action being taken with regard to the office of Fund president, the minutes continue: "Mr. Hoffman then left the meeting." The following resolution was thereupon adopted: "Resolved that Paul G. Hoffman be invited to serve as Chairman of the Board of the Fund for the Republic."[7] Five days *before* his official resignation as president of the Ford Foundation, Hoffman was formally approached by his friends and colleagues at the Fund.

Considering Hoffman's presence "by invitation" and the close ties between the Ford trustees and the Fund's directors, the latter were unquestionably aware of the Foundation's very recent decision to invite the resignation if its chief executive when they met on the 29th.[8] The resolution, approved unanimously, was actually an intraorganizational pledge by the directors to select Hoffman as their chairman at a later date and was no doubt a private demonstration of confidence and affection.

Hoffman had, after all, waged a long, self-incriminating campaign in support of Hutchins's brain child. The president's docket of July 15–16, 1952, furnishes one example:

> Events since October, 1951 make the Fund for the Republic no less necessary than it was when it was authorized. On the contrary, some of the movements and attitudes that it was designed to combat seem to be gaining strength. Private censorship accompanied by organized boycott is spreading. The loyalty procedures of the Government are causing more difficulty. Colleges are having more and more trouble with groups that demand that all teaching be completely orthodox and that free discussion on the campus be inhibited. Minority groups are handicapped or menaced by prejudice.
>
> In view of the specific statements in the Trustees' Report, which have been given wide publicity, the Foundation should not further postpone taking action in the field.[9]

Another is the long lecture on freedom, the cold war, and the obligations of the Foundation, contained within a monthly report to the trustees in late January 1953.[10] Even on the day of the public revelation of his resignation, February 4, he continued to prod the trustees for action.

> At the Chairman's suggestion, Mr. Hoffman read to the meeting the communication which he had made to the Chairman on the previous Monday, after which he said that, before taking up the matter of his resignation and any announcement that was to be made, he would like to have discussed further the matter of The Fund for the Republic and what the Trustees desired to do about it.[11]

At this time Hoffman informed the trustees of the Fund's overture. He felt deeply responsible, of course, for the directors' corporate commitment; they had climbed out on a precarious limb at his request. Moreover, he had received national acclaim for the Foundation's pronounced intention to assist in the restoration of respect for constitutional protections. The Fund for the Republic had the potential for being one of the brightest stars in his administration's record and Hoffman believed sincerely in its purpose. He was not about to submit tacitly to the possibility of its future debilitation by a timorous board of trustees. At the same time, even though the authorized version of his resignation involved nothing more harsh than a longing for home, there would be skeptics, and it might well look better for Hoffman's reputation as a world-famous administrator and man of affairs if there was at least indirect evidence of a friendly parting. Hoffman's message was clear: it would be less disagreeable for all to insure the Fund's general future by approving his inclusion on its board. Ford required each trustee to express his own view of the proposal. All having approved, it was time to call in reporters, talk about Pasadena, and smile a lot.

Two weeks later, on February 18, the directors of the Fund held their third meeting. Corporation lawyer Bethuel M. Webster was retained as counsel and Paul Hoffman was officially, though again not publicly, elected a director and chairman of the board. Hoffman, whose resignation from the Foundation became effective March 1, proceeded to appoint a three-man committee to request on behalf of the Fund the large sustaining grant from the trustees. The board then resumed the drafting of a letter of intention for the committee to carry with them.

No doubt responding to a new desire by the Foundation for specific proposals, the directors approved a nine-page prospectus which leaned heavily on Ketcham's earlier memorandum and told the trustees, with a maximum of candor, what they had in mind. The Fund would be research-oriented, educational, dedicated to the study—by itself and others—of the strengths and weaknesses of American democracy. Four methods of operation would be employed:

1   Studies on a research basis for informational purposes and for possible eventual publication.

2   The development of activities in terms of education and action to be conducted by the Fund itself.

3   Aiding other agencies and working with them in carrying out projects and activities. These would be projects initiated by the Fund but would be done with other agencies because of their special qualifications.

4 Disbursing—not in the form of general grants but for specified projects in certain areas coming within the objectives of the Fund.

And what would be studied? Under the heading "Due Process and Equal Protection of the Laws," for example:

> Topics covered include: the extent to which information obtained by wire-tapping, third degree, unlawful search and seizure, or other unlawful police methods are permitted; rights of witnesses in quasi-judicial proceedings, including availability of counsel, opportunity for cross-examination, etc.; use and mis-use of the privilege against self-incrimination; availability of qualified counsel for indigent or unpopular defendants; and the extent to which the press influences judicial or quasi-judicial decisions by giving unequal coverage to sensational accusations and subsequent denials.

Under "The Scope and Procedure of Congressional Investigations":

> This heading contemplates a study of the activities of the House Un-American Activities Committee, the Senate Internal Security Committee, and other Congressional investigating committees. Sub-topics might include: right to refuse to testify on grounds of self-incrimination, right to cross-examination, right to counsel, contempt proceedings, treatment of informers, whether investigations should be confined to developing new legislation rather than investigating individuals, extensions of scope of investigations beyond their original purpose, rules of conduct, granting of immunity, and publicizing of testimony before accused is given chance to answer.

Under "Investigation of the Loyalty of National and International Civil Servants" the directors wrote:

> This field includes the procedures and effect of Federal, state and local government loyalty and security programs, the use of the FBI to conduct investigations, the non-disclosure of informants, burden of proof and procedures in loyalty hearings.
>
> This field includes current investigations of UN personnel being conducted by Congress, the Department of State, the United Nations and other governments.

Further proposed topics of concern included domestic Communism ("Communism will find in the Fund for the Republic no haven for its subversive activities"), censorship, blacklisting, government secrecy, academic freedom, discrimination in restaurants and transportation facilities, equal voting privileges, immigration laws, the problems of Indians, and released time for religious activities in the public schools.[12] If Henry Ford and the trustees agreed to throw a goodly portion of their vast financial resources behind the Fund for the Republic they could not later plead ignorance of what its directors proposed to examine. Armed with this prospectus, directors Griswold, Brownlee, and Parten, along with attorney Webster, journeyed to Pasadena.

Over a dozen Foundation officials, including the trustees and the associate directors, sat before the four as they were admitted into the plush conference room of the executive mansion on February 24. The meeting was not simply a ritual, even though the trustees had decided to go ahead with the Fund by allowing Hoffman to be its chairman. The vital question of the degree of financial support remained. The difference between a token payment laden with strings and a clear multimillion-dollar grant such as the directors desired was the difference between stultification and invigoration of the Fund for the Republic.

Paul Hoffman contributed to the awkwardness of the unique occasion by declaring immediately that in view of his resignation from the Foundation he preferred to be considered one of the Fund's representatives. It was so agreed. Dean Erwin Griswold, perhaps the most prestigious and certainly the most eloquent of the four chosen by the board, was the first to speak on behalf of the Fund. He reviewed the Fund's short history, discussed the prospectus, described the corporation's independent construction, and expounded upon the need to have firm financial support, in part to assure the selection of a superior president and staff. At the conclusion of his speech, Griswold proposed a grant to the Fund of $15,000,000.

The other directors and Webster were then called upon individually for additional commentary, but their remarks were brief and mostly elaborative. Erwin Griswold, the essence of

sound, dispassionate scholarship, stability, and academic emi-
nence, had been forceful and persuasive before the trustees.[13] The
financial request was both reasonable and, in view of earlier
estimates, minimal. Surely with directors like Griswold the
Fund would contain Hoffman's supposed "propensities" and attract a bare minimum of unpleasant publicity. Its independence
would insulate the Foundation from the responsibility of directly entering the second category of the *Study Report* itself.
And the prospectus had been reassuring, in spite of its lists of
specific intentions.

> Since these problems are persistent and complicated, the Fund
> cannot hope to make an important impression on them quickly.
> The problems and degrees within the problems are so complex
> that time will be needed for the members to get themselves oriented
> so that they can come out with a unanimous opinion. Intellectual
> honesty and judicial impartiality will be needed to reach real
> agreement.

Everyone but the trustees and H. Rowan Gaither, Jr., (already
named Hoffman's successor) was then ushered from the room
while the decision was being made. Upon their return it was
learned that the trustees, on the motion of Henry Ford II, authorized for the Fund for the Republic a sum of $14,800,000 to
supplement the $200,000 granted from the appropriation of 1951.
But only $2,800,000 was to be made available immediately; tied
to the remainder was the warning that further payments would
be suspended if the grantee should for any reason lose its tax
exemption.[14]

Though America's foundations were relieving themselves of
several hundred million tax-exempt dollars annually, and though
in 1952 alone some 14,000 new exemptions were awarded to a
variety of organizations, up to now very little money had been
invested in the fields of civil liberties and civil rights.[15] This was
no doubt due in part to the relatively thorough national disinterest in these matters prior to the pangs of postwar read-
justment, and partially to the foundation tradition of selecting
conservative trustees whose visions of the good society harmonized
more closely with the thoughts of Herbert Spencer and Calvin

Coolidge than with those of Louis Brandeis, Roger Baldwin, and Gunnar Myrdal.[16] The Fund for the Republic was widely recognized as a pioneering effort, and unprecedented attempt to sail beyond the safe waters of hospital charities and university building into the uncharted regions of legal and social malaise. And once again, when the $15,000,00 grant was announced, the nation's press expressed pride in the Ford Foundation for its gallant foresight and willingness to innovate.[17] But news of the large allocation of money also brought grumbles, portending later reaction from pro-McCarthy sources against involvement—even studies—in areas of American life where it was believed that they alone were masters of the truth. Wrote the Washington *Times-Herald* and the Chicago *Daily Tribune*: "It is hard to discern what this expedition is intended to accomplish. All we have to say is that 15 million dollars would be a high price to pay to 'get' Senators McCarthy and Jenner and Rep. Velde."[18]

The day after the Fund was enabled to begin extensive operations, Paul Hoffman sent a jubilant telegram to each director, describing the grant and seeking assistance in the selection of possible presidential candidates.[19] Indeed, the most important requisite for getting under way now, before there could be a definite program, a public-relations policy, or even a firm commitment regarding employee benefits, was the acquisition of a chief executive officer.

The haggling continued for weeks. The full backgrounds of dozens of distinguished citizens were collected, explored, and debated by the directors, with no complete accord. On March 6, Orm Ketcham had lunch with James Brownlee and Malcom Bryan's replacement on the board, attorney and author John Lord O'Brian.[20] The two directors described to Ketcham their view of an ideal president. He would be a man "personally well known to the public [with] a reputation for fair-mindedness. . . . someone who can work well with the Board of Directors," someone with broad experience, preferably not a full-time attorney or a professional educator. The operation was envisioned as

a single person at the head of the staff who will be responsible for preparing and presenting projects, programs and tentative policies to the Board of Directors for consideration . . . the Board will review and decide upon these projects, programs and policies and will express its decisions publicly through its Chairman (Mr. Hoffman).

While they were at it, they discussed the credentials of fifteen notables. Of one prospect, Ketcham noted: "Mr. Brownlee has changed his mind and does not think that ———— is a suitable candidate for this job although he likes him personally." Of another, proposed by Hoffman: "Both men agreed that there was no possibility that he would take the job."[21] And so it went.

By March 18 the two most desirable nominees appeared to be Justice Robert Jackson of the United States Supreme Court and Earl Warren, governor of California. If they were unwilling to accept, which was believed likely, Erwin Canham, editor of the *Christian Science Monitor* was to be offered the position.[22] But a combination of refusals and personality clashes continued to plague the board's efforts to find a president who could win their unanimous approval.

The directors were heartened in late March by news that the Treasury Department had made an exception in its procedures for the Fund. Foundations ordinarily applied for tax exemption only after a year's operation, having made a series of grants on which the government based its decision. But in this case, believing that tax exemption would qualify the Fund for the complete $15,000,000 appropriation, Paul Hoffman and Bethuel Webster delivered an application for exemption on March 20, only four months and one grant after the Fund's incorporation. They asked Treasury officials for accelerated action and emphasized the Fund's need for its entire grant to establish independence, lay out a five-year program, and attract an outstanding president. Within a week the Treasury Department issued an unusual "temporary" certificate of exemption, to be converted into the "full" statement after a year of acceptable activities. A Ford Foundation attorney soon informed Webster, however, that his employer was in no hurry and that the Fund would receive its total grant upon reception of the government's final decree and not before.[24] The Fund was, however, eligible for the initial installment of $2,800,000, and the board received it shortly.[25]

The directors had few clear ideas about what they would do with the sum, but were acutely aware that future decisions would have to be carefully considered. Not only was the Foundation scrutinizing their actions to the point of asking for periodic reports,[26] but the Treasury Department had to be satisfied of the Fund's intentions. If the department felt that the Fund's work was designed to influence legislation, or that it involved propaganda rather than education (vague terms, all), and if it decided not to confirm the tax-exempt status at the year's end, according to the Foundation's grant "the Fund shall promptly on request of the Foundation pay over to the Foundation the balance of the amount of the above grant then held by the Fund" and go out of business. Damage to the personal reputations of those even indirectly involved with the Fund, not to mention the disastrous effect on the ideals propounded by the participants, would be incalculable in such an event. The Fund's lawyers would soon warn:

> Applying the lessons of the above cases to the Fund for the Republic, Inc., we take it to be clear that the Fund is free to engage in partisan advocacy for the principles of the Constitution of the United States and the Declaration of Independence. Such advocacy is merely to support existing systems and not to promote reforms.[27]

So in spite of advice to the contrary by *The New York Times*,[28] it was likely that the Fund's first efforts would be, as outlined to the Foundation in February, "Studies on a research basis for informational purposes and for possible eventual publication." The question of whether or not such studies would have any effect on grave problems of American society was, for the time being, academic. Given the Fund's conservative board, absence of full-time leadership, and its encirclement by critics and vaguely defined legal restrictions, it appeared that for at least several months there would be few headlines.

But by the time the board met, on April 9, to consider methods by which studies could begin, Senator McCarthy had already made inquiries. "I understand that you have just been elected President [*sic*] of a new foundation," he wrote to Hoffman on

March 31. "My questions No. 2 and No. 3 would apply to the new organization which I understand you now head. I would appreciate it if you would give me this information as soon as possible and also advise when you can appear in Washington without too much inconvenience."[29] A few days earlier Congressman Donald Jackson of California, protesting moves to oust Harold Velde from the chairmanship of HUAC, had declared: "The Ford Foundation might well devote some of its efforts to public disclosure of the substantial and vital work performed by the committee in its attempts to preserve the American system under which the Ford company acquired the millions being spent in investigation of the U.S. Congress and its committees."[30] Out of Southern California in March came a small magazine bearing the headline: "WHAT ARE HOFFMAN AND HUTCHINS UP TO WITH THE FORD FOUNDATION? 15 Million Dollars Granted for Smear Against Anti-Reds." Its editors felt obliged to appraise the historical and economic considerations of the Fund's creation: "This is the most incredible piece of insanity in the history of American capitalism's befuddled evasion of its clear and obvious responsibility to courageously stand up to and intelligently fight the criminal Communist conspiracy, which openly boasts that it will destroy all capitalism and liquidate all capitalists!"[31] About the same time, the Reverend Gerald L. K. Smith, now head of the Great Nationalist Crusade, presented "The Henry Ford [Sr.] Plaque" to the anti-Semitic segregationist George W. Armstrong of Mississippi at ceremonies in Los Angeles. Rev. Smith had been quoted earlier as stating that the Ford Foundation, directed "by those two well-known Communists Paul Hoffman and Dr. Hutchins," was a betrayal of the ideals of Henry Ford, Sr. "I should think," an irritated Foundation official wrote to Gaither, "that some legal action could be taken to prevent these people from using the Ford name in this manner."[32] By the end of March, Paul Hoffman was assuring Vice-President Nixon that the Fund's primary study "will be directed toward as accurate a determination as possible of the extent and nature of the internal communist menace and its effect on our community and institutions."[33]

Two committees had been at work during the month between the fourth and fifth board meetings, and their reports were discussed at the April 9 gathering. A three-man committee on the study of domestic Communism, headed by Elmo Roper, suggested using a variety of research techniques, as the result "must not only be as thorough and as objective as we know how to make it, but [that] to do the maximum amount of good, it must be believed by the maximum number of people." Five possibilities emerged:

1   A questionnaire type of study among a broad cross-section of the public to discover popular attitudes on the extent of domestic Communism and its impact on American life.

2   Studies on the findings of the FBI, congressional committees, Communist trials, and the revelations of confessed Communists.

3   A study of the infiltration and influence of Communists in the trade-union movement.

4   Investigations into the Communist leanings of teachers and professors.

5   A study of "the question of whether or not Communists in or out of Government have had much or little to do with certain basic decisions which are commonly supposed to have played into the hands of Communists."[34]

The board approved of these suggestions and added a sixth field of concern, the publishing and entertainment industries.[35] It was agreed that the studies should go on simultaneously and be under the watchful eye of a director of research—as soon as one could be found. The second committee, under Huntington Cairns, had not yet completed its report on methods and procedures for studying the legacy of American liberty.

Discussion then was held on the desirability of undertaking action programs. While no formal vote was taken, it was the "sense of the meeting" that the "basic research" should come first.[36]

Before long, Paul Hoffman thought of a possible candidate for Fund president no one had mentioned. Congressman Clifford P. Case of New Jersey was young (forty-nine), attractive, Republican, had been an ardent supporter of General Eisenhower in 1952 and was known to have Administration support, and had a reputation as a staunch defender of civil rights. He had served four terms in Congress and during his last campaign had been thought liberal enough to earn the support of the American Federation of Labor and the Americans for Democratic Action. His availability was possible, for in early 1953 he had withdrawn as a candidate for the nomination for governor of New Jersey because of a lack of campaign funds—one of the penalities of being a "maverick" Republican.

Acting President Freeman was authorized to make an initial contact with Case on April 22.[37] Director Charles W. Cole talked with the congressman a few days later and informed Freeman that he was "*very favorably* impressed. . . . Hold everything."[38] Cairns and O'Brian next met with Case on May 6, were pleased, and sent him along to Linton and Shuster for further discussions.[39] While the Fund presidency had not yet been offered to Case, in Freeman's opinion he would accept the office if the board posed the question.[40]

When the directors next met, on May 18, it was "Resolved that Congressman Clifford P. Case be and hereby is elected a member, a director, and President of The Fund for the Republic, subject to the negotiation of mutually satisfactory terms of employment between Mr. Case and the committee of the Board appointed for that purpose."[41] A week later Case accepted formally, stipulating that he would resign from Congress and take office on or about September 1. In the interim he would be pleased to be a member of the board.[42]

Perhaps at last the Fund for the Republic might begin broad operations at a reasonable pace. But if the $15,000,000 grant drew fire from certain "patriotic" quarters, the announcement of the Case appointment on May 27 could have been expected to do likewise. Shortly, Westbrook Pegler was describing Case to his millions of readers as "one of a mysterious group in president-elect Eisenhower's headquarters last fall, who secretly got Ike's signature on a 'testimonial' for Arthur J. Goldsmith who tried to win control of Congress for undisclosed eastern financial backers by sending money into states of small population to defeat anti-Communist candidates and all who stand against unrestricted immigration."[43]

The directors, no doubt realizing the probability of the selection of a president, furthered their proposed studies on May 18. The Committee on the Legacy of American Liberty under Mr. Cairns received $25,000 for summer studies, laying the basis for further inquiry into past and present concepts of American freedom. Elmo Roper's committee on the Communist menace received $10,000 to enable Dr. Samuel A. Stouffer, professor of sociology and director of the Harvard Laboratory of Social Relations, to prepare an outline and sample questionnaire in preparation for the first part of the committee's report. Another $10,000 was appropriated for a similar outline for part two (studies on the known record of Communism in America), under the direction of Dr. Arthur E. Sutherland, professor of law at Harvard.[45] For the present, then, the board would develop its own research and study programs; these would be limited and conducted by unimpeachable scholars from the most highly respected universities.

New York's Carlyle Hotel was the site of the board's meeting of June 16. The directors agreed to increase Dr. Stouffer's allocation to $29,500 for a "trial run sampling of his questionnaire." Professor Sutherland's appropriation was also raised by $2,500.[46] A grant of $55,000 was made to the American Friends Service Committee for its program in race relations—largely because the Ford Foundation had handed this responsibility to the Fund, refusing further support.[47] Early in the meeting Paul Hoffman urged "a study of nonconformity" but received little response. The board was even unwilling to make funds available to President Case for contingencies, even when "dispensed with the advice of a committee of the Board." The Fund for the Republic had been in existence for six months, had made two grants and approved small sums toward the creation of future studies. It had elected a president who had not yet officially taken office and whose only comment of record, on June 16, was the suggestion to adjourn until August.

The Fund opened its first office, at 1 East 54th Street, in the third week of July.[48] Scores of requests for employment were received immediately, along with appeals for money.[49] Treasurer I. M. Stickler's resignation shortly afterward coincided with plans to transfer the Fund's records from the Foundation's quarters.[50] Perhaps the Fund was now ready for business.

On August 1, Clifford Case read his farewell address to the House of Representatives. The brief, rather pallid speech concluded:

> I am especially conscious of my personal responsibilities for the work of the Fund for the development of its program, the building of its organization and the management of its operation. If I am to meet that responsibility adequately, I shall have to draw on all the resources which are available to me. The experience gained in this body will, I am sure, be invaluable. Especially, I shall look to you, my colleagues, for continued help and counsel.[51]

His colleagues, however, had already approved a new congressional investigation of tax-exempt foundations, to be under the direction of Representative Brazilla Carroll Reece of Tennessee. In his speech to the House, Reece cast shadows of subversion on, among others: the Ford Foundation, the Ford Motor Company, the Rockefeller Foundation, Americans for Democratic Action, Arthur Schlesinger, Jr., Eric Sevareid, Walter Gellhorn, Carey McWilliams, Bernard L. Gladieux, Bernard Berelson, Ernest J. Simmons, Philip C. Jessup, the National Education Association, the Progressive Education Association, and the Encyclopedia of the Social Sciences. As to the Fund for the Republic, "this king-sized Civil Rights Congress," Reece contended:

> There can be no question that Hutchins is behind this new Ford Foundation project, for he has consistently expressed his concern for the civil liberties of Communists. Since we know Hutchins' attitude toward communism and we know that his conception of civil liberties is similar to that of the Communists, we can be sure that the new Ford Foundation project will aid the Communist conspiracy and will try to discredit all those who fight it.[52]

A *New York Times* reporter noted at the time of the vote: "A decision by the Ford Foundation to grant $15,000,000 to inquire into the methods of Congressional investigations into Communist infiltrations and civil rights appeared to rankle a large segment of the House."[53]

The directors next met on August 4 and were called to order, as usual, by Chairman Hoffman. They accepted the resignation of Mr. Cairns, who left to attend to personal affairs, and turned to a discussion of future policy.[54] Little accord was reached beyond the conclusion that the basis of their efforts would be the presentation made to the Ford Foundation the previous February. Grants-in-aid were thus approved in principle and, as was the common procedure, a committee was appointed to study possibilities and produce recommendations. A further committee was named to "work with the President in the formulation of plans with respect to educational and major projects." An allocation of $4,500 was made to Columbia University for an impending conference on civil liberties under the auspices of the Association of the Bar of the City of New York. Two committee reports were read, the terms for Case's employment were agreed upon, and after more discussion, there being "no further business," the directors adjourned for a month.[55]

The board made two grants when it assembled on September 10. Forty thousand dollars went to Columbia University's Bicentennial Committee for a documentary film, radio programs, an exhibit pamphlet, and a pamphlet series in connection with the theme "Man's Right to Knowledge and the Free Use Thereof." An additional sum of $8,000 was appropriated for the pamphlet effort, to be awarded at Case's discretion after a study of the series' contents. The four items (the original request had listed seven, costing $145,000) were recommended by the Committee on Grants-in-Aid, which also agreed to support for one year (instead of the requested three) the Voluntary Defenders Committee, Inc., of Boston, a tax-exempt body designed to aid indigent criminal defendants. Thirty-five thousand dollars was allocated (along with the promise of a further $10,000, if it appeared appropriate to Case) to add promotional expenses. President Case, who took time off from a vacation to attend the board meeting, was also authorized to hire temporary consultants and three or four assistants to aid him in preparing proposals for the board's consideration.[56]

The Fund, by late September 1953, had not issued a press release in seven months.[57] Its organizational and administrative expenses, due largely to the salaries of the directors, almost equaled the total amount of appropriations and grants.[58] The president, four months after his election, had not yet begun to devote his full attention to the Fund's efforts. Legal counsel continued to preach caution in anticipation of the government's final ruling on tax exemption.[59] Nevertheless, critics continued tirades against the clear and present danger facing the nation in this "anti-anti-Communist" corporation. The American Legion's newsletter, *Firing Line,* referred to the Fund as "a huge slush fund for a full-scale war on all organizations and individuals who have ever exposed and fought Communists." The *Williams Intelligence Summary* of Los Angeles saw the dark specter of Dr. Hutchins behind it all and asked its readers to send evidence to support the suspicion that he was actually Jewish.[60] The Committee For McCarthyism of the Constitutional Education League issued a pamphlet in November claiming that "the master-minds of the Communist conspiracy have been so diabolically clever in their machinations and in the manipulation of their witting and unwitting dupes and stooges that, even at this late date, 1953, they have been able to enlist the support and cooperation of two supposedly super-intelligent, ultra-respectable and all-powerful allies—the Ford Motor Company and the American Bar Association."[61] The general counsel of the Reece committee would soon come calling on Mr. Case with an armful of loaded questions.

Robert Hutchins, in the meantime, had been carrying on as an associate director of the Foundation. The task was no doubt lonely and unexciting since Hoffman's departure, and he had been left in Pasadena to handle whatever administrative duties might be shuffled his way from New York. A close friend visited him in October and reported Hutchins busy, continuing to represent the Foundation on the Pacific Coast. Hutchins claimed to be in constant contact with people interested in the Foundation's gamut of interests, especially within the educational programs and the Fund for the Republic. The telephone seemed busy and the cellar traffic appeared heavy.[62]

By early November, Hutchins was privately expressing dissatisfaction over the Fund's relative inactivity, "even though I know that the reason for it is that the President is very new." Writing to a board member, he suggested:

How about getting started on the local level? For example, we could organize a corporation with the same base as The Fund for the Republic but limited to Southern California. We could raise money locally to match a grant from the Fund. The advantages of this are, (1) you would get some action, (2) you would tap other resources, (3) you would move in one of the two regions that needs it most, and (4) you would conduct an experiment in local operation. I am inclined to think that the Fund will eventually find that it will have to work through local and regional groups. I talked about this with Joyce and Hoffman. Bill was enthusiastic. Hoffman seemed primarily interested in other matters, such as getting your tax exemption and the balance of the money due from the Ford Foundation.[63]

The first "annual meeting" of the Fund's directors was held on November 18 at the Hotel Roosevelt in New York City. Following the formal re-election of board members and officers and the handling of several business matters, the discussion turned once again toward policy and the state of current projects. The Summer Planning Committee on the Legacy of American Liberty, independent consultants who had cost the board over $10,000, had had a difficult and frustrating summer. Most of their recommendations—a study of anti-intellectualism, for example—were either thrown out by the directors or sent to the Ford Foundation. The one suggestion that did catch the board's eye moved it to decree "that the staff of the Fund investigate the work of the Advertising Council . . . with a view to possible assistance by the Fund in the dissemination of the materials developed by the council." Few dangerous radicals seemed to have infiltrated the Fund for the Republic to date.

A series of articles from the Houston *Post* on the "Minute Women of America" had been sent to each director earlier in the month and created interest in the possible study of "the intellectual security of teachers." The president would appoint a committee on the matter, said Hoffman, as soon as he "had an opporunity to ascertain which Board members would be able to give time to meetings of such a committee." Case was furthermore authorized to work with Sutherland's committee and to consult with officers of Adler's Institute of Philosophical Research to determine the worth of supporting its continuing studies on a "Philosophical Analysis of the Meaning of Freedom." The Summer committee and Mr. Cole's regular Committee on the Legacy of American Liberty were dissolved.[64]

The Fund's other major planning committee, on the study of the internal Communist menace, reported substantial progress on plans for one of its two projects, studies on the Communist record. Two recommendations were made and approved by the directors. A sum not to exceed $35,000 was allocated

> to proceed with the execution of the three short-range projects recommended in its report: a digest of public proceedings concerning communism; a microfilm library of transcripts of trials and other proceedings; and a bibliography . . .

For a comprehensive history of Communism in the United States, to be published within three years, $250,000 was appropriated. Anti-Communist studies, to be published at some later date, seemed the safest and least complicated way to set the stage for the request for tax exemption, to be submitted on December 10.

At the conclusion of its first year, the Fund for the Republic had issued no printed matter, had produced two press releases, and had made cash grants to four tax-exempt recipients for a total nearly equaled by "Organizational, planning and administrative expenses" and consultant fees.[66] Elmo Roper wrote to Dr. Hutchins:

> Frankly, at this moment I can't tell you how The Fund for the Republic is getting on. I think it is probably fair to state that progress is being made, but frankly, it is being made at what to me is a discouraging rate. But I think it is fair to add that no judgment ought to be passed for another three months' period. After that . . . ?[67]

CHAPTER FOUR

The Case
Interlude

While the Fund for the Republic struggled haltingly to its feet, the new Administration and the Republican-controlled Congress were vigorously in pursuit of "un-Americans." As conservatives viewed recent history (or said they did), under Truman the Christian leader of China had been betrayed; the American military had been shamefully stopped short of victory and glory; Communism had been coddled in Europe; business initiative at home had been stifled by New Deal bureaucrats; government eggheads and pinkish liberals in the schools, churches, and the mass media had twisted familiar moral standards and sneered at old-fashioned common sense. The nation had repudiated failure and weakness in November and the corruption and treason—"the mess"—in Washington was giving way to the "great crusade." National redemption was at hand.

On April 27, 1953, President Eisenhower unleashed a sweeping expansion of the security system which compounded and extended the Truman program in order to end the "softness" on Communism the new Chief Executive described in his State of the Union address. Executive Order 10450 resumed the highly dubious assumption that a prospective traitor could be identified by outward qualities; that certain attitudes, habits, beliefs, and associations evidenced a likelihood that an official was susceptible to treason. The order listed scores of characteristics—general, without qualification or limitation—any one of which could be used to dismiss a man from government service as a *security risk*.

It applied to all federal employees regardless how far removed their job was from classified data or important decision-making. It contained no specific procedural rights and abolished the loyalty-review program. The heads of all executive departments and agencies were given summary dismissal power. The burden of proof lay with the accused to prove his innocence.

Grounds for termination included "any behavior, activities or associations which tend to show that the individual is not reliable or trustworthy," as well as "any criminal, infamous, dishonest, immoral or notoriously disgraceful conduct." One category included "Establishing a continuing or sympathetic association with . . . any representative of a foreign nation whose interests may be inimical to the interests of the United States." The Attorney General's list (a mysterious device in itself) was no longer the exclusive standard for judging the disloyal character of organizations; federal officials responsible for security supervision could construct their own lists and were not required to make provision for time and duration of membership or knowledge of the organization's aims.

In short, government employees could now be discharged at the whim of a superior, without appeal to a higher authority, on grounds so amorphous as to dazzle all but the imagination. A forest ranger, for example, dismissed for excessive drinking, could suffer the destruction of his reputation by being included in the list of departed security risks. It was his responsibility to prove that he was not a security risk. Such, too, could be the fate of a postman whose wife had attended a Communist rally in 1936, an embassy clerk whose brother was once convicted of forgery, a diplomat discovered having cocktails with a Yugoslavian secretary, an academic consultant found subscribing to a radical magazine.

And a man's loyalty was never securely established, for no one could be fully trusted. Hundreds of officials were to suffer multiple security investigations by different agencies for different reasons. Scores of able, talented, independent-minded public servants left government service rather than submit to constant and arbitrary harassment.

The length of the list of the departed was politically important.

Democrats in mid-1953 were complaining of a "numbers game," the Republican device to convince Americans of the Administration's success in rooting out Communists and fellow-travelers held over from the "twenty years of treason." The White House told the press in October that 1,456 persons had been removed from the federal payroll. Two weeks later a special counsel to the President "clarified" the announcement by claiming in a speech that "1,456 subversives had been kicked out of government jobs since the President assumed office." Following considerable uproar, the official confessed that the number was correct but that the term "subversive" was mistaken. Such figures would increase, however, accompanied by the term, as the 1954 congressional elections approached.

Joining the Administration's security crusade were a number of members of Congress. In 1953 three of the most fanatical super-patriots of the decade assumed key positions on congressional committees: Harold H. Velde of Illinois took the reins of HUAC, William Jenner of Indiana became chairman of the Subcommittee on Internal Security, and Joseph McCarthy named himself chairman of the Subcommittee on Investigations of the Committee on Government Operations.

Harold Velde was an ex-FBI agent given to such observations as "The basis of Communism and socialistic influence is education of the people," and "The influence of Eleanor Roosevelt in the promotion of Communism, of immorality and indecency among so-called minority groups in Washington, should be explored." Under his direction, HUAC, its files bulging with well over a million names of persons cited for "un-Americanism," traveled the country widely, getting banner headlines for its "exposure" of the Red menace in education, the church, and the Democratic party.

For five months in 1953 intermittent hearings were held on Communist infiltration of education. Teachers were suspended or fired for past associations and for refusing to answer committee charges; academic freedom was slandered when not ignored. The hearings sparked further investigations into textbooks, lectures, and the personal lives of teachers by state, local, and university authorities.

In March, Representative Donald L. Jackson supported Chairman Velde's desire for a probe into subversion in the churches by claiming that liberal Methodist Bishop G. Bromley Oxnam "served God on Sunday and the Communist front for the balance of the week." A member of Senator McCathy's staff, J. B. Matthews, then published an article which even drew grumbles from the President, claiming that 7,000 Protestant clergymen were servants of Communism. (Earlier, Matthews had harried Robert Hutchins before an Illinois state investigating committee on loyalty at the University of Chicago, and had the distinction of casting suspicion on Shirley Temple for allegedly endorsing a French Communist newspaper.) Supported actively by a number of right-wing hate groups, HUAC held hearings on the clergy and its social concerns in July. It soon released the statement of one witness who said that some 600 Protestant ministers were "secret party members" and that from 3,000 to 4,000 more were in the "fellow-traveling category." Bishop Oxnam (who believed the Communist party to be a conspiracy and the FBI rather than HUAC qualified to unmask it) was interrogated before the committee (and radio and television) for ten hours before its members would admit he was not a Communist. Even then the bishop was not cleared from the charge of "serving Communism."

Following highly controversial charges by Attorney General Herbert Brownell, Jr., that President Truman knew Harry Dexter White was a "Russian spy" when appointing him to the International Monetary Fund, HUAC subpoenaed Mr. Truman, former Secretary of State James F. Byrnes, and former Attorney General (now Supreme Court Justice) Tom Clark. Apparently no one was above the Committee's grasp.

The Senate Judiciary's Internal Security Subcommittee, under Old Guard stalwart William Jenner, completed investigations on Communism in education and the United Nations, and held extensive hearings in 1953 on subversion in government. In July it issued 110,000 copies of a report which deeply implicated the Democrats in a "breakdown in the loyalty machinery." (The Republican National Committee purchased an additional 50,000 copies, as did ultraconservative Texas oilman H. L. Hunt.) Attorney General Brownell, assisted by J. Edgar Hoover, used the subcommittee and attendant television cameras to air his doubts about the patriotism of Truman and Clark. Hearings were also held on Communism in labor unions and Communist press facilities.

The biggest headlines, however, were being made by Joseph McCarthy, whose star was still in its ascent. The senator had apparently crushed his most dangerous opponents, Senators Tydings and Benton, at the ballot box; he had been a major figure in the 1952 Republican victory, even being selected as the party's climax speaker on nation-wide networks; John Foster Dulles was friendly toward him; and Senator Taft, until his death, was highly sympathetic with his "fight for America."

In February hearings began on the condition of State Department personnel files, which resulted in an interim report condemning the Truman Administration for failing to remove "persons whose interests were contrary to the national security." Soon, with the aid of two young assistants, Roy Cohn and G. David Schine, a "patriotic survey" of literature in the overseas information program was made for the subcommittee, culminating in the charge that over 30,000 books by Communists and "pro-Communists" had been discovered. Hearings were also held on the Voice of America program, featuring a reckless display of unsubstantiated accusations and intimidation.

The senator felt powerful enough to tackle unfriendly journalists directly, submitting James Wechsler of the New York *Post* to an intensive grilling, ostensibly for his membership in the Young Communist League at Columbia two decades earlier, and for the fact that two of his books were discovered in American overseas libraries. McCarthy called for an investigation of the liberal Washington *Post,* whose owner, he claimed, had "prostituted and endangered freedom of the press by constant false, vicious, intemperate attacks upon anyone who dares expose any of the undercover Communists."

In August he moved to a probe of Communist infiltration of the armed forces. In October hearings were initiated on alleged espionage at the Army Signal Corps Radar Center in Fort Monmouth, New Jersey. Attacks also fell, in 1953, upon Harvard University, the Government Printing Office, and the United

Nations. The subcommittee even made an agreement on its own with Greek shipowners to halt trade with Communist China, North Korea, and Soviet Pacific ports. When President Truman was given network time to refute the charges made by Herbert Brownell, Senator McCarthy demanded and received equal time to answer Truman.

MCarthy had a "Loyal American Underground," a corps of "true patriots" throughout the government feeding him information; the President of the United States promised to make no more appointments displeasing to him; the Gallup Poll would soon indicate that only 29 per cent of the American people held an unfavorable opinion of him. Though the senator had not uncovered a single certifiable Communist (he never did) he had become one of the most powerful men in America, passionately followed, as Richard Rovere put it, by "a coalition of the aggrieved—of men and women not deranged but deeply affronted by various tendencies over the preceding two or three decades." That the morale of government employees was low, that flexibility in foreign policy had all but vanished, that many Americans dared not say or read what they chose for fear of becoming suspect, that reform legislation was casually equated with "creeping socialism" at every hand, that scores of Americans were sentenced to unemployment and disgrace without recourse at law—these matters concerned the zealous not at all.

The Bill of Rights meant nothing to McCarthy and his followers. Said the senator of the Fifth Amendment, for example: "Even the most soft-headed and fuzzy-minded cannot help but realize that a witness's refusal to answer whether or not he is a Communist on the ground that his answer would tend to incriminate him is the most positive proof obtainable that the witness is a Communist." Sternly anti-intellectual and fearful of the complex world of uncertainties, McCarthyism sought to restrict traditional liberties in the name of a higher good: Truth. The Republic's true enemies, believers contended, were ambivalence, debate, dissent, unorthodoxy—and they would rid the nation of them. By definition McCarthyism would have to lock horns with the Fund for the Republic—that is, if the Fund were ever to carry out its mandate.[1]

On January 22, 1954, Clifford Case reported happily that an unqualified ruling of tax exemption had been received from the Department of the Treasury. In this same memorandum to the directors, Case declared his "strong belief" in the "harder, slower job of education" and wrote of "our greatest resource,—the innate decency, sense of fair play and basic common sense of the American people."

> Can the Fund call upon these strengths? Can we, by the means available to us as an "educational" organization, alert the American people sufficiently to keep the balance on freedom's side?
>
> The answer depends in great part on whether we are able to gain and hold public confidence. When we present facts, the public must believe we are giving it the true story and the whole story. When we present points of view, the public must believe we are fairly presenting both sides. . . . It would be unrealistic not to recognize that some suspicion exists that the primary concern of the Fund itself is not the preservation of our freedoms as such but the special interests of the liberal and intellectual groups whose freedoms are currently under particular attack.[2]

Clifford Case saw the Fund's ideological role, in the words of one of his assistants, as "a net in the center of the court, whoever might be serving."[3] Whether the generalities in which this view was framed would prohibit meaningful action remained to be seen. There might surely be room for doubt by the Fund's fourteenth month.

The president was hard at work throughout January. He hired three temporary consultants to advise him on a variety of possible projects, and spent much effort on the development of means by which the Fund might use the mass media "to create a better climate for freedom."[4] Stouffer's analysis of public opinion was getting started, the short-term projects on the Communist record were under way, and several additional ideas were under serious consideration.[5]

On the 25th, Case had an assistant interview Henry Steele Commager for suggestions on the development of one of Hoffman's ideas, a study of American dissenters. The historian had been one of the most persistent and eloquent opponents of the current craze to restrict freedom of thought, speech, and association. To assist in reversing the national mood, Commager advised, the Fund ought not to subsidize books. They "would be reviewed, bought, and read by people that already reviewed, bought, and read such books." The problem was, he said, to get the mass-circulation magazines interested in the field of civil liberties. Furthermore, "A lot of good might be done by getting veterans groups and other patriotic groups to see that freedom and civil rights are conservative ideas, not radical ideas. Getting the right people from such groups to participate in undertakings in defense of freedom was good—though risky."[6]

The board, at its meeting three days later, listened to the new consultants and discussed several future actions. It agreed to only two allocations: $5,000 to the Southern Regional Council for the summarization and distribution of a report on segregation written for the Ford Foundation, and $1,000 to the New York Public Library (whose services were "frequently used by the Fund's staff").[7]

The Reece committee, in the meantime, had written two letters to President Case, inquiring into every detail of the Fund's operation. One investigator wanted to know

> The full story of its birth. If you cannot piece this together and would prefer me to address myself directly to the Ford Foundation, I shall do so, but it would seem to me wise for you, yourself, to know the generative, prenatal and obstetrical facts; they should be important as background atmosphere in your work. . . . I would like to know what persons suggested the Fund, and how; what discussions there were concerning its proposed field of operations and objectives; and whatever further material might bear directly on the accusation, frequently made, that the Fund was created to attack or weaken the Congressional investigations.[8]

In his reply, Case hedged on the more specific questions pertaining to the Fund's origins; he was aware that the committee was up to more than securing evidence on which to propose legislation. He quickly assured the committee's research director, however, that "The project furthest advanced is one concerned with the nature and extent of the internal communist menace."[9]

In a thirty-one-page addendum to his letter, Clifford Case summarized the Fund's activities and unwittingly wrote the epitaph to his presidency. The Fund, it was revealed, had turned down forty-six applications for grants from reputable scholars and organizations such as the National Education Association, the American Council of Learned Societies, Tuskegee Institute, and the Scientist's Committee on Loyalty and Security (which had requested $500). The four grants made to tax-exempt bodies (two of which were sanctioned by the Foundation) totaled only $174,-500 and had been made prior to Case's active participation as president. No radical effects were visible or immediately foreseen. The Fund's projects, most of which were respectable, scholarly studies of Communism, had produced nothing tangible as yet and were not expected to for several years.[10]

In response to a further query from the committee, the president replied, a few weeks later:

> The Board of Directors, which has the responsibility for approval, looks . . . not only to the substance of the proposal and its relation to our basic objectives, but to the standing and character of the applicant organization or group, the work it has done in the past, its sources of financial support, and the quality of its leadership. . . . In many instances as, for example, the grant to the American Bar Foundation, individual members of the Board have had extensive acquaintance and knowledge of the activities of the proposed grant recipient.
>
> By the terms of its grants, the Fund receives periodic program and financial reports as well as informal interim reports.
>
> The Board of Directors has authorized the staff to reject proposals which are deemed to fall outside the scope of the Fund's program and has directed that periodic reports of such action be made to the Board.[11]

How the Reece committee could continue to see a left-wing menace set loose on society in light of all observable evidence is difficult to comprehend. True, the corporation had well over $14,000,000 to spend in the next three and one-half years, but on the basis of every aspect of its short history, it should have seemed reasonably likely that few citizens, not enveloped perpetually by library walls, would ever hear of the Fund for the Republic.

On March 4, Paul Hoffman sent an emergency night letter to each director:

> You have no doubt seen newspaper stories connecting Clifford Case with the United States Senate Election in New Jersey. He has not yet decided to run but he is under heavy pressure to do so. He presently feels he may be obliged to make himself available and knowing something of the situation I cannot disagree. If this should happen we both feel he should immediately resign as President of the Fund, but he would be available to help in any capacity in order to prevent interruption of our program. The decision must be made within the next few days and if he is a candidate I will promptly call a meeting of our Executive Committee. I will keep you advised.[12]

The "heavy pressure" had come from President Eisenhower. The next day Clifford Case resigned.

The executive committee of the board met on March 16. It accepted Case's resignation, effective March 5, and appointed him a consultant, at his regular salary, through April 1, when the full body of directors would meet. George N. Shuster was made acting president and directors Roper, Griswold, and O'Brian were selected to seek a new president.[13]

Clifford Case did not assume his full duties as the Fund's chief executive until early October, following his resignation from Congress and a vacation. His leadership was not truly felt, judging from the Fund's official minutes, until mid-November—six months after his election, over three months after his departure from politics, and only four months before his resignation. His role in formulating policy and originating programs was minimal. If the bibliography of the public record of Communism would fall short of expectations, if the Voluntary Defenders would fail to spend their entire allocation, if several of the early studies turned into dusty tomes, it can be argued that little of the blame should rest on Case's shoulders. He was surely aware of the Fund's inadequacies and later notified the new president that he would have authorized an annual report "but felt that [it] would have much more meaning if we could illustrate the statement by pointing to at least several significant programs which were already under way. We were just about at the point where we could do this when my decision to run for the Senate was made."[14]

Case has been criticized for timidity: Dwight Macdonald in his lambent survey of the Fund described him as "both a Republican and a liberal—in that order, as it turned out," and wrote of the "Case fiasco."[15] But the evidence suggests that once he had actually begun his presidential duties, he was a man of ideas and initiative. Even on March 16, 1954, he recommended two grants to the executive committee, one of which, a program of community education by the Carrie Chapman Catt Memorial Fund, would become one of the Fund's largest and most effective efforts.[16] At Case's last board meeting, on April 1, the directors appropriated $240,000, their most ambitious grant so far, to the Southern Regional Council for support of an expanded program of community education in intergroup relations.[17] Case's staff, especially Frank Loescher, had conducted the required research and made the recommendation.[18] With what degree of boldness and effectiveness Case would have led the Fund had he continued in its highest post can only be pondered. The oversimplifications and generalities of his *confidential* correspondence, and his later reactions to the Fund's difficulties, suggest that he may have sought another calling as the political temperature mounted. But it should not be forgotten that he was a man of integrity and of demonstrated conviction, whose public record revealed a deep concern for the highest values for which the Fund for the Republic stood.[19]

By April 1954, the directors had either explored or entered, if only slightly, most of the general areas in which the Fund was to work. The Stouffer survey of public attitudes toward Communism and civil liberties would be published in a year and provide profound and valuable insights into the mass mind of America during the early 1950's. The bibliography and digest of the public record of Communism in the United States were to be completed in a few months and distributed widely throughout the nation. The projected studies of Communist influences in major segments of United States society would produce many highly acclaimed volumes. Allocations to the American Friends

Service Committee, the Southern Regional Council, and the Carrie Chapman Catt Memorial Fund would be increased in later years to provide additional education and service. The papers delivered at the Columbia University Bicentennial celebration were published in the *Columbia Law Review*. The American Bar Association's Special Committee used half of its grant to create an important 45-page report (plus a 166-page appendix) which was absorbed into a proposed code of investigative procedure. The Voluntary Defenders Committee provided legal assistance to a large number of defendants.

The board, in its first sixteen months, under Paul Hoffman and David Freeman and, for a short time, Clifford Case, had achieved complete tax exemption and acquired the balance of the $15,000,-000 from the Foundation.[20] Its insistence on reputable studies and scholars had caused a minimum of perilous publicity.

Dwight Macdonald is correct, however, to point out that the five years between Ford's study committee's report and Case's departure were "just those years that the Bill of Rights was being most rapidly eroded."[21] And by the fourth month of 1954 the Fund had made little social impact. Journalist I. F. Stone lamented: "The premises of free society and of liberalism find no one to voice them, yet McCarthyism will not be ended until someone has the nerve to make this kind of fundamental attack upon it."[22] Perhaps the Fund could discover a new president who would provide the necesary inspiration and leadership to enable the directors to fulfill effectively their original goals.

Within a few weeks the history of the Fund for the Republic would begin to alter sharply; the new president was to be Robert M. Hutchtins.

CHAPTER FIVE

The Right Man

*T*he authority of Robert Hutchins within the Ford Foundation became secondary after Paul Hoffman's retirement. The associate director sat in the rump office in Pasadena, looked upon by many insiders as an unnecessary vestige of turbulent times, an overly outspoken crusader whose retention was due solely to the corporation's unwillingness to invite controversy. No one within the Foundation offered any positive suggestions about the future of the fifty-four-year-old administrator, and Hutchins himself seemed unready to seek other employment voluntarily. His advice was sought on several occasions,[1] but he provoked ill will by insisting repeatedly that the Foundation had higher responsibilities than it currently recognized, and should be much more than a pliant device of a recreant donor.[2] The already strained relationship between Henry Ford and Hutchins became increasingly poor as months passed.[3] By the end of 1953 the educator's presence was becoming intolerable.[4]

In early March 1954, veteran lawyer Grenville Clark heard of Clifford Case's resignation from the Fund for the Republic and telephoned John Lord O'Brian with the suggestion that the directors consider Robert M. Hutchins as a replacement. Clark was a friend of long standing, and Hutchins had been instrumental in securing Foundation support for his monumental study, *World Peace Through World Law*.[5] O'Brian informed Clark that he had recently received a similar proposal by letter from Erwin Griswold in response to a complaint about the Fund's lethargy and ineffectiveness. O'Brian concluded: "Well, I can say this much to you at any rate, that Hutchins' name will certainly be very seriously considered."[6]

Robert Hutchins maintained, he later recalled, but "very slight" contact with the directors following the Fund's incorporation. He had, of course, along with the Foundation's other officers, observed their early efforts with considerable interest—and more than his share of impatience. When offered the presidency by directors Roper and Joyce in the latter's spacious home outside Pasadena, he accepted "with willingness and pleasure."[7] Several directors soon told him they were depressed by Fund inactivity and wanted "to get going."[8] They no doubt knew that the right man had been selected to fulfill such a task.

> When I innocently accepted the Presidency of the Fund for the Republic . . . I made two mistakes: I overestimated the public knowledge of foundations and the way they work; and I overestimated the public knowledge of and interest in the Bill of Rights. My only excuse, in the first instance, is that nothing in my experience had prepared me for the public effects of the campaign of misrepresentation that began as soon as the program of the Fund became known. . . . For [the second] mistake I have no excuse at all. The Chief Justice of the United States was not giving the results of any secret research when he expressed doubt as to whether the Bill of Rights could be adopted today. He was saying what everybody knows and what I forgot or chose to ignore when I began to work on the program of the Fund.[9]

One should not be lured into error by the irony and deliberate overstatement in Hutchins's style of writing, however; he was fully aware of the turbulence risked in executing the Fund's stated goals during the McCarthy era. He was conscious of the fact that on one Monday during the immediate future the Supreme Court, under its new Chief Justice, would issue a profoundly important decision on school integration; that the controversial Oppenheimer case would soon be concluded; that the turmoil surrounding the junior senator from Wisconsin was boiling at an increasing tempo; that the Reece investigation, openly aimed, at least in part, at the Fund for the Republic, was about to conduct public hearings on why foundations "do not support projects of a pro-American type."[10] In *Look* magazine on March 9 he wrote:

> Education is impossible in many parts of the United States today because free inquiry and free discussion are impossible. In these communities, the teacher of economics, history or political science cannot teach. Even the teacher of literature must be careful. Didn't a member of Indiana's Text Book Commission call Robin Hood subversive?[11]

Hutchins was, in short, keenly sensitive to the highly charged political climate of the time when assuming the Fund's presidency. He had not lost touch with the increasing tendency to restrict the Bill of Rights that had lain behind the Fund's creation. Nor was he unmindful of conservative critics waiting in the wings to attack the Fund as it began the second act of its existence.

His would be the task of informing the public, for the first time, of the Fund's programs, as the first studies rolled off the presses and as new ways for spending millions of dollars were conceived and carried out. That such activity would be met with outcry, that he would be the object of considerable acrimony, was predictable. But Hutchins had been involved in the struggle for human rights before and was not known to suffer from such clatter. Moreover, the adversaries would probably be familiar; they were the same right-wing phalanx that most leaders of the respectable intellectual community had condemned since the Depression for their enmity toward the free association of ideas and the redistribution of wealth. And leading the Fund for the Republic was certain to be more attractive and challenging than merely "associating and directing" for Ford's Foundation.

On April 15, 1954, the board elected Robert Hutchins a member, a director, and president of the Fund, "subject to, and effective upon, completion of arrangements" enabling him to assume office. It was decided to hand the "public relations problems which might arise" to Chairman Hoffman.[12] On May 25, during a recess in the Army-McCarthy hearings, and only days after the Reece committee's blasts against the "subversion" of the Fund for the Advancement of Education, it was publicly announced that Robert M. Hutchins had been elected to be the Fund for the

Republic's new president.[13] Hutchins chose to continue living in Pasadena for the time being and to fly to New York when necessary. "Due to the confusion," he recollected later, "it was felt that the Fund could be best operated in that fashion. There would be an advantage in being represented on both coasts and I still had duties with the Fund for Adult Education."[14]

For assistance in arriving at far-reaching, significant projects for the board's consideration, Hutchins, within two days of his own decision to join the Fund, called on W. H. Ferry to offer him the Fund's vice-presidency. Reluctant at first to leave his handsomely paid position as a New York public-relations executive, Ferry finally succumbed to the persuasive powers of his friend and mentor, accepting as of July 1, 1954. Employed half-time on June 1 was Paul Hoffman's son Hallock, executive secretary of the American Friends Service Committee.[15] The staff recruited by Case was dismissed.

The directors did not meet again until June 30; and when they sat down across from President Hutchins to discuss and vote upon the recommendations and proposals sent to each of them in advance, it was as though a whirlwind had suddenly swept away the slow, argumentative, routine ways to which the participants had become accustomed. No figure had ever so clearly dominated a board meeting. The president's presence appears in virtually every paragraph of the minutes. Past programs were re-examined, new ideas scrutinized, and future possibilities explored at length.

The sum of $5,000 was approved to complete the work of the Committee on the Study of the Communist Record. But an evident dissatisfaction with the Fund's current emphasis appeared when the board then resumed discussion of the need for "a clear statement in contemporary terms of the legacy of American liberty."

In the board's eagerness to express the purity of its intentions by financing massive studies of American Communism, it had almost forgotten executive committee chairman Erwin Griswold's statement to the press when the $15,000,000 grant was announced in February 1953:

> One of the first activities to be undertaken by the fund is a thorough study into the many difficult concepts and problems

which are encountered in the field of civil liberties. We see a pressing need for a clear statement in contemporary terms of the legacy of American liberty. We propose to help restore respectability to individual freedom.[16]

Anti-Communism was a simple enough stance to assume; for almost a decade the tiny, shrinking American Communist party and its partisans had been studied, hounded, pressured, and restricted with rigor and fervor by virtually every element within the nation's government and industry. Much was known of the "internal menace," and perhaps more should be. But what exactly was the Fund for the Republic *for*? What were the modern perimeters within which it should function in light of the heritage of freedom responsible, in large part, for the creation and maintenance of history's most prominent democracy? What clearly ought the Fund to defend? Robert Hutchins thought that answers to such questions would be of valuable assistance in the planning of expenditures avowedly in defense of the Constitution. The directors agreed that a statement on the matter would be useful "if one could be produced."

The result of the discussion was the "sense of the meeting" that inquiries into Communism should be modified by the staff. It was suggested that they be limited to "an analysis of communist espionage, infiltration and indoctrination methods, with emphasis on the study of infiltration of groups such as unions, teachers, etc., and the methods used by such groups to turn back communist infiltration." These were not severe restrictions; it was simply time to proceed with other activities.

Hutchins then recommended, and the board approved, $25,000 for expenses leading to the creation of a commission on security which would examine the basic issues of loyalty-security programs. Members were to be chosen by the board's executive committee, subject to approval by the entire board. Twenty-five thousand dollars was also appropriated for preliminary research and planning of a study of "right fringe" extremist groups.[17]

Then the American Friends Service Committee was granted $86,500 to support four projects of its community relations program.[18] The Common Council for American Unity was authorized to receive $15,000 to expand its work in protecting and publicizing the legal rights of aliens.[19] And, finally, $10,000 was granted to the Catholic Interracial Council of Chicago, the first in a long series of sums invested in projects directed by Roman Catholic clergy and laymen.

President Hutchins turned the discussion next toward future possibilities: a study of fear in education; uses of the mass media; investigations into blacklisting in private industry; experimental community-level activities; increasing public awareness of civil liberties and civil rights by means of awards, essay contests, and television. When John Lord O'Brian brought up the problem of the loss of individual rights through actions by administrative tribunals, "The President stated that recommendations for work in this area would be presented at the next Board meeting."

Before adjournment, the nominating committee was requested to submit recommendations for four new directors when the board next met—the first additions in over sixteen months. There would also be no need in the future for monthly meetings, the directors learned: "The President stated that he would *submit* a schedule of quarterly meetings for the coming year [emphasis added]."[20]

All told, it was a spectacular display of executive leadership. Staff recommendations and suggestions were based on extensive investigation and careful research, and bear unmistakable evidences of Hutchins's pen.[21] The board accepted each in almost exact detail.[22] Dr. Hutchins later recalled:

> We had several commitments left over from Case which we were willing to fulfill. But we were determined to see how far we could go to help people and at the same time maintain our tax exemption. That was the major difference.[23]

Paul Hoffman had been expecting to testify before the Reece committee on June 29, but since the hearings had been suspended on the 17th he was unable to present what he felt would be an accurate view of the Fund's origins and purposes. He completed a six-page statement to the committee a few weeks later, submitting it "not because the Transcript of Hearings contains evidence concerning the Fund—for none has been offered so far—but because Representative Reece's speech of

July 27, 1953, now a part of the record of the 'investigation,' contains references to the Fund, and to me, personally, which, in the interest of accuracy and fairness, require comment." Hoffman attacked Reece's notion (protected from legal action by congressional immunity) that the Fund was a Communist-led, "king-sized Civil Rights Congress," patiently proffered an outline of the Fund's creation and its operations to date, and explained carefully the facts of the grant enabling the Special Committee of the American Bar Association to conduct the study on individual rights as affected by national security.[24] "I am happy to say," he concluded, "that it has been the purpose of The Fund for the Republic since it was established to reexamine, with a view to greater understanding and wider application, the sources of strength in our society . . . and that projects suggested for this purpose are being considered and advanced as rapidly as circumstances permit."[25] And indeed they were.

Hutchins and his staff sent six mailings to each director before the next board meeting, scheduled for September 14. The first was a memorandum from the New York *Herald-Tribune*'s talented editorialist and historian Walter Millis, a full-time consultant since August 1. An eloquent, highly articulate statement on the proposed Citizens Commission on the Federal Security Program, it began:

> . . . we have developed a Federal security system which, with its wider ramifications, is bringing into an increasingly large area of American life political and administrative procedures and attitudes which plainly resemble those of a police state much more than those of a normal democratic society. And this development carries with it far-reaching implications of a political and social character which are seriously disturbing. . . . in many ways the system is working against the national interest—not only in its impairment of democratic concepts and our ideas of justice, but in some more tangible ways. It is burdensome; it tends to reduce the government's efficiency in the performance of vital tasks; it tends to distort the processes by which the nation reaches decision in the most serious issues of high policy. Some have raised questions as to its possible long-run effects on economic organization, industrial relations, and other very wide fields of our national life.

Millis recognized the dilemma that many viewed the system as an invaluable shield against totalitarianism. The critical task of the proposed commission, he contended, would be the discovery of ways to reduce or eliminate drawbacks within the federal program without destroying necessary safeguards against actual Communist subversion. To do this he suggested a concentrated effort along "three broad avenues of attack":

> . . . the *need* for a personnel security system; the *description* of the system which has been evolved to meet this need, and a *weighing* of the gains and losses, the real benefits and the real costs, which have come in its train. From these three major lines of inquiry it should be possible to develop *recommendations* as to what can, or should be done about the situation as a whole.[26]

There was more to this proposal than a routine academic exercise; it involved the inevitably controversial process of seeking facts, making judgments, and broadly publicizing recommendations for reform—a course of action favored repeatedly by the Hutchins administration.

Directors may have contemplaetd the year's political events as they read Millis's memorandum, for the loyalty issue continued to rage unchecked—heightened, in fact, by impending congressional elections.

Responding to demands by the President to limit the First Amendment in certain areas for reasons of national security, and urged on by liberal Democrats desperate to rid themselves of the "softness" label, Congress hurriedly passed (so hurriedly that the lawmakers did not see the proper text of the bill until days after the vote) a vaguely worded and confusing Communist Control Act, designed to virtually outlaw the Communist party. Congress also weakened the Fifth Amendment by authorizing the courts to use grants of immunity to force witnesses to testify before its committees. Distinguished atomic scientist J. Robert Oppenheimer was denied a renewal of his security clearance on the basis of old evidence substantiating prior associations which the government claimed tended to make him actively disloyal sometime in the future. Republicans played the "numbers game" to full advantage, Vice-President Nixon soon claiming that "We're kicking the Communists and fellow travelers and security risks out of the Government, not by the hundreds, but by the thousands."

HUAC continued its far-reaching pursuits, with hearings emphasizing subversion in committee members' home states and districts for maximum effect on the ballot box.[27] Its tactics were without alteration: In Ohio the committee summoned one teacher from his position in a southern university to answer charges that he had driven to an American Youth Congress meeting thirteen years earlier; hearings were held on the patriotism of liberal Antioch College at the behest of the Ohio American Legion, a local hate sheet, and a Republican state senator who saw friendly interracial relations between students as an example of "communistic subversion."[28] The Senate's Internal Security Subcommittee provided a platform for the tirades of several retired generals against the Truman State Department and the United Nations, and busily investigated alleged subversion in the armed forces, labor unions, the Progressive party, and the Southern Conference Educational Fund.

On the other hand, Senator McCarthy seemed to be in trouble in the Senate for turning on the Eisenhower Administration, and his national popularity was slipping.[29] But his followers had thrilled at his conduct during the Army-McCarthy hearings, and he could still charge with relative impunity that those who wore the Democratic label "wear it with the stain of a historic betrayal; wear it with the blood of dying men who crawled up the hills of Korea while the politicians in the Democratic Party wrote invitations to the Communists to join them in the United Nations."

Writer and critic Brooks Atkinson surveyed with acerbity what he called "a growing compulsion toward totalitarian attitudes and practices" in a letter to *The New York Times* of August 9:

The Government refuses passports to citizens it does not like.

It blocks the free exchange of ideas by denying visas to eminent European scientists and writers who have been invited by American citizens to attend professional conferences here.

It has repudiated the scientist who led the world in the construction of the atom bomb because he is not a standardized man.

It maintains an organization of investigators who collect, among other items, facts concerning the newspaper reading habits of citizens and the mail that goes into their homes.

It employs political informers.

It blackmails citizens into informing on each other.

It summons citizens before Government committees to answer for their personal ideas, associations, friends and their relatives.

Government committees presume to give absolution to citizens who confess their political sins and promise not to violate the committees' party line in the future.

The Government has permitted a Senator to set himself up as public prosecutor.

It has accused the national foundations of underwriting revolution, threatened them with tax reprisals and denied them equal rights to defend themselves.

It sacks or rusticates foreign service officers who do not parrot the party line at home.

It tries to consolidate itself in power by denouncing its predecessors in office as traitors.

I wonder if Americans really want it this way.[30]

It was becoming increasingly clear by mid-1954 that the officers and directors of the Fund for the Republic did not.

On September 1 the directors received a detailed account of projects under way. The officers, it reported, had made an agreement with Cornell University's moderately conservative professor of government, Clinton L. Rossiter, to direct a thoroughgoing study of Communist influence in the United States; the report noted that he was already at work on the project.[31] Professor Sutherland's committee on the "public record" of Communism had made available records and briefs of twenty-three legal proceedings for microfilming and was laying plans to disseminate widely its bibliography and digest volumes. The Stouffer attitude survey had been completed at the end of July and an analysis of the results was in preparation. The Catholic Interracial Council of Chicago was hard at work coping with complex and dangerous problems of urban slums. Columbia University was distributing the educational materials which grew from its bicentennial meetings, and had received many requests for its documentary film "Freedom To Read" and four radio scripts presented earlier on national network dramatic productions. The preliminary study by Columbia's Bureau of Applied Social Research on community pressures on public schools had been incorporated as background material for a larger study. The National Council of the YMCA was about to distribute nationally a paper entitled "Toward Freedom and Security" and was developing a program on freedom of inquiry and discussion. The Southern Regional Council was recruiting additional personnel, and reported that the first printing of 20,000 pamphlets on the Ashmore report on racial integration in southern schools would soon be exhausted. The Voluntary Defenders Committee was expanding its services and had completed a valuable review of criminal court cases in each county of Massachusetts. The study of extremist groups had been handed over to Columbia University's Bureau of Applied Social Research, which hoped to complete a study plan within the next two months. And, the account concluded, the radio series on education presented by the National Citizens Commission for the Public Schools (about one third of which dealt with civil liberties) had been presented to approximately 4,928,000 listeners.[32] Board members then received seven recommendations for appropriations and grants totaling $780,000.

The ugly practice of blacklisting, in which the directors had expressed previous interest, was most egregious in the fields of motion pictures, radio, and television, Hutchins contended. "It is an area in which there are many flagrant cases in which persons of undoubted competence have lost their positions because of charges, often unfounded, about their political opinions. It is also an area in which the nature and scope of Communist infiltration can be studied." Much political hay had been made (notably by HUAC) upon allegations of "brainwashing" in motion pictures. Charges were common that innocent people had been barred from employment for their beliefs (often simply liberal), and there were rumors of a right-wing clique which raked in considerable sums of money for "clearing" or "weeding out" actors, writers, and others on the basis of their "Americanism." Hutchins sought $100,000 for the production of a statement of the facts. There was, of course, the possibility that a display of the facts would result in reform: ". . . the Officers would plan to obtain the consideration of the report by the industries in such a way that action might be expected."

The officers then requested an appropriation for an inquiry into the intellectual basis of censorship and the possible establishment of a commission on the right to read. The directors were informed that Dr. Paul Lazarsfeld of Columbia had been retained to develop the study of fear in education, and were asked for funds to cover expenses.

Individual court cases involving civil liberties had received little attention from the Fund thus far, and "The Officers are advised on every hand that it is more and more difficult for people of unpopular political views to obtain counsel." Overtures to the National Legal Aid Society and the American Bar Association had gotten nowhere. Hutchins and his staff asked for $10,000 "to continue their search for proper means of Fund participation in this field." To ease board fears, they added: "The Officers . . . are not seeking methods for providing defence of all persons charged with unpopular viewpoints either in Court or through administrative or Congressional hearings, but principally for a way of assisting in exemplary cases."

The uses of television for the Fund's purposes had been explored, the board learned. Three activities were suggested: (1) "a series presenting the contemporary situation with regard to civil liberties and racial and religious discrimination," (2) "assistance to networks or stations in the presentation of programs of interest to the Fund that might not otherwise be shown," and (3) "a series in which through history or fiction in dramatic form the Fund endeavors to show the importance in the development of the principles for which the Fund stands." The total bill might run as high as $2,750,000 a year, but for now the officers would settle for $500,000.

An elaborate scheme for the development of a national editorial competition aimed at "the best discussion of the Bill of Rights in the United States today" was then proposed to further the

American legacy project, which had sputtered along for months without any progress. It would be "the first of what the Officers hope will be the series of competitions in different fields already discussed with the Board, all designed to bring attention to those problems and areas of interest to the Fund."

Lastly, the directors were asked for $10,000 to enable the director of the Rockefeller Foundation studies on civil liberties, Professor Robert E. Cushman of Cornell, to prepare within six months an account of the current state of civil liberties for public or private circulation.[33]

This tour de force was followed by eleven detailed suggestions for preliminary discussion at the next meeting, a report on the grant applications rejected by the staff since June 30 (as well as those under consideration), and a recommendation for an additional appropriation for the Committee on the Communist Record.[34] The directors had sought performance by hiring Robert Hutchins; they could hardly complain about the current rate of acceleration.

The board took almost six hours to wrestle with the weighty agenda when it met on September 14. It approved a great portion of the ideas submitted, and committed the Fund to some daring and potentially significant undertakings. The requested $100,000 for the blacklisting study was appropriated, and Hutchins reported that negotiations were already under way for a director of the project. The board then agreed to the proposed study of fear in education, and appropriated $50,000 for preliminary expenses. The requested sum for the television proposals was lowered to $200,000 by the president, due to a delay of detailed plans; this amount was authorized for "the production of three or four pilot films of a historical-fictional nature and for participation in the presentation of television programs of interest to the Fund where such support is indicated." The editorial competition was viewed favorably, and the full sum of $100,000 agreed upon. And Dr. Cushman was to receive up to $10,000 for his studies on civil liberties.

The board failed to agree to an appropriation for a commission on freedom to read, but encouraged further study and future recommendations. It turned down a request for $10,000 to explore ways of supporting legal assistance in civil-liberties cases, but only on the technical ground that such expenses, "as in other subjects in which the Board had expressed interest," could be channeled through another, more convenient accounting category.[35] The staff was also encouraged to find methods to publicize the Stouffer survey when it was completed,[36] to explore the feasibility of utilizing the National Civil Liberties Clearing House for better distribution of materials of interest to the Fund, to continue the study into the possibility of establishing a commission on the performance of television and the press, to look into the effects of loyalty oaths and state FEPC legislation, and to continue exploring the creation of a study on Negro housing.

One by one the plans of President Hutchins and his assistants were viewed enthusiastically by the directors. The line was drawn, however, at proposed studies of local police and law enforcement and of the FBI. Sensing the volatile effects of such probes, these suggestions were "considered by the Directors to be too large an undertaking for the Fund to handle at this time," and were "postponed."[37]

Within two days after the board members had left the Hotel St. Regis for home, Dr. Hutchins hired a director for the blacklisting study.[38] John Cogley, thirty-eight, a graduate of Loyola University, was the executive editor of the liberal Catholic journal *Commonweal* and former editor of *Today,* a national Catholic student magazine. He had edited one book, written numerous articles, and had lectured at several Ivy League universities. A humble, friendly, perceptive, and keenly intelligent man, Cogley would prove to be a wise choice to head this difficult and delicate study. He proposed to undertake his duties full time in mid-November (he was running for Congress), and in the meantime hired as an assistant a brilliant young Socialist writer, Michael Harrington.[39] These two possessed deep sensitivity to social injustice, and would not hesitate to bare the least glamorous machinations of an incredibly wealthy and influential entertainment complex. Patterns were being woven for an open confrontation with powerful critics who had so far been able only to grumble about "investigations of investigations."

Several directors were becoming concerned about the legal

position of the Fund after two board meetings under Robert Hutchins. The Internal Revenue Code fails to provide any definitions of "education," and simply warns against "propaganda" and attempts to "influence" legislation.[40] The Fund was something new to American philanthropy, and with all of the projects and grants approved, with no doubt scores of others ready to appear for consideration, the staff attorneys were asked for a legal clarification of the Fund's possibilities. A report was submitted by Thomas W. Chrystie on October 1 which amplified and broadened slightly the original tax memorandum of December 17, 1953.

The Fund, Chrystie judged, could not sponsor candidates for political office or develop and support a precise legislative program. It would have to be cautious about entering the "twilight zone" of specific situations. Beyond that, assuming honesty and fairness, the board had little to fear from the government.

> In spite of the obligation to operate with careful regard for the tax exemption requirements, it is believed that the tax limitations present no serious obstacle. The primary problem, we take it, is to convince large numbers of people that American concepts of freedom and democracy are as important in 1954 as they were in 1776. This they will believe not because the Fund or anyone else says so, but because they themselves see and understand that it is so from their own comprehension of current events. And when people are awakened to the importance of applying these fundamental principles to the living problems of today, the detail of how the principles are to be implemented becomes relatively unimportant. The pressure of the tax law towards holding the Fund to fundamental principles, leaving it to the pupils (in this case the public) to work out the application of those principles in the myriads of complex situations in which they become involved, may very well be the course the Fund would wish to take even if there were no tax restrictions at all.[41]

But some board members might have questioned the extent to which the Fund could function successfully on the level of "fundamental principles." The Ford Foundation *Study Report* spoke of defining issues and alerting and educating the citizenry, entering "controversial areas boldly and with courage." The prospectus placed before the trustees in early 1953 listed many specific ills the Fund would encounter. And was it possible, for example, to look into the facts of congressional investigations and ignore HUAC's parodies on proper legislative conduct? Could the federal national security program be examined without reference to individual abuse? Could the blacklist study be written in the abstract? Could attention be called to discrimination in housing and intimidation of teachers merely with innocuous appeals to "American concepts of freedom and democracy"? It must have been obvious that Robert Hutchins thought not.

But by late 1954 much optimism could be found among moderate and liberal Americans. The Supreme Court had defended racial equality as it never had before, Congressman Reece had received pandemic ridicule for his right-wing assault against tax-exempt foundations, McCarthy appeared headed for oblivion, many articles predicted the end of the Red scare. There seemed no cause for alarm over the future of the Fund for the Republic. Dr. Hutchins and his staff worked on without interruption.

Within his first few months in office, Hutchins replaced Clifford Case's three consultants and hired nine more. They and their specialties were: Walter Millis, federal loyalty-security programs; Paul Lazarsfeld, the fear in education project; Frank Loescher, intergroup relations; Robert E. Cushman, civil liberties; Clinton Rossiter, studies on Communism in America; Samuel Stouffer, the survey of public attitudes on Communism and civil liberties; Howard Chernoff, television; John Cogley, blacklisting; George Overton, legal assistance programs; Conrad Arensberg, extremist groups; Philip Woodyat, editorial competitions; and general consultant Elmer Davis. It was a distinguished collection of scholars and experts, and Hutchins deemed it advisable to begin the practice of holding consultant meetings prior to board meetings to inform one another and the staff of developments within individual areas and to facilitate the preparation of factual progress reports.

They met first on October 27 at the offices of the Association of the Bar of the City of New York, and participated in seven and one-half hours of reports and discussion.[42] Several days later the directors, nearing their second annual meeting, received an imposing report from the Fund's officers documenting the alacrity with which the Fund's many programs were developing. The Communist record project was nearing completion: the publication and distribution of the *Digest of the Communist Record* and the *Bibliography on the Communist Problem in the U.S.* were scheduled for early 1955; the microfilm collections of the records of court proceedings involving Communism were to be ready in three weeks. The Stouffer survey was completed and being checked; publication was only a few months away. Dr. Lazarsfeld's study of educational freedom was progressing, and plans were developing to devote the initial effort to a limited survey among selected college and university teachers. Professor Cushman reported that his survey of current issues in civil liberties was "well under way" and that it too should be ready for publication early in the coming year. Clinton Rossiter had obtained firm commitments from six highly respected writers for as many studies into the influence of the Communist party in the United States. Frank Loescher said that as of October 1 the Southern Regional Council had six southern state organizations functioning with full-time executives; that the American Friends Service Committee was counseling Negroes on job opportunities and holding seminars on integration for teachers, parents, and community leaders; and that the Catholic Interracial Council of Chicago was running six workshops on race relations in Chicago.

Several projects were just beginning. Philip Woodyat, former English professor and director with the Institute of International Education, and since October 21 a full-time consultant to the Fund,[43] had several constructive preliminary recommendations for the essay awards, including the suggestion that "it may be found advisable to enlarge the scope of participation, not limiting it to editors and editorial writers alone." Experiments in television were being made in Los Angeles by supplying film clips on developments in civil liberties and civil rights for newscasts. A preliminary survey of blacklisting in the entertainment industry was nearing completion. Explorations into possible projects in legal assistance to individuals had come along so successfully that a recommendation to the board had already been prepared.[44] But it would have to wait its turn, for the recommendations designed for the directors' next meeting took twelve pages and two appendixes to present, and requested a total of $579,610.

On November 18 board members initiated their session by going through the legal actions required of them at their annual meetings. Before turning to the agenda, they proceeded to elect three additional directors.

Harry Ashmore was a much-needed representative from the South. The executive editor of the *Arkansas Gazette* and author of *The Negro and the Schools* was known widely as a highly intelligent and personable spokesman for liberal reform and integration. The second new director was Chester Bowles, celebrated author, wartime director of the OPA, former governor of Connecticut, and former United States ambassador to India and Nepal. Completing the list was the four-time Pulitzer Prize-winning playwright and historian, Robert E. Sherwood.[45]

The board then began to consider the long list of recommendations before them. The Carrie Chapman Catt Memorial Fund, with $45,000 granted by the Fund in April, had created several popular pamphlets on civil liberties which were widely distributed and used in its freedom agenda discussion programs. Sixteen national organizations now asked to cooperate with the programs, and the Fund was approached for additional money. As was often the case, Hutchins and his staff trimmed a huge request to a fraction of its size and the directors accepted the revision.[46] A terminal grant of $66,610 was to go to the "CCC," and an additional $20,000 was allocated for use by other tax-exempt organizations wishing to offer complementary programs.

Most of the school-segregation incidents in the early months following the Brown decision had occurred in the border states of Deleware, Maryland, and West Virginia—states in which the Southern Regional Council had no offices. The National Council of Churches of Christ in America asked for $10,000 to assist in providing staff for community counseling work in these states through the opening of the schools in the fall of 1955. The officers and directors of the Fund agreed on the value of the request, and granted the desired sum.

The Fund's staff had learned of the availability of a quantity of unsold volumes on civil liberties edited by Robert Cushman and originally underwritten by the Rockefeller Foundation. Professor Cushman sought $2,000 to acquire a number of the four major books for distribution to Fund directors and "to college department heads, newspaper editors, and others." The studies were several years old, but comprised the finest scholarly indictments of right-wing exploitation of the domestic Communist subversion issue. One in particular, Robert K. Carr's *The House Committee on Un-American Activities 1945–1950,* remained acutely relevant, and was a standing challenge to the committee's very existence. The board agreed to become associated with these so-called "Cornell Studies in Civil Liberties" by approving the request, but W. H. Ferry, during discussion of the matter, felt it prudent to note that "a large number" of the books would go to libraries.

A proposal was then entertained for the creation of a commission on race and housing to undertake a large-scale fact-finding study of the housing problems of minority groups. To persuade the directors of the wisdom of a $150,000 appropriation, an appendix was affixed to the recommendation containing data accurately reflecting one of the grave problems of American life. It stated, in part:

> It is believed that Negroes pay higher rents than whites for equivalent housing and, if they purchase homes, have to make larger down payments and pay higher interest rates. . . .
>
> There is evidence of "gentlemen's agreements" among property owners, financial, real estate, governmental and sometimes religious institutions that keep Negroes out of new housing developments and define the areas where Negroes may or may not live. . . . Considered typical of most large northern metropolitan areas is Philadelphia whose 400,000 Negroes constitute 20 per cent of the city's population. "Practically no new, privately-built housing was made available for Negro occupancy in recent years," is the finding of a recent study of private housing in the Philadelphia metropolitan area. "Although 140,000 new homes or rental units have been built since 1946, only 1,044 or less than one per cent were made available to Negro purchasers or renters. Of these

1,044 dwellings 578 were in Philadelphia; only 45 of the dwellings built in Phialedlphia were offered for sale to Negroes. During this same period almost 23,000 Negroes bought second-hand homes in Philadelphia under terms which customarily are more demanding than those required for new housing."

About a million dwelling units are being built every year. The pattern of segregation grows as Negroes are barred from new neighborhoods and communities.[47]

Hutchins sought a commission composed of men of "the highest repute" to conduct a "comprehensive, impartial study" which would gauge the nature and extent of the discrimination and report to the board and to the nation.

The Officers believe that the Fund ought to establish this Commission on the same basis that they recommended appointment of a Security Commission. If the Board authorizes a Commission, the Officers plan to find the best possible chairman. The aim would be to get a Commission made up of people of standing in the business and banking communities.[48]

The Fund's directors, for the first time, approved a proposal "in principle" and appropriated only $25,000 to enable the president to present a few examples of his Solid Citizenry.

The next recommendation resulted from investigations by consultants George Overton and Walter Millis. They found a need for a summary of existing laws and regulations under the federal personnel-security system to assist attorneys with loyalty-security cases. Ten thousand dollars was requested and approved to initiate its preparation.

Also approved was an appropriation of $100,000 to implement fully the creation of a commission on security. Walter Millis had had great difficulty in finding even a chairman for an independent commission, and it now appeared probable that the project would be undertaken by the Association of the Bar of the City of New York.

Hutchins then turned to his proposal for a continuing agency to appraise the performance of the mass media. He had sought such a body for several years, knowing that McCarthyism was, in great part, a result of the irresponsibility of elements within the mass media.[49] Charges of Communist subversion, no matter how bizarre, were often exploited by owners and managers in the communications industry because, like items on sex, they sold papers and raised ratings; they made startling headlines and supplemented accident and crime reports on newscasts. When the suggestion was made in 1947 for an independent agency, as Hutchins put it, "to appraise the performance of the press in discharging its responsibilities for public enlightenment," the National Conference of Editorial Writers, among others, howled it down. Henry Ford II (not one to tackle the likes of Hearst and McCormick) disliked the idea intensely when Hutchins later submitted it to the Foundation.

The Fund's president now phrased his recommendation with great care, even dropping the names of directors Shuster and Roper into the proposal. But the board "deferred" the $50,000 request, in spite of Hutchins's explanation that "this was not a proposal for a commission, but for a working party to instruct the Fund on what problems might arise if a commission were formed." He was to try again.[50]

Another possibility for the Fund, earlier conceived but left dormant, was the use of fellowships and grants-in-aid to scholars, lawyers, and journalists for work within areas of interest.

As a result of conferences with Henry Allan Moe of the Guggenheim Foundation and Professor Robert E. Cushman of Cornell, the Officers conclude that fellowships and grants-in-aid should be awarded not only to young people and unknown scholars, but also to established authorities who may need only a small amount of help to complete an important piece of work.[51]

The requested $115,000 for 1955 was appropriated, and the program, as accepted by the board, was to be under the direction of the officers in consultation with Professor Cushman.

The directors concluded the meeting by granting $6,000 to the American Library Association for assistance in the production and distribution of its faltering *Newsletter on Intellectual Freedom*; granting $15,000 to purchase and distribute a paperback edition of Erwin Griswold's forthcoming book *The Fifth Amendment Today;* and appropriating $100,000 to allow the officers to pursue an unspecified number of suggestions from Columbia's Bureau of Applied Social Research for studies of extremist groups.[53] Two proposals, a pamphlet series to be published by the Fund, and an award to a Los Angeles YMCA, were received warmly, but were delayed for further preparations.

In opening up several new avenues for grants and projects, and by appropriating almost half a million dollars at a single sitting, the directors could perhaps conclude that by its second anniversary the Fund for the Republic had made a sound start toward defending and propounding principles too often forgotten in a decade of cold-war frustration and rapid change. The Fund's administrative expenses for the first two years were extraordinarily high and open to criticism, but the percentage was expected to loom less large as further ideas were enacted and when actual expenditures were able to catch up with the board's recent appropriations.[54]

Robert Hutchins had proven quickly that he possessed the imagination, the vigor, and the will to be an effective leader. By November 1954 it was common for "the President" to appear in almost every important paragraph of the corporation minutes. The generous quantity of surviving correspondence from that time centers largely around this one man and his wishes. The Fund's delay in becoming fully operative and the directors' willingness to encourage performance explain much of this circumstance. The domineering character and genius of the president explain the rest. Almost from May 1954, the Fund for the Republic and Robert Hutchins were one. It was unthinkable to lay praise or blame on one and ignore the other. Whether or not this arrangement was advantageous would appear in due time.

CHAPTER SIX

For
the American
Dream

O n November 23 the first installment by the Committee
on the Public Record of Communism was unveiled.
Nine libraries received a microfilm collection of the records and briefs of twenty-three trials involving Communism
in the United States. The eighty briefs, representing 170,000
pages of trial transcripts and exhibits, were from materials
made available by the Attorney General, the Department of
Justice, and counsel in the cases. They were assmbled by Charles
E. Corker, formerly of the Stanford Law School faculty, under
the supervision of the four-man committee chaired by Professor
Arthur E. Sutherland of the Harvard Law School.[1] The proceedings ranged from *People v. Lloyd,* which confirmed the sedition
conviction of eighteen members of the Communist Labor party
in 1919, through the recent trials of Hiss, Coplon, Dennis, Sobell,
and the Rosenbergs. "The microfilm library, in the view of
the committee, will help meet the present need for factual, accurate and carefully compiled information on the Communist
problem," declared the Fund's press release.

The collection might not have an immediate effect on the
national state of civil liberties, but it provided a worthy aid
to the serious student of American Communism.[2] Such a research tool would have profoundly bored the figure who, within
a few days of the microfilm collection announcement, became
the third man in the history of the Senate to be censured.

The forces which underlay Joseph McCarthy's dazzling rendez-

vous with American history are complex and not easily iso-
lated. Sheer political gain is the least obscure ingredient in the
compound. McCarthy stumbled upon a combination of public
frustrations which he exploited for political power; he was encouraged and tolerated by fellow Republicans as long as he
garnered or appeared to garner votes for the party. When his
Gallup rating dropped as a result of his nationally televised display
of reckless tactics and boorish manners, when he became a nonpartisan demagogue by turning on the President and on Senator
Arthur Watkins's Select Committee To Study Censure Charges
with allegations of treason, when the 1954 congressional elections
went against Republicans after McCarthy's call for a personal
referendum, the Wisconsin senator became expendable. For certain
relatively minor insults to fellow congressmen, he was "condemned." His official deflation was sealed by the President, most
forcefully by social ostracism.

But exultant liberals might have though twice about pre-
dictions of a rapid improvement in the nation's respect for individual liberties. The *-ism* was more than the man, and the
poison McCarthyism spawned was not to be subdued easily.[3]
The very heart of the legal strictures on freedom of thought
and expression—for example, the federal loyalty-security program (which Chief Justice Warren soon noted affected twenty
million Americans)—had been altered by not one line; its administration by security officers installed in every agency of the
federal government and in much of industry continued to be
severe and damaging to the public interest. An illustration of
the program's radical departure from traditional standards of
fair treatment was disclosed in late December.

Wolf I. Ladejinsky was an agricultural expert working for
the State Department in Tokyo when he applied for a transfer
to the Department of Agriculture. Secretary of Agriculture
Ezra Taft Benson vetoed the proposal, labeling Ladejinsky a
security risk. A newspaperman revealed that the State Department had granted Ladejinsky a security clearance using information found objectionable by Benson. Conservative Congressman
Walter Judd called attention to Ladejinsky's anti-Communist
writings and his labors for democratic land reform in the Far

East. A government security officer then felt compelled to explain Benson's action: It seemed probable that the Russian-born attaché had written and acted on orders from Moscow because his father and three sisters lived safely in Russia! That was the substance of the case; Benson adhered to his decision with confidence and pride.

Ladejinsky had no record of disloyal conduct; he had been described, in fact, as "the most effective man in Asia" and "the chief architect of the post-war land reform program in Japan" under MacArthur. No evidence suggested that he was a spy whose continued employment endangered the security of the United States. Even his personal habits were above reproach. That an American who dedicated years of his life to preventing the spread of Communism could suddenly find his job and reputation in jeopardy on the basis of mere whimsy seemed to critics typical of many cases involving the federal security system's disregard for sound evidence and due process.[4] Subsequent damage to the quality of government personnel and to the flexibility of United States foreign policy was incalculable but certain.

Instances similar to the Ladejinsky affair had come to light, and complaints were in abundance from former government employees whose careers were shattered without benefit of such minimum constitutional safeguards as the power of subpoena, the right to confront hostile witnesses, the right to examine adverse evidence, and the right to appeal. How common such cases were, how necessary the bypass of legal protections had become for the purposes of internal security, no one could (or would) say with certainty. Few statistics were available to the public, for most of the ferreting was done in secret. Political considerations aided in insulating the security processes from scrutiny. Well-publicized "trials" like that of Dr. Oppenheimer, however, revealed confusion, contradiction, and abuse in the government's aims and procedures.[5]

More than one prominent citizen had called for a review of the program. The board of directors of the American Association for the Advancement of Science, for example, recommended basic revisions in the security system.[6] Participants at a conference held by the American Assembly called for a "commission of outstanding citizens to review the problem."[7] On December 22, *The New York Times* made a front-page story of the $100,000 grant by the Fund for the Republic to the Association of the Bar of the City of New York for an examination of the federal loyalty-security program.

Dr. Hutchins had given the controversial program top priority shortly after accepting the Fund's presidency. Walter Millis was engaged to do preliminary research on it; a 101-page description of federal statutes, executive orders, and regulations was prepared for distribution by Sandra Weinstein and Ralph S. Brown, Jr., of the Yale Law School; and Washington attorney Adam Yarmolinsky was granted funds to make the first collection of loyalty-security case histories.[8] The president had negotiated the agreement with the New York Bar Association personally, and took pride in the fact that the grant went to an organization "of unimpeachable competence and integrity."

The purpose of these inquiries was the acquisition of facts to illuminate persistent questions—among them, as Walter Millis put it: "Can the necessary ends of the personnel security system be adequately provided for by some means less costly, less obstructive and less damaging to our basic ideas of individual right and due process than the system as it now exists?"[9] It was fitting that the Fund for the Republic, true to its mandate, should sponsor the first intensive nongovernmental studies of federal efforts to balance national security with individual freedoms.

The fund made news again early in 1955 with a press release heralding the impending publication of one of the important studies of the decade. Under the supervision of Dr. Samuel Stouffer, director of the Harvard University Laboratory of Social Relations, the most expensive survey of public opinion ever made had been conducted by George Gallup's American Institute of Public Opinion and the University of Chicago's National Opinion Research Center. For the $125,000 project 530 interviewers visited nearly 8,800 homes and made 15,000 telephone calls to arrange for and complete interviews during May, June, and July 1954.[10] Among those questioned about their views on civil liberties were 1,500 selected local leaders (mayors, Community Chest chairmen, regents of the DAR, PTA presidents, and others) to compare their opinions with the public at large. The results, compiled by Dr. Stouffer and published in one volume as *Communism, Conformity, and Civil Liberties,* provided a fascinating view of the national temper during the Army-McCarthy hearings as well as a clear look at the public's understanding of constitutional protections.

The Communist threat and civil liberties were not uppermost in the minds of Americans;[11] less than one per cent were primarily concerned about either, preferring, quite naturally, personal over national problems. But when the public did consider the subjects, it had little sympathy for the principles and safeguards cherished by civil libertarians. Among the findings were the following: 77 per cent of the respondents would have taken away an American Communist's citizenship (51 per cent would have had him jailed); 64 per cent approved of wire-tapping to secure evidence against Communists; 73 per cent thought it wise to report suspicious neighbors or acquaintances to the FBI as possible subversives. Only 3 per cent said they had known a person who admitted being a Communist, but another 10 per cent told of having suspicions. Some of the reasons given for such fears were: "I saw a map of Russia on a wall in his home"; "He had a foreign camera and took many pictures of New York bridges"; "He was always talking about world peace"; and "He didn't believe in Christ, heaven or hell." Said one respondent: "My husband's brother drinks and acts common-like. Sometimes I kind of think he is a Communist."[12]

Reflecting the craze for loyalty oaths (at least thirteen states required them of teachers), 94 per cent of the national cross-section would refuse to allow an atheist to teach in a college classroom, and 67 per cent would deny that opportunity to a Socialist. At least 30 per cent said they would not even permit a loyalty suspect the right to make a speech; only 58 per cent would grant that privilege to a Socialist.

The better-educated were more favorable to civil liberties than the general population, but 50 per cent of the attorneys interviewed believed that the invocation of the Fifth Amendment was a clear sign of guilt.

The study was later reviewed with enthusiasm, and described

as both objective and valuable. Dr. Gordon Allport of Harvard's department of psychology wrote of it:

> There has never been a more careful, more reliable, or more costly survey of a cross-section of American opinion on an issue of deep ideological significance. Every known safeguard in the interest of accuracy was employed . . .[13]

Summaries of the findings would appear in newspapers and popular magazines, stirring widespread commentary.[14]

The survey achieved its purpose exactly: it documented the extent of public prejudices and mapped a solid path for future ventures by responsible advocates of civil liberties. Dr. Hutchins believed it to be of value, and later wrote that it "confirmed the Board of Directors of the Fund in its conviction that the principal function of the Fund should be to uncover the facts about the state of civil liberties today and to promote discussion of them."[15]

The public's fear of Communist subversion, of course, was tightly interwoven with its dim appreciation of the Bill of Rights. Dr. Stouffer wrote in the conclusion of his study:

> People have a table fare of vague and distorted information about the Communist danger. They exaggerate present-day conversions of Americans to Communism and they have little awareness, let alone concern, about many of the harmful counteractions to such dangers as do exist.
>
> If a more balanced and palatable diet of information and education were to be made available, what does the study show about the prospects of acceptance? . . . the author offers his considered judgment that the prospects, on balance, should be good.[16]

Two further steps in that direction by the Fund for the Republic were announced on January 10.

Two unprecedented source books on the thirty-five year history of the Communist party in America, the second and third projects compiled under the direction of the Sutherland committee, were receiving free distribution to more than 700 libraries throughout the nation. One volume of over 500 pages, entitled *Bibliography on the Communist Problem in the United States,* consisted of a topical listing, with an author index, of books, pamphlets, magazine articles, and public documents on party antecedents, literature, and activity. The larger *Digest of the Public Record of Communism in the United States* was a guide to laws designed to control Communism, and information about Communism provided by public records. It included federal and state statutes, regulations and decisions, and public documents issued by federal and state governments. Within state legal materials, for example, it explored the following areas:

A Treason and acts bordering on treason.
B Rebellion and insurrection.
C Sabotage.
D Crimes of advocacy.
   1 Criminal anarchy.
   2 Criminal syndicalism.
   3 Sedition.
   4 Red Flag laws.
E Obstruction of justice, unlawful assembly, disorderly conduct, perjury, etc.
F Exclusion from ballot.
G Exclusion from state office, elective and appointive, and state employment.
H Communist registration laws.
I Exclusion from bar admission.
J Teachers' loyalty and oaths.
K Defamation.
L Litigation over control of labor unions.
M Investigatory power and contempt cases.

The book's appendix covered legislation of the second session of the Eighty-third Congress up to August 1954.[17]

The first four scholarly projects conceived by the Fund's directors in the spring of 1953 were now completed, leaving a rich legacy for generations of earnest students. The many volumes in the process of being written, on "Communist Influences in Major Segments of U. S. Society," would likewise be of invaluable assistance to, among others, the legal, political, and historical professions. It was hoped that irresponsibility would be less respectable in the future. The Fund for the Republic was fulfilling adequately one of its two immediate goals: "Research into the extent and nature of the internal Communist menace and its effect on our community and institutions." This task was perhaps less difficult and by all odds less controversial than direct entanglement with the very alive and outspoken non-Communist enemies of civil liberties and civil rights. But several plans in this direction were under way, and 1955 was young.[18]

All was going well for Robert Hutchins: the Fund's programs were developing satisfactorily in both quantity and velocity, predictable critics had lodged few complaints, and the board of directors had repeatedly expressed their affection and confidence. His requests were rarely trimmed or refused. In December, for example, he had called upon the executive committee twice to approve proposals, and its members consented to the rental of luxurious offices on the sixteenth floor of a new building on Fifth Avenue, the purchase and distribution of publications on civil liberties, a $75,000 appropriation for a television script competition plan just completed, and several other items.[19]

No doubt enjoying the security of his position as well as his freedom from the censorious scowls of the Ford trustees, Hutchins, in early 1955, began to turn his considerable skill with words against certain prominent foes of the freedoms he believed essential to the development of a just society. He told a Chicago American Legion post, on January 9, that he saw no discernible difference in the motives of the American Legion from those of the Grand Army of the Republic, and that members of the latter organization "were interested chiefly in increasing their personal incomes at the public expense." He also spoke out against Senator Bricker of Ohio and the proposed Bricker amendment.[20] A few days later, before the National Press Club in Washington, D.C., he attacked the Reece committee and its final report with the boldest and most caustic public comments yet expressed by an officer of the Fund.

The 432-page Reece report, published in late December, had already received widespread disclaim as a weird conglomeration of immoderate charges and ultraconservative diatribes. At its core was the contention that large foundations such as Ford, Rockefeller, and Carnegie were promoting socialism, subversion, and "Moral Relativity," and should be more closely supervised by federal authorities. A 189-page appendix listed dozens of prominent (usually liberal) persons and organizations "whose names had appeared in the body of the Report in a distinctive kind of type indicating that they had been cited by the Attorney General of the United States or by various other government agencies for having associations and affiliations of a questionable character."[21] Two Democrats on the committee had called the report "shocking" and "barbaric." The American Civil Liberties Union had urged congressional study of the "investigative practices involved" in the report, the union's executive director declaring that "The threat of governmental assault, punishment and control has been directed against ideas which happen to be disliked by certain Congressmen."[22]

When Dr. Hutchins stepped up to the rostrum on the evening of January 26, Representative Reece sat at the head table to his right, five chairs away. In the audience were Supreme Court Justices Felix Frankfurter and William O. Douglas, as well as Representatives Wayne Hayes and Gracie Pfost, who had filed the Reece committee's minority dissent. The speech began with a disclaimer:

> These remarks have been written for myself alone, and not on behalf of the Fund for the Republic, the Directors of which I have not consulted; nor the Ford Foundation, of which the Fund for the Republic is completely independent; nor for other foundations.

What a reporter from the Washington *Post* called the next day a "classic roasting" then commenced, a paradigm of the biting sarcasm and considered disdain Robert Hutchins reserved for those blatantly unencumbered by a liberal education. He said, in part:

> The Reece Committee achieves some of its gaudiest effects by the simple process of giving old words new definitions and then pinning the old words on the foundations. This is the way that empiricism becomes subversion. Subversion now means, the Committee says, a promotion of tendencies that may lead to results that the Committee will not like. Hence support of the New Deal

could be subversion. Social engineering, planning, world government, the United Nations, William James, John Dewey, the American Friends Service Committee, Dr. Kinsey and reform are all subversive in the bright new lexicon of the Reece Committee. And of course all these things are socialistic, if not communistic, too . . .

The appendix of the Reece Committee's so-called majority report is an endless carnival of good clean fun—it is almost two hundred pages long; but I must pass on. I cannot regard the Reece Committee as having more than symbolic or symptomatic importance. Its wild and squalid presentation affords a picture of the state of our culture that is most depressing. Its aims and methods are another example of the exploitation of public concern about Communism and subversion to further political ambition and to work off political grudges.

We may as well state it plainly: the Reece investigation in its inception and execution was a fraud . . .

However true that may have been, no employee of a tax-exempt corporation had ever so boldly condemned a congressional committee, let alone one authorized to pry into the legitimacy of philanthropic foundations. The guarded and benign letters of Clifford Case to Representative Reece stand in sharp contrast to Hutchins's casting of the gauntlet.

Then, in spite of the disclaimer, Hutchins proceeded to speak at length of the purposes and achievements of the Fund for the Republic, concluding:

> [It] is a kind of anti-absurdity fund, a fund to remind us that we can't have things both ways. We can't brag about the Bill of Rights and talk about Fifth Amendment Communists. We can't say that every man has the right to face his accusers and go on using what the Denver Post has called "faceless informers." We can't proclaim our devotion to due process of law and then deny it to people we don't like.
>
> The Fund for the Republic is a sort of Fund for the American Dream. I do not think the Fund can make the American dream come true; but perhaps it can help keep it alive and clear. Perhaps it can show where we are forgetting the dream as it once was dreamt and can point out those places, and they are numerous, where the progress toward the realization of the dream has surpassed our most expansive expectations.[23]

Several months earlier, Hearst's Fulton Lewis, Jr., and West-brook Pegler had begun research on the Ford Foundation and its offshoots. Pegler had mentioned the Fund for the Republic specifically during his initial inquiries.[24] Controversy was something Robert Hutchins sought, enjoyed, and found useful. The time was approaching when he and his board of directors would have a supply sufficient to occupy their attention.

The board convened again on February 17, 1955, and faced once more an extensive list of recommendations supported by several reports and studies. Dr. Hutchins initiated the deliberations by presenting an application for $9,000 by the National Book Committee for a preliminary study of the theory of censorship.

The president might have pointed out, had he thought it necessary, that for the last few years the right to publish and to read freely had been seriously abridged in America. In the winter of 1954, for example, one authoritative report documented the removal of hundreds of books from library shelves and classrooms on grounds of "controversiality," and the closing of bookstores throughout the nation by police (often on their own authority) for the confiscation of "obsene" publications. The post office in Providence, Rhode Island, notified Brown University it was holding up delivery of seventy-five copies of Lenin's *The State and Revolution* as "subversive literature"; a bookseller in St. Louis was fined for possessing copies of *Solaire Universel de Nudisme* and *Sunshine and Health;* a New York pharmacists' association yielded to pressure from the "National Organization for Decent Literature" and agreed to take from its newsstands some 530 comic books, periodicals, and paperback volumes, including works by Ernest Hemingway, Emile Zola, William Faulkner, Lilian Smith, and James Jones; in three months alone censorship ordinances were passed in twenty-eight cities from New Orleans, Louisiana, to Central Falls, Rhode Island, and "Newspaper reports indicate activity against newsstand publications in varying degrees by diverse community groups in at least 99 other cities and towns during the same period."[25]

The Fund's directors had for several months been wary about confronting the difficult, emotion-packed issue of censorship.

But the president's insistence, coupled with a favorable investigation into the request by director George Shuster, caused them to approve unanimously the small grant which, the minutes carefully noted, "did not commit the Fund to undertake an extensive study of the subject, but was rather designed to learn whether an extensive study would be desirable."

The board also approached the proposed policy of Fund awards with caution. Several directors questioned the usefulness of awards, others were wary of sanctioning past programs of specific organizations. After considerable discussion, Chairman Hoffman was authorized to appoint three directors to serve as an advisory committee to the president in developing criteria for future awards. And by the board's first badly split vote, the new program was inaugurated with a grant of up to $5,000 to the University YWCA at the University of California, Los Angeles, "in recognition of its maintenance of the open platform policy."[26]

The president had little difficulty in obtaining the board's approbation of other recommendations. An additional $11,000 was appropriated to assist in the financing of a legal service on security regulations to be published by the Bureau of National Affairs. The Commission on Negro Housing was given an additional $75,000 following the presentation of a list of eight eminent citizens who had agreed to accept membership on it.[27] Another $75,000 was appropriated for Professor Lazarsfeld's fear in education study.[28] A $5,000 request from the Association of the Bar of the City of New York Fund, Inc., was approved for an experimental program in supplying counsel for civil-liberties cases in the United States courts.

The board further appropriated, on the president's commendation, $25,000 to reprint and distribute articles and books dealing with civil liberties. General response to the earlier distribution of Dean Griswold's impressive defense of the Fifth Amendment had been encouraging, as it had been to the mimeographed transcript of a nonpolitical but friendly interview between J. Robert Oppenheimer and Edward R. Murrow which the Fund had been circulating free of charge.[29] This "general authorization," as was the case with most appropriations, was "to be expended at the direction of the Officers."[30]

A recommendation for $50,000 was then approved in support of a two-year group discussion program by the American Heritage Council, "devoted to producing a better understanding of such basic documents as the Declaration of Independence, the Constitution and the writings of Jefferson and Lincoln." The council's board included prominent attorneys, businessmen, educators, and clergymen, and it had previously received sizable contributions from other foundations, including the Fund for Adult Education. The council concentrated its efforts on labor unions, high schools, and the American Legion. (Of approximately 350 Legion posts in Cook County, seventy were participating in the program.) Here was an opportunity to spend money, to educate, and to assume ties with one of the Fund's most certain antagonists. Hutchins wrote earlier to his directors:

> Forecasts differ as to the enthusiasm that this program will enlist at national offices of the Legion, but it appears to have taken root in Illinois. It is difficult to argue against a free discussion of the Declaration of Independence and the Constitution. Legionnaires active in the program feel they are "bulletproof" against attacks by those whose chief interest lies in the Legion's "anti-subversive" efforts.[31]

Irving Breakstone, commander of the Illinois department, described this educational effort as a "positive approach" to anti-Communism. Hutchins looked upon Breakstone as a "hopeful figure" in the Legion.[32]

The final major resolution passed at this quarterly meeting of the directors was for $50,000 to be added to previously authorized monies for the commission on security project. Part of the sum was for further support of Adam Yarmolinsky's surprisingly successful case-record study, under way since early December.[33]

A few days later Brazilla Carroll Reece had his chance to respond to Dr. Hutchins before another luncheon of the National Press Club. The soft-spoken Tennessee congressman, exhibiting the anti-intellectualism fundamentally characteristic of McCarthyites, launched an impassioned, vituperative attack on the former university chancellor. It was as though Robert Hutchins exemplified everything Mr. Reece found foul and subversive; in smiting "one of the nation's most publicized educators" he could again strike out against a body of men who had drained the nation of its patriotism, courage, honor, and morality.[34]

> As this man of wisdom spoke [he said, in part], I was somehow reminded of Elbert Hubbard's definition of egotism. He defined egotism as "the anesthetic that nature gives to deaden the pain of being a damn fool.". . .
>
> As this great and dedicated man rose to address us, an aura of academic distinction radiated from his person, an aura reinforced by the soft effulgence which radiates from the wealth and power which support him . . .
>
> What a great shock, a distinguished academician turning politician, before our very eyes. His utterances appear as endless rewrites of a central theme of the professional intellectuals found in the foundations. The artful propagandist, dressed in the attire of an intellectualist, rides again.

Reece warned of the menace of "social scientist reformers" seeking "to introduce Fabian socialism into the United States," and portrayed an immense "intellectual cartel" which expends "vast millions of foundation money under their control to determine opinion, academic and public, in the leftish directions they favor." At one point his thoughts turned toward syllogism:

> You know, these planners, of whom Dr. Hutchins is an outstanding example, have clearly adopted a communist tactic.
>
> Communist[s] charge that the *rest* of the world is "aggressive."
>
> Similarly, these planners accuse the Committee on Foundations of wishing to suppress freedom of thought.

The congressman was also critical of the Fund, depicting the Murrow-Oppenheimer film as merely "an opportunity for Dr. Oppenheimer to make a defense of his conduct." A note of possible importance was raised when he turned his attention to the relationship between Hutchins's address and the Fund's board of directors.

> Despite Dr. Hutchins' fervent disclaimer in the title and first paragraph of his speech, Fund for the Republic is repeated four

times, once more than the number of times the sponsor's product needs to be mentioned in a radio commercial.

This disclaimer hardly balances the impression, and, by the way, if he was speaking without even consulting his trustees, he reduces them to the level of impotent window dressing.

He avers, however, that the foundations have been doing "a good deal of talking lately." Does he mean through their presidents and without consulting their trustees? Does this activity indicate the overt evidence of a hitherto covert condition?[35]

Ranks were slowly but steadily closing among opponents of the Fund for the Republic in early 1955, as its activities (especially those of its president) became more widely followed. At least one newspaper columnist was moved by Reece's speech to call for another investigation of foundations. The last one, he explained, had been undermined by a Democratic committee member, "all to the tittering applause of the pinkos and the New Deal one worlders of press, radio, and lecture platforms."[36]

On April 7 the executive committee held its second meeting to handle details and consider recommendations referred to it by the board for rapid expedition.[37] Among actions taken were the approval of a $10,000 appropriation to Columbia University (along with Harvard, one of the Fund's favorite universities) for exploration of an academic freedom study, and a $20,000 allocation to sustain efforts by new consultant Ben Segal (former associate director of the CIO's educational department) in developing interest in civil liberties among labor unions.[38]

As May approached, Robert Hutchins was completing his first year as the Fund's president—twelve active months filled with the excitement and bustle accompanying new, expensive, and often daring ideas. Under Hutchins the Fund's appropriations and grants were in excess of one and one-half million dollars. By this fifth month of 1955 a few of the projects and grants had borne fruit, and many more, representing the Fund's two and one-half years of existence, were in the making, as a review of selected activities reveals.

In intergroup relations, the Southern Regional Council had been enabled to strengthen its Atlanta headquarters and to staff twelve state affiliates with full-time professional personnel. It was bringing out an enlarged monthly magazine and reported its information services in heavy demand. A grant to the National Council of Churches was facilitating the creation of programs of community education in small border cities and towns to assist school integration. Seventeen distinguished citizens had accepted positions on the Commission on Race and Housing, which would soon begin its novel and much-needed study.[39] The Catholic Interracial Council of Chicago had held six human-relations workshops for three hundred teachers, and could report that for the first time Negro Catholic families living in the troubled Trumbull Park Homes housing project were attending masses in the local church without incident. The American Friends Service Committee was doing remarkable work with Indians in the Southwest, as well as with integrated PTA's in Washington, D.C., and Maryland, and reported progress in its job opportunities programs in Dallas and Greensboro.

In civil liberties the Fund had been even more resolute. Professor Stouffer's book had been distributed (2,500) copies), marketed, reviewed widely, and serialized in seven newspapers. Now in print were 1,500 copies of the bibliography and digest, of which 1,100 had been distributed free of charge to public, school, and armed-forces libraries. The Fund also distributed 2,000 transcripts of the sympathetic Oppenheimer interview, and 100 prints of the film were seen by thousands around the country.[40] As part of the appropriation for the dissemination of civil-liberties materials, 116,000 reprints of eight articles and speeches, along with 38,450 books, had been mailed to a wide assortment of citizens.[41] These materials contained strong criticisms of the federal loyalty-security program and the Radical Right, and included Telford Taylor's *Grand Inquest,* a carefully documented and highly rated thrust against congressional investigations.

The $100,000 blacklisting study was scheduled for completion on June 1, and plans were made to put the findings of the staff into book form. The reaction was guaranteed to be extremely heated. John Cogley told a reporter for an advertising magazine:

Virtually everyone interviewed says he's against blacklisting. But further probing shows that political criteria for hiring radio-TV personnel do exist. The criteria vary from agency to agency, from client to client, but exist they do.[42]

Said one important radio-television director:

This group won't accomplish anything. They'll have a hard time getting a reaction from people about this—people will just clam up. No one's going to be completely truthful.[43]

The fear in education study had progressed satisfactorily; 2,305 social-science faculty members in 158 colleges had completed questionnaires. A pilot study was under way with high-school social-studies teachers, principals, school-board members, and community-organization leaders.

More than 500 communities were using the freedom agenda discussion programs. The National Education Association alone wrote to 5,600 teachers urging them to be leaders or participants. The Carrie Chapman Catt Memorial Fund had distributed 125,000 pamphlets, and was now able to produce a newsletter relating to the progress of freedom agenda groups which included reports on pertinent films, recordings, pamphlets, and books. Additional grants had been awarded to the National Board of the YMCA and the Universalist Service Committee to aid in their participation with the program.

A revised and printed version of a federal loyalty-security handbook was being distributed to attorneys and libraries. Adam Yarmolinsky's case studies were proceeding on schedule and were expected to be available to the Committee on Personnel Security of the Association of the Bar of the City of New York in the fall. The Bureau of National Affairs relayed hopes of completing the preparation of its legal service on security regulations by the end of June.

Twelve grants, totaling $48,750, had been approved under the fellowship and grants-in-aid program since its inception in early November. One scholar was finishing a book on the Kentucky and Virginia resolutions, another was completing his Ph.D. dissertation, entitled "The Eisenhower Security Program: A Study in Public Policy," and a third was conducting interviews in Europe "with former leaders and opponents of fascism to help determine the potential leadership of the Extreme Right and the opposition to it in this country."

Fifty-six entries had been received by early May for the television script competition authorized by the executive committee in December. Seven judges were selected, and a special consultant to the project, Howard Barnes, former drama and film critic of the New York *Herald Tribune,* had been employed. Plans were announced to offer nineteen prizes totaling $29,000 for dramas and documentaries involving subjects of interest to the Fund. It was hoped that winning scripts woul be produced by the Fund on a current nationally televised program.[44]

In Pasadena, Hallock Hoffman was busy developing news clips for television broadcasts, while in New York negotiations were under way with Herblock, the brilliant editorial cartoonist of the Washington *Post,* over the possibility of a fifteen-minute weekly program.[45]

The awards program had begun on March 23 with the presentation of a $5,000 award to the Young Women's Christian Association at UCLA.[46] Another award, this time for $10,000, was presented a few days later by Paul Hoffman and Eleanor B. Stevenson to the citizens of Waverly, Iowa, for providing housing for the family of a Negro Air Force captain who moved into the all-white, predominantly Lutheran community.[47]

There had been a few disappointments within the past year. Two pilot television films by Al Capp, for example, were judged to be of poor quality, and a proposed series by the cartoonist was dropped;[48] the American legacy project had fizzled; no one could be found to undertake the extremist study. But failures, like criticisms, were bound to occur; to date the number of both had been surprisingly low.

Dozens of qualified, enthusiastic, and eminent Americans were actively pursuing the Fund's objectives by mid-1955, and many programs were satisfactorily in progress. It seemed, as recommendations, memos, and reports poured into the directors' offices and homes in preparation for the May 19 meeting, that the Fund for the Republic was about to become an almost undisputed success.

CHAPTER SEVEN / *Perils of Prosperity*

T he board meeting of May 19, 1955, was the most momen-
tous yet held. The recommendations, completed by the
officers on May 5, took forty-four single-spaced pages
to outline, and required, for the first time, a table of contents.
After two and one-half hours (by lunch) the total of appropriations and grants had reached $474,000; the final figure added up
to $861,000. Several items approved at this meeting were to have
great effect on the Fund's future.

The proceedings began with the formal announcement of
director Richard J. Finnegan's death.[1] Elected to replace him
was Arthur H. Dean, succesful New York attorney, Panmunjon
representative, former United States ambassador to Korea, and
a director and trustee of twelve corporations and foundations.[2]

Before turning to the regular agenda, Dr. Hutchins first presented a request of his own, a desire for "discretionary funds" to
enable the president to investigate and authorize various programs between meetings of the board and without the assistance
of the executive committee. The directors had, of course, relied
heavily on the judgment of the president during the past year,
expressing their confidence in word and deed. They had also
approved increases in the executive committee's duties to hasten
decisions and intensify the Fund's effectiveness. In this case,
however, the board members balked: the line was drawn at
actions involving major appropriations and decisions taken
solely by the officers. Their conclusion, based on a sense of per-

sonal responsibility to the Fund, was that "proposals which it was not possible to submit at this meeting should be submitted during the summer to the Executive Committee. Board members would be kept informed of all actions taken." This general policy was to remain permanent. The twelve directors present at the Hotel St. Regis this Thursday morning then turned to the numerous recommendations awaiting their consideration.

Several grants and appropriations were approved which need not be dwelt upon here: $5,000 to the American Friends Service Committee to record radio programs featuring civil-liberties and racial-integration messages for rural radio stations and school systems; $5,000 to finance a summer project on a civil-liberties project by members of the *Stanford Law Review*; $11,500 to underwrite the production of four phonograph records "selected from the great classics on Freedom"; $10,000 to the Public Education Association to assist in the cost of a survey on segregation in the New York City public-school system; and $5,000 to meet expenses incurred in discussing the possibility of a commission on censorship.[3]

One project was given additional funds: the study of the influence of Communism received $50,000 for the creation of two volumes on the history of the Communist party from 1917 to 1945. (Contained within the recommendation was the fact that negotiations were in progress to make use of "the knowledge and background" of Earl Browder, deposed head of the Communist party, U.S.A.) One former grantee, the Catholic Interracial Council of Chicago, was judged worthy of an additional $10,000 for its work toward reducing interracial tensions. The Common Council for American Unity, was also given a second grant, $32,000, to support a research project on aliens in America.

Money was made available for several new projects. It was widely known that postal officials were practicing censorship, barring *Pravda, Izvestia,* and other Russian publications from the mails, burning pacifist literature, and prohibiting the mailing of such "obscene" works as *Lysistrata.* To Hutchins such actions were intolerable, and the recommendation for a "Commission on Post Office Interference with the Flow of Opinion and Information" was offered. The president assured the board that

"Editorial comment through[out] the country has become increasingly critical, and centers on the arbitrariness of the restrictions and the fuzziness of the authority involved." Furthermore, he included a list of thirteen prominent people who might be called upon to make up the commission, noting that the group's report would be made exclusively to the board. The requested $35,000 was appropriated.

In the field of communications it was recommended that a new series of awards be given "to the best shows produced during the regular television season beginning in September." The idea, having the purpose of maximizing public attention to the Fund's general areas of concern, included enough cash incentive to "attain some of the prestige of the Pulitzer and Nobel prizes." The projected price tag, deemed acceptable by the board, was $65,000.

After viewing a pilot film, the directors appropriated $200,000 to underwrite a twenty-six-week series of fifteen-minute television programs by the Pulitzer Prize-winning cartoonist Herbert Block (Herblock), on condition that the officers might discontinue the programs after thirteen weeks if they lacked popularity or proper commercial sponsorship.[4]

The executive committee was empowered to expand the successful television news-clip experiments in Los Angeles into a national news service, costing as much as $150,000 a year.[5]

To increase the interest and activity of the legal profession in civil-liberties problems, the Fund became concerned once again with specific legal cases. Adam Yarmolinsky's case studies suggested that most of the defendants in federal security cases were not represented by an attorney. Consultants to the Fund were developing methods to implement legal-referral services in New York and Chicago, and an initial $65,000 was appropriated for that purpose. An appropriation of $17,500 was authorized to enable the officers to make grants to bar groups for the defense of civil-liberties cases. In addition, the American Friends Service Committee was granted $150,000 to provide funds for the legal costs of cases involving "freedom of conscience," "described as including rights of conscientious objection to military service, to loyalty oaths, to demands to inform on the activities of one's friends; and right to public or private employment without discrimination based on conscientious beliefs which do not conflict with job performance." Hutchins declared that the AFSC would assume responsibility for the selection of cases. John Lord O'Brian suggested that informal reports be made to the directors at future meetings.

Hutchins slipped his oft-rejected plan for a commission on the mass media into the middle of the recommendations with the simple explanation that "some evidence has developed that many editors would welcome the creation of [it]—or at least would not object to having the possibilities investigated." He was no doubt referring to responses to his recent speech before the American Society of Newspaper Editors, at which time he restated the proposal.[6] His request was for $50,000 "to appoint a working party to explore the possibilities" of a commission. The directors agreed to appropriate $25,000 to determine the feasibility of a working party. They remained obviously less willing than Dr. Hutchins to cross swords with the generally conservative and enormously influential fourth estate.

The Council for Social Action of the 1,200,000-member Congregational Christian Church had introduced civil-liberties literature into more than 300 discussion groups in 1953 and 1954, and applied for $20,000 to further efforts. The Fund's officers carefully outlined the council's intended use of the money, and devoted an appendix of the recommendations to the names and credentials of the council's directors. Everything seemed in order and the grant was approved. This method of assuring the board of a prospective recipient's authority and orthodoxy was employed frequently and with success.

The two proposals of most profound significance to the Fund's immediate future did not appear overly inflammable when discussed. Paul Hoffman alone seemed reluctant to endorse a $25,000 analysis of the testimony of key witnesses in loyalty-security cases. Each director had received a memorandum on the subject by Walter Millis which should have revealed the delicate nature of such an inquiry. Millis was clearly skeptical of much of the evidence produced by government witnesses before various congressional committees, and strongly criticized the FBI and the Attorney General for accepting it at face value and defending it. (The recent confession by ex-Communist Harvey M. Matusow that he had falsely connected 244 persons with Communism before congressional hearings "for money" and with the encouragement of Senator McCarthy, plus Matusow's "belief" that he was not the only government witness who had lied, raised questions in many quarters.[7]) What was needed, Millis wrote, was an attack upon "the total picture of subversion and conspiracy as developed by the committees."

> The foregoing considerations suggest the utility of going back over the entire record—and analyzing (a) the instances in which they contradicted themselves or each other or facts ascertainable from other sources; (b) the gaps in their records and testimony, some of which might turn out to be significant; (c) the failures of the committees and the FBI to follow up hints and leads which might have resulted in a more accurate appraisal of their reliability; and (d) the extent of what actually has been proved, and also what has not been proved, by such of the testimony as has been corroborated or may be considered upon examination as probably worthy of credence.[8]

With the encouragement of the officers and director Chester Bowles, the appropriation was approved unanimously. This study was designed to be one of the Fund's most direct challenges to proponents of the Red scare; it could not fail to bear a strong reaction, even though the specter of Senator McCarthy no longer grinned from each evening's newscast.

Of equal future importance was an award made at the recommendation of the newly formed Committee on Special Awards, consisting of directors Stevenson, Linton, and Sherwood.[9] The story leading to the award was first called to the attention of Dr. Hutchins a few weeks earlier by John Roche, a political scientist in charge of a study for the Rossiter project.

In October of 1953 the library committee of the Plymouth Monthly Meeting of the Society of Friends employed Mrs. Mary Knowles as a temporary replacement for the librarian at its William Jeanes Memorial Library, just outside Philadelphia. It did so with the knowledge that from 1945 to 1947 Mrs. Knowles had been a secretary in a Boston school that had been placed on the Attorney General's list in 1947, that FBI undercover agent Herbert Philbrick had claimed she was a member of a Boston Communist cell in about 1947, and that she had been discharged by a Massachusetts library for refusing to answer questions before the Senate Internal Security Subcommittee in 1953. Mrs. Knowles explained her unwillingness to cooperate with Senator Jenner and his associates in a letter to her Massachusetts employer:

> In the first place I have committed no crime, nor am I facing criminal prosecution, but it is entirely possible that by testifying I could provide a link in a chain of events, or supposed events, which would render me liable to prosecution. . . . In the second place, the investigating committees no longer uphold the validity of the First Amendment, and recourse to that Amendment by the witness before the committee could very easily lead to contempt of court citation and ensuing jail sentence. In the third place, if, under compulsion, I testified concerning my religion and politics, but refused to answer questions about others, I would also be held in contempt of court. . . . Fourth, if I refused to answer questions on moral or ethical grounds without invoking the Fifth Amendment, I would also be held in contempt of court and again face a jail sentence.

Her contentions were accurate, and pointed to what Frank J. Donner would later call "rules of a game as weird as the legal proceeding described in Kafka's prophetic novel *The Trial*, in which an arm of the state, moved by dark, concealed and vengeful compulsions, plucks out and punishes men for phantom crimes."

Congressional loyalty committees placed before witnesses an intimidating tangle of uncertainties clearly inconsistent with legal safeguards surrounding judicial proceedings. Charges were vague, the boundaries of inquiry were nebulous, and standard rules of evidence and procedure were ignored. If a witness had associations he felt might be used against him, he was faced with difficulties puzzling to the most experienced attorneys. The courts had thrown out his right to plead the First Amendment in lieu of testimony. Under the Supreme Court's "waiver doctrine" a voluntary contribution of "materially criminating facts" meant the waiver of his recourse to the Fifth Amendment. He might then be forced to give testimony for which he could be prosecuted under the sweeping language of the Smith Act. How much could be said before a committee chairman arbitrarily waived the Fifth Amendment? No one knew exactly, but admission of former party membership or a simple profession of one's beliefs almost automatically eliminated further protection against self-incrimination. Far less, however, had accomplished the same end. Senator McCarthy often asked a witness if he had ever been engaged in Communist espionage. Hearing a denial, the senator would then claim that the witness had waived the protections of the Fifth Amendment and must answer all further questions at the risk of contempt of Congress charges. Thus, as Mrs. Knowles made note, witnesses at these proceedings, though they had committed no crime for which they could be properly tried, were often forced to take the Fifth Amendment almost immediately to protect themselves from dangers greater than the disgrace and economic hardship surrounding the inevitable label "Fifth Amendment Communist."

Her personal beliefs, Mrs. Knowles continued, were above suspicion.

> I believe wholeheartedly in the brotherhood of man; that we are here to help one another in whatever ways we can, and to be helped; that service to others is a source of one of the deepest satisfactions we have. I believe in the freedom of the individual within the framework of the law; and that such freedom can best be attained by free access to knowledge and truth. . . . I am opposed to all forms of discrimination and censorship on any grounds whatever. I believe in the basic goodness of man and in the limitless potentiality for good in the human race, given an opportunity to exercise their minds and hearts. I believe that peaceful and honorable settlement of worldwide situations is not only possible, but imperative; that war is barbaric, stupid, uncivilized, and needless. I believe firmly in the United States of America and in the documents upon which it is founded; the Declaration of Independence and the Constitution. I believe it is every citizen's duty to uphold these documents and the United States. This duty I have performed.

Her own case, she wrote,

> is a straight civil liberties issue, since at no time have my professional qualifications as a librarian been questioned; nor, I might add, my integrity as an individual. The issue seems to be whether or not an individual can maintain his means of livelihood and his conscience at the same time.

She was employed by the Plymouth Monthly Meeting's library committee after an interview and a careful review of her past associations, professional credentials, and character references.

In February 1954, Mrs. Knowles declined out of principle to take a Pennsylvania loyalty oath (not required of private employees in Pennsylvania), but enclosed a signed statement with her refusal which read:

> I believe firmly in the United States of America and in the documents upon which it is founded—the Declaration of Independence and the Constitution of the United States, and do support, obey and defend them. I do also support the Constitution of the State of Pennsylvania.
>
> Since leaving the Samuel Adams School, I have had no connection formal or otherwise with any so-called left-wing or "subversive" organization.

The minutes of the Plymouth Monthly Meeting recorded that "it was the unanimous feeling of those present that we should be motivated by our Quaker principles and that any compromise at this time would be wholly incompatible with our basic faith." In April the regular librarian returned to the Jeanes library and Mrs. Knowles left to seek other employment.

The permanent librarian, however, soon decided to resign, and during the early summer the library committee advertised for a replacement. The most attractive application came from Mary Knowles, a professional librarian since 1928, and the committee offered her the position, effective September 1. She accepted, and on September 22 offered a notarized statement to the library committee:

MARY KNOWLES, being duly sworn according to law, deposes and says that she is not a Communist or a member of any subversive organization.

Before long, however, city officials publicly challenged her loyalty for the failure to take the Pennsylvania oath. Following press accounts of the controversy, the boards of commissioners of two townships and the local Community Chest cancelled gifts to the library; city school boards curtailed the practice of sending school children in classes to the premises. The Valley Forge chapter of the Daughters of the American Revolution expressed its "wholehearted commendation" of the punitive actions. The local American Legion post went on record as opposing the employment of Mrs. Knowles.

But the Quaker Meeting had no intention of altering its position. Its December minutes read: "The Meeting is in accord with the Library Committee's employment of Mary Knowles. . . . Since Mary Knowles bears a strong conviction against Loyalty Oaths, and the Library Committee is completely satisfied as to her fitness for the position, the Meeting concurred in the decision that other plans for supplementary support be made which would not subject our basic testimonies to political pressure."

In January 1955 a smear campaign began in the community, led first by the Citizens for Philbrick and subsequently by the Alerted American Group. Monthly newsletters appeared demanding the librarian's dismissal, and by April 19 the Alerted Americans claimed to have 561 signatures supporting their cause, including 22 from members of the Meeting. The current newsletter contended:

In asking for her removal, Alerted Americans are fighting for a principle. That principle is that no Security Risk should be employed in a sensitive post of honor and esteem where she is in a position to harm the community. Mrs. Knowles, proven Security Risk, is in such a position. Her controversial beliefs and unpatriotic behavior have already disturbed the peace, set a bad example for our young people and caused widespread suspicion and criticism of the whole Friends Meeting. Her presence in the Library poses a possible future threat to our security.

The May 13 newsletter contained even more philippic:

> At best some of her supporters are anti-anti-communists of the most destructive, hypocritical, self-righteous type. In almost every instance, their "reasons" for supporting her closely follow the approved Communist line specifically designed to build up public sympathy and support (among the mistaken) for those accused of being somehow involved in the conspiracy to overthrow our American Way of Life. The Communists started all this furor and screaming about "academic freedom" and "civil liberties." In upside-down, communist language, this screaming advocates freedom and liberty for reds, not freedom and liberty for loyal Americans.

A petition containing sixty signatures of adult members of the Meeting was soon presented to the library committee. Only thirteen of the signers, it was quickly discovered, regularly attended the meeting; twenty-nine had not attended worship services in twenty years. The leader of Alerted Americans, Mrs. Phillip Corson, was neither an attender nor a member of the Society of Friends.

As the clamor mounted and pressure on the Quaker Meeting increased, the library committee felt it necessary to issue a public clarification of its position.

> Should an accusation of association with the Communist Party eight years ago be disqualification for employment? We think it should not. Certainly, in a Christian and democratic nation, the individual has a right to be judged on the merits of his particular case. If he is a person of evident character and there is nothing to indicate any recent association with the Communist Party, it would be a denial of the very ideals on which our form of government is founded, to so disqualify him.

> Is it a disqualification for employment if a loyalty oath is declined? Loyalty is a fact which goes beyond any particular form of words. The state does not require a loyalty oath of Mrs. Knowles. As Friends we have not, and shall not require an oath of her, believing that truth is no stronger under oath.

> Should a plea of the Fifth Amendment give rise to unfavorable inferences? We think not. The right to be silent (Fifth Amendment) is equal to the right of freedom of speech, free press, and

freedom of religion (First Amendment). These rights must be respected for all persons or they are endangered for each of us.

Finally it is suggested that one who does not cooperate with a Congressional Committee should be penalized by exclusion from employment in his chosen field. But, when silence is the exercise of a constitutional right, to penalize that silence would jeopardize that constitutional right. We think it impossible, in the name of the defence of democracy, to penalize in any way the exercise of rights guaranteed by our Constitution. Such rights, however unpopular, must be available without penalty to all, or they will mean nothing to any of us.

Communications from the Alerted Americans soon contained, along with the usual attacks upon Mrs. Knowles, pamphlets, folders, and reprints displaying such titles as "The Power To Tax Is the Power To Destroy," "United Nations' Sole Concern Is Spread of World Socialism," and "National Education Association Defends Filthy Books in Public School Library."[10]

Upon learning of the case, Dr. Hutchins sent a staff member, Maureen Black, to the Plymouth Meeting community to conduct an investigation. The library committee cooperated fully and made its files available to Miss Black.[11]

At the board meeting in May the president presented the facts and a collection of newspaper clippings on the matter to the directors. That they were obviously moved by the Quakers' strength of principle—both religious and constitutional—in the face of the concerted right-wing assault was revealed by their unanimous agreement to present an award of $5,000 to the Plymouth Monthly Meeting "in recognition of its forthright stand in defense of individual freedom." Furthermore, "The Directors expressed the hope that suitable attention be drawn to the presentation of this award."[12] Dr. Hutchins soon released the story of the award to the press, announcing that it was for "courageous and effective defense of democratic principles" before an organized pressure group. "I hope that Plymouth Monthly Meeting's example," he said, "will be followed elsewhere in America, particularly when our libraries—which seem to be a special target of self-appointed censors and amateur loyalty experts—are involved."[13]

The award itself was presented by Mrs. Eleanor B. Stevenson on July 6.

> . . . I would like to make very clear that this $5,000 award is being given because the Fund for the Republic wishes to pay tribute to the Friends for their realization that whatever Mrs. Knowles' past associations may or may not have been, she is a loyal American and a highly qualified librarian; that she has every right to earn a living and to be treated with the respect accorded a human being in these United States.
>
> American democracy is in serious jeopardy when one group would stigmatize an individual not in terms of the present situation but in terms of the past, often based on careless assumptions and irrational thinking and thus deprive him of his basic human rights.[14]

The long quiet months were over for the Fund for the Republic.

Possibly the most influential and certainly the most widely followed political commentator in America at that time was Fulton Lewis, Jr. Over 16,000,000 people, each weekday evening at seven o'clock, heard the familiar voice on the radio; many watched him on one of fifty television stations; millions read his syndicated columns in Hearst newspapers. Lewis's audience was not only numerous, but much of it was devoted. Time and again he had called on his listeners to exert pressure on behalf of favorite personalities and issues with striking success. His broadcasts started over a dozen congressional investigations; they assisted appreciably in the retention of Richard Nixon on the 1952 Republican ticket when the Californian's private fund was uncovered by others.

Lewis was a prosperous and consistent defender of the Far Right. For over a decade he had bitterly attacked intellectuals, New Dealers, integrationists, civil libertarians, liberal theologians, social workers, "one-worlders," a galaxy of "pinks" and "leftists" who were "destroying Americanism" and "selling the country down the river." Predictably, Lewis was a close friend and staunch supporter of Senator Joseph McCarthy. "You'd expect the *Daily Worker* to be against him," Lewis once said.

But look at the rest. Not Communists, of course, but those who oppose the anti-Communists—the anti-anti-Communists. The apologists for Alger Hiss, for instance. Look at them—the Washington *Post,* the New York *Times,* the Alsops, Drew Pearson, Elmer Davis, Marquis Childs, Frank Edwards, Cecil Brown, John W. Vandercook . . . and all the rest of the so-called liberal columnists, whoever and wherever they are.[15]

He had no discernible sympathy for those concerned with assaults upon civil liberties. His view of the issues was simple: there were Reds in this country, perhaps at the highest levels of decision-making, and they should be exposed and punished; anyone interfering with this process, as carried out by some of the finest Christian Americans he had ever met, were (at least) doing the work of the Communists and should be stopped. It was inevitable that the Fund for the Republic would attract his rabid attention.

Lewis had taken several swipes at the Ford Foundation in recent years for its alleged liberal bent, but by mid-1955 he concluded that the greater menace to freedom was the Fund for the Republic, and he devoted entire newspaper columns to it. On June 14 he contended that "Every act of the Fund for the Republic has been aimed directly at stopping all investigations of Communism and its agents, at undermining the Government's personnel security program and generally at discrediting any effective anti-Communist activities."[16] For two more days he hammered away at the Fund, claiming that it was linked with the Americans for Democratic Action, and maintaining that "this leftist-supported campaign is using the money of yours and mine and all other taxpayers." Hutchins was an "ultra-liberal"; Clifford Case, "a darling of the ADA"; Paul Hoffman, a "Fair Dealing Internationalist." All three must have been startled when Lewis informed his readers that "Reports are circulating that Henry Ford II . . . has become so disgusted with operations of the Fund for the Republic that he is considering making a public statement."[17] David Freeman followed Lewis's columns closely, and wrote to Vice-President Ferry: "I see no grounds for suit in these articles—he's a pretty cagey gent."[18]

Lewis's reprobations seemed to be infectious. The *American Legion Magazine,* in an article defending the Reece committee, caustically referred to a "surprising use of Ford Foundation money," meaning the Fund's distribution of the filmed Murrow-Oppenheimer interview.[19] J. B. Matthews published a vitriolic tirade against Dr. Hutchins in the *American Mercury.*[20] Congressman Donald Jackson inserted a George Sokolsky article critical of the Fund into the *Congressional Record.*[21] But this caliber of commentary was to be expected; the Fund's chief publicity officer, Joseph Lyford, informed Adam Yarmolinsky privately that "we are not taking alarm."[22] His calm may have been shaken a few days later when Congressman Reece gave a blistering speech on the floor of the House against the Fund and its award to the Plymouth Friends. Shortly, Mrs. Knowles was subpoenaed by the Senate Internal Security Subcommittee and questioned at length in an executive chamber hearing.[23]

On August 21 the Fund issued its first annual report (dated May 31, 1955), which released news of several hitherto unrevealed activities, including the government witness study (to be undertaken by the Stanford Law School), the Herblock television show, and the Commission on Post Office Practices. It also disclosed that the Fund had spent $2,514,738 on 34 grants, 26 projects, 13 fellowships and grants-in-aid, and the distribution of literature and expenses.

Several personal judgments were expressed by the Fund's president in the course of the report. At one point he declared: "Although in some particulars the atmosphere is better than it was five years ago, the misunderstanding of civil liberties, the indifference to them, and the violations of them, to which we too easily grow accustomed, are still such as to give cause for alarm." He was highly critical, in a statement on general Fund policy, of the post-war anti-Communist crusade.

> The range of suspect persons has been enormously extended by resort to guilt by association. The evidence offered to show that a man is a danger to American institutions has been farcically remote. The treatment accorded suspected persons in Congressional investigations and administrative hearings has not always been that contemplated by the Sixth Amendment. A kind of continuous

propaganda and social pressure has been kept up that has tended to suppress conscientious non-conformity. Political advantage has accrued from claiming that others were indifferent to the threat of communism. The result has been that governmental officers, university presidents, and ordinary citizens have felt it necessary to exhibit inordinate anxiety on this score.

These were assertions that a growing body of evidence had affirmed persuasively. Preliminary findings from several Fund projects were replete with supporting data. What would soon become Hutchins's most controversial statement, however, involved the American Communist party.

A political party in this country has been identified with the "enemy." Those associated with this party have therefore come under suspicion as an imminent danger to the state. In view of the weapons now available and of the examples of subversion that other countries have offered, the danger has seemed great, though often mysterious and intangible. It has appeared that the peril to the country could be dealt with only by methods that drastically departed from those which have characterized Anglo-American jurisprudence.[24]

His position on the "political party" issue was unpopular but technically correct. Congress, in the McCarran Internal Security Act, in the Communist Control Act, and in a recent 84–0 roll-call vote by the Senate, had charged the American Communist party with being part of a world-wide conspiracy rather than an agency of legitimate political expression, but had failed to make membership or office-holding in it a crime. The party had not been clearly outlawed, perhaps out of fear that the Supreme Court would refuse to alter the constitutional precedent which does not permit legislative conviction of specific individuals or groups. Public sentiment had undoubtedly been influenced by the scores of former party members and agents who made headlines (and considerable cash) by charging from the lectern, pulpit, and witness stand that the American Communist party was not, as Whittaker Chambers put it, "an organization like other political parties," but rather "an instrument of conspiracy" with purposes "utterly different from those of other political parties."

To the Fund's president this view was a gross oversimplification; credible evidence in its behalf was thin and often stemmed from unreliable and reactionary sources. But even if true, it did not follow that all past and present members were by definition conspirators. Intellectuals and reformers by the score had joined the party for the highest of reasons only a few years earlier when a callous indifference to poverty, racism, and the threat of perpetual war was curiously equated by many with patriotism. Altruism, or a belief in or desire to study the Marxist dialectic —these were legitimate motivations for which no American should be locked up or pursued and harassed.[25] The hard fact remained, moreover, that past and present membership in the party was not a crime *per se*.

Robert Hutchins had never been a Communist ("I was neither sufficiently poor nor stupid," he once mused[26]), had revealed no attraction to party members or sympathizers, and repeatedly opposed the ideology, particularly for its interference with freedom of thought and expression. But, he maintained, members, former members, and those who had ever associated with members should not be denied every constitutional right protecting American citizens from arbitrary punishment. As he later stressed:

> Due process and the equal protection of the laws are the basis of our society. The Constitution provides for emergencies. The laws prohibiting espionage and subversion must be obeyed and enforced. If I insist that every person accused of crime must be given a fair trial, that accusation is not proof, and that the presumption of innocence extends to every man accused of anything, I do not expect to be called a criminal or pro-criminal or anti-anti-criminal. . . . I should have supposed that the test of one's Americanism would have been whether one was prepared to insist on justice under law for the scurviest and most unpopular persons around. They are the ones who need it. And if they don't get it, we may be certain that, if events run riot, eventually nobody will get it.[27]

Such a stand was far from radical; it was in conformity with traditional attitudes on civil liberties tenaciously defended by virtually all proponents of the freedoms of the Bill of Rights

throughout the cold war—attitudes which had brought forth a
Fund for the Republic in the McCarthy era.

The appearance of the Fund's first annual report was a declaration of war for many McCarthyites. Never before had an agency
so vigorously challenged premises they identified with love of
country. Never before—as the lists of grants, projects, staff
members, consultants, and directors made obvious—had ultra-
conservatism been faced with an equally determined combination of intelligence, prestige, and money. The "pro-Communist"
deviltry possible with the remaining millions of dollars was inestimable. The Fund for the Republic was a menace to be confronted promptly and halted. Fulton Lewis, Jr., led the way.

On the day after the report appeared, Lewis began a series
of nightly broadcasts devoted in part or in whole to "exposing"
the Fund. During his second program he described the foe with
a breathtaking sentence:

> The fact is that it's an extreme, ideological political propaganda
> organization, promoting the doctrines of the Americans for Demo-
> cratic Action and points to the left of that, fighting the security
> programs by which the Federal Government tries to protect itself
> against enemy infiltration, fighting also the Congressional investiga-
> tions who [*sic*] seek to expose Communism, and the methods the
> Communists have used in the past to infiltrate our government up
> to the very highest levels—fighting in fact to discredit those former
> Communists who have had the courage to renounce Communism
> and come forward and tell their own experiences and thus expose
> others, some of whom are still in high places.[28]

Each project, every grant, each piece of literature distributed by
the Fund warranted his attention as a link in a deliberate plan
to undermine the nation's security. "If this outfit is operating
in the interests of all the people of the United States, I am the
King of Siam."

The commentator's facts were often greatly in error. He
claimed, for example, that Paul Hoffman ("the dilettante left-
winger") was the Fund's first president, drawing a salary of
$75,000 a year.[29] He overlooked few tricks: "Now let me quote

from the DAILY WORKER for Friday July 7, 1950 . . . this is an interview with Dr. Hutchins . . ."; "Please note in all I have read to you, from these projects of the Fund for the Republic, there is not one penny for anything to benefit the farmers of the nation, the man and his wife who run the corner grocery store and provide jobs for a couple of other neighbors. . . . nothing about bringing up healthier kids, or better education, or better salaries for school teachers and policemen and postmen . . ." An interview with Ferry on August 24 ("he sat with both feet at the top of his desk, a short distance from my face," Lewis growled), immediately following an embarrassing incident in which he was discovered prowling through the Fund's office files, seemed to intensify the acrimony with which the broadcaster spoke of the corporation and its officers.[30]

Lewis's major target, well into September, was the Stanford study of government witnesses. It was not, he said, to be a scholarly pursuit ("Study—my grandmother!"), but was an effort, through a Fund agent planted at the Stanford Law School, to discredit and slander the truths about Communist internal subversion. The project had been accepted on provision by the university until its trustees held their next meeting on September 11. Lewis badgered the trustees and university officials with telephone calls and telegrams in an effort to defeat the proposal, reporting nightly to his millions of listeners. Even the dean of the law school seemed part of the plot: "He . . . made a great profession of his friendship with Alger Hiss, for whom he gave a cocktail party, I am told, in San Francisco shortly after the war. . . . my informant thinks that it was at the time of the United Nations Conference there, in 1945, but was not absolutely sure."

Clamor from the right began to mount in the heat of the summer. Columnist David Lawrence submitted: "Judging from its annual report . . . the 'Fund for the Repubic' is primarily interested in investigating the investigators—the persons and institutions who recognize that a Communist conspiracy has existed in the United States and still exists."[31] On August 26, Chicago television personality Tom Duggan openly criticized the Fund's grant to the American Friends Service Committee for the assistance of defendants in civil-liberties cases.[32] Two days later radio network commentator Paul Harvey spoke out strongly against the Stanford Law School study and the Fund.

> Russia will never have to take us into a shooting match if she can poison us while we sleep. It is time to destroy the tax-exempt status of these outfits that manufacture the poison. I do not expect the Internal Revenue Service to initiate action, but your congressman can. He may be away from his office this summer but you write him there; your letter will find him.[33]

Republican Congressman August E. Johansen, whose district approached the outskirts of Detroit, soon charged the Fund with being a one-sided propaganda outlet. He predicted that many members of Congress would take an increased interest in it.[34]

Part of the bellicosity which greeted the Fund's report probably stemmed from right-wing frustrations over the dissipation of the Red scare by mid-1955. McCarthy's censure had been a severe blow. The Matusow confessions had badly shaken the credibility of paid informers. Former Senator Harry P. Cain, at one time an arch-conservative and currently a member of the Subversive Activities Control Board, now called publicly for sweeping changes in the government's security programs, citing the Ladejinsky case to illustrate the "shortsightedness, ruthlessness, smugness, and brutality of bureaucracy." By March, Attorney General Herbert Brownell, Jr., consistently a vociferous defender of federal loyalty measures, offered his first mild proposal for reforms. There was definite stirring in the new Democratic Congress. Senator Hubert Humphrey, safely re-elected and renowned as an anti-Communist, opened hearings in the Subcommittee on Reorganization to discuss his proposal for a commission to examine the country's security system. Senator Olin Johnston received $125,000 for his Post Office and Civil Service Committee to investigate complaints against the Federal Employee Security Program. Senator Thomas C. Hennings, Jr., an energetic if sporadic defender of civil liberties, formed the Subcommittee on Constitutional Rights which in April was granted $50,000 to study the erosion of the Bill of Rights. The Fund had contributed to the retreat from frenzy most recently with the publication in August of two timely and significant studies.

The first was *The Draftee and Internal Security*, by Baltimore attorney Rowland Watts. It was a path-breaking, two-volume report on the Army's practice (tightened after the confrontations with Senator McCarthy) of giving "undesirable" discharges to drafted servicemen on grounds of their pre-induction activities and associations. Scores of cases, acquired from defendants and their attorneys, were presented in detail, documenting appalling examples of military ignorance and fear for which young men suffered shame and denial of future employment opportunities without adequate recourse to their legal and constitutional rights. Men were branded by the Army as "almost subversives" on such evidence as the past beliefs of relatives (in one case, those of a deceased mother-in-law), chance remarks at school, and associations with organizations listed by the Attorney General or cited by a witness before an investigating committee. Security officers were often careless with their facts and held the liberal and radical opinions of their suspects with less than enthusiasm. (One question asked of a hapless lad was: "Why did you, a white person, belong to the National Association for the Advancement of Colored People?") And little could effectively be done in one's defense. Only seven days were given to answer charges in writing, Watts noted, and "few could do more than pit their own written word against the unrevealed 'information' in the Confidential file."

The author summarized the most serious injustices current to the Army's Military Personnel Security program thus:

1   Denial of any hearing to many men.

2   Denial of a valid hearing to all of the men charged with allegations of derogatory information.

3   Imprisonment without trial.

4   Punishment without conviction of crime.

5   Deprivation of property rights.

6   Imposition of attainder.

He called for a new military security system in which the Army granted discharges solely on the basis of service rendered while on active duty, one which would give soldiers in security cases "the same full hearing rights that are guaranteed him by the Uniform Code of Military Justice in defending himself against any other charge."[35] Watts furthermore advised against passage of the Butler bill, an ultraconservative attempt, then being weighed by Congress, to require a security clearance of all citizens having access to "defense facilities."

Adam Yarmolinsky's *Case Studies in Personnel Security* was an unprecedented presentation of 50 federal security cases, taken from a collection of over 200 gathered from 12 cities by 123 lawyer-interviewers. The study, published by the Bureau of National Affairs, was part of the New York City Bar Association's project on the federal loyalty-security program. The case histories were used with the consent of the employees involved and their attorneys; government files, of course, were not available to the interviewers. "While we realize that the usefulness of a study of this kind is circumscribed by the limitations on the available material," Yarmolinsky wrote, "we feel that it will provide useful and indeed essential material for an understanding of how the security programs operate from day to day."

The cases were damning evidence of the suspicion, confusion, haste, and lack of scruple that went into producing the Administration's latest count of "security" separations: 8,008. In case after case, government employees were faced with vague and often irrelevant charges; were forced to hire attorneys while suspended without pay, for weeks and even months; were denied access to evidence used against them; were denied the opportunity to cross-examine anonymous informers; and were denied any real right of appeal. Grounds for suspension and discharge might be a slightly unorthodox comment, a joke, a rumor about homosexuality—might be anything read or said in one's entire lifetime that could be found objectionable in the effort to "defend national security." One Government Printing Office security officer, for example, charged a GPO employee with "left-wing" leanings because he had allegedly used the expression "second-class citizen." It turned out that the accused had said he would "rather be a second-class citizen in Mississippi than a first-class citizen in Russia." One postal worker was accused of having Communist art and literature in his home. The hearing revealed reproductions of paintings by Picasso, Matisse, Renoir, and Modigliani, along with a single copy of *Das Kapital,* recommended years earlier for a college course. One clerical worker with twenty-six years of government service was suspended from his position for, among other reasons: (1) expressing unspecified "pro-Communist" remarks; (2) having "consistently embarrassed" his agency by not paying his debts promptly; and (3) for being a "trouble maker, antagonizer, and braggart."

Senority, previous security clearances, a nonsensitive position —there were no certain protections from the most ludicrous accusations by unknown sources with secret evidence. The burden of proof lay with the accused; he was guilty until he could prove himself innocent. And how does one substantiate innocence to the charge of having spoken in a "pro-Communist" manner? The elderly clerk mentioned above, Russian-born and possessing a slight accent, before entering a mental hospital from the strain of the prolonged, expensive, and mysterious proceedings, protested frantically:

> I am an ultra-conservative. I am a God-fearing man . . . my background is anti-Socialist, anti-Communist. My family were small property owners, branded by the Reds as "burjois," "exploiters." My father was a journalist. . . . He was tortured by the Cheka, beaten by a lead-filled whip. My mother, the epitome of saintliness and piety, was killed by Tarashchantzy, members of a Red Military Division . . . She protested the nationalization of our printshop— a devious trick of the Communists to deprive the property owner of his property and converting it into national commune. I was not given a chance to bury her. I fled from the Red Terror. . . . I solemnly swear that I am not, nor have I ever been, a member of the Communist Party, nor a fellow-traveller, nor a member of any subversive organization, that I have never subscribed to any subversive publications, never attended meetings, that I fled from Red tyranny . . . I am 100% American. . . .[36]

Was this Orwellian pursuit of peculiarity really necessary? Was it an invaluable part of what Attorney General Brownell proudly called the "drive to exterminate the Communist Party and Communist espionage in this country"? There was very little if any evidence to sustain the affirmative. Federal authorities had provided no concrete public information of late on the nature and extent of internal subversion. Congressional committees continued to drag before the television cameras the reliable cast of characters used in the past to garner publicity and generate suspicion. The most persistent seekers of treason, it seemed, were at the same time the most consistent seekers of personal fame and power, and the most eager to identify liberal thought and legislation with Soviet designs on the freedom of man. The extreme peril of Communist saboteurs, the fear employed to justify the utilization of police-state methods against millions of Americans in government service and private industry, was becoming increasingly questionable by mid-1955 in the absence of supporting evidence. The Yarmolinsky study, while it contained no final judgments or conclusions, reaffirmed the suspicions of many who thought the government's violations of constitutional safeguards unwarranted, politically inspired, and dangerous to the future of liberty.

The New York Times lauded both the Watts and Yarmolinsky studies, proclaiming "it is apparent that the curtain of mystery that has to a large degree unnecessarily descended upon this field is at last about to be penetrated."[37] A right-wing Brooklyn newspaper, the *Tablet,* condemned the books (and *The New York Times*) vigorously, and wondered: "How the living members of the Ford family can stand by while the Fund for the Republic . . . uses the inheritance of their great progenitor to sabotage efforts to expose the Communist conspiracy to take over the United States is incredible."[38]

On September 1 the Fund's executive committee assembled and made two appropriations (previously approved by Fund attorneys) to assist the work of Senator Hennings's Subcommittee on Constitutional Rights. The sum of $7,000 was granted for assistance in typing, editing, and distributing transcripts of the hearings; $15,000 went to American University's Bureau of Social Science Research for tabulation and analysis of subcommittee questionnaires.[39]

Within days Fulton Lewis, Jr., learned of the appropriations and asked his listeners "whether this Fund for the Republic, with the decidedly slanted preconceptions [of] its leaders and directors, is infiltrating the investigating committees of Congress, and whether, if that is so, it is entitled to its tax-free status.—Commissioner T. Coleman Andrews of the Bureau of Internal Revenue should be interested."[40]

About the same time the directors received a collection of recommendations from the officers of the Fund so large that it not only contained a table of contents (the progress report even had one now), but also an index and summary. Requests added up to an unprecedented $1,412,200.[41] In the face of increasing hostility, Dr. Hutchins had accelerated operations.

Highlights of the docket were proposals for a telephone contest on the Bill of Rights, an educational series to be run in *The Progressive,* and a study of the American Legion and civil liberties. The latter inquiry was hopefully to be carried out by Princeton University's award-winning historian Eric Goldman.

> Mr. Goldman believes that from this material would emerge the "Legion Mind" and its impact on the 1950's—"a description of what the Legion generally has come to mean by civil liberties, the difference between that conception and the traditional American view, and a quite specific pointing up of the effects on present-day American Legion activities in the field of civil liberties."[42]

President Hutchins had little fear that the board might take alarm at the proposals. His confidence was expressed in a radio interview two days before the September 15 quarterly meeting:

> . . . the directors were chosen because they are conservatives. They recognized that the essential characteristics of what we call the American way of life are those liberties which are promised to us through the Declaration of Independence, the Constitution and the Bill of Rights. And they are dedicated to these principles.[43]

But before the directors could congregate, more controversy broke out. Fulton Lewis, Jr., had somehow discovered Hutchins's proposal to study the American Legion and shared the news with the nation, expressing shock and anger.[44] In response to Lewis's broadcasts and telephone calls, the chairman of the American Legion's Illinois State Committee on Subversive Activities presented a resolution to the annual state convention strongly denouncing Dr. Hutchins and the Fund, and calling for new congressional investigations of all tax-exempt foundations, which "have diverted sums of tax-exempt money to the propagandizing of alien philosophies, and to engage in left-wing political activities." It passed unanimously. State commander Irving Breakstone was forced to use parliamentary maneuvers to deter another resolution repudiating the local Legion's participation in the American Heritage Council's lectures and discussion groups.[45]

On September 11 the national commander of the 2,800,000-member American Legion, Seaborn P. Collins, issued a strongly worded statement to the press, which said in part:

> I hope that the American Legion elements at the State and local levels will have no truck with Fund for the Republic enterprises. . . .

> The American Legion has consistently advocated and fought for a strong and united nation. By shrewd grants and expenditures, the Fund for the Republic is threatening, and may succeed in crippling the national security. . . .

> Hutchins is entitled to an opinion that communists should be given jobs in teaching and in government. He is entitled to his evident opinion that the Supreme Court law makers and the FBI are evil when they are intolerant of communists.

> By the same token, Legionnaires are entitled to know and be alerted against an operation, directed by Hutchins which, in our judgment, will not serve the cause of American unity and strength.[46]

Similar sentiments were echoed on that Sunday afternoon by Clarence Manion, one of Senator McCarthy's most ardent followers, over his nation-wide radio program on the Mutual Broadcasting System.[47]

"As if responding to the baton of a hidden conductor, all the champions of the Neanderthal wing have begun a concerted attack on the Fund for the Republic and Robert M. Hutchins," sighed Max Lerner.[48] To several directors of the Fund, arriving in New York for the board meeting, the bombardment of past weeks was not in the least humorous.

CHAPTER EIGHT

Not
That Kind of
Doctor

Dr. Hutchins faced but eleven directors in the Fund's plush suite atop the new building at 60 East 42nd Street when he called the meeting to order. He must have sensed immediately a new uncertainty and edginess about them; these distinguished businessmen, educators, and authors were troubled, cautious, perhaps even a bit frightened. Almost every day for weeks their radios had questioned their loyalty, integrity, and common sense; newspapers had pondered their long-established trustworthiness; customers and acquaintances had seemed puzzled and wary over what had been portrayed as assistance to the nation's enemies. Of the eleven, only Paul Hoffman and Harry Ashmore had previously been targets of the smears and insinuations of the Far Right, and being fired at in this unsophisticated and libelous manner (unless you were Hutchins) was not at all a pleasant sensation. Though their task with the Fund seemed no less noble, the disruption, the directors strongly indicated, would have to be quelled. This could be achieved, perhaps, by a public reaffirmation of the Fund's ideals, another recitation of the directors' credentials, and a cutting-back on actions likely to grist for Fulton Lewis's widely observed mill. The reduction of provocation seemed especially desirable— perhaps that was the key to the restoration of peace and quiet. And taking reasonable precautions was not, after all, retreat.

The board's first action was the approval of a draft of a statement on the Fund's high purposes, in reply to the charges of Commander Collins.[1] Following some routine business, the president's recommendations were then considered.

Efforts toward the elimination of segregation, which Dwight Macdonald would rightly call "politically safe," received the board's welcome attention. (It was curiously unfashionable for the Far Right to expend great overt effort against racial integration.[2]) The Southern Regional Council, rapidly becoming one of the nation's most effective instruments for moderation and tolerance in the struggle for racial harmony, was granted an additional $150,000, following an extensive review of its activities within the recommendation. A $200,000 grant was awarded to the Law School of Vanderbilt University to finance a legal service on school desegregation for a three-year period. Grants for similar purposes were made to the Christian Life Commission of the Southern Baptist Convention ($15,000) and the Board of Social and Economic Relations of the Methodist Church ($25,-000).[3] The Commission on Race and Housing, having held its first meeting and appointed a research director, received an additional appropriation of $135,000.

Further recommended and approved (this time with one dissenting vote) was a $100,000 appropriation to establish a commission on the rights and liberties of American Indians. Up to $50,000 in matching funds was granted for the support of the Alianza Hispano-Americana, an old fraternal society newly interested in the civil rights of Mexican-Americans.

The directors were also willing to approve a request for "$50–60,000" to support television programs on race relations to be produced by the Council for Civic Unity in San Francisco. They were assured that "the program would be sponsored by a group of important San Francisco citizens and would have the cooperation of most of the local organizations in the civil liberties and civil rights field."

The officers' attempts at "popular education" were viewed with less enthusiasm by the board. The previous appropriation of $200,000 had been used, in part, to produce the Al Capp films (which had failed), a half-hour dramaic film (which as yet had no sponsor), the Herblock show (about which there were already reservations among certain directors), and to circulate the "See It Now" interview with J. Robert Oppenheimer (one of the favorite subjects of David Lawrence, the American Legion, and Fulton Lewis, Jr.). The officers, said the recommendation for another $200,000, "continue to believe that television can be extremely useful to the purposes of the Fund. They continue to discover new ways to adapt the medium to those purposes." They received an additional $50,000.

Certain requests involving civil liberties seemed entirely too risky to undertake. Morris Rubin, editor of the staunchly liberal magazine *The Progressive,* was among the most tenacious and capable foes of McCarthyism and had recently sought a grant for the creation and distribution of a series of studies on civil liberties in the United States. The Fund's officers were favorable toward the request, and the corporation's lawyers approved of it, "as long as the aim of the grant is educational." But the directors had no desire to create further pyrotechnics and "tabled" the recommendation.

Plans for studies of right-wing extremism suffered a like fate. The officers were requested to explore further one such request they had supported from the Board of Social and Economic Relations of the Methodist Church. The minutes record soberly that Dr. Hutchins then informed the board that Professor Eric Goldman had, for certain unexplained reasons, decided to drop his well-formulated proposal for a study of the American Legion.

The officers' selection of books and articles for the distribution program had been the object of particular reproach by Fulton Lewis, Jr., and other critics. In seeking $50,000 for the continuation of this activity, the officers noted plans to disseminate "a Congressional Record reprint of a statement by Senator Humphrey on government secrecy and freedom of the press, such books as John Lord O'Brian's Godkin Lectures, to be published this month by Harvard University Press, and other printed materials." But the familiar paeans to respectability this time were good only for a $30,000 appropriation—which would at least dampen plans to "reach well beyond . . . present audiences and undertake distribution of appropriate materials on a much larger scale." The spirit of confidence and daring displayed by the directors in May had waned very noticeably.

Later items before the board were approved as recommended. The sum of $20,000 was appropriated to underwrite the creation and distribution of a handbook on immigration law by two well-qualified attorneys. An award of $50,000 was made to the tax-exempt Legal Defense and Educational Fund of the NAACP to defray costs incurred in implementing the Supreme Court's decisions declaring segregation in education unconstitutional. And awards of $5,000, $3,000, and $2,000 were granted to three New York civic groups to assist in alleviating expenses stemming from a fracas with a local American Legion post over the alleged radicalism of a Columbia professor employed part-time by a guidance center. The board's courage had not entirely collapsed.

At Paul Hoffman's insistence, a request which had been rejected by the executive committee in June was reconsidered and approved, over the objections of Elmo Roper. New evidence, Hoffman claimed, revealed that it was not likely to be controversial.[4] The grant of $5,000 went to the Committee on Ethics and News Objectivity of Sigma Delta Chi, the national journalism fraternity, "to determine on what basis, of any, an objective appraisal of the performance of the press during the 1956 campaign might be possible."

Finally, the Bureau of National Affairs was authorized to receive an additional $5,400 for its legal service on security regulations. A $5,000 award was approved for the YMCA at the University of California at Berkeley in recognition of its race-relations program and open-platform policy. Hallock Hoffman's television news-clip program was authorized to receive $200,000 for expansion to a nation-wide basis. Several last-minute requests were deferred until a subsequent meeting.[5]

It had been a long, sometimes heated, and extremely busy session. In retrospect, the directors showed more perspicacity than temerity in their deliberations of proposals, though there was, of course, the deepest concern among them about the effects of the adverse publicity on themselves and the Fund. They were men and women of Impeccable Reputation—and liked it that way. To Dr. Hutchins, needless to say, the clamor was nothing extraordinary and came from familiar sources, though he must have been sharply disappointed by his board's hesitations. Within days he was delivering a rousing speech which taunted "the extreme right wing of American politics . . . who are constantly in full cry against all efforts to extend the scope of governmental action." "How do you become controversial?" he asked. "By being attacked," he answered, "and it makes no difference how innocent you are or how silly, stupid, or irresponsible the attack may be."[6] He was soon on his way to Europe to give a few lectures and enjoy a vacation.

While the board met in New York, Mrs. Mary Knowles was in Washington, D.C., seated before Senator Jenner and the Senate Internal Security Subcommittee. In what appeared to be pure harassment, she had been subpoenaed to appear before the subcommittee in early August but was dismissed without being publicly questioned. Now, on September 15, she was asked the old questions answered many times before. No, she was not a Communist, and, she repeated, "for many, many years I have had no connection, direct or indirect, with any organization on the Attorney General's Subversive List." She refused to invoke the Fifth Amendment, but said that in view of the fact that she was a private citizen employed by a private institution under the direction of a religious organization, the subcommittee lacked the authority to question her. Getting to the point, subcommittee counsel Jay Sourwine asked her who applied for the award from the Fund for the Republic. She replied that she did not know but that the money was not used to pay her salary. Fulton Lewis, Jr., broadcasting each event in detail, chortled:

> So continues the case of Mrs. Mary Knowles, the 5th Amendment librarian, whose case was considered by Dr. Hutchins and Mr. "Ping" Ferry to be worthy of 5 thousand dollars of money which is supposed to be spent in the general public interest and welfare. The question is whether you agree that this falls in that category.[7]

That same day, Lewis publicized a fact revealed by syndicated writer Victor Riesel two days earlier: the "employment" of Earl Browder, former head of the Communist party. All of the Fund's directors, except the most recently appointed, Arthur Dean, had learned in May of the possibility of Browder's inclusion as a consultant to the Rossiter project, but the actual event went unrecorded and was not made public in the Fund's first annual report.[8] Said Lewis: ". . . might you feel that you don't want Mr. Earl Browder on your payroll, or to have any truck with him in any connection and for any purpose?"[9]

Fulton Lewis, Jr., had spent several broadcasts assailing the loyalty of Dean Carl B. Spaeth of the Stanford University Law School, with whom preliminary arrangements were made for the proposed study of the testimony of important witnesses in judicial and legislative inquiries dealing with Communist activities in the United States. Determined to squelch the study, Lewis went so far as to describe the dean as a friend of Nelson Rockefeller, "State Department New Dealer during the war, and office mate of the named Communist, Gustavo Duran."[10] The telephone calls to university trustees, previously noted, elicited some information, but apparently had little damaging effect, for on September 15 the $25,000 grant to the law school was accepted by the full board of trustees. The statement by Stanford's President J. E. Wallace Sterling acknowledged the pressure he and his colleagues had experienced.

> In accepting this grant, about which questions have been raised by certain commentators and newspaper columnists, the University reaffirms that one of its chief functions is to encourage research into problems which individuals or departments within the University deem worthy of investigation. The University is concerned only that its faculty should adhere to those rigorous standards of independence of judgment, exact inquiry, and impartial evaluation of findings which have always motivated true scholars.[11]

Lewis replied feebly: ". . . it still is very suspect from a realistic standpoint," and turned his attention to other "startling, if not shocking angles on which I am working presently."[12]

On September 21, Senator Joseph McCarthy, in one of several endeavors to rehabilitate his luster, released a letter to President Eisenhower expressing concern over the "mounting assault on the Administration's security program by, among others, left-wing Democrats and the 'civil liberties' cultists." He rapidly turned his attentions to the Fund for the Republic, concluding with the plea:

> The left-wingers are having a field day at the expense of the Nation's safety. It is our imperative duty to the American people to resist their unprincipled campaign—a campaign that, if successful, will open the door once again to large scale Communist infiltration of our government.[13]

By now the New York *Daily News* had called for a congressional investigation of the Fund,[14] and several newspapers were covering at length the uproar—in part over the Fund—between liberal and ultraconservative factions within the American Legion.[15] The burgeoning turmoil was beginning to wear badly upon the newest director, Arthur Dean. A violent letter from an obvious crank had caused him considerable irritation in August.[16] And when, on September 19, President Hutchins announced privately that he had added temporarily to the Fund's public-relations staff one Amos Landman, who had pleaded the Fifth Amendment a few weeks earlier before a Senate investigating committee, Dean exploded. In a letter to Hutchins he blustered: "Mr. Landman ought not to be employed in any capacity by the Fund for the Republic, Inc." "Mr. Landman," the former law partner of Secretary of State John Foster Dulles argued, "has of course his individual right to invoke the Fifth Amendment but it seems to me that as long as he stands on that right there must remain a question whether he is or is not a communist or whether once having been a communist he has completely severed all of his relations."[17] A week later he resigned, "effective immediately."

The letter of resignation revealed that Arthur Dean had several misgivings about the operations of the Fund. The retainment of Earl Browder and Amos Landman (the first, in actuality, by Clinton Rossiter and the second by Ferry) headed the list. Communists and fellow travelers, he wrote, owe their allegiance to a foreign government and are not free to indulge in honest scholarship. He did not challenge the constitutional right of an individual to take the Fifth Amendment but thought "that others have the right to draw certain inferences in connection with that plea, the circumstances under which it is made and the individual's continued fitness for jobs."

He also objected to the award given to the Plymouth Monthly Meeting, as Mrs. Knowles "had pleaded the Fifth Amendment and to a certain extent had persisted in refusing to answer certain questions at her second appearance." The American Friends Service Committee, he had read in *The New York Times*, was using some of its grant to deal with cases involving passport denials, discriminations against naturalized citizens, the right to refrain from becoming an informer, and conscientious objectors. These were issues with which he simply did not want to become personally involved.

> . . . the Fund does not or may not in fact have sufficient control over the money it is spending so as to prevent organizations to which grants are made from using the money in a way which is at variance with the expressed intention of the Board of Directors in authorizing the grant.
>
> In sum, it seems to me that we are becoming over-identified with a particular set of views.[18]

The last sentence was particularly damning, coming not from the Far Right—still howling against the New Deal and the United Nations—but from Solid Citizenry itself. Unless Dean could be persuaded to retract his resignation, or at least to soften his parting remarks, the publicity surrounding his departure might be severely damaging to the Fund's reputation.

Hutchins replied that he had asked for an executive committee meeting on October 6 and hoped Dean would attend. All other members of the board were urged to be on hand.[19]

In the meantime, the flow of hostile speeches and articles increased steadily while Fulton Lewis, Jr., nightly dissected parts of what he claimed was a "carefully designed, heavily financed project" to weaken and destroy security procedures "that would safeguard the country against the infiltration that our friends the British are now up in arms about."[20] Walter Winchell asked his large network radio audience:

> Why in the world with hundreds of organizations on the U.S. government's list of subversive outfits—there's a lot more which

should be—does this Fund for the Republic single out the American Legion for appraisal, for study, for even an inquiry? There is talk too that they plan to probe the FBI. All they have to do is read the record of the American Legion which unfortunately is written in stone, headstones from New Guinea to Normandy, from Tunis to Iwo Jima. . . . there would be no Fifth Amendment to plead if the men of the American Legion hadn't been ready to bleed. . . . the men and women of the American Legion make up about eight per cent of the fighting reserve of this nation, the only real bulwark against Reds' global domination.[21]

The next day two agents from the Bureau of Internal Revenue visited the Fund's New York office, informing David Freeman that they had been assigned to check the corporation's information returns for the fiscal years ending September 30 of 1953 and 1954. They described their task "as a more or less routine audit."[22]

Shortly, the ultraconservative Washington newsletter *Human Events* featured a scathing attack on the Fund by a member of Fulton Lewis's staff, stressing the need for Henry Ford II to repudiate or disassociate himself publicly from the Fund. "Such action . . . would go far toward discrediting the Fund as a parent's disowning of a wayward child discredits the child."[23]

On October 3, J. Edgar Hoover employed unusually vituperative language in a speech before the sixty-second annual meeting of the International Association of Chiefs of Police. Without citing any names, he said:

It is through the "pseudo liberals" that the Communists do some of their most destructive work. These fictitious liberals are the individuals who through insidiously slanted and sly propagandistic writings and reports oppose urgently needed internal security measures; conduct a one-sided campaign to discredit Government witnesses; present the menace of Communism as a myth of hysteria; urge that we tolerate the subversive acts of Communists because Communists are only "non-conformists"; contend that the Communist Party is a "political" movement and that it is improper to consider it a criminal conspiracy linked to a world conspiracy to overthrow our Government by force and violence.[24]

The allusions to the beliefs of Robert Hutchins and to the Fund's loyalty-security studies were not overly subtle, as Fund critics were quick to note. The same day, before the same audience, William F. Tomkins, the Assistant Attorney General of the United States, took severely to task Richard Rovere's "The Kept Witnesses," sponsored and distributed by the Fund.[25]

The horizon seemed not entirely bleak, however. The Fund had received support throughout the current melee from several prominent sources of opinion, including the Washington *Post and Times-Herald* and *The New York Times*; Nathan M. Pusey, president of Harvard University, gave an address expressing strong confidence in the Fund and its president and spoke of the nation's need to be "saved from ill-informed, unqualified protectors";[26] and the Ford Foundation issued a private statement to the Fund's board stressing its independence of the Fund but concluding that "The over-all program of the Fund for the Republic as it has thus far evolved appears to be within the general terms and purposes of The Ford Foundation's grant."[27]

But the Fund's officers were becoming convinced of the necessity of some sort of defense strategy. Spot advertisements were placed on several large radio stations following the Fulton Lewis, Jr., broadcast, inviting listeners to send for the Fund's annual report. And Dr. Hutchins held a news conference in Los Angeles in late September at which he defended the freedom and objectivity of the scholars engaged in Fund-sponsored projects, and emphasized the varied and extensive nature of the Fund's expenditures. He lashed out at the "kingmakers" of the American Legion whose vested interests in the Red scare caused them to take the view "that anybody who raises a question as to the imminence of the threat of communism to this Nation is in some way subversive." The Fund's critics in general were "opportunists, afraid the truth may disprove the assumptions they've used to gain fame and political fortune. In short, they're afraid of their jobs."[28]

However true these accusations were, this type of splenetic rejoinder was dubiously necessary and certainly not in keeping with the board's desire to evade further provocation of the Fund's antagonists. A press release crisply presenting the facts of a matter and including a proclamation of the directors' faith in the Constitution and the Declaration of Independence was the customary and more dignified was to respond coldly to right-wing clatter. And it augured less retaliation.

On the very day the participants in the executive committee meeting were gathering over cocktails, minus Arthur Dean, the Los Angeles *Times* carried an editorial (later retracted) involving the Fund with jury "bugging";[29] and American Legion conventions in two Idaho communities demanded that the University of Idaho cancel a speech by Dr. Hutchins scheduled for the campus. Fulton Lewis, Jr., proudly shared the public statement by the legionnaires with his millions of listeners:

> Hutchins' public utterances and testimony before Congressional Investigating Committees have indicated that he and his associates are trying to propagandize Americans into believing that communism never has been and is not now a serious threat to this country, and that similar forces under the pretext of fighting communism are the real danger and threat to the civil liberties of Americans.[30]

The eight officers and directors present for the October 6 meeting in the Fund's conference room were in a somber and petulant mood. No matter how much they admired and respected Dr. Hutchins, no matter how firm their belief in the principles which underlay his actions, the hard reality to be faced was the necessity of arresting the Fund's constantly mounting public-relations problem. The president's heady and often daring programs had exacerbated an unduly large number of citizens; rumors persisted in the directors' newspapers, their mail, and within the walls of their exclusive clubs that the Fund was close to losing its tax exemption, that Congress was about to investigate it and the Ford Foundation, that Henry Ford II was displeased and irritated. Measures had to be taken to quash the bad publicity—and it was regrettable if Dr. Hutchins seemed dejected by the retrogression.

For an opening, the contract for the weekly television program "Herblock's Week" was terminated. Fulton Lewis, Jr., had devoted an entire broadcast to Herbert Block's cartoons, describing them as "Always anti-Republican, but not always pro-Democrat.

. . . only when the Democratic policy is in line with the party line of the Americans for Democratic Action which, for your information, coincides very closely with the Communist Party line."[31] Elements of the American Legion had also denounced the $200,000 appropriated for this project. A short time earlier Herblock had been widely criticized for a cartoon portraying President Eisenhower carrying Vice-President Nixon on his back, the latter exclaiming: "You're going to run again, aren't we?" The artist had drawn the cartoon before the President's heart attack, but several newspapers ran it on the day Mr. Eisenhower was stricken. The Fund's official explanation later tendered: "Herblock's initial scripts showed that his effectiveness as a news commentator would depend in large part on his complete freedom to discuss current issues and particular legislation. Their review of the initial scripts made it apparent to the Fund and Mr. Block that it would not be practical to limit Mr. Block's field of discussion to the boundaries set by the charter of the Fund."[32]

Then the awards program was scheduled for a complete review at the November annual meeting of the board. For the time being, awards to the New York community centers for their bravery against pressures by the American Legion were suspended.[33] Moreover, the wording of the September 15 resolution for the award to the NAACP Legal Defense and Educational Fund was changed from:

> RESOLVED that the sum of $50,000 be and hereby is appropriated for an award to the NAACP Legal Defense and Educational Fund, Inc., in recognition of the persistent, courageous, and successful efforts to define, secure and protect the legal rights of the Negro minority, and that Officers be and hereby are authorized to arrange for appropriate presentation of the award.[34]

to the milder

> RESOLVED that a grant of $50,000 be and hereby is authorized to the NAACP Legal Defense and Educational Fund, Inc., to support its educational work in defense of the legal rights of the Negro minority.

The distribution of publications program, managed by President Hutchins personally, was suspended, pending review of the program at the annual meeting. The officers were asked "to review all grants to other organizations and report to the Board whether the funds granted were being used for the purposes originally intended." Counsel was requested to review activities by the American Friends Service Committee; the Fund had not been, as promised, apprised in advance of certain causes they had selected to defend which had drawn intensive criticism from Fulton Lewis, Jr., and others.[35]

The executive committee meeting closed with the request (omitted from the minutes) that president Hutchins draft a detailed memorandum to the board exploring in depth the Fund's past and current activities in relation to the maintenance of tax exemption.[36] This was a stern demand, not yet an ultimatum or a threat, for evidence that the corporation was not bent on self-destruction.

This shocking *volte-face* was more than a temporary panic— it was a revolt. Hutchins said little, choosing no doubt to defer his comments until the hoped-for return of some tranquility among these flustered friends.

As October ground on, the national hubbub over the Fund for the Republic became more intense. Right-wing hate sheets and smaller ultraconservative newspapers joined in, newly apprised of a major source of "un-Americanism."[37] For the Fund's officers, each day seemed to bring its own troubles. On October 7 it was made known widely that the steady verbal barrage against the Fords had been increased by former congressman Hamilton Fish, who had written to Henry Ford II asking if Ford endorsed the Fund, in view of its allegedly unpatriotic bias.[38] Two days later, the board of directors of the California Republican Assembly called publicly for a congressional investigation of the Fund.[39] On October 10 the national convention of the American Legion met in Miami, busily denounced India, UNESCO, and the American Civil Liberties Union, and watched its executive committee issue a report condemning the Fund and Robert Hutchins.[40] The Herblock departure was announced on the 13th, and on the same day the Hearst newspapers broke the story of

Amos Landman. "As you know," said Ferry, affecting his usual brusquerie, "he took the 5th Amendment before the Senate Internal Security Committee. This fact alone did not appear to the officers sufficient reason to bar him from temporary employment."[41] The Detroit *Free Press* commented:

> Defenders of the Fund for the Republic haven't had their task made any easier by its employment of Amos Landman. . . . taking Landman in on any capacity certainly reveals an ineptness, a head-in-the-clouds imperviousness to reality, which can raise legitimate doubts as to the Fund's capacity for meeting problems in the field of security which confront this Country.[42]

By October 18, Arthur Dean had seen enough, and he reaffirmed his resignation in a letter to Paul Hoffman.[43] When the story hit the newsstands a few days later ("he didn't have time to read all the documents," a spokesman for Dean said), the Fund's critics expressed unanimous delight. J. Addington Wagner, new national commander of the American Legion, declared that he was "pleased and encouraged" by the news.

> Evidently Mr. Dean recognized, as did the American Legion several months ago, that the Fund for the Republic is becoming increasingly identified with the sponsorship of projects contrary to the best interests of America and its citizens.[44]

Paul Hoffman could only say lamely:

> I don't know the reasons for his resignation, and it would be presumptuous of me to speak for him . . . whatever his reasons, I am sorry to lose him as a director, because we need the services of men like him.

When asked if Dean's resignation might have been the result of controversy over several Fund projects (as the Hearst papers and Fulton Lewis, Jr., were repeating daily with obvious satisfaction) Hoffman replied: "No comment."[45]

On the 19th, Dr. Clinton Rossiter explained publicly that Earl Browder, even then under federal perjury indictment, had indeed been hired as a "source of information and raw material" for the Fund's project on the history of domestic Communism.

Browder was being paid, the Cornell University professor explained, to answer questions posed by the various historians. "He does not control a single word or comma or comment in any book which may be put out by the project. . . . He is a paid source of information, commenting on events in which he took a leading part." Both the Fund and Rossiter emphasized that this project, like all of the Fund's projects, was completely free from controls or pressures by the donor. Rossiter admitted that he had obtained Hutchins's approval before taking on Browder.[46]

The Hearst newspapers quickly concluded:

> It gives offense to any decent and honest sense of propriety for a man with Mr. Browder's record as a Communist and in his present position of still unresolved accusation to have any part in the preparation of the reference books and texts from which American children may shape their political and economic philosophies in even the smallest part.
>
> Does it not justify equal offense that an organization capable of assigning such a role to such a man should undertake the tasks and responsibilities of publication in that field?[47]

The Scripps-Howard chain of newspapers included similarly critical columns.[48] Several papers ran headlines such as "FORD FOUNDATION PAYS BROWDER AS RED HISTORY AID,"[49] and "FORD FUND PAYING BROWDER FOR DATA."[50]

By now it was apparent that Mr. Hutchins would have to step into the forefront. He and the Fund had received public encouragement from many sources, including attorney Abe Fortas,[51] broadcaster Edward P. Morgan,[52] and syndicated columnist Marquis Childs.[53] but the persistent and thriving attacks upon the Fund called for a more forceful response than the corporation's officers and directors had yet been willing to launch. The Fund's staff was planning an appearance by Dr. Hutchins on NBC's popular "Meet the Press," and soon additional ideas for publicizing the Fund's purposes, personnel, and activities began to be considered.[54]

Dr. Hutchins's immediate challenge, however, was his prior obligation to the board to prepare a private defense of his administration. It had to be a superior effort, for if he was to face the mass media at length with the Fund's story he must be certain that the directors were behind him to a man. Their most recent performance was discouraging; one more Arthur Dean and the Fund's enemies could no doubt topple the unique citadel of civil liberties and civil rights in which Hutchins had for several years invested great quantities of time, effort, and hope, and to which his reputation was now securely attached. He wrote to his fellow directors with a vigor akin to passion, with a sense of self-righteousness combined with indignation and dismay over the board's failure to match his energy and devotion to principle with confidence and support.

The first draft of a memorandum to the directors, presented privately to Paul Hoffman, later tempered by reflection, and read by the board only in altered form, is one of the most significant documents of the Fund's history. It is a reclarification of the corporation's role and duty by the man most responsible for its existence, a reprimand to the board for its fear under fire at the October 6 executive committee meeting, and, in retrospect, a valuable insight into the complex mind and guarded emotions of Robert M. Hutchins.

The directors had been warned in 1952, Hutchins wrote, that the Fund was, by the nature of its mandate, headed for trouble. "We could have named then the columnists, commentators, politicians, and organizations who would attack the Fund if it had a program that meant anything." The fact is, he continued, that the Fund has had a surprisingly good press. (He had a point, for a survey conducted a few days later revealed that many of the nation's most important and influential newspapers had defended the Fund, including *The New York Times,* the *Christian Science Monitor,* the Boston *Herald,* the Atlanta *Constitution,* the Chicago *Sun-Times,* the Louisville *Courier and Journal,* the St. Louis *Post-Dispatch and Globe-Democrat,* and the San Francisco *Chronicle.*[55]) "We are trying to help save the Republic," Hutchins declared. "We can expect few cheers from those we are saving it from."[56]

Every action undertaken by the board, wrote the president, had been first approved by counsel (the highly respected and conservative Bethuel Webster), who was paid to keep a sharp eye on the provisions of Section 101 (6) of the Internal Revenue Code.

> I have been unable to think of anything worth doing, to say nothing of anything the Fund has done, that might not lead to pressure on the Commissioner of Internal Revenue.
>
> Southerners can object to work in race relations; we have been criticized by Congressman Reece and others for the grant to the Bar Association to study congressional investigations; a growing number of American Legion posts has attacked the Freedom Agenda program of the League of Women Voters; the Voluntary Defenders Committee has drawn the fire of a District Attorney in Massachusetts; the study of Communist influence in the United States is certain to incur the continued disfavor of vocal groups. The same is true of the analysis of fear in education, the prize-winning television plays, the censorship projects, and the investigation of the Post Office Department. What we have heard so far is nothing to the storm that may break when the study of black-listing is published.
>
> The reason why it is impossible to think of anything the Fund might do that might not produce pressure on the Commission is found in the nature of the field. The essential concern of the Fund is justice. If powerful persons or groups were not profiting by injustice, if they did not have a vested interest in it, it would not exist. . . . This is the first time that an organization dedicated to civil liberties has had any money. That fact alone, as soon as it appeared that the organization meant business, would account for the clamor we hear today.[57]

Point by point and issue by issue, Hutchins responded to criticisms he had heard from the directors. The Herblock series? The board had approved a pilot film. A sponsorship agreement was on the verge of conclusion with a national corporation. The Eisenhower cartoon had nothing to do with the Fund's agreement with Herblock and could not legitimately be used to threaten the Fund's tax exemption.

> If considerations of good taste make it desirable to postpone a Herblock program until the President has recovered, that is one thing; cancellation based on fear of resentment arising not from the program but from official dislike of the man is another.[58]

The award program? The board accepted every phase of it. If it was outside the Fund's charter so also would be the television awards, which the executive committee did not mention, as would be the Stiles Hall award with which it voted to proceed. The wisdom of the Plymouth Monthly Meeting award?

> The answer depends on the importance that the Board attaches to the principle that loyal and qualified persons should be allowed to earn a living, even if they have resorted to the Fifth Amendment, and their employers should not be intimidated.[59]

The distribution of literature? Each progress report contained a list of the selections, and counsel had expressed the judgment that the program was within the Fund's proper limits of action.

> Members of the Board have often expressed concern over the lack of accessible information, ideas, and discussion about the state of civil liberties. Some of them have suggested that the Fund publish a magazine or news bulletin. Others have wanted to encourage writers and publishers. The program for the distribution of literature has seemed the least expensive way of experimenting in this field.[60]

What about charges of "one-sidedness"? Hutchins's tone became sharper in the last few pages of the memorandum.

> The Fund is entitled as part of its educational work to bring to the attention of the public material that it feels should not be overlooked or neglected. The balance that it seeks is not necessarily balance within a list of books that it distributes, but balance in the discussion of the country.

This provocative assertion warranted elaboration, and Hutchins continued:

> The logic of balance cannot require the Fund to distribute one of Gerald L. K. Smith's publications every time it sends out an article against anti-semitism or to circulate statements favoring segregation in the South to balance statements opposed to it.
>
> If the Board is concerned about the selections made by the Officers, it might make future distribution contingent on the approval of each item by a special committee.[61]

Should not the Fund have more control over its grantees? (Ironically, Fulton Lewis, Jr., considered all recipients of Fund monies not unlike puppets of the master manipulator, Dr. Hutchins.) Foundations in general had not sought to dominate the decisions of grantees. Counsel Webster, Hutchins wrote, asked to have a knowledge of the plans of the American Friends Service Committee before they were put into effect. The committee violated its agreement to supply this, and new arrangements were made, following an official apology to the Fund. "Meanwhile it should be noted that the actions of the AFSC to date are not outside the terms of the docket item approved in May."[62]

What about the officers themselves? Their discretionary powers were limited to fellowships, grants-in-aid, the distribution of literature, and the appointment of staff, the president reminded the directors. Amos Landman was highly qualified for his position, was needed by the Fund, and came recommended to the officers by Stanley Isaacs, Republican leader in the City Council of New York.

> To make an award that can only have the effect of encouraging others to retain or engage qualified, loyal persons who have taken the Fifth Amendment and then to decline to hire such a person on the ground of possible criticism would seem to me a refusal to practice what we preach. It would be like the Urban League's opening an office in Atlanta to promote the employment of Negroes and then failing to hire one itself because of what people might say.[63]

Hutchins concluded this draft to the directors by curtly suggesting the possibility of longer quarterly meetings, "to disclose the considered judgment of the Board."[64] His final words were exhortative, tempered by earnest demand; they summarize the strict sense of duty and devotion to principle, of moral crusade, which exist in almost every speech, every article, every book, on every subject, by this Presbyterian minister's son.

> The objects of the Fund require it to expose injustice, encourage justice, and speak the truth. No lesser mission would be worthy of such a Board as this. We can have no illusions about the conse-

quences to every one of us of persisting in the performance of this task. But we did not promise one another an easy time. We promised one another an important enterprise.[65]

Hutchins had failed to specify any personal mistakes, and had slightly oversimplified the composition of the Fund's opponents. But the memorandum, even in its softer final form, came directly to grips with many issues which the directors would have to settle among themselves before the Fund could take the offensive.

Hutchins then decided to set the record straight before the Southern California public, submitting to three hours of questions by four editors of the moderate Los Angeles *Mirror News*. Several of his responses came verbatim from the memorandum he was polishing for the Fund's directors and dealt with the barrage of complaints against the Fund which was causing interest and alarm throughout the nation. Others contained platitudes virtually required of all citizens choosing to defend he Bill of Rights—"If we had a Communist regime we couldn't expect to have civil liberties. That's all there is to it." He attempted self-effacement ("I'm not the kind of doctor who ever does anybody any good"), praised the "sense of fair play" of America's publishers, and said of the Fund's unnamed critics: "These people are fighting a rear-guard action. They don't know when they are licked." It was not a particularly enlightening or informative interview, but the generous coverage, including smile-filled pictures, no doubt assisted public relations as intended. The first of three published installments of the interview cited Hutchins as "one of the nation's most forthright defenders of the U.S. Constitution and the rights of the individual."[66] There was little time for applause, however, for more trouble soon broke out.

On October 28, Fulton Lewis, Jr., quoted an article by Frederick Woltman, staff writer for the Scripps-Howard newspapers, summarizing recent criticisms of the Sutherland committee's highly praised *Bibliography on the Communist Problem in the United States*. Novelist James T. Farrell, Chairman of the liberal, anti-Communist American Committee for Cultural Freedom, had charged the authors with "inexcusable sloppiness." Professor

Phillip Taft of the department of economics at Brown University was quoted as having told Professor Sutherland: "You deserve a vote of thanks from the communist party."[67] Several important anti-Communist references were omitted from the book. Dr. John Sessions, in a fiery review for the *New Leader,* noted the absence of works by Dwight Macdonald, Arthur Koestler, Bertram Wolfe, Max Eastman, Norman Thomas, Joseph Wood Krutch, and Angelica Balabanoff, first secretary of the Communist Internationale.[68] If the bibliography's faults did not merit the reviewer's often intemperate language, they were all the same quite real. In fact, Dr. Hutchins told the board shortly, the authors of the project had been discussing revision for six months.[69]

Dr. Sutherland replied to critics by saying that no more than "a few dozen omissions at most" had been pointed out to date. "When you consider the thousands of entries, that does not appear too bad, and we certainly will include those omissions which appear worthwhile in the revision."[70] Committee member Clinton Rossiter, reached by reporters at Cornell, said: "I am taking full responsibility for a revision and expansion to correct some of these mistakes."[71] The Reverend Joseph M. Snee, S.J., professor of law at Georgetown University, and another member of the Sutherland committee, responded with a letter to the Fund on November 2 which was released to the press the following day. "I am not at all surprised that a pioneer work of this kind should contain omissions and imperfections." Honest criticism was welcome, he wrote, but it ought not to warrant attacks upon the motives of the bibliography's compilers.[72] (To Fulton Lewis, Jr., the possibility was very real "that somehow, the anti-anti-communist attitude has touched this work."[73]) Privately, Rev. Snee echoed Professor Sutherland's sentiments: it was time to "take courage rather than take cover."[74] A weary spokesman for the Fund exclaimed to reporters: ". . . the bibliography was prepared independently of the Fund. We had absolutely nothing to do with its contents and never touched the manuscript."[75]

Throughout the past months of controversy (Joseph Lyford referred to them as "these troubled times") Paul Hoffman had been busy handling his duties for the Studebaker Corporation, traveling around the country completing speaking engagements, and keeping up with his enormous correspondence. In September he had mailed a form letter and a copy of the Fund's press release responding to the charges of Seaborn Collins to hundreds of professional men and organizations. Of the dozens of replies there was but *one* clearly critical response. The publisher of the Harlowton (Montana) *Times* wrote:

> When you begin combatting Republicans of stature such as Senator McCarthy and when your objectives are frankly New Dealish and Democratic as they obviously are you have sacrificed your right to be considered as an organization devoted to America.[77]

Scores of the most prominent and respected citizens in the nation joined with their counterparts in towns and villages in every section of the country in enthusiastic and complete support of the Fund's purposes and deeds. The letters illustrated the relatively small quantity to date of the Fund's severe critics. But this minority, most of which was predictably defiant, was vociferous and determined, and there was no telling what damage it might cause in the future.

"I think we should try to put our Directors to work telling the Fund's story," a staff member confided to Hutchins and Ferry. "They are reacting now by modifying our program. If they could be given more opportunities to react by defending it in public (or by persuading others even more prominent and powerful to do so) they might be less inclined to modify it further."[78] Chairman of the board Hoffman took the initiative and flew to Berkeley to present the award to Stiles Hall and hold a press conference.

Before 3,000 students assembled in front of the university's Divinelle Hall, Hoffman presented the campus YMCA with a check for $5,000. "For 25 years," he said in his brief remarks, "Stiles Hall has practiced the old American doctrine of appraising people as individuals."

> Stiles Hall has stood for freedom of speech. Through times that include World War II and that hysterical rampage of the Tenney

Committee, Stiles Hall has believed in free discussion as the way to seek the truth and has helped provide a forum for it.[79]

Copies of laudatory letters by University of California President Robert Gordon Sproul and Major-General William F. Dean of the Sixth Army were mailed to each Fund director—as was a letter by ultraconservative Senator William F. Knowland, who sent his regrets at being unable to attend.[80]

At the press conference in San Francisco's Fairmont Hotel, Hoffman said that criticisms of the Fund ranged from "silly" to "mere misunderstanding." Loyalty oaths? "I'd just as soon sign them from morning to night." But experience had convinced him that "the people who talked the loudest about loyalty and signed most eagerly were Communists." Earl Browder? "Naturally, you find out about Communism from people who know about it." Communism

is not something that's going to die tomorrow. We're going to have to reckon with it for a long time to come. So we had better find out all we can about it . . .

There is not a man on the board of directors who is not a dedicated anti-Communist.[81]

Once again it was President Hutchins's turn.

Robert Hutchins's first biographer will discover striking similarities between his subject and Woodrow Wilson: family and religious background, education, career, idealism, strength of character and will, a sort of Zoroastrian penchant to divide men and ideas into pellucid categories of good and evil. Moreover, both men, when not behind a lectern, appeared deeply reserved, distant and cold-blooded, unable even to return the confidence and warmth they sought from a few select friends. And Hutchins, again like Wilson, tended to become stiff, rigid, and abrupt when confronted in unnatural situations by individuals whom he perceived possessed both personal and ideological hostility. In 1949, for example, before an Illinois state investigating committee and J. B. Matthews (a man whom he —and many others—considered a fraud), Hutchins answered antagonistic and insipid questions with terse, often wry comments which opponents like Dwight Macdonald later pretended to take literally and used to darken the educator's reputation for high intelligence.[82] It was beyond his powers to share his ideas and eloquently expound upon his ideals before men who cared not a whit for the principles he cherished; men whose sole desire, in his judgment, was to slander the highest causes and the most noble pursuits.

For weeks the Fund's staff had been laying plans for a major news conference for Dr. Hutchins; gathering statistics, nervously anticipating questions, and lining up participants. On November 7, Hutchins yielded to what a reporter for *The New York Times* called "a two-hour cross-examination" by twenty newsmen, including Hearst reporters, Frederick Woltman, Dwight Macdonald, and a representative of Fulton Lewis, Jr.[83] The result was sheer disaster. Consultant Walter Millis, who attended the session along with the officers and many of the staff, recalled: "Bob was just too intellectually arrogant to submit to the pounding they gave him. We all thought, including Bob, that the whole thing was a dreadful show."[84]

The reporters appeared little interested in the Fund's multiform programs and grants involving millions of dollars and including scores of the nation's highest-ranking scholars, organizations, and institutions; they bore down hard on Hutchins's allegedly infamous belief (publicized by Fulton Lewis, Jr.) that neither Communists nor partakers of the Fifth Amendment were by definition immoral, irrational, unpatriotic, or unemployable.

For many years Robert Hutchins had defended the principle "that the progress of mankind depends upon the freest possible expression of diverse points of view"; that diversity of opinion was the lifeline of freedom. He was loath to see government in the business of suppressing "heresy," for the practice was known to be notoriously habit-forming and conducive to varying forms of tyranny. Unless a man be a spy or an advocate of the violent overthrow of the government, he insisted, he should be free to engage in political activities and to earn a living. Anything less and all dissent and unorthodoxy were threatened with penalties accorded treason. As for the Communist party, membership in it was not a crime and it was by no means certain that the thoughts of every party member were rigidly controlled by party discipline. A man should not be deprived of employment for past and current party membership unless his actions were illegal. And each individual should be judged, in accordance with the Constitution, on the merits of his case. Thus if a man was free to think independently, and if he was not guilty of a crime, Hutchins considered him employable—certainly by a university or a foundation. He expressed this clearly when a university president: "If a professor can think and make his contribution to a center of independent thought, that is all that is required of him. One might wish that he were more agreeable or more conventional; but he cannot be discharged because he fails to measure up to desirable standards in these respects."[85]

Dr. Hutchins might have expounded upon this essentially conservative viewpoint with grace and wit; he might have softened his position during the press conference with a fashionable tirade against the Communist conspiracy; he might have alluded to his war record or to the pertinent fact that he had never employed a Communist for any position with which he was connected. But faced with the hostile and suspicious questions shooting out from behind the hot, glaring lights, he was able only to repeat briefly and haltingly his lifelong enmity toward limitations upon independent thought, and contend that under the proper conditions the employment of a Communist was justifiable.[86] What made the news the next day was simply: "I wouldn't hesitate to hire a Communist for a job he was qualified to do provided I was in a position to see he did it."

Seated before a large, framed facsimile of the Bill of Rights, he defended the Fund from each of the charges of past months with taut, crabbed phrases which tended to elevate rapidly into lofty generalizations. When asked if a single Fund project had escaped criticism, he merely replied: "If your object is to promote justice, you're likely to be attacked, because if people weren't profiting by injustice it wouldn't exist."[87]

As had been feared, serious trouble seemed to be developing for the Fund within the Treasury Department. On November 9, Adam Yarmolinsky wrote a memo to Hutchins and Ferry relating a report from "a confidential informant" who was told by two officials of the Internal Revenue Service that a review of the Fund's tax exemption was under way and "by the very nature of things" was "on the top of the pile."[88] The Washington *Post* carried the story from the *Congressional Quarterly* the next day.[89] A Fund spokesman replied to the *Post:*

> Since all of the projects and grants of the Fund are educational, it is very difficult to see how its tax exemption can be properly questioned. The educational nature of the Fund's activities is set forth in its Annual Report, copies of which are available on request.[90]

Paul Harvey cheerfully told his listeners that afternoon of the investigation and predicted that "A decision is to be handed down from Washington any day now."[91]

Joseph Lyford, the Fund's public-relations director, polled many of the officers and staff members to see what they had done to improve public relations of late. The directors were scheduled to meet on November 17 and there were bound to be plenty of sharp questions. Vice-President Ferry, for one, reported that he was spending up to six hours a day with publishers, editors, and newsmen.[92] Report after report by staff members indicated that their intensive efforts at widespread coverage of the facts were being met with willingness and sympathy. Hallock Hoffman concluded: "I think our public relations are in much better shape than we—sitting in our positions—are likely to think."[93]

By mid-November, Lyford had gathered enough data to report that in the past three and one-half months

> the Fund has been the subject of approximately 2,000 stories and editorial comments, and an undetermined number of syndicated columns. About one-third of the news stories were originated by the Fund itself. About two-thirds of the wire service stories concerning the Fund could be classified as favorable. Editorial comment pro and con the Fund was about evenly divided.[94]

His analysis of the over-all situation caused him to suggest several reforms in the Fund's administrative operations, including an intensive short-term public-information program. "The attacks upon the Fund can be expected to lessen somewhat in 1956 because of the general preoccupation of newspapers and other communications media with the national elections. This may conceivably allow the Fund more time to explain itself."[95] The suggestion was further developed and submitted in the form of a rather expensive recommendation to the board, concluding: "A well-thought-out program may help the Fund to be better understood in some quarters."[96]

The ominous rumblings about a government investigation and the noisy challenges of past months had all but obscured daily developments of the many programs sustained or initiated by the Fund for the Republic. The progress report submitted to the board in preparation for the November 17 meeting, among other indexes, revealed that contributions toward the corporation's imposing goals were being steadily developed.

In intergroup relations, a chairman for the Indian Commission had been selected and was expected to accept shortly; the American Friends Service Committee and the Catholic Interracial Council of Chicago continued their diligent efforts to ease racial tensions; and the Southern Regional Council now boasted full-time, paid staff members in every southern state. The latter organization had been attacked with the usual epithets about Communist infiltration by the attorney general of Georgia, the Montgomery (Alabama) *Journal,* and Hearst's New York *Journal American* ("Name 21 Pro-Reds on Board of Dixie Race Study Council"), but reported growing membership—over 300 members in Alabama and 175 in Mississippi.[97] The Commission on Race and Housing reported it now had a research staff of sixteen, including consultants, and was planning vast studies by several major universities. The Public Education Association released its study of discrimination in the New York City public schools on November 7, revealing serious inequalities between predominantly white and nonwhite educational facilities.[98]

In popular education, the American Heritage Council reported widespread use of its discussion materials, including sixty to seventy American Legion posts in Illinois (where the state's Department of the American Legion had repudiated the program). The recordings of the classics of freedom were well under way and it was hoped that the first album would be ready in time for the board meeting.

Only mediocre success could be cited for the Fund's television projects. Little progress had been made by the Council of Civic Unity of San Francisco, only one of nineteen prize-winning scripts had found a sponsor, and Worthington Miner's pilot film, "The Challenge," had gotten nowhere. The news film project was expanding, however, and distinguished jurors had been found to judge programs for the Fund's television awards.

A meeting of six prominent publishers and editors had taken place on September 12 and decided to take no further steps toward the creation of a commission on the performance of the mass media. They did approve, however, of the Sigma Delta Chi project, now in the making, for a survey of press coverage of the 1956 Presidential election. A report commissioned by the Fund on the Swedish Fair Practices Board suggested that this continuous experiment in press appraisal had been of little value.

A freedom agenda conference, held on November 9, described the thousands of recipients of the program's discussion literature, which had the support of many national organizations, including the AMVETS, the American Jewish Congress, the Campfire Girls, the YWCA, the YMCA, and the League of Women Voters. The program had been bitterly attacked in anonymous mailings, by Fulton Lewis, Jr., and by elements within the American Legion, but plans were under way to respond to the attacks promptly and vigorously.[99]

The Association of the Bar Committee on the Federal Loyalty-Security Program, now working in the shadow of a newly formed government commission on the same subject, was continuing its labors satisfactorily and hoped to have a report in final form by May 1956.[100]

Directors must have been amazed by the progress report's discussion of new plans to produce studies on right-wing extremism, including volumes on "veterans' organizations, patriotic societies, and the churches," taking into account "such organizations as the American Legion, the DAR, the Minute Women, etc." Dr. Hutchins at least had to be admired for persistence (in World War I he received a medal for bravery under fire).[101]

The nine-page report also noted the completion of the *Conspectus on Civil Liberties,* by Robert Cushman, Professor Lazarsfeld's study of fear in education, and the near-completion of John Cogley's manuscript of the blacklisting study.[102] All three of these works might soon be before the public and would unquestionably be controversial. The directors must have pondered the disquieting possibility that the strife over the Fund for the Republic had just begun.

On the very day the Fund's board met for their afternoon and evening meeting, American Legion National Commander L. Addington Wagner raised nation-wide headlines by declaring, in an address before the Indianapolis Chamber of Commerce:

> The American Legion formally charges that by its action under its current direction, the Fund for the Republic renders comfort to the enemies of America. . . .
>
> I submit to you that by their own words and actions, the managers of the Fund for the Republic have clearly demonstrated that it is their intention to debunk what they consider to be the myth of the Communist menace in the United States.[103]

CHAPTER NINE

/ *Storm Center*

By the time the directors seated themselves for their third annual meeting, they had had ample opportunity to study President Hutchins's fourteen-page apologia, to consider his appeal for unity, to measure the velocity with which he wished to proceed. While they remained convinced of his good intentions and sympathetic to the general principles he espoused, they were little moved by Dr. Hutchins's belief that sharp attacks were inherent to the Fund's operations. Few of them had anticipated the soaring controversy of recent months: each knew that his good name was periled by the government's scrutiny of the Fund's activities.

The possibility of federal action against the Fund seemed very real. The Internal Revenue Service had recently stripped the Institute of Pacific Relations of its tax exemption on the basis of what appeared to many to be right-wing political pressure; the Ford Foundation had been embarrassed recently by a congressional investigation triggered by Fulton Lewis, Jr.; and the rumors of future hearings and reprisals involving the Fund were in evidence in greater quantity than ever before. Millions of people were reading and hearing daily of the Fund's alleged enmity to patriotism and anti-Communism. Dr. Hutchins had provoked rather than soothed the principal attackers with his polemics, and had no doubt attracted few supporters for the Fund. The board had obviously failed to convince many observers of the corporation's basic conservatism. Perhaps mistakes in judgment by the officers had unduly irritated many well-meaning Americans; perhaps, in fact, the board had relied too heavily upon the president and his subordinates. This was the time for retrospection and retrenchment; the clamor, the charges, the hostility must be terminated quickly and permanently.

The awards program, the board decided, would be maintained, but only on condition that each proposed award first receive unanimous approval by the directors present at two consecutive board meetings. The October 6 suspension of awards to the New York community centers was to be continued indefinitely.

The distribution of publications was allowed to continue, but each item had first to be cleared by counsel and approved by the board both as to subject matter and as to intended recipients. "No publications by political figures are to be distributed," the directors enjoined, "and no unsolicited distributions are to be made to government officials or members of the judiciary." Highly conspicuous among a small list endorsed at the meeting was a *Saturday Review* article by none other than George Sokolsky.

Completing the evening session of the 16th, the board decided to meet every two months (excluding summers) instead of quarterly. More frequent caucuses might inhibit the somewhat ebullient tendencies of the officers.

The next day three new directors were elected, providing the board with welcome additional professional and regional representation: Pulitzer Prize-winning lyricist Oscar Hammerstein II, corporation executive and former mayor of San Francisco Roger Lapham, and Texas oilman J. Howard Marshall. When the officers were routinely renominated, Dean Erwin Griswold abstained from voting for president and cast his ballot against the re-election of Vice-President Ferry, whose gruff and petulant mannerisms, along with his employment of Amos Landman, had incensed many, if not most, of the directors.[1]

The board then turned unenthusiastically to the officers' recommendations. Requests were limited wisely to a small fraction of the usual quantity; appropriations and grants approved fell almost 82 per cent from the September total.

The *Columbia Law Review* received $1,670 to assist a current study of "the problems involved in dealing with former prisoners of war accused of acts prejudicial to the interests of the United States." A grant of $25,000 went to the Committee on Internal Security of the Administrative Law Section of the Bar Association of the District of Columbia to support a study of passport matters. Kenyon College (long familiar to the Hoffman family) was granted $25,000 for a conference on the nature of liberty. The television awards (renamed the "Robert E. Sherwood Awards" in honor of the recently deceased director) were increased by $15,000. And $20,000 went to the Association of the Bar of the City of New York Fund, Inc., to assist a study of methods of representation of criminal defendants. Nothing remotely controversial here. In fact, a heading of the progress report, "Studies of Right-Wing Extremists," was ordered revised so that it "could not be interpreted to reflect on any of the organizations referred to under that heading"—notably the American Legion and the DAR.

A sharp clash took place among the directors over a proposed appropriation for the fellowship and grants-in-aid program, hitherto administered solely by the officers. Its denial would have been an unusually humilitating slap at President Hutchins. Over two negative votes, cast by Griswold and Joyce, the board allocated the requested $115,000.

At the request of John Lord O'Brian, Paul Hoffman had earlier requested Bethuel Webster to draft an official reply to Arthur Dean's letter of September 27.[2] Now approved by the board, the response politely challenged Dean's most potentially damaging objection, that the Fund was becoming associated with a particular set of views.

> To argue that any citizen is entitled to the protection of the laws of the United States is not to argue for whatever views the citizens may hold. The measure of the Fund's concern is the seriousness of the civil liberties issue involved, not the merits of the minority position.

As to the award to the Plymouth Monthly Meeting:

> . . . the Fund did not take any position on the issue that concerns you. One of the major civil liberties of our time is the tendency of private groups to take the law into their own hands, and to

attempt to compel retribution against unpopular individuals. In this case the Fund was paying tribute to the Friends, who were under severe pressure by other private organizations to dismiss an unpopular individual in their employ. The Fund did not attempt to judge the merits of Mrs. Knowles' case. . . .

Similarly, in making a grant to the Freedom of Conscience Committee of the American Friends Service Committee, the Fund is not committed to the position of any defendant who is helped by the Friends to assert a claim of conscience.

"The Fund *is* committed," the letter concluded, "to the proposition that full opportunity should be provided to present such claims, when honestly asserted, to the proper tribunal."[3]

The direcors also approved a letter drafted by Paul Hoffman to Henry Ford II. Ford had been the object of intensive verbal abuse in recent months. Even as the Fund's directors met, former McCarthy aide Roy M. Cohn attacked Ford at a dinner in Yonkers for his "silence" on the Fund for the Republic, which, Cohn said, had "given unrivalled assistance to the cause of Communism in this country."[4] Hoffman had received a letter from Ford as early as October 27 expressing personal objections, prompted evidently by complaints received in his mail, to "some" of the Fund's projects and "some" of the actions of the officers and staff. On November 1, Hoffman asked Ford to delay any public comments until he could formulate a detailed answer.[5] The letter before the board at its meeting on the 17th was flattering and highly conciliatory. It assured Ford that the board was "engaged in a continuous audit, appraisal, and re-appraisal of the program and of the activities of the staff, to the end that mistakes may be avoided and that such changes as experience and judgment seem to require may be made."[6] The directors knew that if Ford ever spoke out against the Fund the damage could be fatal—knowledge they shared with the corporation's most determined antagonists.

Concluding the session, the board was faced with a Hutchins request to commission a study by a scholar who had taken the Fifth Amendment before HUAC. It was clear to Hutchins that no inference of illegal activity could be drawn from a citizen's invocation of the Fifth Amendment before a congressional committee, and that a citizen should not be punished for a crime until proved guilty of one, in accordance with the safeguards and protections of the Constitution. Here was a qualified man eager to conduct a valuable inquiry. To what degree would the Fund operate to the pleasure of its critics? At what point would fear of controversy weaken the board's resolve to defend constitutional rights and elementary justice? The current issue was part of the president's standing challenge to the board to clarify its intent, to make known its will, to create guidelines for the officers to follow so that "mistakes" might be minimized and responsibility for success and failure more clearly apportioned. The directors could conclude only that "the fellowship in question not be awarded."[7]

The next meeting was scheduled for December 2, following President Hutchins's appearance on national television and radio.

The "Meet the Press" interview had been anxiously anticipated for weeks by the Fund's directors and staff. It was the president's supreme opportunity, before millions of Americans, to set the record straight: to call attention to the Fund's major achievements; to clarify the board's authority; to resolve the relatively petty issues involving Landman, Browder, and the bibliography, which critics were exploiting to the fullest in order to sustain charges that the Fund was giving "comfort to the enemies of America."

The day before the interview was to be held, the Hearst press carried a story from its Washington bureau declaring that "A full-scale Congressional probe of the granting of tax immunity on 'educational' grounds to the left-wing Fund for the Republic and other leftist groups was assured today."[8] That evening Joe Lyford had participated in a grueling radio debate on the Fund which revolved around Dr. Hutchins's assertions about the employability of Communists. Lyford argued that this was a personal opinion of the president's and had no bearing on the policies or operations of the corporation. Lyford assured his opponent and the audience that "Mr. Hutchins would be very happy to discuss this and he's doing it tomorrow . . . with four newspaper men, all going after him on a nationwide TV-radio hook up."[9]

"Going after him" was correct. The "Meet the Press" panel was not the most sympathetic group that program director Lawrence Spivak could have assembled. (Ferry protested privately that it was a "bunch of bearbaiters."[10]) Dr. Hutchins was grilled for one-half hour by James McConaughy, Jr., of *Time;* highly critical Frederick Woltman of the New York *World Telegram and Sun;* the suspicious and quarrelsome columnist of the Portland (Maine) *Press Herald,* May Craig; and Spivak himself. Hutchins managed to assert that the Fund considered Communism the nation's most serious menace to civil liberties—a principle consistently held by the board of directors before and during his employment—and did much to clear up the Browder engagement. But most of the questions carried negative implications and were couched in suspicion, causing Hutchins to bristle with anger and become evasive, cold, and spiritless. Even though a team of public-relations men had coached him before the program, the insolent character of the interrogation shattered his unusual imperturbability and incapacitated his celebrated rhetorical brilliance.

Would the Fund hire a Communist? the panel asked repeatedly. Hutchins declared that this would be up to the board of directors, and protested that the question had no relevance to the achievements of the Fund. But was he unaware of the Communist conspiracy? How could the Fund for the Republic be against Communism and be willing to hire one of its followers? Unable and unwilling to teach a short course on his perfectly orthodox and respectable views of the Constitution and the Bill of Rights, expounded in speeches and journals for over twenty years, Hutchins could say little except that "There are many gradients of membership" in organizations. When asked to explain his views on the Fifth Amendment, he made a curt reply, adding derisively: "The Fifth Amendment is part of the Bill of Rights."[11]

One exchange went as follows:

WOLTMAN Would you also hire a Nazi or a Fascist, or a Ku Klux Klanner?

HUTCHINS This question is a real flying saucer; so was the other one.

WOLTMAN Well, you didn't answer it.

HUTCHINS I beg your pardon, I did.

WOLTMAN You would also hire a Nazi—

HUTCHINS No, I didn't say I would.[12]

It was not at all clear why Dr. Hutchins (the Fund) would hire a Communist, but not a Nazi. Neither was it understandable at the end of the interview what the Fund for the Republic had been doing with millions of tax-exempt dollars. The entire encounter was reminiscent of a televised congressional committee hearing, and it was common knowledge that the tight-lipped, unfriendly witnesses in those proceedings were guilty of some kind of criminal activity.

Many friends and supporters of the Fund were stunned and dismayed by the president's television performance. Harry Ashmore, on leave from the board, saw several of Hutchins's former University of Chicago colleagues literally in tears at the program's conclusion.[13] Roger Lapham wrote to Paul Hoffman: ". . . Hutchins' handling was far from satisfactory, and I think he did his cause more harm than good."[14] Mrs. Lapham wrote: ". . . had I not known you, your honesty and your very sincere belief in what you feel the Fund for the Republic can accomplish, there would have been no doubt in my mind but that it was a high-sounding name for a Communist front organization."[15] Hoffman too was unhappy:

> . . . I share your disappointment that Mr. Hutchins did not give an unqualified "no" to the question of whether he would employ a communist. If I had been asked that question, I would have so answered and would have explained that I believe that anyone who is a communist today is either a conspirator or a fool. I would have made this reply despite the fact that there are probably some intelligent people who are intellectually committed to communism and who conceivably might be employable. Whether this is what Mr. Hutchins had in mind, I do not know. I do know that he is a *totally* honest person and a purist. There are times that I wish he were a weak-kneed compromiser like myself.[16]

Said Fulton Lewis, Jr.: "I sincerely hope, ladies and gentlemen, that you took my advice on Friday and watched or listened to the Meet the Press program yesterday . . . it was about as clear a lesson on the subject of Mr. Hutchins and the Fund for the Republic as you would ever find. He proved everything that has been said about him."[17] An old friend confided to Hutchins: "I caught your TV contest last afternoon and kept a round by round score. You lost."[18]

On November 23 the chairman of the House Committee on Un-American Activities, Representative Francis E. Walter of Pennsylvania, confirmed a rumor which had been spreading for weeks: a full-scale congressional investigation of the Fund for the Republic was under way. Public hearings were planned for early 1956.[19]

The committee, for seventeen years the bailiwick of some of Congress's most determined foes of civil liberties and civil rights, had been condemned openly by two Democratic Presidents for its often-ruthless treatment of witnesses and for publicity-seeking, and was widely known to have close ties with southern conservatives, the Hearst press, and Fulton Lewis, Jr. The decline of McCarthy had had no noticeable effect on the committee's zealous pursuits, and throughout the year investigations were held in Los Angeles, New York, Washington, San Francisco, Seattle, Newark, and Milwaukee.[20]

Representative Walter had served in the House since 1932 and was one of the most powerful figures in Congress. During his career he had favored wire-tapping, the power of arrest without warrants for officers of military intelligence, and loyalty oaths for jurors. His co-authorship of the McCarran-Walter Act of 1952 prompted Adlai Stevenson, during his Presidential campaign of that year, to remark of his fellow Democrat: "It is this Walter who is inclined to regard every prospective immigrant as a potential subversive and everyone who disagrees with his views on immigration as a danger to national security."[21]

What legislative purpose could be served by an investigation of the Fund for the Republic? What causes had Chairman Walter to question the loyalty of its eminent board of directors? A man who had taken the Fifth Amendment had been hired for a part-time publicity job (and had been dismissed); a highly respected scholar had agreed, with President Hutchins's permission, to pay Earl Browder less than $75 a week to be a historical source (at the suggestion of Judge Robert Morris, former chief counsel of the Senate Internal Security Committee); Dr. Hutchins had left open the purely theoretical possibility of hiring a Communist to perform a special task for which he was qualified (a position also taken by Senator Robert Taft and State Department security officer and McCarthyite Scott McLeon);[22] and a small award (still to be accepted formally[23]) had been made to the Plymouth Monthly Meeting, upsetting a number of people attempting to deprive an avowedly loyal American of her job.

Where was the faintest trace of treason in these activities? And how significant were they in the full scope of the Fund's three-year history, involving millions of dollars and thousands of distinguished scholars, clergymen, and civic leaders?

Congressman Walter chose only to justify his committee's probe on the ground that a Fund report had "criticized the Congress for legislation branding the Communist party as an 'international conspiracy.'" This charge was based on two sentences of the Fund's annual report, pertaining to the equation by unspecified sources of a political party with the enemy, and cannot be sustained as a fair or reasonable interpretation of the twenty-nine words in question. Had the sentences specifically warranted the charge, however, the need for a congressional investigation by HUAC into this statement of opinion would remain absurd, especially in light of the Internal Revenue Service's current scrutiny of the Fund's conformity with the requirements of tax exemption.

At any rate, the Fund's board of directors, fresh from the sorry spectacle of Dr. Hutchins's television interview, could now relish the thought of appearing before a hostile congressional committee, publicly associated by an arm of the federal government with motives and actions contrary to the best interests of the United States.

The assembled directors graced their board meeting of December 2 with the smallest quantity of allocations yet approved at a regularly scheduled session under the presidency of Robert Hutchins. Consultant Ben Segal received an appropriation of $35,000 to continue his successful educational endeavors with trade unions; the officers were authorized to make grants, aggregating not more than $25,000, to tax-exempt entities within local bar groups to help assure competent defense in individual civil-liberties cases; three church organizations were each granted $15,000 to expand their labors in race relations; $25,000 went to the Board of Social and Economic Relations of the Methodist Church to finance further studies on Communism; and the sum of $3,000 was granted to the United States National Student Association to assist their Academic Freedom Week in 1956.

But the purpose of this gathering was not to spend money, it was to formulate policy which would extirpate the Fund's increasingly grave public-relations difficulties. Two major decisions were made during the morning session.

Counsel Bethuel Webster was given full responsibility and virtually unlimited financial resources "to represent the Fund in connection with any investigation or proceeding pending in or threatened by the Treasury Department, the House Committee on Un-American Activities, or any other branch of Government or Committee of Congress." In addition, Chairman Hoffman was authorized to select from the directors a Temporary Advisory Committee on Information Program, to take whatever steps necessary to elucidate for the public the breadth and importance of the Fund's activities and to counteract the frequently abusive tactics of the growing number of critics. He subsequently appointed Elmo Roper as chairman and included directors Cole, Parten, and Shuster.[24]

The board's actions were far from premature, for on December 6 news of the greatest disaster that had yet befallen the corporation burst from the radio broadcast of a gleeful Fulton Lewis, Jr.: Henry Ford II had publicly expressed dissatisfaction with the Fund for the Republic.

Ford was to have met informally with the Fund's directors on December 15, but suddenly decided to undercut the encounter with a reply to a complaint from the chairman of the Anti-Subversive Committee of a New York American Legion post.[25] When Lewis made the letter public it earned headlines in every major newspaper in the country. Ford wrote, in part:

> Despite the fact that I have no legal right to intervene in the affairs of the Fund for the Republic, I have exercised my right as a private citizen to question the manner in which the fund has attempted to achieve its stated objectives. Some of its actions, I feel, have been dubious in character and inevitably have led to charges of poor judgment.[26]

Why had Ford done it? And what lay behind the timing of the menacingly vague criticism? Elmo Roper knew that there had been heavy pressure from officials at the Ford Motor Company; Roper was given hints that his own business relations with the company might be cut if he failed to resign from the board or to support the removal of the Fund's outspoken president. At one point, Ford himself had asked Roper to leave the Fund's board.[27] This pressure was based, presumably, on the fear of economic boycott brought about by continuous bad publicity. But statistics reveal that the company was breaking all of its records in sales and profits.[28]

The outburst was chiefly due, perhaps, to Ford's high-strung temperament, provoked by what he considered to be an unprecedented amount of personal criticism by dealers, customers, and ultraconservatives. There was evidence of unrest among southern Ford dealers over the Fund.[29] And in his letter of October 27 to Hoffman, Ford wrote of "a great number of letters . . . expressing disapproval of the Fund," adding that "many of them have come from responsible people who seem to be sincere and constructive in their criticism." (Such mail had, of course, contributed to the break with Hoffman several years earlier.) Moreover, Fulton Lewis, Jr., and other McCarthyites had been pounding for months at Ford personally for some kind of censure of the Fund. Just a few days before Ford's letter was written, William F. Buckley, Jr., devoted a full page of his *National Review* to the publication of a letter he had written to Ford on November 29 pleading for commentary on the Fund.

What is your own judgment on those activities of the Fund for the Republic that are at public issue? Do you believe that the present management of the Fund is faithfully and effectively carrying out the intentions of the Foundation in establishing the Fund? . . . A statement from you on these matters is of crucial public importance.[30]

Ford's reprobation was sure to injure seriously the Fund's rather (in the popular eye) the Fund's donor, a foremost supporter of the Eisenhower Republicans, and one of the nation's most widely known and respected leaders of industry.

J. Addington Wagner, national commander of the American Legion, told reporters that Mr. Ford had made a "necessary and commendable move in the right direction" and that his letter struck "a reassuring note for every American who is concerned with the nation's security."[31] The Fund's president was not available for comment.[32]

Hutchins was not in seclusion, however. Shortly before the Ford letter became public information, he made a sincere effort to quell another protest against the Fund, this time from within the intellectual community. On December 1 he sat down with a few leading members of the American Committee for Cultural Freedom to attempt a settlement of matters which lay at the bottom of several recent volleys against the Fund.

The ACCF first became prominent in 1950 as an independent affiliate of an international association of socialist, liberal, and conservative intellectuals dedicated to responsible and vigorous opposition to totalitarianism in general and Communism in particular. Its membership list, while bristling with ex-Communists, contained a fairly broad spectrum of political partisans, including Whittaker Chambers, Milton R. Konvitz, Richard Rovere, Norman Thomas, Peter Viereck, Max Eastman, and Bertram Wolfe. The committee's leaders and more zealous members frequently expressed themselves through the journal *The New Leader,* described by the committee's bulletin as the "foremost weekly of the anti-Communist left."[33]

The New Leader, whose editor, S. M. Levitas, was a member

of the ACCF's executive committee, took very seriously many of the charges of suvbersion in government made before and during McCarthy's bloom. One rather typical editorial of 1950 read:

> Today, as Mao sits closeted in Moscow with Stalin, the Far Eastern Division of the State Department—a division of misinformation ever since Henry Stimson left State—is the last refuge of the Henry Wallace-Owen Lattimore type of "progressive"—the abode of John Davieses, Fulton Freemans and Walton Butterworths, if not of Alger Hisses. The Far Eastern Division still emits the pungent stench of the John Carter Vincent-Institute of Pacific Relations days, and if you sniff real hard, you can detect the odor of the *Ameresia* spy case.[34]

The journal and a large number of its contributors were no more than mildly critical of McCarthy, and only slightly troubled about what many qualified observers described as a contemporary crisis in civil liberties. The Communist party was a monolithic conspiracy whose members were conscious agents of absolute, totalitarian depravity; the Communist peril to America was sufficiently critical and immediate to warrant severe restricions upon the free marketplace of ideas.

Both the journal and leaders of the ACCF appeared disturbed and angered by the Fund for the Republic in late 1955, by implication because of its "softness" on Communism. ACCF members had led the attack against the Fund's bibliography, and the most venomous critique had appeared in *The New Leader;* Arnold Beichman, ACCF executive committeeman, had used the journal to publish a scathing blast against Dr. Hutchins over his November press conference; and ACCF partisan Dwight Macdonald suggested that the Fund's officers and staff become better informed on Communism, "say up to the high-school level."[35] Moreover, Sol Stein, executive director of the ACCF, attempted to deepen suspicions about the Fund by telling *The New York Times* that under Hutchins's leadership it had turned down "at least three projects" submitted by the committee involving anti-Communism.[36]

Indeed, since June of 1954 the Fund had rejected three ACCF proposals; before that time, under Clifford Case, the Fund had declined to accept three others. But a study of the voluminous correspondence of the Fund's officers, staff, and directors, between themselves and with ACCF representatives, reveals not the slightest evidence of a plot to exclude the ACCF from a grant because of its militant anti-Communism. Both Case and Hutchins sought broad counsel before taking action, and the ACCF proposals were given careful and thoughtful consideration before joining hundreds of similar requests in the Fund's "Grants Reject" files. There are indications that the ACCF treasury was sorely in need of replenishment, and that ACCF criticism of the Fund grew in fairly close proportion to the extent of that need.[37]

Important also to the enmity with the Fund felt by leaders of the ACCF was Sidney Hook, one of the organization's founders, a member of its executive committee, and its ideological *Kapellmeister*.[38] Hook, a brilliant, fiery, and extremely self-confident philosopher, had been at odds with Robert Hutchins for a quarter of a century over the issue of progressive education.[39] On matters of freedom and security the two differed just as greatly.

Hook had been a Marxist during the early Depression, intimated an apostate's superior knowledge of the guile and fanaticism of Communism, and was the sworn enemy of "ritualistic liberals" whose alleged naïveté and irresponsibility led them to conclusions other than his own: that American Communists were an intimate part of a world conspiracy, to be barred, along with takers of the Fifth Amendment, from all positions of responsibility under all conditions. Moreover, Hook considered there were few problems in civil liberties during the McCarthy era, only "scattered events of injustice, foolishness and hardship." Congressional investigating committees, federal loyalty-security programs, and blacklisting in private industries were, by and large, reasonable and necessary means for thwarting ruthless maleficence. He also rejected the idea that restrictions on academic freedom were widespread, and thought civil rights to be a minor and rapidly improving social problem.[40] In fact, from Hook's point of view, aside from its opportunity to study and disseminate information on Communism (most wisely via the

ACCF), there was virtually no reason for the existence of a Fund for the Republic.

Dr. Hutchins, along with staff member Paul Jacobs, met with Hook and several other ACCF members at Columbia University on the evening of December 1 to attempt to iron out some of the past misunderstandings and build rapport between the intellectuals of both organizations. Hutchins and Jacobs thought the meeting highly successful.[41] But when in later months two more ACCF proposals were rejected by the Fund's officers (on the advice of a committee of the board and Professor Rossiter), and an innocent comment by Ferry was interpreted by several ACCF members (including Hook) as a slanderous excuse for Fund reluctance to distribute publications by prominent ACCF personalities (including Hook),[42] Hook lashed out at Hutchins in a *New Leader* article, condemning him for "extremism and irresponsible judgment," "his misplaced sense of methodological nicety," his "lack of common sense," and "his total political innocence." Hutchins was the prince of "soapy-minded ritualistic liberals," "a foolish man."[43] A later offer by the Fund to distribute a Department of Defense publication through the ACCF was curtly rejected.[44]

After the session at Columbia University, Hutchins returned to his Pasadena office to continue efforts at answering critics. He was in trouble with a number of his directors, and knew it; much soothing and mending would have to be done to compensate for the unfortunate television appearance, Congressman Walter's announcement, and Ford's letter. As a significant step in that direction, the draft of a lengthy memorandum to the board, requested by the directors and designed "to deal with any question that any Director has raised about the Fund," was submitted to Paul Hoffman for prior approval.[45] Perhaps by coincidence, the next day Hoffman received the following telegram from Hutchins's old friend Supreme Court Justice William O. Douglas:

> I know that the Fund for the Republic and Bob Hutchins have been under fire and criticism in recent months. I want you to know from this quarter that in my opinion the Fund under Bob Hutchins has rendered great public service in helping keep alive

the traditions of civil liberties. The Bill of Rights is a great storm center in all times of tension. Those who defend it are certain to incur the wrath of the narrow minded partisans. That is why I with millions of others congratulate you on the great courage and steadfastness you have shown by helping to keep the great program of the Fund alive and vital.[46]

That same day, the Fund made public a letter by Eugene W. Landy, the young man who, in August, was denied an ensign's commission in the Naval Reserve because his mother had once been a Communist. The Yale law student commended Dr. Hutchins for asserting that there could be different grades of Communists, and that in certain hypothetical circumstances he would employ a Communist party member. His mother was living proof, Landy wrote, that not all Communists "rank with the most degenerate criminals." The Fund's president was congratulated for "being one of the few free men in our time."[47]

But these moves by Hutchins were insufficient to quell the fury of one of the original board members, Dean Erwin Griswold. On December 16, Griswold, by all evidence the most restive of the directors, officially rejected any further financial compensation for his services to the Fund.[48] He then granted an interview to a Rhode Island reporter and publicly condemned the employment of Amos Landman. "It should have been obvious from the beginning," this author of a major book on the Fifth Amendment said, "that it would cause more misunderstanding and do more harm to the interests we're trying to represent than it would do good." He went on to declare that it "was most unfortunate that Dr. Hutchins didn't make it plain that the Fund would not hire a person known now to be a member of the Communist Party for any purpose."

In the same article an unidentified source told of the directors' regret over the Plymouth Monthly Meeting award and cited attempts "to keep a much tighter reign on Dr. Hutchins."[49] The reporter, within a few days, noted accurately that "a difference of opinion has developed within the board of directors as to which action would do more harm at this point—the dropping of Dr. Hutchins or his retention."[50]

On December 19, Dean Griswold wrote a letter to Paul Hoffman, sending copies to each of the directors, calling for the retirement of Robert Hutchins. "With great pain and difficulty," he felt compelled to conclude that the president's inflexible views on civil liberties and his seemingly unquenchable taste for controversy rendered him unqualified for his current position.

He does not primarily seek to explain, to lead, to guide, to speak softly and persuasively, to inculcate wisdom and understanding. On the contrary, his approach tends to be combative, belligerent, provocative, dramatic. Rather than leading to better understanding, this approach evokes strong reactions, and often leads to increased opposition, and to misunderstanding. This, I think, is poor human relations.[51]

Three other directors, M. Albert Linton, John Lord O'Brian, and James Zellerbach, sent letters to the Fund's chairman expressing agreement with Griswold's proposal.[52] Zellerbach added: "I feel it extremely important that this change be made prior to Congress convening and the commencement of the investigations of the Fund, which I am advised are now under active consideration by three separate committees of Congress."[53] Hoffman himself promised to lay aside all personal loyalties, adding: "We must take a long, hard look at our program and remedy whatever we find wrong."[54]

American Legion Commander Wagner, possibly knowing of Hutchins's vicissitudes with several of his "true conservatives," men chosen for the board in part for their personal courage, selected January 3 (three days preceding the directors' next meeting) to speak on the Fund for the Republic before the American Legion Club in Los Angeles. Reversing previous tactics, he extolled the virtues of the Ford Foundation and applauded the aims of the Fund. The villain in the story was quite simply and exclusively Robert Maynard Hutchins, whose sardonic wit had taunted the Legion for almost three decades.

A Communist, whether he is an American or an Outer Mongolian, is an enemy of the United States of America. Anyone who does not recognize and accept that fact is too naïve or too obtuse to be trusted to give away tax-exempt money.[55]

Hutchins, meanwhile, had sent each director a copy of a letter by Supreme Court Justice Douglas, who expressed his willingness and "great pleasure" to join the American Jewish Congress at a tribute banquet in honor of the Fund's president.[56] And on the day before the board meeting an excerpt from the minutes of a special committee of the American Friends Service Committee was mailed to the directors, which commended the Fund and seconded a favorite Hutchins position: "It is to be expected that any program in the field of civil liberties will meet hostile criticism during a period of public apprehension when there is every temptation to sacrifice individual freedom to State security."[57]

A rump meeting of several directors most deeply committed either for or against the retention of Dr. Hutchins preceded the January 6, 1956, conclave. The president's strongest partisans, Elmo Roper, Mrs. Eleanor Stevenson, and Jubal Parten, argued at length with Erwin Griswold and William Joyce over Hutchins's tenure. As Roper recalls:

> Griswold and Joyce honestly believed that Hutchins was searching for people to aggravate, that he was using unnecessarily inflammatory methods to defend principles we all believed in. If Parten or Stevenson or I had even wavered at any time in our belief in Hutchins, he would have been gone. We had no intention of wavering. You could say he came that close to being removed as president.[58]

But the issue was far from settled at this preliminary huddle. The full board of directors met for almost thirteen hours on January 6 and 7 in what was clearly the most important session they had ever held. A few cautious allocations and distributions were approved, but these brisk actions did not obscure the principal reason for the assemblage.[59] To Dr. Hutchins this meeting contained the grim possibility of a refutation of his entire public life—a crushing humiliation relegating him to the outermost fringe of intellectual respectability and national prominence.

Central to the discussion was a twenty-two-page memorandum

to the directors, dated December 21 and read in draft form beforehand by Hoffman and Roper. In it Hutchins discussed many of the Fund's grants and projects, and made several proposals to improve the organization and staffing of the corporation. The letter, requested on December 2 by the board, was an offer containing the conditions by which Hutchins might continue as president.

Critics of the Fund were narrowed to established members of the Right and Left and dismissed. "It is an honor to the Fund to be assailed by Lewis, Hearst, the Legion, and Senator McCarthy. It is a tribute to its work. . . . Congressman Walter," he continued, "appears to be collaborating with Lewis, which seems odd, since Walter is said to be a 'brilliant intellectual.' . . . I would not court attacks from any quarter; but I assume that attacks from this quarter should not disturb us." The campaign from the Right was inevitable. Even without the hiring of Landman and Browder and the remarks about the employability of Communists, the attack upon the Fund would have been substantial. "Evidence for this is that it had been going on for almost two months when the appointment of Landman became public." Criticism from the Left, Hutchins believed, was over, as the result of the December 1 meeting with ACCF leaders. The immediate task was the promotion of understanding of the Fund with the vast public standing in the ideological center. "The audience at which we have to aim consists of those who would be favorable to the Fund if they understood it."

Several recent incidents about which certain board members had expressed alarm were of no major consequence to the Fund, Hutchins insisted. Only 123 letters were received on the "Meet the Press" program, and only 24 of these were unfavorable. Recent statements by ultraconservatives Herbert Philbrick and Scott McLeod supported his position on the hypothetical employability of Communists. And although Fulton Lewis, Jr., had attacked the Fund at least 60 times over 214 stations, the officers had received only about 300 letters, 65 per cent of them favorable.

Hutchins noted the inevitability of fresh attacks upon the release of the forthcoming studies on blacklisting, academic freedom, post office practices, and the testimony of ex-Communist witnesses. He reiterated his belief that

> the problem of the Fund is education, rather than public relations in the usual sense. That is, the process is relatively slow and long; the Fund cannot be operated in terms of tomorrow's headlines. One thing seems fairly clear: if we operate in terms of tomorrow's headlines, we shall be permitting the enemies of the Fund to manage it. They can write more headlines than we can.

The president was clearly unwilling to shoulder much of the blame for the Fund's past difficulties. Directors had complained, for example, that liaison with grantees was inadequate. This was untrue, Hutchins contended, and the board should have been aware that the Fund could not prescribe the detailed methods by which the purposes of a grant are carried out.

> This matter was central in the discussions that led up to Rossiter's undertaking the study of Communism. Good men will not work for the Fund on the studies it wants made unless they are free to select their own staff and reach their own conclusions.

At the December meeting there were complaints that the Fund was overly involved in direct action. In assisting defendants, Hutchins wrote, the Fund was insulated from attack by the organizations which received the grants. No award could be given without the directors' unanimous consent. "At some time the Board may wish to re-examine and clarify its views about intervention in individual cases."

Did the officers create too many of the Fund's grants and projects? Numerically, the percentage of projects was small, the president demonstrated. And if the board wished to live up to its original mandate, it had to realize that often a qualified agency was not ready to step forward with an appropriate request. "Nevertheless," he stated correctly, "most of the work of the Fund has been done through established agencies on their application."

The award to the Plymouth Monthly Meeting now seemed to give the board serious concern. But a committee of the board, having seen all the facts, recommended the award. Perhaps the board's hasty meetings had prevented it from asking further questions.

The hiring of Amos Landman ("The only action of the Officers to which Directors have taken serious exception") was not an ill-considered or reckless move.

> . . . if I had not supposed that the Board regarded persons who had pleaded the Fifth Amendment as employable, if Landman had not been qualified, and if we had not needed him, I would not have authorized his employment. If we had been under attack at the time the appointment was made, or if I had thought that an attack on this ground would disturb the Board, or any members of it, I would have certainly discussed the matter with the Directors in the same way in which at the December meeting I presented the question of a grant-in-aid to a man who had pleaded the Amendment.

Returning to the issue of hiring a Communist, Hutchins noted that his position had been clear since 1934 and that he did not expect it to surprise board members. He had not clarified his belief very well at the press conference or on television, but had written a letter published in *Time* attempting to state it better.[60] "I should be glad to know whether those members of the Board who criticized my rhetoric feel that the letter to TIME meets their objections."

> There are at least three variables in these situations: the nature of the job, the qualifications of the man for it, and the man's relation to the Communist party. These variables are such that it seems stultifying to say that never under any conditions should any Communist be hired for any job.

> The problem is illustrated by the case of the Communist or near-Communist set designer engaged by a subcontractor on "Omnibus." His sets could not possibly have been regarded as propaganda. There was no doubt that he was the best qualified man available. The argument that he should not have been employed seems to me absurd.

> It is also unchristian. In the absence of a showing that a man is a conspirator or spy it seems inhuman to deprive him of a chance to earn a living in a position that he is competent to fill and in which he can do no damage.

Dr. Huchins's general proposals for future public education were to supply information about the Fund to its grantees, perhaps presenting them on radio and television as missionaries for the Fund; and to widen the scope of the Fund's programs, perhaps re-entering the editorial competitions and essay contests abandoned earlier due to their complexities and apparent lack of results. As for organization—there had been very little of it under the president's banner "feel free"—he suggested: (1) moving the president's headquarters from Pasadena to New York, "for as long as necessary"; (2) putting W. H. Ferry in charge of program and planning; (3) making David Freeman responsible for administration (which would mean that he, not Ferry, would manage the New York office, receive visitors, and maintain contact with grantees); (4) appointing a third man, coordinate with Freeman and Ferry, in charge of public information; and (5) "Having these three officers report to me." If this arrangement remained unsatisfactory to the board, Hutchins concluded, "more drastic steps could be taken."

On occasion, creating a striking effect, the language of this significant memorandum softened almost to supplication, and Hutchins appeared willing to compromise, to draw upon the obvious wisdom of the true rulers of the Fund for the Republic. In one instance, on the ground that three members of the board now agreed that the award to the Plymouth Monthly Meeting was a mistake, he even conceded the possibility of error—"regardless of the merits" of the case.

The directors were urged to respond to the challenge of their positions, to recognize the quality of the attack upon the Fund, and to renew their pledge to defend freedom.

My experience and observation of organizations that have been attacked lead me to say that the most important aspect of their public relations is the face that those in control present to the world. The contrast between the attitude of the trustees of the University of Chicago in the Broyles investigation and that of the regents of the University of California in the loyalty-oath fight is instructive. Without a moment's hesitation the trustees of Chicago unanimously told the legislature that they would never permit it to in-

fluence the policies of the University. Broyles could not crack the
solidarity of the University, and the result was that the press and
the public got the impression of a strong and dedicated institution
being insulted by a midget. The differences among the regents
left the University of California defenseless. I know that the Board
of Directors is united in its devotion to the principles of the Fund.
If this can continue, and if it can be apparent on all occasions, the
problem basic to any effective program of public relations is solved.

Robert Hutchins drew heavily upon his considerable talents
to create this letter, and the result was a document of persuasive,
agile, prudently constructed prose, polished to the last word of
a final exhortation.[61]

After an extensive debate throughout the evening of the 6th
and the morning session of the 7th, the board decided to accept
the president's recommendations on organization and personnel,
"on a trial basis." Hutchins would remain. But the directors
affixed several conditions. He would have to present a detailed
plan of organization at the next board meeting. In the selection
of a new vice-president (the "third man") he must work with
the Temporary Information Committee of the board. And,
it was decreed, no member of the Communist party would be
employed by the Fund for *any* purpose, nor would a former
Communist or any person who had pleaded the Fifth Amendment
—"in relevant circumstances"—be employed or receive a fellowship or grant-in-aid, except with the approval of the board.[62]

Two days later a Fund spokesman revealed that on November
17, Dr. Hutchins had been quietly re-elected as president of
the corporation.[63] When asked by a reporter why the story had
not been released at the time of the vote, Hutchins replied:
"It hardly seemed of sufficient importance to take note of."[64]

Congressman Francis Walter promptly announced that within
a short time HUAC would call Robert Hutchins before it.
Walter said that he and the committee wanted to know how a
passage corresponding to the Communist party line got into
the Fund's first annual report. "We're not going into the Fund
for the Republic," he told reporters, "were going into Dr. Hutchins."[65]

CHAPTER TEN

"...To Make or Become Steady"

N ow that the directors had reaffirmed their confidence in administrative leadership of the Fund and forged what by all evidence was a renewed sense of harmony and determination during tedious hours of debate over the corporation's endangerment, the officers could formulate and initiate actions leading to the rapid dissemination of public information about the Fund's goals and programs. Paul Hoffman took the first step less than a week after the board's January meeting.

The chairman of the board of directors mailed copies of letters he had written to Henry Ford II and Roger Lapham to both the trustees of the Ford Foundation and the directors of the Fund. Additional recipients of the Lapham letter (which included three attachments outlining Fund grants and projects) were United States Senators Jacob Javits and Clifford Case, Ford public-relations consultant Earl Newsom, colmunist David Lawrence, publisher John S. Knight, and former Ford Foundation associate director Milton Katz, now teaching law at Harvard under Dean Griswold.

Both letters were full of standard and reliable anti-Communist professions. "Out of our Marshall Plan experience," Hoffman reminded Lapham, "you and I both learned that the Kremlin was and is in deadly earnest about communizing the world. We became aware that the struggle between the Kremlin and the free world is 'the battle of the century for the century.'" The Fund for the Republic, wrote Hoffman, stood in the patriotic middle, admired by neither the Far Right nor the Far Left.

> When the studies now in process have been completed, they will be resented by those persons who think that communism is not a menace, as well as by those persons who are willing to use un-American methods to combat communism. The studies will be attacked by the unbelievers in the Bill of Rights and the segregationists.

Surely few of the letters' readers would care to cooperate with such sullied citizens in condemning a body which had as its mission "the work of promoting an understanding of the vital role that the Bill of Rights has played and must play in keeping our society strong and dynamic."[1]

To strengthen the home front the directors were apprised of the background of a new HUAC staff member, one Karl Baarslag, whose associations with ultraconservative movements went back ten years and included a stint in 1953 on the staff of Senator McCarthy's Senate Subcommittee on Government Operations. He was reported to have a special desire to investigate the Fund.[2] Also, the officers made an extensive check on the past remarks of Fulton Lewis, Jr., which revealed, among similar things, that in 1951 he insinuated that Secretary of State George C. Marshall was senile and that Marshall, together with Acheson and Truman, had handed China over to the Communists.[3]

Few events in the month of January, however, offered comfort to Fund partisans. A syndicated labor columnist made public the fact that staff member Paul Jacobs had been named in charges preferred in two West Coast loyalty proceedings.[4] The "United States Steel Hour," the first television program to purchase a prize-winning script on civil liberties emanating from the Fund's playwriting contest, suddenly canceled the production, "because we have so many scripts like it."[5] Charges appeared in another syndicated newspaper column that one of the jurors for the Robert E. Sherwood television awards, producer Kermit Bloomgarden, seven years before, had participated in a "pro-Soviet" peace conference and was thus unqualified to judge

television programs "dealing with American liberty."[6] And
Sigma Delta Chi, the professional journalistic fraternity, halted
plans for a study of American press performance in the 1956
political campaigns, amidst editorials claiming that the idea was
inspired by Robert Hutchins.[7]

On February 2 the Chicago *Daily Tribune* reported that the
Internal Revenue Service had proposed new regulations to curb
the political and propaganda activities of tax-exempt foundations; ". . . officials revealed they want to be sure they are on
'solid ground' before moving against such giants as the Fund for
the Republic."[8]

The study most likely to cause trouble in the near future was
the Cogley report on blacklisting. This extensive and heavily
documented two-volume work was completed in late December
and in January was presented for consideration to Roper's committee on public relations. Earlier a resumé had been presented
to the full board, telling of widespread boycotts in the motion-
picture and radio-television industries of employees who had
defied congressional probes or had been named as Communists
or "pro-Communists" by individuals or private organizations.

The volumes bulged with case histories of careers destroyed
by inaccurate reporting of political sympathies; of professionals
pressured into political conformity or silence in order to get
or hold jobs. Named in the report as powerful influences in
"clearing" persons seeking re-employment were several of the
Fund's most outspoken antagonists.[9] In fact, said the report:
"If a performer has a strong prejudice against associating with
Hearst columnists or American Legion officials, or rejects their
definition of 'effective anti-Communist,' he will find it difficult
if not impossible to clear himself."

Certain of the Fund's critics, George Sokolsky in particular,
had watched the progress of the Cogley study with great interest.[10] HUAC, in a report of January 18, carefully anticipated
the release of the volumes with the charge that a "Communist
supported" campaign against "so-called" blacklisting existed
which had "completely falsified the true hiring policies applied
to entertainers." The networks, the report stated, "continue to

use the talents of Communist party members because of inadequate information and investigative facilities."[11] Shortly, the committee contended that it had found no evidence to substantiate the existence of a blacklist.[12]

On January 23, Roper's committee turned the Cogley study over to Earl Newsom, W. H. Ferry's former business partner and public-relations consultant for the Ford Motor Company and the Ford Foundation. "This is a terrible chore to drop into your lap out of the blue," Ferry apologized. "But such is my respect and Elmo's for your judgment on such touchy matters that we agreed nothing would be done until we had some expression from you."[13] If Newsom and his associates agreed to the publication of the $100,000 report, there would be room later for considerably less adverse reaction from sensitive sources surrounding—perhaps including—Henry Ford II.[14]

A week later Newsom replied: The Cogley report should not be made public. It was, wrote Newsom with a curious twist of reasoning, "thorough, objective and perceptive in delineating a deplorable situation," but would do little to improve "the present public impression that the Fund for [the] Republic is partisan and not 'objective' in these matters." The study was bound to "revive widespread public controversy and confusion about a complex problem to which no wise solution has yet been found." Perhaps the Fund's directors could turn the data over to a bar association for a future study.

> It seems to me that such fears as we are dealing with here are overcome only by normal evolutionary processes in the kind of democratic society we are committed to develop in this country. It is possible to give these evolutionary processes direction in some cases, but attempts to accelerate them usually result in setting back progress.[15]

In short, the Cogley report was too hot to handle.

The directors were thus faced with a basic decision. The blacklisting study was part of the Fund's original mandate; it had been publicized widely in a host of speeches and news releases and was anxiously awaited both within and without the entertainment industry. To retreat from the public release of this report would involve the denigration of the Fund's very reason for existence. And the peace this pawn would buy could be shattered by the slightest comment or by the most innocuous action of officers, directors, staff members, consultants, or any one of the scores of grantees. Was Dr. Hutchins correct in maintaining that the Fund and controversy were indissolubly wed? Could the Fund operate to the pleasure of its critics?

On February 15 the board elected to proceed cautiously toward the eventual publication of the blacklisting study by asking Cogley to reduce its length (from about 700 pages), and by giving it for review and comment to representatives of the entertainment industry and the professions "for the purpose (a) of catching possible inaccuracies and (b) of obtaining a statement or statements which might be published in or used in connection with the report." The Lazarsfeld fear in education study, long out of the public spotlight, was also permitted to be prepared for possible publication. Several recommendations received favor at the obviously steadier hands of the directors.

A grant of $50,000 went to the National Urban League for the development of a job-opportunities program for Negroes in the South. The highly effective Southern Regional Council, having weathered months of attack by Fulton Lewis, Jr., and the Hearst newspapers, received a grant of $50,000 to finance a program of fact-finding and analysis concerning developments in southern race relations. The Carrie Chapman Catt Memorial Fund was granted $50,000 to finance the freedom agenda community discussion program for another six months.[16] And the New York Public Library received its third annual grant of $1,000 to support the Central Reference Room, frequently used by the Fund's staff and consultants.

Furthermore, at the officers' request, the board expanded the purposes for which previous grants to local bar associations could be used to include direct educational activities in civil rights and civil liberties.

The directors deferred action on (and later forgot) the distribution of *The Right To Read,* by Paul Blanshard, a noted critic of the Roman Catholic Church. A series of Fund-sponsored articles on the American Right by Swedish scholar Herbert Tingsten were judged "not of sufficient general interest to warrant Fund participation in publication." And a request was denied from the president of the Southern Regional Council to use a portion of a previous grant for research preliminary to actions of libel against ultraconservatives.[17] On the other hand, the board flatly refused a request from David Lawrence to distribute a Senate Internal Security Subcommittee pamphlet on Communism, judged earlier by Walter Millis to be "badly written," "badly organized," and "simply an unsubstantiated rehash of the usual allegations."[18]

In general, this meeting revealed the board's slow recovery of nerve, undoubtedly brought about by its determination to ride out the storm with its president. Recommendations and allocations increased and there was a marked decline in fraternal dissension. Dr. Hutchins was soon busy preparing requests of the dimension common the previous year.

But the Fund's external problems remained and continued to worsen. An inquiry was received from the House Committee on Un-American Activities to investigate the corporation's files.[19] Before long, Legion Commander Wagner again made headlines, this time by suggesting that Hutchins and his directors be "deterred" from spending the Fund's remaining principal.[20] And on March 5, Francis E. Walter, at the conclusion of a conference with Bethuel Webster, formally requested the Fund's minutes, employment records, a list of all recipients of financial assistance, and a list of all "projects and grants approved or started" since May 1955.[21]

Lawyers were aware that neither Congress nor the courts had defined the limits or scope of congressional investigating powers within the area of "subversive activities." And seated on this particular version of the committee, chaired by Representative Walter, were three of Congress's most virulent ultraconservatives: Harold H. Velde of Illinois, Donald L. Jackson of California, and Gordon H. Scherer of Ohio. Their fellow committee members were not particularly noted for any desire to clarify and expand civil liberties and civil rights: Clyde Doyle of California, Murray M. Moulder of Missouri, James B. Frazier, Jr., of Tennessee,

Bernard W. Kearney of New York, and Edwin E. Willis of Louisiana.

The Internal Revenue Service was known to be scrutinizing the Fund, and had itself been the object of loud attacks from the Right for its refusal to grant tax exemption to several highly conservative organizations. The effects of an investigation, inevitably laden with sweeping charges, personal attacks, and prolonged publicity, could very well spell the end of the Fund for the Republic and set a precedent that would virtually seal off the Fund's primary areas of concern to further efforts by tax-exempt foundations.

On March 12, Elmo Roper's Temporary Advisory Committee on Public Information officially informed the officers and directors of its selection for the new vice-president in charge of public information. Frank K. Kelly, a bald, rotund, forty-two-year-old Irishman with a genuine and infectious sense of humor, and a striking desire and ability to make friends, was vice-president of a New York public-relations agency, Stephen Fitzgerald and Company. A novelist, reporter, distinguished veteran, Nieman fellow, and Presidential speech-writer, Kelly had had experience in Washington as executive assistant to the Senate majority leader, and in civil liberties as special consultant on book-censorship problems for the American Book Publishers Council.[22] As Kelly recalls the procedures of his employment:

> Each of the directors on Roper's committee interviewed me. Each asked about my opinion of Dr. Hutchins. Though I was familiar with his writings, I had met Hutchins only once, when he asked me if I would help pull the Fund out of its difficulties. I told each director that in my opinion Robert Hutchins was a very great man and that the Fund had to be unpopular if it was to accomplish anything. They seemed to like my response.

> Charles W. Cole asked me how long I felt it would take to turn the tide of public opinion. I guessed it would take about two or three years. He said that it would make all of the directors very happy if it could be accomplished within that space of time.[23]

According to Hutchins's proposed reorganization of the New York office, accepted by the directors on March 22, Frank Kelly was to be in complete command of the Fund's preparation and distribution of public information.[24] David Freeman was advanced to vice-president and treasurer (responsible for office management, the reception of visitors, and relations with grantees, and to assist with the fellowship program), and Adam Yarmolinsky was appointed secretary—such officers, like the president and Vice-President Ferry, "to serve, subject to the pleasure of the Board, until the next annual meeting."[25]

Dr. Hutchins was gravely concerned about the future of the Fund, Kelly recalls. "One day at lunch he told me that he felt we could lose our tax exemption by Thanksgiving. I told him we wouldn't and he looked amused, calling me an optimistic Irishman."[26] Kelly had good cause for his brighter outlook, for significant decisions were made at the March 22 board meeting which, together with allocations of over one quarter of a million dollars, illustrated the heightened resolution and confidence of the Fund's directors.

An appropriation was made to further the preparation of a full-scale public-relations program, under the direction of new staff member James Real. The prospects for the eventual publication of the blacklisting study were improved, following a vigorous defense of the project by John Cogley, with the elaboration of conditions by which it could be released and an appropriation of $20,000 to finance the "final editing, printing and distribution" of 10,000 copies.[27] A bimonthly bulletin was discussed and approved in principle. And it was agreed to hold a special board meeting on May 15 and 16 to plan at greater length for the future.

Allocations included: $25,000 to the Study of Communist Influence project for a revision of the bibliography; $3,500 to the University of Virginia for a summer research program in the field of municipal law; $25,000 to the Association for Education in Journalism for a study of the press treatment of civil-liberties issues (to be conducted after the election and to have "no relation to the election period"); $105,000 divided among four church bodies for community education in civil rights; $15,000 for a six-month syndicated cartoon feature entitled "It's Your America"; $35,000 for an American tradition project which would collect and publicize current examples of the successful application of the Bill of Rights; $6,000 to the American Library Association to support its bimonthly publication on censorship and related civil-liberties problems; $2,500 (subject to clearance by counsel) for the distribution of a report on Mexican labor in the United States; $30,000 to continue the Fund's distribution of materials program; and $4,382 to close the account of the study of the Communist Record.[28]

The distribution of three publications was approved, including a Department of Defense pamphlet entitled "Who are Communists and Why," described by the officers as "An excellent summary of the question." As hoped, the New York *Daily News* soon editorialized: "We applaud Doc for his new line, and hope he keeps it up."[29]

Before the March gathering, Paul Hoffman drafted another suppliant missive to Henry Ford II, this time inviting him to attend the Fund's special meeting in May and requesting a confidential look at letters mentioned by Ford as a cause of his criticism of the Fund.

> While the Fund is a completely independent body, we understand your deep interest in it as a private citizen, and your desire to do everything in your power to help it succeed. We would welcome your comments on any action that has been uncertain by the Fund. We certainly hope that you will speak freely and frankly. . . . We are all anxious to have the benefit of your comments at that time.[30]

Ford coldly declined the invitation, but permitted Frank Kelly to examine the letters.[31]

Kelly soon reported the discovery in Ford's files of some 1,200 letters containing complaints about the Fund, the Ford Foundation, or both. Most of the writers threatened boycotts of Ford Motor Company products; many used extremely intemperate and even libelous language. Bigotry was a common denominator. Many of the partisans appeared to be older people of low income. Fulton Lewis, Jr., David Lawrence, and Hearst newspapers were frequently cited as authorities.[32]

"The idea of checking the letters Ford talked about was

mine," Kelly recalls. "I thought the board should know that they rarely come from informed, sincerely concerned citizens."[33] A subsequent request by the Fund to have the letters objectively studied by a qualified outside agency was denied by Ford, who then expressed disinterest in their existence.[34]

The reserved room at New York's Yale Club was filled to capacity on the afternoon of May 15, 1956, as sixteen directors and seventeen officers, staff members, consultants, and an observer (public-relations expert Stephen Fitzgerald) assembled for the special meeting. The board first accepted without dissent the actions of its executive committee which had, in an earlier session, approved all but one of the officers' well-prepared recommendations for appropriations and grants. Hutchins and his staff had stressed race relations and allocations to church bodies, and with Erwin Griswold on the four-man committee the directors were assured that potential hazards were minimal.

To further efforts toward racial integration in the South, a total of $45,000 was granted to national divisions of the Young Men's and Young Women's Christian Associations; the United Church Women, an affiliate of the National Council of Churches, received $10,000; the Council for Social Action of the Congregational Christian Churches was granted $31,480; and the Anti-Defamation League of B'nai B'rith received $5,000.

For similar actions $5,000 went to the Catholic Interracial Council of Chicago; the free distribution to newspapers and magazines of drawings dealing with segregation was financed by a $2,000 grant to Religious Drawings, Inc.; and the Philadelphia Fellowship Commission received an appropriation of $2,000 to purchase and distribute prints of a film on discrimination against Negroes in industry.

To promote studies in civil liberties, a grant of $5,610 was authorized for the Law School of the University of Pennsylvania; $36,000 went to the University of California's School of Librarianship; the Association for Education in Journalism received an additional sum of $20,000; and the fear in education project was allowed to complete its work by an appropriation of $15,000.

The promising Robert E. Sherwood television awards program (a valuable instrument, of course, for public relations) was continued at a cost of $91,250. And a grant of $28,600 was authorized, over Erwin Griswold's negative vote, to Sarah Lawrence College for student-faculty seminars, community forums, and research projects on civil liberties and civil rights.[35]

The full board then turned to its primary function at this meeting; the determination of methods to strengthen the Fund's reputation. A good public-relations program had for months seemed a vital need. Positive steps in that direction had already been taken by May 15, evidenced by the production of 100,000 copies of the first Fund bulletin—an attractive, informative pamphlet, currently being distributed to educators, libraries, business executives, American Legion posts, Knights of Pythias lodges, Catholic clergymen, 10,500 "opinion leaders," and 7,000 names on the Fund's mailing list.[36] In addition, a three-year report was in the making, Hutchins was preparing a book on the Fund, and both Hoffman and Hutchins maintained a rigorous schedule of speeches. Encouragement had come from Congressman Richard Bolling of Missouri, who inserted a highly flattering article on the Fund into the *Congressional Record*.[37]

But Francis Walter was incensed by the Fund's failure to comply completely with his requests for evidence.[38] And Mrs. Mary E. Knowles had been given a contempt citation by a unanimous vote of the United States Senate for refusing to answer questions before Senator Eastland's subcommittee the previous summer.[39] With her case in the hands of the Justice Department, untold embarrassment might be heaped upon the Fund by the press or Mr. Walter. Moreover, the blacklisting study was complete and the fear in education project soon would be. And the Internal Revenue Service was still "investigating."

The directors endorsed and appropriated $28,000 for a plan of James Real's, a "reporter-researcher" project. Photo-reporting artists or writers were to explore the dramatic content of several studies undertaken by Fund grantees, the results to be made available upon the release of the study. "Heightened impact and wider popular currency of the finished work will result," the directors were assured.[40] They also appropriated $100,000 for a film or films "delineating the advantages and benefits of the

American legacy." The board showed no interest in Mr. Real's suggestions concerning paid advertising campaigns.

The morning session on May 16 began with Bethuel Webster's report that HUAC staff members had requested copies of the Cogley study, "both in original draft form as submitted to the Officers, and in galley sheets." What uses the committee might have for the report, which contradicted its own pronouncements on blacklisting and exposed tactics of several of its members and warm supporters, could well be imagined. After discussion the board directed Webster to deliver the report, but instructed him to attempt a postponement of the delivery date until the study was publicly released. Directors Hammerstein and Joyce chose not to agree to even this tactic, and voted against any suggestion that the unpublished study be turned over to the committee. The board thereupon, for the first time, voted unanimously to publish the report, after clearance by counsel—an ironic conclusion to HUAC's persistence.

In executive session during the afternoon, the directors, following an interim report of the Special Committee on Overhead, retained the Stephen E. Fitzgerald Company as public-relations consultant on a month-to-month basis.[41] The phenomenal expansion of the Fund's channels for self-expression stood in marked contrast to the days when W. H. Ferry fired rapid rejoinders at New York reporters.

The concluding matter of major importance on May 16th involved a curious and provocative eleven-page memorandum from President Hutchins proposing that a committee be selected "to advise the Board of Directors on the desirability, feasibility, program, organization, financing, location, and personnel of an institute or council for the study of the theory and practice of freedom." The cost for such a body, whatever the details of its composition, would be a minimum of $1,000,000 and a maximum of $6,000,000 or $7,000,000 over a five-year period.

The Fund for the Republic, in its first three years, Hutchins explained, had dealt with urgent problems and experimented with every form of popular education. These actions were exploratory, necessary, and on the whole successful. But, "In this effort little attempt was made to relate one study to another or to relate any studies to the clarification of important ideas." This has meant a succession of "commentaries on current events," he continued, which "in the nature of the case, cannot be very significant in time or space." What was needed, *along with* a continuation of the Fund's normal activities, Hutchins argued, was a "full-fledged institute or council" with an object

> to promote coherence and intelligibility in the program of the Fund, to relate every study to every other, to be sure that efforts in popular education were enlightening rather than confusing, to enable the Board to function with confidence even though it could not afford the time for protracted philosophical discussion, to permit the Officers to proceed with confidence in the absence of clear agreement on fundamental principles in the Board, to give the studies sponsored by the Fund permanence and universality, to develop a basis of common conviction in the West, and to show a pluralistic society how it can reach unanimous devotion to justice and freedom.[42]

For many years Robert Hutchins had expressed a personal distaste for "fact-grubbing," research stressing the collection of quantities of data to the exclusion of the larger issues of meaning which entertain and enthuse philosophers. (His own voluminous writings bear few traces of serious grappling with, say, statistics or primary source materials.) What mattered ultimately were the ultimate questions. And the secrets of these questions, he had believed for several decades, could be unlocked by the finest minds engaged in serious, intensive, and continuous discussion. What better way might the Fund for the Republic serve truth than to pursue the perimeters of "justice" and "freedom"? The Fund's previous efforts were useful, to be sure, but what value other than historical would the Stouffer study, for example, hold for the future? Might not the Fund expend the remainder of its resources and go out of business, only to have wasted the precious opportunity to provide lasting contributions toward the answers to some of man's eternal queries?

Moreover, Hutchins might have added, there was growing evidence of a decline in the national fear and suspicion which had, in large part, led to the primary evocation of a Fund for the Republic. While Republicans continued to play the "numbers game" (now up to 9,700 departed federal employees), the Army, the Coast Guard, and the Atomic Energy Commission, for example, were making dramatic readjustments in their security regulations toward the protection of individual rights.[43] (The Army, as a case in point, had greatly limited its use of guilt by association in security cases by requiring that a soldier, to be considered a risk, must be found personally sympathetic with subversive aims, or influenced by them. All previous security discharge cases were being reviewed, and several less-than-honorable discharges had been elevated to honorable.) Two Senate subcommittees had expressed criticism of the federal personnel-security programs. Government charges against Dr. Owen Lattimore were finally dropped. Several lower federal courts were cracking down on the use of secret informers, arbitrary passport restrictions, the loyalty-oath fixation, and congressional investigating committee exposés. And the Supreme Court seemed restive and about to re-examine the Constitution for new (liberals would call them old) truths.[44]

Hutchins's new proposal was an understandable product of his life and thought. And it was the origin of what would become the sole function of the Fund, the Center for the Study of Democratic Institutions. For the time being, Hutchins only asked permission and means to appoint a distinguished committee to study the matter and report in September. The board assented, provided that this committee act "with the advice of an *ad hoc* committee of the Board, to be appointed by the Chairman."[45] Erwin Griswold voted no.

CHAPTER ELEVEN

On Trial

"*I* am an ardent believer in the American free enterprise system," declared the speaker at New York City College's Bernard Baruch lecture.

> . . . I believe it so deeply that I have made an earnest effort to understand it and to identify those elements which give it its strength. . . . Our founding fathers were profound believers in the dignity and worth of the individual. Many of them were deeply religious, holding all men to be children of God with certain inalienable rights as individuals.[1]

Paul G. Hoffman had utilized such pious homilies for many years. But in the spring of 1956 the familiar phrases assumed a heightened value, for Hoffman found himself the victim of an extraordinarily severe verbal attack.

Fulton Lewis, Jr., was enraged upon learning of President Eisenhower's intention to appoint the Fund's chairman of the board to the American delegation to the United Nations. Repeatedly, from April into the summer, he voiced his objections to his millions of listeners.[2] "This I can report to you," he was at one point moved to threaten:

> If the White House persists in sending his nomination through the Senate as it now plans to do, he will face the worst fight that any Eisenhower appointee to anything has faced since the Administration took office. This is the Fund for the Republic, ladies and gentlemen, bidding for a place on the United States delegation

to the United Nations General Assembly. It already has $15,000,-
000 of public money for its propaganda; now it wants to move into
American foreign policy after the coming elections are over and
it's too late for the public to do anything about it.[3]

The President's action had been completely unforeseen by the
Fund's enemies, and it seemed to some of them, at least to
Lewis, to have a smell of conspiracy about it—perhaps involving
Milton Eisenhower or the admission of Communist China into
the United Nations.[4] If Hoffman was allowed, with congressional
sanction, to receive the touch of Presidential dignity implicit in
the nomination, the desired impact of the impending congressional investigation of the Fund could be nullified.

And one must look beyond the details. Ultraconservatives eager
awaited the probe and were planning to put a view of national
life on trial.[5] Paul Hoffman, Robert Hutchins, and their protago-
nists symbolized, in 1956, the demonology of the Radical Right:
the eastern Establishment, Ivy League universities, New Deal
bureaucracy, internationalism, foreign aid, racial integration,
the "liberal press," and social welfare. To "expose" the Fund and
its officers in a widely publicized investigation would be to reveal
much of what had gone wrong with America in the past quarter
century—the "fuzzy-mindedness," the "softness," the "internal
subversion and decadence." If the truth were known about certain men of high repute there might not be another Marshall
Plan or a further "Half Century of Revolution in domestic
affairs."[6] The President—this middle-of-the-road Republican who
appointed Earl Warren, accepted the censure of McCarthy, endorsed the United World Federalists, practiced deficit spending,
and passed civil-rights legislation—was clearly making "another
blunder."

There was the possibility of persuading the President not to
send the nomination to the Senate. Senator Styles Bridges soon
voiced his opposition to the appointment of Hoffman and called
for a nation-wide demonstration of letters.[7] Representative Reece
attacked the Fund on the floor of the House.[8] And Fulton Lewis,
Jr., was soon speaking of "violent opposition" by Senate Republican leaders.[9] The un-American activities hearings might also
be called promptly.

On June 11, Robert Hutchins was startled to read in his newspaper that hearings on the Fund for the Republic were to begin on the 27th.[10] The press release contained some not wholly unpected insinuations.

> The Fund for the Republic is financing a number of activities which have aroused criticism and doubt on the part of members of Congress, prominent patriotic organizations, and individuals, including Henry II himself, who has publicly described some of the activities of the Fund as "dubious in character."
>
> Is this foundation, with its vast reservoirs of funds and power, a friend or a foe in our national death struggle against the Communist conspiracy? Are its extensive and diverse activities strengthening or weakening our security structure in the Communist cold war? Are the leaders of this force, who enjoy the benefits of tax immunity, serving an interest inimical to our basic American tradition?[11]

Immediate reactions varied. The Hearst press was elated.[12] The Washington *Post and Times-Herald* thought the announcement disgraceful and "punitive."[13] Less predictably, H. Rowan Gaither, Jr., president and chairman of the board of the Ford Foundation, was authorized to express the Foundation's "full confidence in the integrity and patriotism" of the Fund's directors.[14]

Dr. Hutchins, having issued a formal reply for the Fund, wryly announced to a delighted University of Chicago audience his campaign to become national commander of the American Legion.[15]

It seemed likely that the Fund's directors would need a sense of humor. Chairman Walter apparently held a personal grudge against the Fund for its plans to prepare a handbook on the rights of immigrants.[16] HUAC's new staff director, Richard Arens, had worked for Senators McCarran, Eastland, and McCarthy, and was a former head of the antisubversive section of the American Legion's Americanism Commission.[17] And the committee was fresh from an inquiry into Local 47 of the Hollywood Musicians Union, which featured a prehearing leak of the names of subpoenaed musicians to the local Hearst newspaper.[18]

The greatest immediate danger lay in the possibility that no Fund spokesman would be able to speak at the hearings. Neither the committee's press release nor its letter to Hutchins offered the Fund such an opportunity. And Arens indicated by telephone that the hearings might be adjourned following testimony by committee witnesses.[19] Hutchins framed a stern message to Walter, stating that he and the entire board of directors would be present at the hearings, and requesting "equal time, on each day of the hearings, to present witnesses of our selection, including members of our board and representatives of our grantees."[20] A dinner party for a select group of reporters was then arranged by Paul Hoffman to insure the placement of the Fund's case within responsible hands.[21]

Suddenly, on June 20, newspapers carried the story that the hearings were postponed indefinitely—to allow committee staff examination of "additional facets of the Fund's activities."[22]

The next day the Fund released an eighty-eight-page three-year report detailing the expenditure of $5,414,201.[23] The report classified the Fund's work into five categories designed to resemble the Ford Foundation's original mandate: "To Study Communism in the United States," "Equality Before the Law and Equality of Opportunity," "To Make the Bill of Rights a Living Document," "To Maintain Due Process and the Principles That Underlie It," and "To Maintain Freedom of Speech and Belief." Hutchins and his staff had labored over the report for several months and it was masterfully conceived, designed, and written —as well as timely.

"The largest single appropriation of the Fund has been made for the study of Communism in the United States," the report declared. "The largest cumulative expenditure has been in race relations." And critics of the Fund would now have to contend with the public knowledge that on the issue of segregation, "Almost every religious organization has received assistance in its efforts to solve this basic problem."[24] Page after page of studies, polls, competitions, awards, fellowships, grants-in-aid, and distributions greeted the reader. The sheer number and accumulated authority of the recipients of Fund monies was staggering.

In a foreward Paul Hoffman pointed out that "The policies

and programs of the Fund have been determined by the Board of Directors"—not simply by the president. (Hutchins conceded that "some of the actions of the Fund have been misinterpreted because they have been stated in such a way as to be open to misinterpretation.") The report stated clearly the Fund's independent relationship with project participants and grantees. And it made the Fund's position on Communism absolutely clear:

> The Fund is studying Communism in the United States in order to determine its influence, direct or indirect, on civil liberties. The Fund regards Communism as a threat to civil liberties, but it was not organized solely to oppose Communism; it was organized to study and disclose the facts about all threats to civil liberties, including Communism.[25]

Congratulatory messages from around the country began to pour into the Fund's offices within a few days.

"I would like to suggest," Paul Hoffman told a New York audience, "that those who attack us are not as fully informed as they might be and that a review of the Fund's three-year program might lead them to revise their comments."[26] Far from showing remorse, Fulton Lewis, Jr., called the report

> a picture of planned attack and sabotage against the Federal Government's loyalty security program, against Congressional investigations into communism and other subversive activities, and a general organized effort in the field of racial relations that follows the standard communist tactic of arousing racial strife and friction as a means of inflating trouble and disharmony on which to play for their own communist advantage.[27]

Hearst's Boston *Post* was more succinct: "It's a little nostrum called Love Those Commies."[28]

The congressional investigators had not counted on the appearance of this report. Nor had they anticipated any Ford Foundation support of the Fund's board or the determination of the directors to attend the hearings. It now appeared more difficult to discredit the Fund's entire operation. The United Press even apologized for previously reporting as fact Chairman Walter's contention that the Fund's 1955 annual report "criticized Congressional investigators for branding the Communist party part of an international conspiracy."[29]

Perhaps some new piece of evidence would arise which could be attacked independently. Thursday afternoon, June 21, Richard Arens received a printed copy of John Cogley's blacklisting study.[30]

The board of directors met on June 22, and routine business was handled with dispatch and unanimity. Hutchins first directed attention to an earlier resolution supporting a handbook on immigration law. In defiance of Mr. Walter, the directors decided to proceed with the project. Appropriations and grants included: $70,000 to the American Library Association for a book-awards program; $2,500 to the National Book Committee for assistance in the publication of a report entitled "Freedom To Read"; a supplementary $7,500 to the Common Council for American Unity to enable the completion of studies on aliens in America; $2,000 to the National Council of Catholic Men for the distribution of a film dealing with racial and religious tolerance; $30,000 to continue the Fund's distribution of materials program; $20,000 to finance the preliminary stages of a study on fair trial and free press, to be sponsored by the University of Pennsylvania and the Nieman Foundation; $60,000 to the Southern Association of Nieman Fellows to administer foreign travel fellowships for southern journalists; and $40,000 to the Pennsylvania Bar Foundation for a study of the right of privacy as affected by current law-enforcement practices. It was also decided to distribute 100,000 reprints of a clement article on the Fund published originally in the *Presbyterian Outlook* and recently inserted into the *Congressional Record*.[31]

On June 24 the two-volume paperback edition of the *Report on Blacklisting* was released to the press. It followed by only a few days a $1,500,000 libel suit by CBS radio personality John Henry Faulk, charging existence of a plot to blacklist him.[32] The study had been combed carefully and repeatedly for injudicious commentary and libelous error. The result was a temperate, fair, heavily detailed account of secret practices, common to all branches of the entertainment industry except the legitimate theater, causing denial of employment and loss of income to hundreds of performers, writers and film workers on both sides (but usually to the left) of the political spectrum who were without recourse to the law. An accusation made by anyone, anywhere, at any time, that an individual had Communist "sympathies or associations" could destroy a career. Through devious channels, usually an assortment of lists of the accused, "controversial" performers were branded unemployable. Resumption of work was dependent upon the approval of several "experts on Communism" ("clearance men"), relied on by employers—leery of local pressures against theaters and sponsors by "patriotic" citizens and groups—to certify "loyalty." To receive absolution from these self-appointed confessors the accused were forced to undergo certain forms of penance: render letters of explanation, divulge information, take out advertisements proclaiming innocence of charges, sign affidavits of regret for past political activity, sign statements supporting right-wing political positions, and so forth. Researchers heard strong rumors of the sale of "clearances," and a few cases appeared in which a public-relations man used his influence to secure a "clearance" and received a "public-relations fee."

The major principle involved was that found in the Plymouth Monthly Meeting incident: private citizens were being maliciously persecuted for failing to comply with an assailant's definition of "Americanism." In both cases those mainly directing the persecution were of the same frenetic and radical political persuasion.

The $127,000 Cogley report was not entirely free of judgments, as its author admitted in an interview, and perhaps could not have been.[33] But interpretations were minimal, beyond the premise that blacklisting was wrong, and no recommendations were offered.[34] Controversy was certain: deeply involved in blacklisting and "clearing" activities, according to the report, were, among others, Hearst columnists Victor Riesel and George Sokolsky, officials of the American Legion, an executive of a major advertising agency, a prominent movie-union leader, several right-wing organizations such as AWARE, Inc., and the House Committee on Un-American Activities. (A careful study by Dorothy B. Jones, a propaganda analyst, was appended to the report, strongly suggesting that HUAC had deliberately instigated a sharp decline in the number of motion pictures containing anything critical of American life.[35])

For eight months ten reporters had gathered evidence from nearly 500 individuals. This material was bolstered with a legal study and a survey of "morale in the radio and television industry." Out into the light came some of the ugliest features of postwar American life: the zealous intolerance, the unsubstantiated innuendoes, the unevaluated and false evidence, the effective intimidation, the reckless equation of any form of liberalism or controversy with treason—the ruthless violation of the constitutional guarantee of freedom of expression and the constitutional safeguards of due process. The most vociferous opponents of the report would be those who had been most ardent in their opposition to the international and domestic activities of the Ford Foundation and the very creation of a Fund for the Republic. The struggle would transcend the accuracy of a single study.

Frederick Woltman of the New York *World Telegram and Sun,* himself cited in the report, initiated the assault. "While not pro-Communist," he wrote, "the report cannot help but bring joy and comfort to the Reds." Its author, he continued, "rubber-stamps the basic philosophy of the Fund's own president, Robert M. Hutchins" and "runs counter to the mainstream of American thought today."[36] Senator Karl E. Mundt of South Dakota said in a Senate speech that the report gave "aid and comfort to the Communists in this country and abroad," and fired off a letter to the Commissioner of Internal Revenue.[37] The Hearst newspapers ran an editorial dismissing the study as "further conclusive evidence of the anti-anti-Communist slant" of the Fund for the Republic.[38] (Frank Kelly decided to investigate the source of the latter editorial and contacted the writer at the New York *Journal American.* He discovered that the author had not even seen the report. "Well, I read a news story, a clipping about it, and I got a note from Mr. Hearst, suggesting an editorial," Kelly was told.[39]) The American Legion's J. Addington Wagner called the report an "utterly ridiculous and highly melodramatic recital." "Dr. Hutchins," he said further, "is not only uninstructed on the subject of communism, but his mind seems to be impervious to any understanding of the Communist meance."[40]

On June 28, four days after the blacklisting report was made public, John Cogley was subpoenaed to appear July 10 for questioning at a closed session of the House Committee on Un-American Activities. The usual procedure was to extend an invitation. In a prepared statement, Chairman Walter (who admitted to an interviewer that he had not read the report) declared that the committee would seek to determine "what the purposes of the Fund and Mr. Cogley truly are."[41]

Dr. Hutchins immediately issued a brief statement, concluding: "While he [Cogley] accepts responsibility for this report as its director and author, the Board of The Fund for the Republic wishes to states its full confidence in the calm deliberation which he has given to its preparation."[42] Cogley himself contended:

> The Committee's action involves freedom of the press. The Question is: should a man be summoned before his elected representatives to defend or explain a book he has written or divulge the confidential sources of his information? The answer is far more important than the future of the Fund for the Republic, the "Report on Blacklisting," or John Cogley.[43]

Frank Kelly mailed a summary of the report to director J. R. Parten, a close friend of Walter's political mentor, Speaker Sam Rayburn. "I hope you will send it to your friends in Washington," he added. "There is a strong possibility that Mr. Cogley will be questioned by people who are not fully familiar with his report."[44]

Frederick Woltman, several days before the hearings were to begin, denied a charge from the report that he was one of several figures involved in "clearing" blacklisted performers. At first unable to acquire the identification of the informant, cited in the study as a "public relations expert" (several of Cogley's sources asked to remain anonymous), Woltman publicized a letter from Arnold Forster, chief counsel of the Anti-Defamation League, stating that he recognized "some material, attributed to such a person by the report, as things which I told an interviewer."[45] On July 6, Fulton Lewis, Jr., announced that Forster had been subpoenaed to appear before the committee.[46]

The evening before the hearings, Lewis revealed the inclusion of two additional witnesses: James O'Neil, director of American

Legion publications, and Vincent Hartnett of New York, both named in the report as prominent in blacklisting and "clearing." He furthermore disclosed a last-minute reversal in the House Committee's procedure: the hearings were to be open to the public.[47]

The next morning Hutchins talked by telephone with Paul Jacobs, in Washington along with Michael Harrington for the hearings. "I don't know what John or you or Mike is going to tell the committee, and I don't want to know. I just want all three of you to know that whatever position you take, all the money the Fund has left will back you up."[48]

Such a guaranty, even though hyperbolic, was welcome, for Cogley and his friends knew that the Radical Right had suffered unusual frustrations of late and was thirsting for a victory over what it called the Liberal Establishment.

Highly irritating had been the continued efforts of former McCarthyite and ex-Senator Harry P. Cain to reform the federal loyalty-security programs. For well over a year Cain had objected loudly to the injustice he had encountered as a member of the Subversive Activities Control Board. In mid-June he had appeared before the Hennings Subcommittee on Constitutional Rights, and in a powerful performance followed closely by the press, described in detail some of the suffering caused by the Eisenhower security program. He contended accurately that in spite of the sweeping character of both the Truman and the Eisenhower loyalty programs, they had discovered not a single disloyal citizen. The federal loyalty program, Cain insisted, was unnecessary; the security system was best restricted to that small number of federal employees with access to national secrets. He reported that a June 7 conference with the President left him convinced that Mr. Eisenhower intended "to protect the individual against any unreasonable encroachment on his movements, speech and mind."[49]

Even more exasperating to the Radical Right than Cain and the President, however, was the Warren Court. In April, in the case of *Pennsylvania v. Nelson,* the Court invalidated state sedition and antisubversive statutes. A week later it ruled that New York educational authorities could not determine a teacher disloyal and unemployable merely on the ground that he had taken the Fifth Amendment before a congressional committee. And on June 11, in the case of *Cole v. Young,* a six-to-three majority dismantled the Eisenhower security program with a decision restricting the use of summary security procedures to federal employees occupying "sensitive" positions.

Cries of outrage were soon heard in Congress. Congressman Walter authored an anti-Cole decision bill in the House (soon endorsed by Attorney General Brownell and the chairman of the Civil Service Commission); separate bills to reverse the decision were introduced in the Upper Chamber by Senators Eastland, McCarthy, and Mundt. The three senators agreed that the Cole decision struck "a mortal blow" to government barriers against internal subversion; McCarthy urged legislation "that will effectively discipline the Supreme Court." In one Senate Internal Security Subcomittee hearing the following exchange occurred:

SENATOR EASTLAND   The Court seems to be issuing just one pro-Communist decision after another.

SENATOR MC CARTHY   You're so right.

SENATOR EASTLAND   What explanation is there except that some Communist influence is working within the Court?[50]

Moreover, on July 9, the Special Committee on the Federal Loyalty-Security Program of the Bar of the City of New York released a scholarly and objective 301-page report, sponsored by a $100,000 grant from the Fund, calling for sweeping revisions in the federal government's personnel security and loyalty programs. Among the proposals advocated by this committee, composed of nine distinguished attorneys from across the nation, was a 75 per cent reduction in the number of persons covered by the five personnel security programs ("We have to choose between a more effective security system in critical posts or a less effective one in all"), and the abolition—or total revision—of the Attorney General's list of subversive organizations. While asserting that the basic structure of the security system was sound, the report urged several changes in the treatment of individuals against whom charges were pending, including the right to receive written findings of fact and conclusions by hearing boards, the right to subpoena defense witnesses, expansion of the right to confront accusers, and the right to remain on government salary during an investigation. Many major newspapers, especially *The New York Times,* warmly applauded the study—and the Fund.[51]

And now this Fund for the Republic, this "anti-anti-Communist propaganda mill" led by "dupes," "foreign-aid squanderers," and "pinkish eggheads," had set out to destroy well-established and patriotic efforts to quash Communist infiltration in the entertainment industry. The President, the Supreme Court, and a number of legal experts appeared to have been "taken in" by the liberals, but there were still "pro-American" congressmen with enough common sense to put an end to this destruction of the nation's internal security. The time to end the Great Thaw was at hand.

Minnesota Congressman Eugene McCarthy accompanied John Cogley past reporters into the hearing room with an arm around his shoulder as a gesture of support.[52] Five committee members, including Chairman Walter, were present, along with Richard Arens and Karl Baarslag. For four hours Cogley was questioned sharply about the details of his study, its relationship with the Fund for the Republic and Dr. Hutchins, its possible aid and comfort to Communism. Doubt was cast upon Cogley's evidence, conclusions, even his choice of words. The witness answered calmly and respectfully, refusing only to give the names of those who had been interviewed for the study with the promise of anonymity. He said that he did not intend to plead the First or Fifth amendments.

Arens challenged the loyalty of Cogley's staff members repeatedly, taking obvious delight in revealing that Michael Harrington was a Socialist and that Paul Jacobs had belonged to a Communist club two decades earlier. When Cogley protested that both men were well-known anti-Communists, Arens informed the hearing audience: ". . . Socialists are only people who are conducting the transition from democracy to communism."[53] As for Dr. Marie Jahoda (selected to conduct a survey, appended to the report, by the Research Center for Human Relations of New York University):

MR. ARENS   Did you know that she was admitted into the United States only in 1945?

MR. COGLEY   She had a pronounced accent. I presumed it was not too long ago.

MR. ARENS   Did you know that prior to her association with the study of which you were director that she had issued reports of studies herself critical of the loyalty programs of this government, published reports?

MR. COGLEY   I had read nothing of Dr. Jahoda's before the grant was made to the Research Center of New York University.

MR. ARENS   Did you know anything about her connection with the Socialist Democratic Party in Austria prior to the time that she became identified with the Fund for the Republic?[54]

Of more interest was the fact, quickly made evident, that Arens and the congressmen believed that show-business figures who took the Fifth Amendment before federal subversive activities investigating committees, as well as those named as Communists or "sympathizers" by any one of a host of fanatics and professional witnesses who frequently testified before the committees (with congressional immunity), *deserved* to be deprived of their livelihoods without recourse to the law. When circulated lists of their names resulted in unemployment, this was not blacklisting, for channels existed through which the reluctant and the infamous could confess, could prove their innocence. And who controlled these channels? Patriotic Americans: friends and admirers of the committees.

Outside of the committee's decision not to require Cogley to disclose confidential sources of information, and Cogley's admission that Arnold Forster was indeed the witness who had named Woltman in his interview, little was settled during the inquiry. Chairman Walter absented himself from the hearing room during much of Cogley's testimony. Cogley responded to the prolonged harassment with a dignity and candor which virtually nullified committee efforts to tarnish his study before the general public. At the conclusion of the hearing, when asked if he had anything further to say, Cogley requested to know why he had been called. Congressman Walter (who had declared, upon becoming chairman, that the purpose of the committee was "to seek out Communism and subversion as related to individuals"[55]) replied, in part: "We called you for the purpose of ascertaining what your sources were in order to determine whether or not your conclusions were the conclusions we would have reached had we embarked on this sort of project."[56]

In New York, Dr. Hutchins declared, with little exaggeration, that the subpoenaing of Cogley "to justify his study" was "an unprecedented invasion of freedom of thought and expression in the United States."[57] In a public letter to Walter he called for "a statement declaring that the Committee's study has convinced it of our patriotic purposes" or "a full and impartial hearing."[58] But such a request did not fit in with Chairman Walter's plans.

The next day the first witness was Arnold Forster, general counsel for the Anti-Defamation League of B'nai B'rith. Forster was clearly selected to appear at the hearing for the purpose of weakening the report's authenticity. Quotations attributed to him, linking Woltman, Sokolsky, and others with the "clearing" process, are cited, however, on but three (of 599) pages of the study and affect its conclusions to no substantial degree.

Forster's testimony revealed that when the Cogley study first appeared he received a telephone call from Jack Wren, a public-relations man cited in the report as a leader in "clearing" accused professionals. When he read aloud material from the report he assumed (accurately) had come from Forster, the attorney then came "under the impression that these were my words," and wrote his letter to Woltman. Forster refused to deny at the hearing, however, that the quotations were accurate. "Yesterday John Cogley, the author of the report, testified that the quoted material is not a composite but are my words to one of his assistants. He may well be right." He contended only that they were "far from complete." The point he wished to make was that "the Anti-Defamation League would like to make an expression of gratitude, as I would to men like George Sokolsky, men like Victor Riesel, and men like Jack Wren, and men like Fred Woltman, to whom we had gone innumerable times to solicit their opinions." While the report said "more than a dozen," Forster recalled "probably eight people who had come to the Anti-Defamation League to help rehabilitate themselves whom we tried to help."[59]

When Arens finished with Forster, Chairman Walter thanked the witness and exclaimed: ". . . you have confirmed the suspicion that this committee has had right along, namely, that this report isn't worth the paper it is printed on. . . . I do not think there is a blacklist. I cannot find evidence of it."

"I think there is, sir," Forster replied abruptly.

> I mean by blacklisting the denial of employment to a man on grounds other than merit without first giving him an opportunity to be heard. I know that in the cases that we attempted to help actors, actresses, and others had been unable to get work and, according to them, had been told quietly, privately, and sometimes bluntly, that they just could not get work because of past records; actors and actresses who had never had a hearing by a radio company or a television company or a motion-picture industry. . . . To my knowledge there are men on the staffs of the networks and on the staffs of radio companies and of the Hollywood motion-picture industries whose purpose is to screen possible talent, to decide whether or no[t] these networks and these radio companies want to use these people for considerations other than merit. . . . this is a dreadful thing, this is a problem that has plagued knowledgeable newspapermen, it is a problem which has plagued the Anti-Defamation League. . . .
>
> Let me add this, if I may: If the Fund for the Republic report results in this kind of public hearing and results in public discussion across this country about the problem to which I have pointed, if it does nothing else regardless of its accuracy or inaccuracy on anything on its pages, I think it will have performed a great public service—wittingly or otherwise, deliberately or otherwise.

"I think you are absolutely correct," said Walter.[60]

The next witness was Frederick Woltman, staff writer for the New York *World-Telegram* (reporting the hearings for the Scripps-Howard newspapers!). While denying the content of references to him in the report, he made it clear that there existed "discrimination in employment practices," and a "process of rehabilitation," led by Sokolsky, Wren, and Riesel. He considered the rehabilitation process especially commendable: "Anybody who breaks with the Communists ought to get a job, I think."[61]

Woltman admitted talking with Arnold Forster about "many aspects of communism and persons involved in the Communist movement." "This was all very informal," he said. "He called me. We tried to check on people."[62]

Woltman expressed serious doubt about the loyalty of Cogley staff member Elizabeth Poe, and said of Cogley and Harrington: "I wouldn't call them Communists or sympathizers. I think, like Mr. Hutchins, they are very mixed up."[63] The study itself he thought "fraudulent." He complained:

> As a result of this report I am sure the guys who are mentioned in there are going to spend less time helping to rehabilitate people— I am talking about Sokolsky and Wren and Riesel and the others —because they were put in a reprehensible light for something which a person like Hutchins should applaud. If it has any effect at all, I am sure it will be to taper off their interest in this sort of business.[64]

James F. O'Neil, publisher of *American Legion Magazine*, a former national commander of the Legion and an eleven-year member of its National Americanism Commission, was then called upon to testify. Though he had not read the report "in its entirety," O'Neil, cited on several pages of the report, stated flatly that "the American Legion has never been engaged in clearance activities, that it has never been associated in any manner with any so-called blacklisting."[65] But he told of the Legion's participation in publishing and distributing the names of "suspects," notably, uncooperative witnesses before governmental subversive activities committees.

MR. ARENS   Does the American Legion in its Indianapolis headquarters and its Washington headquarters keep abreast of the hearings of the House Committee on Un-American Activities and the Senate Internal Security Subcommittee and of other congressional bodies dealing with the question of communism and subversion?

MR. O'NEIL   Yes, sir. I would say that most of the work of the Americanism division in this area is in *implementing and supplementing* the reports in the area of distribution of the House Un-American Activities Committee and the other committees of Congress and State organizations directly concerned with this problem [emphasis added].[66]

At one point O'Neil was moved to declare: "The American Legion . . . feels very definitely that those *identified with* the Communist conspiracy, the Communist apparatus, should not be employed in the entertainment industry [emphasis added]."[67]

O'Neil also described a Legion "rehabilitation project" by which members of the industry, suspected of Communist or "pro-Communist" activities or sympathies, could regain their jobs via the Legion. A letter could be written to an employer documenting or pleading personal innocence of charges. The letter would be turned over to the Legion's national office. (About one hundred such letters had already come to his attention, O'Neil said.) Under questioning by Congressman Doyle (who had read "4 or 5 pages" of the report), O'Neil further explained the process of exoneration:

MR. O'NEIL   Of course rehabilitation, Mr. Congressman, would come, I would say, not directly probably from the letter-writing campaign but from all of the things that went with it. In other words, if the protest arose at the local level, the exhibit or exhibitor became involved, and that built up into the studios. By the same token, when a local post became satisfied with the explanation and in their local appraisal felt there was no longer any occasion for them to protest, they would make their views known to the exhibitor at the local level. Of course that would be transmitted back through the entertainment industry belt to the studio people. We at our level would feel that if there was no further inquiry from the local posts they had become satisfied. If there was another inquiry, then we would try to determine whatever they desired. We tried to determine a method to obtain the answer to any questions which might arise.[68]

The witness was proud "that the American Legion has made a major contribution in helping to reestablish a climate of employment for the innocent, the stupid, and the repentant guilty in the entertainment industry, principally in Hollywood."[69] He was permitted to insert three exhibits into the hearing record, including an article by J. B. Matthews and J. Addington Wagner's condemnation of the Cogley report, Robert Hutchins, and the Fund for the Republic.

George Sokolsky had explained earlier to Arens that a heart condition would prevent him from appearing before the committee. A written statement by the Hearst columnist was thus entered into the record, in which he denied statements in the report attributed to Forster and condemned the study as suffering "from inadequate research, from either an unwillingness or an inability to get all the facts, from a double standard of morals." He admitted, however, participating in what the report called "the burdens of a private citizen judging the political trustworthiness of other privte citizens."

> I do not and cannot know the correct number of those rehabilitated by this process. My rough estimate runs about 300 men and women who are today working in the motion-picture industry who could not work before because of the record they had established of Communist or pseudo-Communist associations. Rather than being a blacklisting effort, this was an effort in rehabilitation.[70]

On the following morning, July 12, Vincent W. Harnett was called to the stand. The Cogley report described Hartnett (a principal defendant in the Faulk suit) as the "most professional" of the "clearance men"; "he makes a full-time occupation out of what for others is merely a sideline." Hartnett took fees for investigating "pro-Communist allegations" against show-business figures, wrote and distributed literature containing the names of "suspects," and lectured frequently to veterans' groups and others on Communism in the entertainment media. Said the report:

> Hartnett may be the most widely criticized man in the radio-tv industry, because he is frankly in the business of exposing people with "front records" and then, later, of "clearing" them—or as the [New York] Times writer delicately put it, "advising them on how to counter pro-Communist allegations."[71]

The witness condemned the second volume of the study for "dangerous slanting," and declared that its author was "either woefully ignorant or he is a rogue."[72] Blacklisting was "a nasty term" and should not have been applied "to honest, intelligent,

222 / *Freedom and the Foundation*

reasonable, and fair patriotic efforts to keep subversives out of radio and television."[73] The truth of the matter was that

> in spite of the tremendous information uncovered by this commit-
> tee, which is, of course, an object of opprobrium to the Com-
> munists—they dread investigations, especially by this committee—
> in spite of that, in spite of all the investigations conducted by both
> State and congressional committees, I would say that not more
> than 5 percent, not more than 5 percent of the past and present
> *Communists* in the entertainment industry have been uncovered
> [emphasis added].

"And we have been accused time and time again, as you know, of exaggerating the menace," chortled Congressman Scherer.[74]

The airwaves were swarming with Communist subversion, Hartnett claimed.

> . . . you will find script after script in which the policeman shoots
> an innocent teen-ager, not the bad teen-ager. It is always the inno-
> cent. The wrong man is identified and sent to jail. An honest
> official abroad is suspected of being a Communist agent and the
> man who points the fingers at him is always a fanatic, disgruntled.
>
> In other words, if you could believe television, our courts are
> incapable of convicting the right man, our witnesses are incapable
> of making a positive identification, our juries are incapable of
> coming in with the right finding, private citizens are incapable of
> making a right evaluation. We are being brainwashed.[75]

Was the witness well paid for his efforts against the Reds? asked Arens. Not at all, claimed Hartnett. "For example, I was asked by a client a month ago about Arthur Miller. That report was more than 33 pages and I charged more than $20 for it. It took about 2 weeks."[76] (In 1958 Harnett would reveal that from 1952 to 1957 he received over $100,000 for his work.[77])

The next witness was Roy M. Brewer, until recently a Holly-wood union representative, who was cited by the Cogley study on thirty-seven pages. He was permitted to attack the report for "a complete falsification," "a distortion," and assorted "omissions" and "errors," but told readily of combatting and helping to re-habilitate "identified Communists." Brewer and the committee members got along famously; their camaraderie was born of several years of collaboration. At one point the witness joined Arens and Congressman Scherer (who had only "scanned" the report[78]) in noting close similarities between the study and articles in the Communist *Daily Worker*.[79] One exchange went as follows:

MR. DOYLE   I want to take advantage, I have not discussed this with you, but I want to take advantage of your presence here. I know that you know the history of this committee over a term of years.

Will you give us out of your experience over a term of years your appraisal in general terms at least of the extent of the usefulness of this committee, say, in this field of exposing and defeating, meeting the problem of subversive activities in the field of entertainment, either in Hollywood or any place that you have in mind?

I do not know what your answer is going to be, but you have appeared here as an expert and I would like to have your opinion as an expert.

MR. BREWER   Well, I have appeared before this committee at various times since 1947 and as the knowledge of the Communist conspiracy grew, I think that this committee has done a very effective work. . . . I think the careful efforts of this committee over a long period of time, and as I say, as the knowledge of the Communist movement grew their techniques improved, and I think they have done a very effective work and certainly I have been a champion of what the committee has done and have defended it and would do so today.[80]

A delighted Fulton Lewis, Jr., told his listeners that evening:

So perhaps our reportorial work over this microphone over the last 11 months is beginning to bear fruit. A Congressional committee looks into one of these phony studies and finds it to be exactly what I have reported to you that the others have been, an ill-disguised and somewhat clumsy propaganda effort to brainwash the American public against the loyalty security program, against investigations into communism and Communist-front activities, and to persuade the public that the Communist conspiracy is a political party like the Republican or Democratic party and should be accepted on the same basis.[81]

The fourth day of the public hearings opened with testimony by Paul R. Milton, a director of AWARE, Inc., "an anti-Communist organization in the entertainment-communications field." The Cogley report had devoted many pages to AWARE; clarifying its close ties with HUAC, Senator McCarthy, and other elements of the Radical Right; explaining in detail its major role in the blacklisting business.[82]

Like other witnesses, Milton was allowed to tear into the report for alleged inaccuracies and "pro-Communist" assumptions. And he entered a lengthy rebuttal by AWARE, Inc., into the record. (When Walter called the study "gobbledegook," Milton added: "That is somewhat an insult to gobbledegook, sir."[83]) Also, like the other witnesses, Milton proceeded in his testimony to substantiate much of the report's findings.

> AWARE believes that a Communist, a fifth amendment witness, and persons with significant and unrepudiated records of association with Communist-front organizations should not be employed. . . . Each individual employer should make up his own mind on the basis of what information he may have or obtain and such advice as he feels necessary as he may do in a legal matter, in an accounting matter, or in a tax matter.[84]

And what was a prominent channel for such information? "We issue membership bulletins and occasionally we issue one beyond the membership, commenting on evidences of Communist influence in the entertainment field."[85]

What about "clearing" practices?

> . . . as Mr. Brewer testified yesterday, the voluntary efforts of people in the entertainment-communications field to help Communists, ex-Communists, and Communist fronters and ex-Communist fronters to "rehabilitate" themselves as the word has been used—those efforts are admirable.[86]

Milton warmly praised HUAC, noting: "This committee provides a wonderful forum in which people may explain themselves."[87]

Next on the stand was Godfrey P. Schmidt, president of AWARE, Inc. To Schmidt (whose organization was a target of the Faulk suit) the Cogley report was simply "the Communist line," "nothing but a partisan and political tract": "I am sure that the Communist Party high command would be delighted to have every week a document like this come out, because this fronts for a line that it seems to me has been increasing."[88]

As the hearing progressed, charges against the report and the Fund became so shrill and so routine that Congressman Velde finally asked: "Mr. Schmidt, do you think the Fund for the Republic is a type of organization that should be tax-exempt?"[89] When Arens asked Schmidt ("as a devout anti-Communist") if he felt it "a legitimate concern of a congressional committee that a tax-exempt foundation with vast resources should be making these allegations to which you have been alluding?" he replied: "I think, from the point of view of our Constitution, it is exactly what the Founding Fathers wanted a congresisonal committee to do."[90]

The committee also heard lengthy testimony from Frank McNamara (to Arens, "an expert in the field of fighting Communism"), former editor of *Counterattack,* a right-wing weekly newsletter mentioned prominently in the report as an instrument of blacklisting. As usual, Arens and the congressmen guided the witness through his attacks against Cogley, his staff, the Fund, and the report ("it aids" a "basic Communist aim").[91] The committee also placed into the record a written denial by Victor Riesel that he had ever been part of a "clearance ring"—a term invented by Woltman.[92]

For a third time Dr. Hutchins requested the right to cross-examine witnesses and to reply at the time charges against the Fund were being made.[93] But Walter would not go beyond the promise that "When we are considering the Fund for the Republic—and we are not now—we are going to permit witnesses to be heard."[94]

That same day, July 13, President Eisenhower sent his formal nominations for the delegation to the United Nations to the Senate. To the anguish of Fulton Lewis, Jr., and Joseph McCarthy, the name of Paul G. Hoffman was included. (McCarthy was boiling with rage at the Administration for proposing Hoffman. In a slashing speech to the Senate he described a writing by the Fund's board chairman as "either the irresponsible twaddle of a halfwit, or the calculated propagation of the approved Communist Party line."[95])

And by now the outrageous procedures of the committee were beginning to arouse protest. *The New York Times* recorded concern "over any and every effort, no matter how it may be disguised, to intimidate a man for writing what he believes."

> If the House Committee on Un-American Activities were really interested in examining all un-American activities it might long ago have used its great powers as an investigative arm of Congress to look into the thoroughly un-American art of blacklisting in the entertainment industry. Instead, it left that thankless job to the Fund for the Republic, but it has now suddenly raised its hackles because it didn't like what the Fund's independent inquiry produced.[96]

The Washington *Post and Times-Herald* excoriated Arens.[97] *Commonweal* asked: "Will a writer who upholds the Supreme Court decision on segregation . . . be subpoenaed and grilled by Senator Eastland? Will Keynesian economists be called to account by Congressional critics who are anti-New Deal?"[98] Shortly, a London reporter wrote of the committee: "At the risk of appearing John Bullish, I must say that such a quasi-legal chamber would not be tolerated for a day in a civilized European state."[99] The *Christian Century* editorialized: "We have the honor to count John Cogley as a friend, whose Christian integrity and ability as a journalist we greatly respect. If Mr. Walter compels us to choose between his brand of patriotism and that of John Cogley, we will choose that of John Cogley."[100]

Following a three-day recess the hearings resumed in Philadelphia on July 17 under a subcommittee consisting of Congressman Walter and Scherer. Called to the stand were two actors named in the Cogley study, among dozens of others, as examples of show business personalities who had been blacklisted. The two selected were hardly typical; both had taken the Fifth Amendment before HUAC in the past and were expected to do so again.

The first to appear was Academy Award-winning actress Gale Sondergaard. She told her interrogators that the questions asked of her were already a matter of record, and complained of being blacklisted since taking the Fifth Amendment in 1951. "For the committee to recall me here at this specific time while I am deeply involved in a creative work, the first in five years, can only be construed as an act of harassment."[101]

Comedian Jack Gilford appeared the next day and, like Miss Sondergaard, again took the Fifth Amendment when asked about former Communist associations. "I would love to supply blacklist information," he shouted angrily in the course of his examination. "Everyone hates the blacklist—the whole TV industry. I have important information for you."[102] When he refused to state whether he had ever been a Communist he was dismissed.

Having thus "refuted" the Cogley study, the hearings now moved to another subject—the Plymouth Monthly Meeting award. It was obvious that the committee was investigating something more than the contents of a specific pair of volumes. Chairman Walter was unusually candid:

> The committee wishes to know more about the factors which prompted the Fund for the Republic to consider the retention of *a Communist*, a defense of "democratic principles" worth $5,000 of its tax-exempt money.
>
> The Communists and their dupes will undoubtedly try to distort our inquiry into appearing as an interference with the great freedom of religion. . . . Our sole concern is with the seemingly dubious ventures of the Fund for the Republic, Inc. [emphasis added].[103]

A week earlier the chairman of the library committee of Plymouth Monthly Meeting was subpoenaed and asked to bring the Meeting's minutes to the hearings. Claiming the protection of the First Amendment, the Meeting refused to submit its minutes (thus qualifying its members in Walter's lexicon as "Communist dupes") and the House committee complied.[104] A Fund researcher who investigated certain facts of Mrs. Knowles's harassment prior to the award, Mrs. Maureen Black Ogden, also received a subpoena.

Mrs. Eleanor Stevenson heard of the impending inquiry into the Fund's award by telephone from Dr. Hutchins while on vacation in Mexico.[105] She immediately wired a request to Chairman Walter on July 17 asking to appear the next day to explain the Fund's position.

The decision of the Fund to make a grant to this Quaker group was based on the unanimous recommendation of my committee, which consisted of myself, M. Albert Linton, Chairman of the Board of the Provident Mutual Life Insurance Company and the late Robert E. Sherwood. . . . I think you should also hear from the Directors of The Fund for the Republic, who accept full responsibility for the Fund's action.[106]

But Mr. Walter had no such desire. At the hearing Bethuel Webster pleaded strongly with the committee's chairman to allow Mrs. Stevenson to testify. Walter refused ("it doesn't fit into the program arranged for today"), finally telling the Fund's counsel in an angry exchange: "You have no rights here, no rights at all."[107]

In a lengthy press release Mrs. Stevenson accused Walter of raising "questions about the patriotism of the Fund which reflect on the members of its board, on its staff, and on the many religious groups, educational institutions, civic organizations and individuals who have received grants from the Fund for work on civil liberty fields."[108] Before returning to Mexico she told a radio interviewer that "As chairman of the Awards Committee, I went over the details [of the award] and to my knowledge it was a very, very American thing to do."[109]

The Plymouth Monthly Meeting was badly split over the award, though no complaints had arisen when Mrs. Knowles was hired permanently or at the time the Fund's award was made known. The $5,000 check was in escrow. A bare majority (thirty-four to thirty) of the active members of the meeting favored Mrs. Knowles's retention.[110] Four of the five witnesses subpoenaed by the House committee on the 18th, however, were violently opposed to the award. One, George C. Corson, was a close relative of the leader of the campaign to have Mrs. Knowles fired.

JUDGE CORSON If we could get rid of the $5,000 Fund for the Republic money, I think maybe we all would fall on each other's necks and say "Let's forget it all and let the woman stay." But it is the $5,000 that holds everything up because everybody says, "What did you ever do to get a Communist $5,000? Everybody is stigmatized. Are you all Communists?" Unfortu-

> nately, it is drawing people who come to the Meet-
> ing who are rather different from people who have
> been accustomed to coming.[111]

Another witness admitted attending Plymouth Monthly Meetings
only occasionally, and a third was a Baptist.[112]

Testimony included charges that the former librarian had been
"pushed out" in 1954 as part of a plot to hire Mrs. Knowles, that
only four of the eight members of the library committee had approved of her permanent employment, and that a majority of the
members of the Plymouth Monthly Meeting and of the residents
of the community had consistently opposed the retention of the
woman in the William Jeanes Memorial Library. The library
committee's chairman was heartily criticized by Congressmen
Walter and Scherer for turning over excerpts of the Meeting's
minutes to the Fund.[113]

Mrs. Ogden, from a long line of conservative New Jersey Republicans, recalled the details of her investigation while an irate
and frustrated Bethuel Webster tried to protect her from misleading questions. She admitted having interviewed by telephone
only one opponent of the award (Mrs. Philip Corson, who refused
to see her), but declared correctly that she had gathered materials
hostile to Mrs. Knowles.[114] "The fact of the matter is," Chairman
Walter exclaimed, "neither you nor the Fund for the Republic
was concerned with whether or not she had ever been a Communist."[115] On that theme the hearings into the integrity and patriotism of the officers, directors, and staff members of the Fund for
the Republic were concluded.

The following day, July 19, the library committee released a
statement, signed by its five members, strongly questioning the
value of the investigation into the award.

> A Committee of Congress has just spent virtually a whole day
> ventilating the unhappy internal affairs of a small religious group,
> Plymouth Monthly Meeting of the Religious Society of Friends.
> Not a single fact has been developed that was not known before.
> The division in the Meeting, the various points of view, all had
> been well known long before. It is hard to see what public service
> is rendered by dramatizing a difference over a matter of con-
> science. . . .

The House Committee accepted reckless statements that many people "in the community" wanted the Meeting's Librarian removed; it gave no opportunity for evidence that there has been strong and enthusiastic support for the Librarian's continued employment.

The House Committee suggested that controversy in a community of itself is bad, ignoring the fact that only by controversy can there be tested the devotion to principle which is essential to democracy.

The Library Committee of Plymouth Monthly Meeting remains satisfied with the qualifications of Mrs. Mary Knowles, both as a citizen and as a librarian.

Mrs. Knowles has sworn she had no subversive associations since 1947, and no evidence has been produced to the contrary. Unless, or until, evidence is produced—indicating activity inimical to our democratic form of government—we envision no change in our relationship with her.[116]

A letter to Chairman Walter from nine non-Quaker residents of the Plymuoth Meeting area, including a prominent Catholic layman, followed shortly. It called the hearings "undignified" and "pointless," concluding: ". . . we feel that you have done irreparable damage to our community, have abused your Constitutional powers, and through cheap theatricals have lessened the respect which should be accorded to the Congress of the United States of America."[117] Nine Quaker leaders then sent letters to the seven absent members of the House committee protesting interference with their religious affairs, and labeling what had taken place "a travesty upon the word 'investigation' and a mockery of the idea of inquiry. It appears rather to have been an organized attempt to present selected facts in the light most discreditable to the Fund for the Republic, Inc."[118]

Francis Walter soon displayed a letter bearing twenty-one signatures stating: ". . . we would like to offer our sincere congratulations on the fair, dignified and extremely patient manner in which the recent House Un-American Activities Committee hearing . . . was conducted. Also we would like to commend Attorney Richard Arens for his kindly and courteous questioning of all the witnesses on both sides of the controversy."[119]

CHAPTER TWELVE / *Turning Points*

O ne of several turning points in the Fund's long battles with its critics occurred on July 20, 1956. Over the heated objections of Senators McCarthy, Bridges, and Jenner (and in spite of a widespread letter-writing campaign based on the subscription list of the archconservative *National Review*), the Senate, by a vote of sixty-four to twenty-two, accepted President Eisenhower's nomination of Paul G. Hoffman as a delegate to the United Nations.[1] He was approved unanimously by the Senate Foreign Relations Committee and was even supported by minority leader William F. Knowland (also named to the delegation).[2]

The Administration, in mustering the determination to defeat a right-wing coalition bent on condemning foreign aid, obstructing reappraisal of the government's loyalty-security regulations, and hindering the orderly evolution toward racial integration, assisted to no small degree, however unknowingly, in the revitalization of the Fund for the Republic's good name. It would be increeasingly difficult to question the loyalty of a man demonstrably trusted and admired by two thirds of the United States Senate and an extremely popular President about to be renominated to the world's most responsible office.

On July 25, Senator Hubert Humphrey placed into the *Congressional Record* statements in support of the Fund from the executive boards of the International Union of Electrical, Radio, and Machine Workers, and the National Agricultural Workers

232 / Freedom and the Foundation

Union, as well as from A. Philip Randolph, international president of the Brotherhood of Sleeping Car Porters.[3] Oregon's Senator Wayne Morse, the following day, inserted a laudatory
editorial on the Fund from the Louisville *Times*.[4] Senator John
F. Kennedy of Massachusetts soon did likewise with friendly
comments from the Boston *Pilot*.[5] On July 30, Emil Mazey,
secretary-treasurer of the United Automobile Workers union,
pointed to HUAC's hearings on the Fund and called for the
defeat of Congressman Walter at the polls.[6]

No little credit should be given to hard-working Frank Kelly
for the gradual emergence of a nation-wide revulsion to tactics
employed against the Fund for the Republic. He encouraged
grantees to issue press releases in support of the Fund. By the end
of July he had prepared and mailed to newspaper editors and
news commentators 5,000 copies of a small booklet of reproduced
editorial comments on the blacklisting report, revealing a favorable ratio of five to one.[7] Copies of the three-year report had been
mailed, with personal notes, to 140 editors in key cities. The
Fund's June bulletin, containing a digest of the report, went to
the editors of 1,800 daily newspapers.[8] Ten thousand reprints of
Paul G. Hoffman's militantly nationalistic address to the Willard
Straight post of the American Legion were being dispatched
across the country.[9]

Whenever possible Kelly gave private briefings to reporters
and editors. One such personal confrontation resulted in an editorial of major significance in *The New York Times,* which
chastised the House Committee on Un-American Activities for
its "hit-and-run tactics," called the hearings "sorry sniping expedi-
tions," and referred to "the tactics employed by the Walter committee and its counsel, Richard Arens" as "deplorable."[10] ("I
supplied John Oakes [of the *Times* editorial board] with full information about what had happened in the course of this 'investigation,'" Kelly reported to Hoffman, "and he drew his own conclusions."[11]) The editorial was soon placed within a special Fund
bulletin and distributed from coast to coast.[12]

Kelly also wrote to the United Press, protesting charges made
by Senator John C. Stennis of Mississippi. In calling on the Treasury Department to restudy the tax-exempt status of the Fund,

Stennis had excavated the long-dismissed and erroneous claim that the Fund financed a "jury-bugging" study by scholars of the University of Chicago.[13] A touch of satisfaction appeared as Kelly passed the cup of wrath: "I understand that the Ford Foundation financed some such project, but I wish to remind you that the Fund is an entirely independent organization, with an entirely separate board of directors and an entirely separate group of projects."[14]

The vice-president's efforts were made less difficult when, on August 6, the close relationship between Francis Walter and Fulton Lewis, Jr., became widely evident. On that evening Lewis, rushing to defend Senator Stennis, cited over the air a memorandum from W. H. Ferry to Joseph Lyford and read, in its entirety, a handwritten letter from Mrs. Eleanor B. Stevenson to Ferry. Both documents had been subpoenaed by Congressman Walter and were thought to be in his possession exclusively.[15]

Bethuel Webster had recently learned that Walter had requested and received all information and papers given by the Fund to the Internal Revenue Service for its investigation.[16] When he learned of the link between Walter and Lewis, he sent the following telegram to HUAC's chairman:

IT IS AN INEXCUSABLE VIOLATION OF THE INVESTIGATIVE PROCESS THAT YOU SHOULD HAVE MADE AVAILABLE TO A RADIO COMMENTATOR DOCUMENTS OBTAINED UNDER SUBPOENA FROM THE FUND FOR THE REPUBLIC THAT WERE NEVER MADE A PART OF THE RECORD. THE FUND CANNOT BE HARMED BY YOUR IRRESPONSIBLE USE OF THIS MATERIAL, BUT THE PRESTIGE OF CONGRESS CANNOT FAIL TO BE DAMAGED BY THIS ABUSE OF THE POWERS LODGED IN YOU. THIS IS ANOTHER EXAMPLE OF THE HIT AND RUN TACTICS PURSUED BY YOU AND MR. ARENS IN YOUR DEALINGS WITH THE FUND FOR THE REPUBLIC.[17]

Hutchins mailed copies of the telegram to each of the members of the House committee. To House Speaker Sam Rayburn he wrote:

We believe that you as the chief officer of the House will wish to be informed of this epsode. We venture to hope that in conformity with your long and distinguished record of honorable dealings you will find it possible to check the excesses of the Chairman of the House Un-American Activities Committee and its staff.[18]

Representative Walter responded to his critics on August 7 with a letter to *The New York Times,* contending that the hearings for which he had been so soundly condemned by the *Times* had established important facts about "the activities of the Fund for the Republic." They were: (1) that only "a number of people who have been identified as hard-core members of the Communist conspiracy have been refused access to mass media of communications," (2) that Mrs. Mary Knowles "was not at any time employed by the Plymouth Quaker Meeting," (3) that the Meeting "at no time evidenced a sympathy" with her employment, and (4) that the "vast majority" of the residents of the community were opposed to the librarian's retention.[19]

Such statements indeed appeared during the hearings, but remained largely unchallenged, due to the chairman's refusal to permit cross-examination and testimony by the Fund's directors or officers. Each of the contentions, in fact, was false.

The Cogley report and the author's testimony provided ample evidence of blacklisting tactics employed against many persons holding a variety of political opinions. Moreover, it was the study's implicit assumption that the mere identification of a man with a Communist or "pro-Communist" idea was not parallel to a conviction according to due process for subversive activities.

Members of the library committee that hired Mrs. Knowles were appointed by the Plymouth Monthly Meeting. The permanent employment of Mrs. Knowles was submitted to the membership of the Meeting and received the unanimous consent of those who attended the scheduled session. Moreover, the yearly Meeting of Friends, representing ninety-three monthly Meetings, unanimously backed in principle the Plymouth Meeting's stand on the retention of Mrs. Knowles. The population of Plymouth Township was over 4,000, and signatures on petitions against the librarian were variously represented during the hearings as running between 243 and 884; even the highest figure would hardly represent a community majority.[20]

In a reply to the *Times,* Cogley mused:

At the time I was questioned by the committee Mr. Walter admitted that he had not read [the report] nor had the majority of the committee. Mr. Walter's latest letter leads me to believe that he has still not got around to it.[21]

The harrowing clashes characteristic of so many of the board meetings of the past had been replaced by a solid spirit of confidence and unity when the executive committee assembled on August 14. Erwin Griswold, who at one point had even scolded Vice-President Ferry over the use of an excessive quantity of postage stamps, had been wooed unremittingly by Hutchins and his staff for the past few months.[22] The dean still refused financial remuneration for his services on the board and had, with others, some reservations about the president's plans for the future of the Fund. But personal letters and unanimous votes illustrate the harmony and assuredness nurtured by common attack.

The committee's initial grant, $20,000, went to the AMVETS, the American Legion's major rival, to finance a "Positive Americanism" program. The national chairman of this veterans' organization advertised the program nationally in letters to newspapers as "an examination of our heritage as derived from our famous documents and the ideas of great Americans and how that heritage gives meaning to our present." He added: "There is no witch-hunting, no flag-waving, no name-calling."[23]

Further committee approvals were: a $47,000 grant to the St. Louis Bar Association to cover the cost of several open-forum programs, a $70,000 appropriation to complete the work of the Commission on Race and Housing, and a $29,000 appropriation (urged by Dean Griswold) to extend for a second year the Bureau of National Affairs' loyalty-security loose-leaf service.[24] Before adjournment the committee authorized the publication of a strongly worded Fund bulletin to be entitled "Congressman Walter Investigates." It would describe the recent history of "the deliberate scheme" by Francis Walter to discredit the Fund, and reproduce the *Times* editorial as well as Bethuel Webster's telegram to Walter.

The Fund was, of course, taking a great risk; there was no precedent for such a public attack on a congressman by a tax-exempt foundation. But there was no precedent for a Fund for the Republic; its officers and directors knew that pressures from the Right had placed the corporation in serious jeopardy and that

236 / *Freedom and the Foundation*

the possibility of its extinction remained very real. (On July 25, Bethuel Webster had met with an officer of the Internal Revenue Service, who appeared puzzled and suspicious of the Fund's activities. "Like others who seem to want to be friendly, he talks about bad public relations, saying that we have not 'sold' the Fund, that we are losing friends, etc., and that some of our officers and directors [and not just one or two] are controversial or provocative."[25]) With well over half of the Fund's financial resources remaining to be spent, even survival might mean months, perhaps years, of threats and harassments by the federal government unless the corporation took forceful measures to defend itself; to convince the public and government authorities of its fervent dedication to the highest and most orthodox principles of the Constitution. The Fund's officers and directors knew that they could document a good case against HUAC; the facts surrounding and contained in the hearings condemned Walter and his associates before any fair observer; the press had rallied to the Fund's support. This was as good a time and place as any to intensify the Fund's counterattack.

The bulletin was released on August 28 and was used by such highly reputed newspapers as the Louisville *Courier-Journal,* the Pittsburgh *Post-Gazette,* and the St. Louis *Post-Dispatch* to condemn soundly what the latter called "Mr. Walter's Dirty Work."[26] The Hartford *Courant* demanded:

> Let Mr. Walter bring his charges in open hearings, and with a free flow of witnesses and information for defense as well as offense. In the present circumstances Mr. Walter is discrediting the whole legislative investigative process. If he does not himself follow through, to allow a rebuttal to the attacks he makes, then Congress should act at the first opportunity. In the interests of its own reputation, it should remove Mr. Walter. For, strangely enough, the most un-American thing about this entire matter thus far has been the acts of the committee itself.[27]

Congressman Walter hastily issued a statement calling the Fund a "multi-million dollar propaganda machine," and promised new full-scale hearings to determine whether it was "friend or foe in our death struggle with Soviet communism." Previous hearings, he declared, had revealed the use of tax-exempt funds for "political subversion." "The investigation by the Committee of the Fund for the Republic will continue in an orderly, objective manner," he said.[28]

J. Addington Wagner was soon heard from again, boasting to the national convention of the American Legion that "Our work to expose the danger to America represented by the Fund for the Republic has borne good fruit."[29]

Paul G. Hoffman told a luncheon meeting of the Overseas Press Club the next evening that charges that the Fund was engaging in political subversion were "strictly nonsense." He accused "some Congressmen" of making "irresponsible charges." To reporters afterward he admitted that he "clearly" included Francis E. Walter in the list.[30]

On September 11, Hoffman and Roger Lapham had lunch with William Randolph Hearst, Jr., attempting to convince the newspaper tycoon of the Fund's value and integrity. Hearst had refrained from attacking Hoffman's nomination to the United Nations delegation, and it was hoped that the two Republican leaders could reach some degree of accord. Perhaps Hearst could at least be persuaded that a majority of the Fund's directors had the best interests of the nation in mind.

The next day Hearst sent a copy to Hoffman of a letter he had just received from J. Edgar Hoover, congratulating him for an editorial entitled "One-Track Reds." In the letter,[31] Hearst gloated to Hoffman in an attachment that the nation's outstanding authority on the Communist menace had acknowledged the wisdom of the newspaper owner in regard to the infiltration of subversives into the American way of life. Yet neither Hoover nor Hearst, the latter complained, had been consulted by the Fund for the Republic in its studies of communism. Hearst expressed grave suspicions about the reason, and confided the personal belief that Hoffman and Roger Lapham were being cruelly deceived, perhaps by Dr. Hutchins.

It appeared certain that Hearst's position was inflexible. Further negotiations with him were attempted, without success.[32]

The Fund's board of directors assembled at the Plaza Hotel in New York on the afternoon of September 12. Following a report by Bethuel Webster on the Walter committee hearings, the shuffling of committee assignments, and a break for dinner, the board discussed recent developments of Hutchins's basic-issues proposal. Further consideration was planned for the annual meeting in November.

The next morning the directors turned to the officers' recommendations, approving them in order and unanimously. A supplementary grant of $30,000 went to the Stanfard Law School's analysis of testimony of principal government witnesses. The Southern Regional Council, following an oral report on its excellent work by the Fund's consultant on intergroup relations, Frank Loescher, received an additional $110,000. A grant of $25,000 was authorized for the University YMCA at Berkeley, California, with Chancellor Clark Kerr's encouragement, for a two-year program of popular education in civil liberties directed toward the students and faculty of that branch of the University of California. The American Friends Service Committee was authorized to receive a grant of $33,000 to finance civil-liberties conferences for high-school students. A grant of $4,000 went to the United States National Student Association for support of its 1957 Academic Freedom Week on campuses throughout the nation. The Fund's extensive fellowship and grant-in-aid program was continued by an appropriation of $115,000. And the blacklisting study was closed out with an additional appropriation of $21,090, which included $2,000 to be used to prepare an analysis of reactions to the report.

The directors also found the supplemental recommendations to their liking. The Carrie Chapman Catt Memorial Fund was awarded a grant of $10,000 to finance a training course on the Bill of Rights for New York City teachers. And the prestigious Alexander Hamilton Bicentennial Commission received $10,000 to support a commemorative, nation-wide scholarship and fellowship contest program for high-school and college students.[33]

Within a few days Dr. Hutchins "heaved" what a friend thought would be "a five-gallon can of kerosene" on "the embers of controversy" over the Fund.[34] Readers were just finishing a newly published book entitled: *Freedom, Education, and the Fund. Essays and Addresses: 1946–1956.*

Although half the pages were devoted to the author's uncompromising and oft-repeated criticisms of American education, the heart of the paperback volume concerned the Fund for the Republic, its role in the nation's turmoil over human rights, and its critics. Brilliant aphorisms decorated an outline of the Fund's creation, its aims, and its contributions. Opponents such as the Reece committee and the American Legion (not HUAC) were handled with blunt sarcasm and towering disdain. A case for the Fund, and for Robert Hutchins—no attempt was made to distinguish between the two—was articulated with zest and acuity. Near the end of the volume he wrote:

> The point of view of the Fund for the Republic is conservative. It wants to conserve the Republic by conserving its essential attributes, which are freedom and justice. These ideas rest on a conception of man. According to that conception the ideal man is one who thinks for himself; who respects the convictions of others, but who will stand up for his own against any power whatever.
>
> In this country we do not have to take anybody's word for anything. The citizen does not have to take the word of diplomats about foreign policy, of military men about military power, of policemen about security, of informers about the disloyalty of persons, or of the Attorney-General about that of organizations. He does not have to take the word of legislative committees about the prevalence of witches. Though he is supposed to take the word of the Supreme Court about what the law is, he does not have to stop trying to get it to change its mind; and in America we recognize the claims of a higher law. We have only to recall Thoreau to be reminded that civil disobedience has a long and honorable history in this country.
>
> Our reliance is upon the intelligence and character of the independent individual. The greatest dangers to the ideals that we cherish are fear and conformity. Courage and independence are the best guarantees of freedom and justice. We cannot feel free and feel frightened. The motto of the Fund for the Republic is "feel free."[35]

The book was a stirring, persuasive, highly provocative, and totally partisan declaration of a philosophy of freedom, as well as an aggressive counterattack against many of that philosophy's most implacable foes. Reviews were almost unanimously favorable.[36] Along with Hoffman's appointment to the United Nations delegation, the bulletin on the Walter hearings, and the public-relations efforts with the nation's press, this book no doubt contributed greatly to the general deflation in the credibility of accusations shown by the Fund's opposition.

Robert Hutchins becàme convinced in the early 1930's that there was little prospect for creating within the United States the kind of university he desired. A philosophical idealist thoroughly schooled in scholastic philosophy, a clergyman's son deeply committed to moral and ethical considerations, Hutchins believed it the proper task of teachers and students to abandon pragmatism for the study and discussion of the "underlying principles" of man's life and institutions. In an early book he wrote: "To determine the good and the order of goods is the prime object of all moral and political education."[37]

He envisioned, but was not able to implement at the University of Chicago, a sort of Platonic academy in which twelve to fifteen thinkers from a variety of disciplines would be provided with a central location and the necessary finances to study together subjects of their own choosing, to transcend their specialties in an attempt to shed light upon and stir discussion about the eternal questions. These distinguished scholars would be free of the workaday encumbrances of academic life which hinder sustained, significant intellectual effort; they would be free to consider the existence of God if they so desired; they would be free.

This idea traveled with Hutchins to the Ford Foundation. After considerable effort the Institute for Philosophical Research was created in the spring of 1952. The institute, headed by Mortimer Adler, was devoted to the creation of a *Summa Dialectica* ("a dialectical summation of Western thought"), but in addition was planned to play a major role in the establishment and operation of Hutchins's academy. In March and May of 1953 two conferences were held at which several of the world's leading thinkers were invited to express their views on the desirability of a new institution devoted to the advancement of understanding. The overwhelming response was affirmative. But the rapid deterioration of harmony between Hutchins and the Ford Foundation's trustees following Paul Hoffman's resignation canceled the elaborate drafts for the academy.[38]

When Hutchins moved to the Fund for the Republic his desire for an academy was subdued by the many duties and controversies surrounding his new position. But by early 1956, firmly established as president of the Fund and in fair command of the board of directors, it returned to him. On April 5 he telephoned John Cogley and asked him to fly to Pasadena for a conversation on the Fund's future. After lengthy discussion between Hutchins, Cogley, and Hallock Hoffman, it was agreed to keep the matter a secret until a formal proposal for the academy was presented to the board.[39]

The immediate problem to solve was the discovery of language to convince the more pragmatic members of the board to alter radically the Fund's remaining efforts, to persuade them of the academy's relevance to the corporation's mandate.

In early May, as we have noted, the directors received a memorandum from the president in which he contended that the past activities of the Fund had not been properly educational. The handling of disparate issues and cases, Hutchins wrote, was based upon the false assumption that people had some common understanding of the principles of the Declaration of Independence and the Constitution. "The underlying problem of the Fund, the United States, and the West may be the same. References to freedom, justice, civil liberties and the Bill of Rights are inadequate to convey a meaning sufficiently precise and inspiring to arouse or maintain the devotion of the masses or to guide the policies of their leaders." What the Fund ought to do with its resources, he contended, was to create an institute or council to clarify the "basic issues," the political and moral principles underlying civil liberties and civil rights; to arrive at common convictions in spite of profound historical and philosophical differences to the end that mankind might know how to attain "unanimous devotion to justice and freedom."

Details of the institute or council were not worked out much beyond the suggestion that it might become "something like a university, except that it would be limited to the study of freedom, it would do no classroom teaching, it would not confer degrees, and it would not require them of its members." This "ideal or ultimate form" would require an organization of full-time men.[40]

The directors authorized further study of the proposal and provided funds to gather an advisory board to meet during the summer.

The five-man board, selected by Hutchins in consultation with a committee of directors, consisted of historian Eric Goldman of Princeton University; philosopher Richard McKeon of the University of Chicago; theologian John Courtney Murray, S.J., of Woodstock College; anthropologist Robert Redfield of the University of Chicago; and political scientist Clinton Rossiter of Cornell. The *ad hoc* committee, selected by Paul Hoffman, was composed of George Shuster (openly in favor of Hutchins's plan), [41] Meyer Kestnbaum (a board member of Adler's Institute for Philosophical Research), and Howard Marshall (one of Hutchins's most consistent partisans).[42]

Three sessions of the advisory board took place. In addition to the appointed members, several other prominent individuals were invited to attend the meetings, including Mortimer Adler, philosopher Jacques Maritain, and Joseph Klein of St. John's College. (Logical positivism was somewhat poorly represented!) More opinions of Hutchins's proposal were solicited through interviews.[43]

Hutchins reported the summer's findings in a fourteen-page memorandum to the board dated September 6. The recommendations were almost precisely those submitted earlier by the Fund's president, altered slightly to appeal more directly to the board members. The Fund should continue to provide the nation "with reports on the operations of American institutions connected with freedom and justice," but the effort "should be directed and conducted by a group of men of the highest distinction, aided by assistants and consultants, who will devote full time over a period of years to examining the state of the free man in the United States and ideas and institutions associated with the terms 'liberty' and 'justice.'"

> . . . we are not suggesting the establishment of an ideological center. It should not get bogged down in metaphysical or theological super-

stition. The American Idea is directed to action—the functioning of a free society—and the effort we propose would have to limit its concerns to ideas which relate directly to action in the political and social orders.

We have faith that once the issues are clarified, the good sense of the American people will be brought into play, with highly beneficial results. We believe that issues now fogged in useless controversy will be satisfactorily resolved according to time-tested principles of justice and freedom, once the people see clearly what the issues are.

Hutchins requested authorization to prepare a plan (with the advice of the *ad hoc* committee of the board) to implement the proposals for presentation to the directors at the annual meeting in November.[44]

In response to expressions of dissatisfaction from several directors, Hutchins submitted, on October 15, a forty-four-page memorandum to the board, defending and elaborating upon his proposal to transform the Fund for the Republic. It began with a brief review of the genesis of the idea.

My reconsideration of the program of the Fund began with the three-year report. It did not lead me to conclude that what the Fund had been doing was wrong. On the contrary, it confirmed the view that the program was inevitable and desirable. It did, however, suggest that we had reached a stage at which we should look around, take stock, and decide whether the methods we had used in the past were necessarily the best for the future.

I did not come to this conclusion for public relations reasons, because of a wish to avoid controversy, to propitiate the Treasury and the House Un-American Activities Committee, or to evade the responsibility of making some contribution to education on current, practical problems. I was impressed by the tremendous range of the Fund's work, and I was compelled to admit that the criteria used to arrive at the recommendation or rejection of grants and projects were not altogether clear or consistent. It seemed to me to follow that if more intelligible standards of action could be developed the Fund would be better understood. . . . My effort has been prospective, rather than retrospective, and in my opinion should have been made even if the work of the Fund had been obviously perfect in every way. It seemed to me that if we could figure out what civil liberties needed, we could arrive at what the Fund needed with relative ease.

The Fund's collection and presentation of facts, Hutchins continued, evoke a valuable but insufficiently enlightening effect due to the prejudices inevitably read into the facts. Clear standards of truth are lacking nowadays; there is no commonly understood frame of reference in which the complex issues of civil liberties may be seriously discussed. Two readers of, say, the blacklisting study could come away with entirely different reactions. Merely "to collect the facts and to expect education to result from their publication and discussion when there are grave differences about the significance of the facts is shown by our experience to be somewhat less profitable than we had hoped." What is needed in addition to the Fund's presentation of data on current events of consequence is serious thought about what *ought* to be done in civil liberties and civil rights. The Fund should ask: "Given the law, the facts, the history, and the aims of our society, what should we do? The reply is not a theory, but a program of action."

> The point is that the facts would continue to be presented, but in such a way that they might be better understood, and, *in addition*, an effort to comprehend and explain the basic issues would be made. The effect of this should be to promote discussion that would be less heated and more enlightening than what we would be likely to get otherwise.

Hutchins then presented a series of proposals, still quite general, for implementing his recommendation. In total they comprised the framework of his long-sought academy.

A center should be created, preferably in or around New York City, in which a number of "qualified" individuals of diverse backgrounds and points of view, selected by the president, would be involved full-time "in the examination of institutions and practices and in the study and clarification of ideas relating to action." This "central group," or "faculty," would be given the authority, subject ultimately to the approval of the board of directors, to plan and carry out the future activities of the Fund for the Republic. Its chairman would be Robert M. Hutchins.

The central group could create and direct its own studies (employing fellows, assistants, and outside participants as it desired), establish discussion groups composed of experts to critcize work in progress, sponsor public meetings, arrange for visitors and conferences, award fellowships and grants-in-aid, and produce and distribute publications. It would have the power to decide what past programs the Fund would discontinue. Its members would receive the same degree of financial independence they would enjoy as full professors in leading universities, and "would have to be free to speak and write as they chose."

The board of directors would determine the Fund's "general policies" and be "roughly analogous to the board of trustees of a college." It would approve the "major members" of the central group, the group's general "areas of work," and an annual budget. Directors could share in the interrelated studies as participants in the discussion groups, through *ad hoc* committees, and as individuals.

> The relationship of the Board to the program of the Fund would be more intimate than it is now. In general the grantees, projectors, and fellows of the Fund are now independent contractors with whom the Board has no contact, beyond progress reports, after it has approved the appropriations. For example, Rossiter will spend $400,000 or more of the Fund's money and publish 13 books without any control from the Officers or the Board and without the approval of any academic group or faculty.

The Fund's officers would be consulted in formulating the center's over-all program. Primarily, with the exception of President Hutchins, they would "be to the Fund as the administration is to a college."

The operating procedures of the center would not be complex. The central group (which Hutchins suggested be called "The Council on Rights and Liberties") would arrive at a theme for consideration and would present it to the board, together with an estimate of costs. If the board approved, the group would determine how the subject could best be handled, and might commission, or undertake themselves, legal and historical investigations to shed light on their labors. These studies, as they developed, would be criticized by the discussion groups composed of outside experts and directors. Meanwhile, the central group would be discussing the deeper aspects of the topic in regular meetings. The studies, as they came in, would be fitted into the group's discussions if considered worthy. Outside studies, works by central group members, or both, would be published and distributed as the group saw fit. The goal would be a series of authoritative and durable publications illuminating the "basic issues" of complex and significant topics in civil liberties and civil rights and setting forth the basis of a sound public policy with regard to them. The Fund's efforts would cease to be scattered "all over the lot."

How would the Fund pay for the addition of a center? Many projects supported by the Fund were almost completed and were not likely to be duplicated. And certain current activities, such as the television news-clip service and the award program, might be discontinued. The Fund would channel its remaining monies into the center, and to "make the Fund last longer" would actively begin to seek additional financial resources.

This key point in Hutchins's recommendation was startling—far beyond anything emanating from the summer advisory board or the *ad hoc* committee. No longer was the Fund for the Republic to be a short-lived grant-making body; it was now planned to be self-sustaining and permanent. The president's attempts to gear his proposal to the Fund's historical development were wisely brief.

Hutchins knew his board members well and framed this memorandum carefully. He used the word "practical" eighteen times in the first fourteen pages; his style became charitably repetitive. The directors were promised less controversy ("The first effect of this plan would be to take the Fund off the defensive"), while at the same time they were assured that the Fund could not be thought to be retreating from the line of fire. Moreover, they were offered an active role in the center's studies; they were referred to as "experts." Although Dr. Hutchins suggested that the central group be composed of men like George Kennan, Robert K. Carr, Robert Redfield, John Courtney Murray, and Reinhold Niebuhr ("The common characteristic of these men is that they have spent their lives wrestling with practical problems"), he wrote:

The recommendation of this memorandum would not be necessary if the Directors, who are the kind of people who would be sought for the group proposed, could drop everything and devote themselves to the Fund.[45]

In spite of this cajolery, and the challenging offer to participate in the search for universal truth, several directors greeted Hutchins's plans for the Fund, fully apparent in the October memorandum, with disinterest. Before the annual meeting this disinterest, compounded with several personal considerations, led to the retirement of John Lord O'Brian, Chester Bowles, and James D. Zellerbach.[46] Roger D. Lapham, deciding reluctantly to remain, complained to Paul Hoffman:

> Perhaps I'm not educated enough to deal in the abstract along the lines Bob seems to enjoy. . . . I've been trained in the school of getting down to brass tacks. Maybe Bob will find it hard to adjust himself in a school where you have to watch the cash till instead of appropriating cash which flows from contributions not accumulated by personal effort.
>
> When I consider this proposal to study the theory and practice of freedom I'm reminded of what I believe Thomas Huxley said about philosophy; "Philosophy is a hunt in a dark room of an empty house at midnight for a black cat that isn't there." . . .
>
> Aside from any changes in the board it will be very much of a new picture if Bob's proposal is adopted. Frankly, I hope it won't be.[47]

Rebellion, rather than dissent, burst from the ranks of the Fund's officers when, two weeks before the board's annual meeting, Adam Yarmolinsky and David Freeman prepared an unsolicited seventeen-page counterproposal, soon revealed to the directors. Unlike the Hutchins plan, this memorandum contained much detail and an attention to statistics. It was directed toward methods by which the Fund would be liquidated in 1961 with "the greater likelihood of leaving a legacy of continuing interest and activity" to workers in the fields of civil liberties and civil rights. Its emphasis was on the Fund's original mandate.

The writers agreed with the Hutchins contention that a change in the general political atmosphere of the nation during the past four years warranted a major encounter with the "basic issues" of civil liberties and civil rights. They disagreed, for two major reasons, with the new method proposed to achieve this end: (1) there was little likelihood that more productive scholarship on the basic issues would emanate from a continuous group effort than from the studies of a widespread assortment of individuals, useful and productive in their own universities and communities; (2) group members might not be the most qualified to do the planning and grant-making assigned to them in the president's proposals, bringing on a host of thorny problems. The two authors of the memorandum were also concerned about increasing the ratio of overhead to program expense, carefully scrutinized by the Treasury Department: "To the extent that the group plans other people's work and makes policy decisions, it could be said to be engaged in the normal administrative functions of a foundation."

The Fund's emphasis, they maintained, should be on making grants to strengthen and encourage independent tax-exempt organizations with similar interests.

> Particularly in the civil rights area, we suggest that a program of grants assumes what we believe to be the case—that no individual or group of individuals can find *the* answer to the problem, but that many groups, with different approaches, will help to work out common-sense solutions. We believe that the Fund, for practical as well as public-relations reasons, should eschew the position that it knows best how to solve the major problem in its field.

Copious and carefully conceived suggestions for utilizing future grants consumed almost half of the memorandum. Included was a promise to cut the current yearly overhead of almost $750,000 (made up, in large part, by staff salaries, legal fees, and the public-information program) by at least 50 per cent.[48]

But the future of the Fund for the Republic belonged to Dr. Hutchins. The board had given him firm control of the reins in January and he had held them with distinction. Several significant contributions had appeared within the last year and more were on the way; most of the directors were obviously pleased with the manner (however expensive) in which the Fund had discredited its opposition. The time was perhaps in sight when it could combine meaningful achievement with even greater safeguards against credible attack. The president's suggestion, while not yet detailed, was reasonable; its presentation was authoritative and attractive.

Moreover, with Zellerbach and O'Brian leaving, Griswold's voice would be less commanding. The two distinguished citizens invited to attend the November meeting as prospective directors were known to think very highly of the president, and Harry Ashmore, returning to the board after duties with the Democratic party, was a personal friend.

Freeman and Yarmolinsky had made a daring gamble with their frank and determined memorandum. Their future with the Fund was likely to be, at the least, circumscribed.[49]

During the first day of the annual meeting in New York's Plaza Hotel, the board of directors appeared quite receptive to the heavily detailed grants and appropriations recommended by the officers.

The unprecedented study of communist influence in American life, of which the directors had been so justifiably proud when under fire, received an additional $130,000 to complete the costs of the eleven or twelve volumes (scheduled for total completion by August 1959). Further grants of $5,000 each went to the National Boards of the YMCA and YWCA to assist their work in race relations on the campuses of southern colleges. A 1955 grant to the Board of Social and Economic Relations of the Methodist Church for interracial work and conferences was renewed to the sum of $25,000. The Council for Social Action of the Congregational Christian Churches receive a renewal grant of $7,500 to promote discussion of civil-liberties issues among its members. Ben Segal received an appropriation of $35,000 to further his program on civil liberties with trade unions. A supplementary grant of $20,000 went to the Association of the Bar of the City of New York Fund, Inc., for study of methods of representation of indigent criminal defendants.

The first item on the agenda for the next morning was the election of two new directors. Joining the board were Alicia Patterson, editor and publisher of Long Island's *Newsday,* and the Pulitzer Prize-winning historian of the American Civil War, Bruce Catton.

The docket of new requests then came under consideration.[50] Dr. Hutchins had not been able to acquire board approval for a specific study of right-wing extremists, even though several studies, notably the Cogley report, had penetrated many of their activities. He now presented a proposal approved by President Henry Heald of New York University, before Heald resigned to head the Ford Foundation. It was an inquiry to identify and describe extremists taking part in hearings on the fluoridation of New York City water, an analysis of the press coverage of the hearings, and a study of the arguments on the constitutionality of public water fluoridation. The $25,000 study was to be supervised by New York University's department of sociology.

On the board's first evenly divided vote, the recommendation was turned down. Directors Parten and Marshall, integral members of the Hutchins coterie, then entered the room, barely missing the show of hands. The president would not come that close again to victory on the issue of right-wing extremism.

The board then went into executive session. When the full meeting resumed, Elmo Roper assumed the chairmanship held by Paul G. Hoffman since February 18, 1953. Hoffman would continue to be a director, but his many responsibilities no longer allowed him the time to be the vigorous chairman he had always been.[51]

The Hutchins proposal for a basic-issues center was then discussed, each member being asked to express his view. There was little disagreement over the suggestion to concentrate much of the Fund's resources on the clarification of basic issues, but considerable argument took place over the superior method for doing so. While the Freeman-Yarmolinsky appurtenance went unexplored (according to the record), Hutchins was forced to accept much less than he desired.

The president was authorized to employ temporary consultants, with the advice and consent of the *ad hoc* advisory committee of the board, to assist in identifying the most important areas for study. One or more areas would be submitted to the board at its next meeting in February and would be considered on a project basis. Griswold and Lapham voted against the $20,000 appropriation.

Hutchins told the directors determinedly that "this approach could be a first step which, if successful, might lead to the establishment of the kind of council recommended in his memorandum." Ultimately, of course, he was correct.

After lunch the directors again turned to the thirty-two-page "Recommendations to the Board." The sum of $100,000 was authorized to assist, with the help of other foundations, a complex program to recruit and train personnel in the field of intergroup relations.[52] The National Planning Association was authorized to receive a grant of $10,000 as a contribution to a study of effects of racial tension on the location of American industry.[53] The board vetoed the officers' recommendation to continue support of the cartoon feature "It's Your America," and voted $1,079 to close out the project. The National Council of the Protestant Episcopal Church was granted $19,250 to assist its Church and Freedom celebration. The distribution program was continued with an appropriation of $50,000, and a dozen articles and books were approved for dissemination. The board chose not to include "Patriotism on the Far Right, by Gordon D. Hall. A documentary analysis of certain extremist groups."

The concluding business embraced an appropriation of $15,000 for continued experimental work in radio and television, and a grant of $4,850 to the Association for Education in Journalism for a study of the foreign press treatment of civil-liberties issues in the United States.

By the close of 1956 the fury of the Fund's critics was waning noticeably. Frederick Woltman belatedly questioned the loyalty of Michael Harrington in his syndicated column, but the story was used neither by other newspapers nor by the wire services, and was dropped from the final edition of his own *World Telegram and Sun*.[54]

On December 9 the Fund issued a pamphlet by Walter Millis entitled "Communism and Civil Liberties." It warned Americans of new dangers from the pathetically dilapidated American Communist party.

. . . it will resume "the fight for legality"; it will now operate in the open; it will eschew "left-sectarianism"; it will endeavor to strengthen its appeal to Americans by working less exclusively in the interests of Soviet Russia and in blind adherence to Marxist-Leninist dogma.[55]

How could anyone any longer seriously consider the Fund "soft" on Communism? Who could declare that it considered the Communist menace to be "just another political party"? Was there a doubt whether the Fund was a "friend or foe" in the struggle against Soviet Marxism? The large headline in the New York *Herald Tribune* read: "FUND FOR REPUBLIC CHALLENGES U.S. REDS' NEW LOOK"; *The New York Times* trumpeted "FUND FOR REPUBLIC SCORES REDS IN U.S. AS STILL CONSPIRATORIAL."[56]

With the internal problems of the Fund settling down, with the external din subsiding, and with the Rossiter project on American Communism about to produce its first fruit, the future appeared much more likely to be tranquil than it had a year earlier.[57]

The directors had a specific reason to be optimistic as they assembled for their first board meeting of 1957. For months Frank Kelly and a committee of the board had been planning a gala demonstration of confidence in the Fund for the Republic. In November it had been attached to the American Tradition awards, the program inviting citizens to send letters describing extraordinary achievements by groups or individuals in defense of freedoms within and beyond the Bill of Rights. Scheduled to attend the American Traditions dinner on February 21 were federal judges, members of both branches of Congress (including Speaker Rayburn), leading clergymen, labor leaders and businessmen, and the project's distinguished panel of judges: General William F. Dean, U.S. Army (Ret.); James B. Carey, president of the International Union of Electrical Workers; Mildred McAfee Horton, former president of Wellesley College; the Right Reverend Henry Knox Sherrill, presiding bishop of the Protestant Episcopal Church; the Most Reverend John J. Wright, Catholic bishop of Worcester, Massachusetts; Henry Nunn, retired president of the Nunn-Bush Shoe Company; and Judge Samuel I. Rosenman. Newsmen, five hundred of them, were also invited.

The dinner was especially timely, for Fulton Lewis, Jr., was heating the atmosphere once again over his network radio program. In early January, Mrs. Mary Knowles was convicted of 52 counts of contempt of Congress and sentenced to 120 days in jail and a $500 fine. Lewis took great joy at the conviction and pounded away at the Fund's award to the Plymouth Monthly Meeting. Noting that the sentence handed Mrs. Knowles was the heaviest ever given a woman for contempt of Congress, he called attention to the fact that the judge in the case was from Oklahoma, and only temporarily sitting in the federal court in the District of Columbia. His action, Lewis philosophized, "suggests perhaps that Judicial perspective from the grass roots of America holds Communism in somewhat different importance than the routine judges of the East seem to do."[58]

Representative Gordon Scherer took the cue to lash out at the Fund in a letter to the director of the Council for Social Action, made public on January 27th. HUAC's investigation of the Fund "was barely started," wrote Scherer, and instead of criticizing the committee "it is time that some people . . . join with us in chasing the criminal instead of always attacking the policeman." Pointing to the conviction of Mrs. Knowles, he asked the letter's recipient if he approved of the $5,000 award, "and do you feel that such funds should be tax-exempt?"[59]

The day before the dinner was to take place, the board held a meeting at the Shoreham Hotel in Washington, D.C. Three eminent additions were made to its ranks: Dr. Henry P. Van Dusen, president of Union Theological Seminary, author, professor, and trustee of the Rockefeller Foundation; Msgr. Francis J. Lally, editor of *The Pilot,* the weekly newspaper of Boston's Roman Catholic archdiocese; and the former governor and senator of New York, Herbert H. Lehman. The principle business of the afternoon consisted of reports by staff members and the authorization of a $16,000 grant to extend the American traditions project through May 30 and to pay for the following evening's activities.[60]

The next morning the meeting recommenced, and the president initiated discussion of his latest recommendation, dated February 6, for the basic-issues studies. The board had revealed

254 / Freedom and the Foundation

obvious reluctance toward Hutchins's desire to dedicate the remaining half of the Fund's money to the pursuit of philosophical verities, but the president procedeed persistently in his campaign for the academy, continuing to adjust the mechanics of his proposal slightly to meet the practical inclinations of the directors.

In compliance with the motion passed in November, Hutchins requested a $100,000 appropriation to retain full-time consultants to the president, who would attempt "to work out and clarify the meaning and significance of civil liberties in the United States today." To do this they would, in part, gather information on and study the operations of the nation's "principal institutions": the government, the corporation, the union, the church, the voluntary association, the mass media, and the educational system. Consultants would hope to ascertain the effects of rapid change within these institutions on civil liberties, contributing to clarification of the basic issues.

The consultants would meet "frequently and regularly"—possibly up to six weeks at one time in the summer—and serve at least until June 30, 1958. One or more of them would have "a special responsibility for each study" and each project would have its own advisers. Board members would be "liaison directors" for various studies, and the chairman and vice-chairman would be "invited to attend all meetings and should receive all materials discussed."

Three potential three-year studies were described: "The Corporation and the Freedom of the Individual," "The Common Defense and Individual Freedom," and "The Church in a Democratic Society." Within the latter project, for example, such questions could be encountered as:

1   What are the limits of religious eccentricity?
2   What role do the churches play in enforcing patterns of conformity? . . .
3   To what degree can political attitudes be traced to religious commitments?

Hutchins recommended that the projects be approved "in principle," on the understanding that further details would be submitted later. "The sample projects indicate that any fears that the attempt to clarify basic issues would mean a retreat from reality are groundless."

To reduce overhead, Hutchins proposed the closing of the Fund's Pasadena office and assured the board that the present staff could administer the new program without substantial increases in cost. In fact, he asserted, if the Fund were to devote itself entirely to a complete reorientation as soon as possible ("This is a preference and not a recommendation"), reductions in overhead could be in the hundreds of thousands of dollars.[61]

Following discussion, Chairman Roper summarized "the sense of the Board": The directors were "not at this time voting on the president's expressed preference to obligate the uncommitted balance of the Fund's assets for the study of the basic issues," but recognized that certain grant-making activities could no longer bear fruit. The $100,000 appropriation to retain consultants was approved with but one dissent (Lapham), and the three projects were accepted tentatively—with the addition of "The Labor Union and the Freedom of the Individual." Elmo Roper asked the officers to prepare and present at the May meeting an over-all plan for the future of the Fund for the Republic. Its contents should not have been entirely unpredictable.

The last order of business concerned a recommendation by the board's Public Information Committee to advertise stories gathered in the American traditions project as well as publications and activities of Fund grantees. The board appropriated $240,000 for this public-relations effort, and gave the five-man committee almost total authority to direct its expenditure.[62] That no board member voted against this costly proposal is a clear indication of the depth of the directors' remaining fear. (A short time earlier, when asked if HUAC intended to include a public probe of the Fund and Dr. Hutchins in its forthcoming agenda, Francis Walter threw back his head and laughed. "I shouldn't be surprised!", he said.[63])

The dinner that evening was described later by Frank Kelly, its designer, as "the turning point in our relations with our critics."

When the stories reached the papers, bales of mail in our favor came pouring in. Critics of the House Committee on Un-American Activities screamed. Sam Rayburn and many others realized who we were and what we were doing.[64]

Behind this realization lay something other than a cold display of facts.

Chairman Roper, eager to impress his large and distinguished audience with the Fund's highest motives, gave a lengthy introduction to the evening's major address, in which he dropped a score of names and titles and poured quantities of treacle.

The chairman of the board of judges was General William F. Dean (U.S. Army, Retired), holder of the Congressional Medal of Honor, the Distinguished Service Cross, the Distinguished Service Medal, the Legion of Merit, and the Bronze Star. General Dean has suffered for America—in battle and in Communist torture chambers. He proved, by his endurance in body and in strength of soul, that he carried the American tradition in his mind and heart.[65]

Hundreds of letters had been submitted to the program's judges. They selected for the first-place award the dramatic story of a courageous Florida politician, John Orr, Jr., who risked his political future by telling his state legislature that segregation was morally wrong and casting a lone negative vote on a bill designed to circumvent the Supreme Court's ruling on school integration.

To illustrate the spirit of this action, the evening's principal speaker, Bruce Catton, delivered a blatantly unctuous address entitled "The American Tradition."

If any one word tells what America really is, it is that one word—freedom.

This is a word that is eternally growing broader. If any single thing gives us reason to have confidence in the infinite future of the American people it is the fact that this most basic of our traditions is capable of infinite expansion. It does not limit us. On the contrary, it forever invites us to grow—to see beyond the horizon, to look ahead to a fairer and a brighter day, to develop and to strengthen the noble concept of brotherhood by which we live. The Fund for the Republic is founded upon this living concept of freedom—and that is why I am proud to be a director of the Fund and to take part in this dinner tonight.[66]

"That speech drew tears from the audience," Kelly later recalled with a twinkle.[67] The Fund's vice-president had it attractively printed and mailed to hundreds of prominent citizens throughout the nation. Paul Hoffman sent dozens of copies to eminent friends in corporation circles, receiving glowing responses.[68] Representative Stewart L. Udall, who was present at the dinner along with fifteen other members of Congress, later called the address "perhaps the highlight of the evening," and inserted it into the *Congressional Record*.[69] Excerpts were published in the *Christian Science Monitor*.[70] The reactions to Catton's speech comprised another of the wondrous and seemingly never-ending reminders of the power of the patriotic platitude in America.

The campaign to muster friends amidst the ominous undercurrent of congressional and Treasury Department ferreting was running smoothly. On March 7, Elmo Roper announced the election of the three new directors and issued a lengthy statement on the Fund's purposes and achievements, including: "I submit that any one who reads the record cannot possibly come to the conclusion that the Fund for the Republic has been anything but a healthy force for the preservation of the best in American traditions."[71]

Two days later Congressman Morgan M. Moulder, second-ranking Democrat on the House Committee on Un-American Activities, who had attended the dinner and been greatly impressed by the Catton address, stated publicly that he did not agree with statements by Chairman Walter assailing the Fund. He declared that the earlier questions doubting the Fund's loyalty were made without his knowledge. "I was not in agreement with them," he said. When asked if he shared Mr. Walter's open distrust of the Fund, he replied: "I'm not suspicious of it."[72] Paul Hoffman and Dr. Hutchins granted interviews to a highly sympathetic "reporter" from the New York *Herald Tribune* who compounded their praise of the Fund's tasks with an emphasis on its research into American Communism.[73]

The next afternoon the first volume of that $250,000 survey was released. Theodore Draper's 498-page *The Roots of American Communism* covered in elaborate detail the complex party developments in America from the primary impact of the Bolshevik Revolution to 1923. With expert and dispassionate care, ex-Communist Draper portrayed the "birth and early childhood" of the futile attempt to weld Marxism onto an open American Left relatively unconcerned with serious ideology or class consciousness and unwilling to surrender its individuality to the Kremlin.

Granville Hicks was quoted by the publishers as writing: ". . . from now on no one will have a right to talk about Communism in America who has not read this book." Reviewers from Irving Howe, Norman Thomas, Bertram Wolfe, George Kennan, and Arthur Schlesinger, Jr., to Max Eastman, Sidney Hook, William Henry Chamberlain, and *Time* magazine were soon unanimous in their praise for Draper's exhaustive scholarship and judicious interpretations.[74] The valuable "employment" of Earl Browder for the study went unmentioned.

In a note prominently displayed within the volume, Clinton Rossiter wrote:

> The entire survey has been made possible through the foresight and generous support of the Fund for the Republic. All of us who have taken part in it are grateful for this exceptional opportunity to study the most confused and controversial problem of the age and to publish the results exactly as we find them.

Though the editors of the New York *Daily News* would determinedly contend that the Fund *and* Draper's book were highly suspect,[75] proponents of the Fund could now declare justly that it had contributed genuinely and effectively to an unprecedented and first-rate analysis of the origins of the nation's greatest political fear. Up to eleven more volumes were in the making.

Perhaps fearing that his charges against the Fund were becoming increasingly untenable, Congressman Walter made his next, long-awaited move on March 29. In a lengthy letter to Bethuel Webster, he asked the Fund to provide office facilities for members of his staff "to review documents relating to the

Fund's activities since December, 1952," and demanded the immediate surrender of scores of documents, including those relating to the blacklisting study which John Cogley had refused to produce at the hearings. The committee had been working with materials from the Fund's files for well over a year and the chairman knew exactly what he wanted. As Webster noted in his reply, the emphasis was on preliminary reports and appropriations that had not been put into effect. The total cost of the items warranting Walter's major attention was slightly over $5,000—of the $7,000,000 allocated. One item involved payments totaling $350 to an attorney in 1954 for research that was not used.[76]

Webster agreed to submit the request for office facilities to the Fund's board, but added that he would not advise that the request be granted. Almost all of the requested documents were mailed to Walter, except for the materials collected by Cogley and his staff. Webster pleaded for a moratorium on requests by HUAC of from two to three months while he was engaged in handling a federal suit.[77]

Within a week a letter was sent to Webster by another member of the House committee, Congressman Clyde Doyle, stating that he had learned from the American Legion's *Firing Line* that the Southern Regional Council had been identified before a state of Louisiana investigating committee as a "Southern Red front." "What investigation does the Fund for the Republic make," Doyle asked, "of the background or control of the personnel and policies of a proposed recipient of funds from the Fund for the Republic by way of a grant?"[78] Webster responded with an extensive defense of the Council, assuring the California congressman that the Fund "makes a careful and thorough investigation of all proposed grantees."[79] Doyle thanked Webster for his prompt reply, adding: "OUR BELOVED NATION DESERVES THE BEST OF WHATEVER WE ARE."[80] Very shortly John Cogley received a subpoena to appear before HUAC on May 15 with virtually all of the documents gathered during his research for the blacklisting report.

Cogley pondered the invitation for a few days and then replied. A majority of the committee members had agreed on July 10, 1956, to respect the confidential nature of his sources. "It seemed to me at the time that the Congressmen were upholding an American tradition according to which writers and journalists, as well as scholars, are not subject to harassment, are free to keep their sources confidential and in a very real sense enjoy the liberties guaranteed by the First Amendment." But now, he noted, that very same source material had been subpoenaed. After citing many of the newspaper editorials favoring his former stand, he wrote:

> When members of my staff interviewed people or wrote to them —and hundreds were consulted—it was with the understanding on both sides that we were free journalists writing in a free country. No one we interviewed or corresponded with had any idea that what he said or wrote would be turned over to a Governmental body. Were I to supply you with the material you demand, I would feel that I had betrayed these people. . . . I do not believe you want to investigate me personally. I have never belonged to any group that might be deemed subversive, even by the most elastic standards of the day. There is nothing in my record, nothing whatsoever, to justify suspicion. However, I will report to your Committee on May 15 and answer any questions your committee may want to ask about my life, my actions or my affiliations. I will do so willingly.

> But I will answer no more questions about anything I have written and published. I will not supply you with the documents you demand. In stating this, I know that I may be asking for a great deal of trouble. There may be a high price to pay. Please God, I will be ready to pay it.[81]

The Constitution implicitly forbids Congress to abridge freedom of the press by calling an author to account for what he has written; it was extremely doubtful that a congressional committee could compel Cogley to divulge his sources. No one was sure. Within a few days and without explanation the hearings were postponed until June 5. The postponement would shortly become indefinite.

CHAPTER THIRTEEN

Toward the Other Side of the Curtain

A lthough the Fund for the Republic would continue throughout the two years of what a spokesman called its "second phase" to support previous projects and to assist by small grants exceptionally worthy efforts in its fields of interest, the bulk of its attention was turned toward the inquiry into the basic issues of individual freedom and civil liberty. The board meeting of May 15–16, 1957, marks the formal point of the Fund's change of direction; it is here, in the wake of the unwavering persistence of Robert Hutchins, that the directors agreed to devote the corporation's major resources to the support of efforts by ten consultants to identify and clarify fundamental issues underlying the contemporary tumult over freedom and justice.

For weeks before the meeting Hutchins bombarded the directors with the newly developed particulars of his recommendation. In the case of the study of unions, for example, the outline designated labor authority Clark Kerr special consultant; liaison directors were Oscar Hammerstein II, Paul G. Hoffman, and Meyer Kestnbaum; the staff assistant was Paul Jacobs. A research committee for the study was already formed, consisting of Benjamin Aaron, associate director of UCLA's Institute of Industrial Relations; Walter Galenson, professor of industrial relations at Berkeley; Seymour Martin Lipset, sociologist and labor expert from Berkeley; Norman Jacobson, a political theorist from Berkeley's department of political science; and Philip Selznik, professor of sociology at Berkeley. In addition, twenty-seven of the nation's top leaders and students of labor and management were currently being consulted.

The nine-page proposal contained a lengthy list of possible basic issues in this area; under one heading alone appeared six "questions under consideration," including "Should there be the right of completely free entry into the union?" and "Should the rights of individuals and factions be protected by a judicial system within unions?"[1]

Committees were formed and in operation, guidelines had been discussed with specialists from around the country at informal conferences and meetings, further sessions were planned to decide upon future topics for study. The proposal (each project had its own elaborate outline) was presented to the Fund's directors as a well-considered, currently functioning package which they could accept, reject, or alter, the latter being the most complex and difficult.

The president had also considered the over-all question of finance: if the board approved his suggestions for the cancellation of unexpended appropriations and a series of terminal grants and appropriations, there would be over $7,000,000 with which to operate.

The board was informed officially of the identities of the central group of consultants: A. A. Berle, professor of corporation law at Columbia University; Scott Buchanan, philosopher and former dean of St. John's College of Annapolis, Maryland; Eugene Burdick, assistant professor of political science at the University of California, Berkeley; Eric Goldman, prize-winning professor of history at Princeton; Clark Kerr, labor expert and chancellor of the University of California, Berkeley; Henry R. Luce, editor in chief and publisher of *Time, Life,* and *Fortune*; John Courtney Murray, S.J., professor of theology at Woodstock College in Maryland; Reinhold Niebuhr, world-renowned theologian and vice-president of Union Theological Seminary; Isador Rabi, Nobel Prize-winning physicist and chairman of the General Advisory Committee of the Atomic Energy Commission; and Robert Redfield, professor of anthropology at the University of Chicago.

This enormously impressive and diverse collection of some of the nation's most capable intellects agreed with Dr. Hutchins about the advisability of the proposed labors; they were willing practically to donate their time and energy to undertake the basic-issues studies. Over a hundred other well-known Americans had also been consulted.

Many of the directors' favorite projects, which they might argue were indispensable, could simply be assimilated into the proposed studies, thus eliminating objections. The board's committee on overhead was not yet prepared to issue a report, but the president had a forecast already formulated and waiting to be approved. Board members found themselves not only promised but assigned more active roles in the Fund's work than they had ever enjoyed, as "liaison directors between the central group and the Board and between the various sub-groups and the Board."

Wrote President Hutchins:

> The purpose of the enterprise is to determine the essential requirements of a free society in the contemporary world and to show how these requirements may be met in the United States today. Paul Hoffman has taught us to say that the object of the Fund is to make the Bill of Rights a living document. The object of the group is to find out what it would mean to do this and how to do it.
>
> Their labors will therefore cover the range of interests of the Fund. Their attention is focused on the present situation, and their aim is to produce something immediately useful in understanding the present situation and in correcting it where correction is needed. . . .
>
> It would be pretentious to suppose that a group many times as intelligent as this, with many times the money that the Fund has left, could solve the problem of how to maintain a free society in an industrialized, polarized world. Even the problem of indicating the conditions under which such a society might flourish may exceed the powers of a group with a limited life and limited funds. But it should be possible to straighten out the issues, to show what the questions are, and to offer some preliminary answers that might be debated in the country. If the group did no more than make intelligible debate possible and get it started, it would create a lasting memorial to the Fund.

But the president had never been able to persuade all of the strong personalities on the board to accept the full breadth of his vision immediately. On the 15th, following much discussion, sixteen of the eighteen directors present (Griswold and Lapham voting in the negative) resolved to "concentrate" the Fund's efforts for one year on the study of the basic issues. The next day, "concentrate" was interpreted by the board to mean "the main effort but not the exclusive effort."[2]

The first two proposed projects were accepted unanimously: $189,750 was appropriated for a one-year study of "The Individual and the Corporation," and $142,275 was appropriated for a year's study of "The Individual and the Union."

Several objections appeared during the discussion of the third proposed study, "Religion in a Democratic Society." "It will deal with the relationship between Church and State," the directors read, "the role of religion in public life, the rights of religious dissent or non-conformity and, in general, with the meaning of freedom *from* as well as *for* religion." The title was softened by the board to read "The Individual and Religious Institutions in a Democratic Society," and a statement in the outline critical of the Supreme Court was deleted. But in spite of the precautions, the appropriation of $134,530 for a one-year study drew negative votes from directors Lehman, Linton, Lapham, Griswold, and Patterson.

The fourth study, on the impact of the government's defense policies on individual freedom, was accepted unanimously, and the requested sum of $88,300 authorized.

The board's Public Information Committee, along with the officers, was instructed to present a preliminary plan and budget at the next meeting for implementing the findings of the four studies. The officers were also requested to prepare a report on the assimilation of present personnel into the basic-issues program and a forecast of administrative overhead.[3]

A summary of the votes clearly reveals an overwhelming support for the fundamentals of Hutchins's view of the Fund's future; the commitment was now made to support what director Joyce called "the new direction the Fund was taking." Shortly, Adam Yarmolinsky, David Freeman, and Roger Lapham submitted their resignations.[4]

Two additional proposals for study were submitted by the

officers at the request of the consultants on September 19. The first concerned the relationship between the television industry and the Federal Communications Commission; the second, a revised version of the project on the Voluntary Association, focused on political parties, political pressure groups, and professional associations.

The directors rejected both projects, the first due to a reluctance to concentrate solely upon a federal agency, the second because they thought the outline "vague" and insufficiently attentive to the political pressure groups of the Left. On November 21, with reconstructed outlines, the proposals were accepted unanimously. The study of the mass media would concentrate not only on the relationship between government and the broadcasting industry, but also concern itself with standards of programming, the use of audience-rating systems, the handling of news and censorship, and the functioning of newspaper critics. The sixth study was designed to examine contemporary American political practices and procedures, and would soon bear the title "Study of the Political Process."[5]

Big trade unions; big industrial corporations; big government, particularly in relation to national defense; church and state; the mass media; the American political structure—these were the awesome matters confronting Dr. Hutchins and the consultants. "The world is hidden from us by the cliché curtain," Hutchins was soon to write. "The object of the Consultants is to get the issues clear so that rational debate may become possible. . . . The basic premise of the Republic is that the people shall judge. They cannot judge unless they have standards of judgement derived from principles firmly grasped and clearly understood."[6]

The framers of the Constitution had written their protective guarantees in terms of the government they knew—a small, closely knit structure employing less than five thousand persons. The Fund for the Republic was now dedicated to discover how the Bill of Rights could apply to institutions and situations Thomas Jefferson and his colleagues could not have imagined. What was happening to the individual in the nuclear age? Was he being manipulated by the mass media? In what ways were his freedoms compromised by bureaucracies over which he had no control? How was democracy holding up? Such questions are "conservative" in the truest sense.

The basic-issues program was the culmination of a lifelong desire of Robert Hutchins. The tasks might not yet involve a search for evidences of God, as his academy could have, but they were sufficiently formidable. No one was sure what would come of the experiment, including its author, but many wished it well. *The New York Times* editorialized:

> The fund has been spending its money by and large in some exceedingly useful directions despite ill-informed and often irresponsible criticism that has been directed against it. In so doing, the fund has helped strengthen American democracy, and the new study . . . gives every indication of being a major contribution to this end.[7]

W. H. Ferrry wrote to Mrs. Eleanor B. Stevenson:

> We have struck the mother lode, I think, in the Basic Issues Program. I confess my amazement at the amount of excitement and interest it is generating. What's more, everyone seems to understand what it is about, more than could be said of some of the other undertakings of the Fund.[8]

George Sokolsky lamented:

> Too bad that Voltaire is not alive to investigate the investigators, or, Marx to curse them for the poverty of their ideas, or Joe McCarthy to haul them before his committee to discover their foibles.[9]

On May 15, Bethuel Webster informed the directors of Francis Walter's request to review all of the Fund's files and of his own recommendation against allowing it. The board agreed to "hereby instruct Representative Walter that the Fund will not permit the general search of its files requested in Representative Walter's letter of March 29, 1957."

Webster visited the House committee's staff director Richard Arens on May 24, informing him of the board's decision. Arens questioned Webster's contention that he had "already supplied substantially all documents and information specifically requested," and called in one Donald Appel, a committee investigator doing a report on the Fund. Appel suggested that a meeting be held in Webster's office at a later date to examine and supplement his findings. The meeting took place on June 4, and the Fund's counsel, after much discussion, was asked to submit additional documents and information the committee had not gathered in eighteen months of intensive inquiry.

Webster complied in a stinging letter to Mr. Walter dated July 2. The requested materials were, in fact, obscure and of miniscule importance to the Fund's over-all operations. Wrote Webster:

> This final voluntary submission is made not because the data is reasonably pertinent to subjects of investigation assigned by the Congress to your Committee but to attempt further to make it possible, consistent with the desire expressed by Mr. Arens and Mr. Appel, for Mr. Appel to prepare a fair report of his investigation of the Fund and thus to put an end to false charges and fruitless investigation.

The Fund would not continue, Walter was informed, to supply internal papers and information irrelevant to a proper inquiry.[10]

By now John Cogley's appearance before HUAC had been postponed three times, the last time indefinitely. Cogley had written a moving article in *Commonweal* explaining the principals behind his refusal to comply with the committee's demands.[11] And Frank Kelly had mailed personal notes to scores of editors, along with copies of Cogley's letter to Walter, adding: "It seems to me that the Cogley case goes to the heart of the American tradition of freedom of the press."[12]

Indeed it did, and newspapers large and small throughout the nation roared with indignation over Walter's demands to secure Cogley's sources of information for the blacklist study. The Salt Lake *Tribune* editorialized: "This case should be watched closely by all interested in freedom of information. This freedom will be seriously abridged if writers stand in fear of being hauled before a congressional committee whenever controversial opinions are expressed."[13] Wrote *The Wall Street Journal*: "Where the principle of freedom of the press is involved, we see scant difference between one Congressional committee demanding the names of people who buy books and another Congressional committee demanding the names of people who helped write books."[14] *Editor and Publisher* declared: "If authors, researchers, scholars, editors, reporters or publishers cannot write and publish the facts as they see them, the opinions of others, or record their own opinions, without danger of inquisition then we have no freedom of press or thought."[15] "The spirit of American democracy," the Minneapolis *Star* pronounced, "flows from free inquiry and free expression—and congressmen should know this."[16]

Reached in Washington by *Variety*, Walter explained that he and his confreres had other business in San Francisco but expected another Cogley hearing at some undetermined time. He said he was unaware of Cogley's letter to him and of the *Commonweal* article. "He [Cogley] had information he tried to sell and is not so much concerned about protecting his sources as he is with not cooperating with the Government," was Walter's comment.[17]

Within a few weeks Senator Hubert Humphrey told the United States Senate: "Mr. President, I have been happy to notice lately in the public press that instances of unfriendliness toward, and misunderstanding of, the purpose of the Fund for the Republic have nearly died out."[18]

But Francis Walter would make one last serious attempt to rescind the Fund's tax exemption. In early February 1958, he gave copies of a HUAC staff report on the Fund to two reporters, one from the New York *Daily News* and the other from the Scripps-Howard newspapers. The report, said the subsequent articles, alleged that "working level" officials of the Internal Revenue Service had urged the revocation of the corporation's tax exemption nearly a year earlier; it requested that the government enforce this decision on the ground that the Fund had been engaged in propaganda activities.[19]

The report, unsigned by the committee's members, was not released; its charges were not documented publicly; its leak to the press, while not without precedent in HUAC's history, was far beyond normal congressional practice. The Fund's officers, unaware of the specific allegations lodged against the corporation, were unable to reply formally, but Dr. Hutchins protested Walter's tactic to each congressman on the committee.[20]

Fulton Lewis, Jr., obviously privy to the report, told his readers that "the galley proofs are already in hand from the Government Printing Office." The report "finds that everything that was ever charged against the Fund for the Republic—by me, the American Legion, or its hosts of other critics—was all true and a lot more." Loss of tax exemption "would mean, oh happy day, that the Fund for the Republic is out of business, under the terms of its charter."[21]

On March 26, Walter wrote a letter, soon released to the press, to Secretary of the Treasury Robert Anderson, urging the termination of the Fund's tax exemption. By "attempting to influence legislation," he contended, the Fund had given "aid and comfort" to America's Communist foes. Walter declined to make public the staff report, also submitted to Anderson, on the ground that its contents were "not entirely within the jurisdiction of the committee."[22]

Shortly, following a brief hearing at which no officer or director of the Fund was permitted to speak, the Internal Revenue Service asked the Fund for the Republic to "show cause" why its tax exemption should not be revoked.

This action was indeed as "shocking" as an editorial in the Washington *Post* described it.[23] The Treasury Department appeared to be knuckling under to pressure from a powerful congressman whose charges were cloaked in secrecy, beyond his committee's proper jurisdiction, without the official support of his fellow committeemen, and contrary to a fair and reasonable interpretation of the facts.

Walter had not objected to the proclamations of a recent convention of the tax-exempt Daughters of the American Revolution calling for repeal of the federal income tax, American withdrawal from the United Nations, severance of diplomatic relations with the Soviet Union, and the cessation of all foreign aid. These proposals were no doubt in the nation's best interest, in Walter's view. Yet he contended that the Fund for the Republic had been "a hindrance" in the struggle against Communism because it chose to test the balance of individual liberty and national security by sponsoring reputable examinations into congressional investigations of subversion, government security procedures, loyalty oaths, and the regulation of immigration. To what degree could individual congressmen enforce private definitions of patriotism? By what criteria was the federal government henceforth to determine subjects legitimate for foundation scrutiny? These questions reached far beyond the fate of one foundation, of course, for with the Fund's demise further efforts by tax-exempt bodies in the area of human rights would virtually disappear; the word "education" in the federal tax laws would carry ominous connotations for serious students and scholars.

A few years earlier Walter's strong-arm methods would perhaps have been successful. But McCarthy was dead and Washington had largely recovered from the poison he and his cohorts had injected into the atmosphere. HUAC itself had been slapped down hard by the Supreme Court for its often reckless and ruthless "exposures." Moreover, the Fund's intensive public-relations efforts had been highly successful, and few well-meaning citizens cared any more to link the corporation's programs in civil liberties and civil rights with subversive activities.

Following a meeting on April 10 between Bethuel Webster and Assistant Commissioner of Internal Revenue Justin F. Winkler, Paul Hoffman and J. R. Parten visited Secretary of the Treasury Anderson, who, as Parten later recalled, "gave assurances that he had no intention of embarrassing in any way the Fund's distinguished board."[24]

As late as July 1959, the Treasury Department received a letter from a congressman demanding that steps be taken against the Fund.[25] A month later the American Legion again called for the revocation of its tax exemption.[26] Fulton Lewis, Jr., would continue the harrassment until his death in 1966.

There were two principal parts to the new effort by the Fund for the Republic: support of the consultants—whom industrialist Cyrus Eaton admiringly dubbed the "Refounding Fathers"—in their attempt to discover and clarify basic issues, and the effort to create and distribute publications useful to public dialogue. The link between the two was a decision by the consultants that a paper presented to them for consideration was worthy of nationwide attention. Although individual consultants might write a few of the documents, it was declared publicly that Fund publications did not necessarily represent the views of the group. Moreover, on the advice of an executive from the Viking Press, the Fund attached a disclaimer to each of its publications asserting that the corporation was responsible only for deciding that the work should be printed and distributed. This was a measure employed by the Council on Foreign Relations and others to thwart pressures from critics of foundations.[27]

By October 1, 1959, fifty-four pamphlets, shorter "occasional papers," transcripts, and reports to the Fund had appeared, of which a million and a quarter copies were distributed.[28] A great many of the highly popular pamphlets were of superior quality, generating overwhelmingly favorable responses from the press and intellectual circles, and no doubt evoking much public discussion. Adult-education classes, colleges, high schools, and seminaries all over the country were eager to secure copies.

The first four pamphlets set the pace: "Individual Freedom and the Common Defense" by Walter Millis; "Unions and Union Leaders of Their Own Choosing" by Clark Kerr; "Economic Power and the Free Society" by A. A. Berle, Jr.; and "The Corporation and the Republic" by Scott Buchanan. Their common feature was a deep and intelligent concern for individual liberty.

Millis brilliantly analyzed government security measures in relation to contemporary world conditions. Kerr argued for greater democracy in trade unions. Berle warned of the emerging power of welfare funds and pension trust funds—drawing praise even from the New York *Daily News*.[29] Buchanan described our "passion for indiscriminate togetherness" and contended that individual freedom was threatened by the domination of institutions and organizations.

Among other authors of Fund publications were Andrew Hacker, assistant professor of government at Cornell University; Frederic Meyers, a member of the economics department at UCLA; Leo Bromwich of the research staff of UCLA's Institute of Industrial Relations; Herbert Mitgang, an editor of *The New York Times*; and political scientist Stephen K. Bailey of Syracuse University. Edited segments of discussions by the consultants were presented in book and pamphlet form; proceedings and excerpts from several conferences held in conjunction with the six projects were also published.

The new course of Fund activities also included the production of two television series. One, "The Press and the People," was presented over 640 kinescopes and 850 audio-tapes, and was broadcast overseas by the Voice of America. The other, perhaps the more important of the two, was the Mike Wallace program—the first time in the history of American broadcasting that a series of intellectual discussions was shown on prime time by a major network without commercial interruption. Interviewed by Wallace were Reinhold Niebuhr, Cyrus S. Eaton, William O. Douglas, Aldous Huxley, Erich Fromm, Adlai E. Stevenson, Sylvester L. Weaver, Jr., Arthur Larson, James McBride Dabbs, Harry Ashmore, Mortimer Adler, and Dr. Hutchins. More than 18,000 letters were received by the Fund, 99 per cent of them favorable. Edited transcripts of several of the interviews were distributed in pamphlet form; senators and representatives requested copies and inserted favorable comments into the *Congressional Record*.[30]

(On one of the Wallace programs millionaire industrialist Cyrus Eaton strongly criticized the FBI's alleged disregard of civil liberties. J. Edgar Hoover—soon to acknowledge that his bureau was operating ninety telephone wiretaps—rejected an offer by Dr. Hutchins to appear on the program and reply. The network then gave equal time, at Francis Walter's request, to Richard Arens, who defended Hoover, said that Eaton's remarks were "typical of a campaign of villification which the Communist conspiracy is promoting in the U.S. against our security agencies," and announced the signing of a subpoena requiring Eaton's appearance before HUAC! The subpoena was never served, and after a considerable number of editorials in the nation's press about freedom of speech and statements on Eaton's behalf by the American Civil Liberties Union and Senators Thomas Hennings, Paul Douglas, Hubert Humphrey, and Joseph Clark, Walter dropped the matter.[31])

The television programs and the literature, however, took second place in Hutchins's mind to the work of the consultants. ("These pamphlets must be regarded as incidental sparks from the anvil.")[32] The major task of the Fund was the clarification of the issues involved in maintaining a free and just society in the second half of the twentieth century—the premier effort by a major tax-exempt foundation to define the social, economic, and political pressures tending to limit individual freedom in contemporary America.

The consultants were called together for weekends at six-week intervals. The first discussions were, of course, exploratory and preliminary and full of the conflicts and clashes expected from dialogue between great teachers. Was light emanating from the friction? Elmo Roper, after reading the transcripts of several meetings, expressed skepticism as early as July 9, 1957.[33] Mortimer Adler studied the record of a session in September and became so disturbed that he wrote a thirteen-page letter to Dr. Hutchins, contending that "Collectively, the result is almost zero. There is almost no evidence that any member of the group learned anything from anything said by anyone else or was even stimulated to say something important and new by something said by someone else."[34] The disappointment was such that W. H. Ferry and Hallock Hoffman soon clashed over what it was the consultants were supposed to do.[35] Dr. Hutchins looked on hopefully, telling Adler of the consultants: "I don't say that they will do better. I say only that their inadequacy in the past does not prove that they will be inadequate in the future."[36]

In early 1958, Scott Buchanan confessed to "a kind of despair for the Consultants and their projects."[37] Several staff members urged Hutchins to take firmer control of the discussions.[38] By May even attendance at the sessions was causing Hutchins great concern: Rabi had suffered a heart attack and then became scientific adviser to NATO, Niebuhr and Redfield had been seriously ill, Kerr had become a university president, and Luce had been persistently unavailable.[39]

But Hutchins seemed confident that after seven consultants' meetings there had been "the gradual clarification of some basic issues for the members." He told his board on May 6:

We have a good deal yet to learn about the methods of making the most of the intellectual resources at our command. The procedures for the conduct of meetings, of relating the work of the projects to that of the central group, and of using outside experts can, and I hope will be improved. . . .

I believe that the effectiveness of the group would be enhanced if the members knew that the Board of Directors was committed to the program for a longer period than one year. I think we are now entitled to say that the program, in spite of the imperfections and uncertainties in it, is soundly conceived and will be successfully carried out. Even if it succeeds beyond our hopes, it will not solve all the problems—or even clarify all the issues—that plague our society. But it is already an important educational force, and there is every sign that it will continue to be so. I therefore suggest that the Board make a three-year commitment to it.[40]

The board—now including attorney Arthur J. Goldberg—had received edited transcripts of the consultants' meetings, as well as full reports on the busy and potentially fruitful activities within the six projects. Its decision at the May 21, 1958, meeting would be based on a sound knowledge of the progress of the basic-issues program.

The directors' hopes for the work of the consultants could not dim seriously on the basis of only seven brief meetings. Perhaps, as Dr. Hutchins contended, the sense of impermanence was a serious handicap; perhaps with more support the difficulties shared by the ten thinkers could be dramatically decreased. Moreover, the board was proud of the Fund's new printed materials; hundreds of organizations had swamped the corporation's mailing facilities with requests, and the reviews were almost unanimously favorable. For the first time in years, the Fund for the Republic seemed out of danger and on a solid path toward lasting contributions to an American understanding and appreciation of the heritage of freedom. Without a dissenting vote the board voted to appropriate $4,000,000 for a three-year continuation of the basic-issues program.[41]

But a steady disintegration of the consultants' efforts at outstanding discussion commenced shortly. On October 16, 1958, Robert Redfield died.[42] Meetings began to be canceled as members found themselves forced to be absent because of other commitments. One consultant resigned in a huff over philosophical differences of opinion with his colleagues. The conversations (to be analyzed in the concluding chapter) pleased virtually no one.

Hutchins experimented with various formats for the consultants' meetings to ease tension among participants and strengthen contributions. He invited his old friend William O. Douglas to become a consultant and assist the group's concentration on constitutional and legal considerations.[43] He repeatedly asked for suggestions to improve the discussions. But by March 15, 1959, only five consultants attended one of the much-delayed meetings.

It was evident to all concerned by early 1959 that the heart of the Fund's "second phase," the sessions of the central group, had failed. The consultants had met twelve times for a total of thirty days; their conversations, bound in blue, were placed in storage.

In a May 5, 1959, memorandum to the board Hutchins described the Fund's method for identifying and clarifying basic issues as "experimental and expensive."

> On the basis of our experience it is clear that though part-time men can be effective critics they cannot be relied on to develop and guide a program in this vast and complicated field. They are under too many different pressures. The more famous they are, the greater the pressures.

The star-studded sessions had resulted from a compromise with the board; Hutchins had asked three years earlier for a residential center, inhabited by full-time thinkers devoted to intensive and sustained dialogue. He now repeated his request: he proposed his academy anew.

The Fund should sponsor, wrote Hutchins, a "Center for the Study of Democratic Institutions," located somewhere outside New York City to insure freedom from distraction. It would undertake on a permanent basis for an indefinite period the tasks which had confronted the consultants in their hurried and harrying confrontations on occasional weekends.[44] The funds had been appropriated, the board was committed to the goal; there remained only matters of detail.

On the evening of May 20 the board met at the Biltmore Hotel in New York City. President Hutchins formally announced the opportunity for the corporation to purchase a magnificent residence on a forty-one-acre estate high above the lovely coastal city of Santa Barbara, California, to accommodate the new center. Donors in California had offered to contribute $100,000 to make a move possible; director William Joyce, a resident of Santa Barbara (as was Hutchins), assured the board that the purchase would be a wise financial investment.

The directors voted unanimously to purchase the California property for $250,000, to establish an office there, and to change the title of the basic-issues program to the Center for the Study of Democratic Institutions. George Shuster was employed as a consultant to devise and direct measures to raise money to supplement the remaining balance of about $4,000,000 for the Fund's continuous operations.[45] The center was to be the object of the Fund's complete attention.

On June 18, 1959,[46] the new headquarters was established in the neoclassic white stucco villa surrounded by towering eucalyptus trees and blessed with the fragrance of lush gardens and the refreshing breezes of the Pacific Ocean. (Greek philosophers noted twenty-five centuries ago that one thinks better in beautiful surroundings.) Robert Hutchins at last had his academy: the Fund for the Republic was in what may be called in retrospect its "third phase."

During the remainder of the year the organization of the center took shape. Four of the staff members and officers who administered the basic-issues studies—Frank Kelly, John Cogley, W. H. Ferry, and Hallock Hoffman—now became integral members of the small corps of resident intellectuals selected by Dr. Hutchins for the collective pursuit of wisdom. Harry Ashmore, now a Pulitzer Prize winner, soon left Arkansas to join them.[47] The consultants became important primarily for the prestige their names and titles showered upon the center. Their formal meetings were suspended and they played little or no part in the center's activities.[48] The six projects soon began to fade into the expanded concerns of the center, and their large and expensive advisory committees were abolished.

At John Cogley's suggestion, the practice of a daily conference of the residents of the center began in late September.[49] For an hour and a half each day, staff members and visiting intellectuals, under the relaxed guidance of Dr. Hutchins, presented and discussed learned papers relating to the survival and strengthening of democracy. A major purpose of the sessions, soon called together by the ringing of a monastery bell, was the distillation, by continuous and hard-hitting dialogue, of publishable documents designed to provoke and promote thought by the American people.

By October, Ferry described the atmosphere at the center to a friend:

> Our schedule is already heavy and getting heavier. Last week three days were devoted to discussion of the theory of democratic institutions. There was a seminar last night on the preamble to the Constitution. At noon today Gerard Piel (Scientific American) comes to lunch and spends the rest of the day with us on Technology and Law. We expect Aldous Huxley and others from the University of California also to be on hand. On Friday we begin discussions of the Trade Union, based on a paper prepared by [Paul] Jacobs. . . . Walter Gellhorn will spend a day with us the following week, and we hope to persuade him to enlarge on the idea that non-action by the State is official action in a different form. We have additional discussions coming up on [Walter] Millis's memorandum on Abolition of the War System, and so on and on.[50]

The demand for Fund publications increased steadily—55,000 copies of Berle's pamphlet had been sent out by December, and 10,000 more were printed.[51] Center literature—including excerpts from the daily discussions—would soon come pouring from the presses into the homes, schools, churches, and offices of millions of Americans who sought to make intelligent judgment of issues deeply affecting their lives.

The new enterprise soon enlisted "Founding Members," interested citizens, corporations, or foundations that would contribute $1,000 or more to the center. By October 1 gifts and pledges of donors totaled $155,000.[52] The William Benton Foundation had assisted the mass-media study, and there was some optimism that other tax-exempt bodies would render financial assistance. Much of the money-raising fell to Dr. Hutchins.

At an age when most men think fondly of retirement, Robert Hutchins had launched a facility unique to the modern world— a place where fine minds might come together regularly for a relatively uninterrupted and intensive examination of matters critical to the preservation of individual liberty. The aim of the center, he wrote, was that of the basic-issues program: "To clarify the issues of the free society so that a reasonable debate can take place, and then to promote the debate."

The clarification of issues so complicated and so important is a long and ardous task. The work that has been done so far and the spirit in which it has been carried on give some hope that it may eventually be accomplished through the Center for the Study of Democratic Institutions in cooperation with interested individuals in business, labor, religion, education, and government. The maintenance of a free and just society requires nothing less.[53]

CHAPTER FOURTEEN / *Conclusion*

*I*t is impossible, of course, to write an adequate conclusion to the study of a corporate body designed to sponsor, create, and disseminate ideas. One cannot even total the number of articles, pamphlets, books, films, speeches, advertisements, discussion groups, and seminars involved in the Fund's allocation of $11,000,000, let alone gauge their effects. What results in the struggle for racial equality may be attributed to the Fund's small grant enabling several southern journalists to travel throughout the world? What countereffect did a Fund-supported study on race and intelligence have against the widely publicized findings of a Villanova University professor which "demonstrated over and over" the mental inferiority of Negroes?[1] No one can weigh the results of a grant to the American Book Publishers' Council to found a censorship bulletin publicizing actions and attempts by public authorities and private groups to separate literature from readers.[2]

What may be achieved is a modest summary and evaluation of the Fund's strengths and weaknesses, its ideas, its friends and enemies. As for its efforts, the most obvious and probable successes and mishaps may be assayed and an overview provided by the careful selection of illustrative examples. First, however, two considerations must be interjected.

Harry Kalven, Jr., professor of law at the University of Chicago and long-time friend and colleague of Robert Hutchins, expressed the view in late 1957 that the Fund for the Republic "had not been a great success" largely because it "started too late" to do much against McCarthyism and because its studies "finish too late."[3]

It is true that the circumstances surrounding the Fund's implementation delayed a direct response to many of the decade's most outrageous attacks against civil liberties. But no one charged with the Fund's activities may be blamed for that. Moreover, a tax-exempt foundation would not have dared to attempt rapid and direct action against congressional proponents of McCarthyism. Dr. Hutchins told a television interviewer in 1956: ". . . what the Fund does is to get things studied. . . . to have a good conversation you have to know what the facts are."[4] This function was necessary; it also was unavoidably time-consuming. And who would contend seriously that McCarthyism was dead once and for all at the close of 1954 with McCarthy's tepid censure? The stormy field of civil rights, it should not be forgotten, was also part of the Fund's mandate.

From the very live issues it encountered, the critics it drew, and the hundreds of proposals it turned down, the Fund may be judged fairly by what its officers and directors did rather than by circumstances over which it had no control, consigning its efforts to failure without benefit of the evidence. There were sufficient tasks for the Fund's resources.

Kalven added to his conclusion: "For an institution to speak with a powerful voice in a crisis, it must carry a pre-existing reputation and prestige with it into the forum." The Fund's establishmentarian directors, each approved originally by the trustees of the Ford Foundation, brought the corporation instant reputation and prestige. Many major newspapers, moderately conservative and pro-Eisenhower, like *The New York Times,* doted on the distinguished composition of the board from the beginning. The Fund should be judged on the basis of its achievements rather than according to a false assumption that it was severely handicapped from its inception. The Fund was sufficient for the tasks.

The most imposing figure in the Fund's history is, of course, Robert Hutchins. From the creation of the very idea of the Fund, through the selection of the original directors, through his presidency, to the transformation to the basic-issues program, to the Center for the Study of Democratic Institutions, this one man dominates the story.

After the spring of 1954, Hutchins and the Fund were one. It could not have been otherwise, for Hutchins was not constituted to be a subordinate. His intellect, will, charm, his uncompromising views, equipped him only for leadership. Henry Ford II discovered this fact tardily; Erwin Griswold resisted it. Kalven wrote perceptively:

> . . . like legal heroes such as Holmes and Hand, Mr. Hutchins' power, stature and impact cannot be measured by what he has, from time to time, written. In these cases, the man is larger than his works, and there is something in his personality and style that makes him at times larger than life.[5]

The philosopher Scott Buchanan, whose close friendship with Hutchins spanned almost forty years, expressed frustration at being unable to describe the composition of qualities which provide him with an almost overpowering air of authority. "After all these years," he stated, "my wife still can tell by my reactions that evening when I have been alone in conversation with Bob."[6] There were very few matters about which Hutchins did not have his way concerning the Fund for the Republic.

Hutchins's vision, conviction, and courage necessitated Fund activity. The board was released from torpor only upon his accession to the presidency. It is possible that the directors, without dynamic leadership, would have suspended extensive and vigorous operations indefinitely. Foundations' widely noted evasion of controversial issues to this day confirms that possibility.[7]

A Hutchins presidency guaranteed boldness. Studies such as those of blacklisting, integrated housing, and intimidation of teachers might not have been pursued and published but for the president's persistence and patience. The selection of able (if inexperienced) officers and staff members, with the zeal of W. H. Ferry, the strength of John Cogley, meant that the Fund could not languish in indifference, too timid to authorize studies and present awards that would defend principle and affront opponents.

And yet it should be recognized that Hutchins's unwillingness to soften his language and his occasional inability to clarify publicly the Fund's intentions caused the corporation needless embarrassment. And if the board had allowed him to pursue direct investigations into the Radical Right or the press, the furor would undoubtedly have been greater than it was.

Moreover, until the board became deeply concerned over criticism and turned to the president for answers, the administrative procedures of the Fund were chaotic. Project and grant requests were passed around among officers and staff members almost at random, public-relations responsibilities were confused—one loyal staff member told Hutchins: "No one is sure of who at the Fund is responsible for what."[8] While clear job assignments were never to appear—Hutchins loathed the mechanics of organization—the more serious maladjustments were rectified.

In spite of board efforts, expenses—including "Program Development" and administrative expense exclusive of amounts allocated to projects—mounted by late 1959 to almost 35 per cent of the total amount spent on grants and projects.[9] Acknowledging the fact that the Fund's officers were faced with far more of a challenge than the simple examination of requests for money, that figure is extremely high for a tax-exempt foundation; one sympathetic writer referred to Hutchins, not unfairly, as "the 18th century rationalist with the 20th century expense account."[10]

In retrospect, the tension and heated debates between Hutchins and his fellow directors, integral to so many board meetings, resulted in strengthening the desire for vigorous action with a healthy restraint and a beneficial attention to detail. The often abrasive encounters between the concerned, business-minded men of reputation on the board and the far-seeing, intensely intellectual president enabled the Fund for the Republic to combine achievement with survival.

As late as November 1957, for example, the directors refused a Hutchins proposal to grant $10,000 to a small interracial community near Americus, Georgia, suffering from a violence-enforced economic boycott by local citizens. A few months earlier, however, the Southern Regional Council, a well-established and successful educational organization, had been granted an additional $200,000. From the distressing publicity attending such minor incidents as the brief employment of Amos Landman, the board had learned to veer away from actions promising little more than certain provocation. At the same time, it was perfectly willing to invest heavily, with the possibility of lasting effect, to alleviate the cancer of racial discrimination.

There is little evidence to suggest that the board's wariness on any subject deprived the nation of any exigent or significant display of facts. The interaction between Hutchins and the directors resulted in a well-tempered balance between wisdom and expedience, purpose and practicality, and was both fortunate and productive.

It seems inevitable that the Fund would have been the object of intense clamor even without Hutchins. In the first place, nearly all civil-liberties and civil-rights issues have been controversial through virtually every period of our national experience; only controversial liberties are ever jeopardized. The Ford Foundation recognized this fact by proclaiming the Fund's independence. Secondly, interracial relations were extremely tense after 1954. Perhaps above all, anti-Communism in postwar America had become a vested interest.

The Fund's mandate assumed the existence of excessive encroachments upon civil liberties in the name of patriotism. Walter Millis, in a memorandum to Hutchins in 1955, wrote:

> Politicians, publicists, the FBI, ex-Communists, the security bureaucracy, the ruling group in the American Legion, many elements in the Catholic Church, have combined to make an enormous emotional and political investment in anti-Communism. The anti-Communists have given themselves the label; and have arrogated to themselves a monopoly in the combat against Communism. It is now apparent, though seemingly it was not two years ago, that an organization which, like the Fund for the Republic, sets out to examine the methods of this monopoly, to question what seemed to be the excesses of its methods and to ask just what was the real menace which formed the basis of its power and authority, was bound to meet it in head-on and damaging collision.[11]

The issue of inevitable opposition must be enlarged, for anti-Communism was only one ingredient within a radical movement which had at its center a passionate desire to repeal the present. The embittered tirades of Fulton Lewis, Jr., and the transcript of the Walter hearings reveal more than a hatred of civil libertarians. They were assaults on a view of American life.

The phantasmagorical fears and hatreds of recent American "pseudo-conservatism," or McCarthyism, have undergone considerable scrutiny by historians and social scientists, providing us with provocative, though no doubt only partial, insights into the phenomenon.[12] It is important to note here that in large part the attack was against the effects of urbanization and the power structure commonly associated with it. At the vortex of this deep reactionary resentment against "liberalism" were men like Paul G. Hoffman, Clifford Case, Henry Ford II, and the editors of *The New York Times:* widely quoted, socially prominent, upper-middle-class citizens who had no basic quarrels with the New and Fair deals, who respected academic credentials, who liked Ike (and Adlai), who contributed to *Harper's,* subscribed to *Foreign Affairs,* and read *Time* and *Newsweek,* who professed belief in racial equality, who supported foreign aid and the United Nations, who played prominent (the Far Right frequently used "conspiratorial") roles in national political conventions, and who were often appointed to positions of authority by victorious candidates of both parties. When such men sought to "defend" civil liberties and civil rights with $15,000,000 the reaction was bound to be noticeable. With few exceptions, expressions of fundamental dissent over the Fund came from a zealous minority smarting over the Sixteenth Amendment and the Supreme Court's decision of May 17, 1954.[13]

The Ford Foundation's act of restricting membership on the Fund's board to members of the establishment made right-wing charges predictable and less credible. Furthermore, it almost guaranteed an affirmative response from men of similar stature and persuasion. A Fund bulletin showing support by the New York *Herald Tribune,* the St. Louis *Post-Dispatch,* and the Denver *Post* did much to dilute claims by Hearst's New York *Journal-American.*

That the Fund was forced to spend hundreds of thousands of

dollars on public relations and suffer the indignities of the Walter hearings is a reflection of the force of the "heated exaggeration, suspiciousness, and conspiratorial fantasy" wielded by ultraconservatives within the decade.[14] The record shows that the Treasury Department was appreciative and attentive to the clangor. One can imagine perhaps a more daring collection of Fund directors composed of men like Roger Baldwin, Morris Rubin, and Norman Thomas, but it is difficult, in retrospect, to believe that such a board could have achieved very much and, at the same time, acquired the widespread, powerful support necessary to retain tax exemption.

And, of course, much was accomplished. Many activities of the Fund and its grantees were clearly successful in hastening needed reforms, providing valuable information, and promoting widespread discussion of significant and often controversial issues.

The studies of American Communism, which Hutchins later called one of the great achievements of the Fund's first phase, were authoritative and invaluable contributions to the history of the United States.[15] The series of volumes edited by Clinton Rossiter was long in the making (six volumes had appeared by 1960)[16] and expensive,[17] but each book helped to roll back the ignorance and superstition often exploited for political gain to the detriment of personal liberties. Though buried in libraries, away from the flow of daily events, as Dwight Macdonald and other journalists have been eager to note, these volumes, together with the bibliography, the digest, the Stouffer public-opinion study, the Lazarsfeld-Thielens study of academic freedom, and Herbert Packer's brilliant analysis of ex-Communist witnesses (published in 1962), remain unprecedented and permanent reference works for thoughtful citizens seeking genuine scholarship on the history and effects of the "enemy within our midst." Paul Hoffman could boast with accuracy in 1956:

> I think the Fund for the Republic is responsible for producing more knowledge about the Communist movement than any organization in this country. I except no organization. When we get through there will be available to anyone who wants to take time to find out the real facts about the Communist movement.[18]

With many issues important to individual and community freedoms Fund appropriations and grants had effect. The Yarmolinsky report and the findings of the Special Committee of the Association of the Bar of the City of New York attracted much attention to the Government's loyalty-security programs and resulted in widespread reappraisal of federal legislation.[19] The Public Education Association's study of public-school segregation in New York City caused considerable consternation among parents and city officials, and reverberations are still being felt through such actions as the controversial busing of nonwhite children to predominantly white schools.[20] Rowland Watts's examination of the security screening of drafted servicemen caused the Defense Department to alter unjust standards.[21] An investigation by Ernesto Galarza, an agricultural workers' union official, of the treatment of Mexican contract laborers spurred the Department of Labor and the Mexican government to pay greater attention to the living conditions and civil liberties of migratory workers.[22] The Cogley Report reinforced directly the successful libel suit by John Henry Faulk which virtually halted blacklisting in the entertainment industry.[23] The Southern Regional Council utilized Fund grants totaling over $700,000 to rise from obscurity and become an effective agency unexcelled in its efforts to produce interracial harmony and understanding in the South.[24] The Indian Commission's painstaking and unprecedented research played a role in the Kennedy Administration's plans to improve the situation of the American Indian.[25] Ben Segal's methods of instructing union members in civil liberties and civil rights were productive and well-appreciated.[26] The monumental report of the Commission on Race and Housing shattered several widely held myths by considering experience with racially mixed housing, the effects of minority housing on property values and market demand, and practices of the housing industry in relation to minority groups.[27] Vanderbilt University's *Race Relations Law Reporter* served a very useful function, presenting to thousands of attorneys compilations of court cases arising from desegregation litigation.[28] The American Friends Service Committee and the Toledo Bar Association provided legal assistance to defendants threatened by loss of constitutional protections.[29]

The Fund's support and encouragement were widely distributed, reaching millions of citizens in a variety of ways. The newsfilm operation produced over 115 film clips on civil liberties and civil rights, many of which were shown on network television news programs.[30] The Council for Social Action of the Congregational Christian Churches prepared bibliographies, purchased films, sold thousands of discussion group packets, and conducted leadership-training schools and conferences on civil liberties.[31] The St. Louis Bar Association financed a series of hour-long televised "town meeting" discussions, featuring citizens' views on national and local matters involving issues of freedom.[32] The freedom agenda program of the Carrie Chapman Catt Memorial Fund, launched and sustained by the Fund for the Republic, promoted discussion groups on American liberties in more than 600 communities in the 48 states and Alaska, made broadcasts on radio and television, and distributed hundreds of thousands of excellent pamphlets on the Bill of Rights written by such authorities as T. V. Smith, Alan Westin, Alfred H. Kelly, Jack Peltason, Richard A. Edwards, Zechariah Chafee, Jr., Robert K. Carr, and Walter Gellhorn.[33] The American Heritage Council also sponsored discussion groups and prepared and distributed civil-liberties literature for Illinois's Department of the American Legion, the National Guard, Veterans of Foreign Wars, Chicago's Jewish War Veterans, the Council for AMVETS delegates from central states, the League of Women Voters, and a variety of trade unions and public schools.[34]

The most obvious disappointment within the long list of activities associated with the Fund was its own work in commercial television. The Fund's executive committee found the Al Capp pilot films unsatisfactory; the board thought the Herblock series too controversial. Others employed broader definitions. Sponsors and network executives, fearful of the slightest drop in profits and used to compliance with the pressure tactics which Cogley's interviewers disclosed, ignored the Fund's desires to stimulate and inform. Writers were often afraid of being branded "liberal."

The television script competition, costing almost $60,000, drew few impressive entries and only a single script was ever produced —it was cut from thirty to fifteen minutes and used on Sunday morning's "Lamp Unto My Feet."[35] A pilot film to promote a series of half-hour programs on current problems in civil liberties, produced and directed by several of the industry's most distinguished figures, found no takers.[36] These failures led to the Sherwood Awards, television's richest and most publicized prizes. The weakness was that the awards could honor only the best that had already appeared. One critic wrote of a victorious entry: "The play was against violence by a mob of psychopaths, a position which is about as 'controversial' as a four-square stand against arthritis, and perhaps even less likely to produce results."[37] The $15,000 independent-station prize for the 1956-7 season (which had a budget of $83,750) could not be given for lack of a worthy nomination.[38] Dr. Hutchins remained optimistic, telling his directors: "Undoubtedly, more programs in the general field of freedom and justice are being written and shown as a result of the Awards."[39]

The timidity of the television industry cannot be blamed on the Fund's officers and staff, whose efforts appear intensive and thorough. Tens of thousands of dollars went to explore every available avenue for reaching the general public through this popular medium. Networks had accounts totaling in the hundreds of millions of dollars. One contemporary observed "an increasing reluctance recently on the part of advertising agencies to use performers or material which 'won't sell toothpaste in Alabama.' "[40] Joseph Lyford recalls:

> We were dealing with a terrified medium. C.B.S. was the worst. You couldn't get anything on the air. Our pilot film by Reginald Rose and Rod Serling involved a bus driver who refused to take a loyalty oath and the response of the community toward this action. It was completely fair and left viewers with a question to think about. It was a terrific film. Not a single station would even talk to us about it.[41]

There were a few more encouraging undertakings in this field. The three-year report revealed an estimate that thirty of the newsfilm project's film clips had reached an audience of 55,581,-000.[42] The Council for Civic Unity of San Francisco used a

$20,000 grant to present several highly acclaimed programs of local interest on civil liberties and civil rights.[43] The Fund-produced "Segregation and the South," a one-hour documentary on developments in race relations since the Supreme Court ruling on public-school integration, was seen nationally, one prominent critic praising it as a "balanced and impressive study of a vital national issue."[44]

It is not altogether surprising that the first studies on the basic issues of the mass media concerned television, "including the question of the application of the First Amendment."[45]

Illustrations of the Fund's extensive efforts should be supplemented by mention of the intellectual and professional stature of those chosen by the officers and directors to carry them out. Almost without exception, the most respected authorities were selected for duties demanding expert judgment. If these authorities shared certain attitudes about the Constitution and human dignity and equality, this was less due to Dr. Hutchins's bias than to the fact that the attitudes themselves were in harmony with the thought and research widely accepted and published by leaders within the scholarly disciplines.

If a controversial book by Telford Taylor on congressional investigations was selected for distribution, it is to be noted that Taylor was qualified to write on the subject, the work received excellent reviews, and the author's position was acknowledged and scholarly. (By 1961 fifteen large American daily newspapers, including *The New York Times,* had called for the abolition of HUAC.[46] That the Fund chose to distribute a book on the Fifth Amendment by Dean Griswold rather than one by, say, Dean Manion, was a decision reflecting a standard not unlike that held by most leading centers of thought which have considered the subject; that Harvard University was considered a "smelly mess" by Senator McCarthy casts no suspicion on those who respect the scholarship of its most distinguished professors.[47] Project consultants like Paul Lazarsfeld, Samuel Stouffer, and Clinton Rossiter, fellowship and grant-in-aid recipients like John W. Caughey, Eleanor Bontecou, Marie Jahoda, and Philip Selznik were established leaders in the academic world and in the pursuit of truth and justice. Many younger scholars with the best of credentials were encouraged by the Fund to do work in fields that might otherwise have been ignored.

The Fund was not neutral or indifferent about the complexities and moral overtones of civil liberties and civil rights. It could not have been. But the selection of authorities and recipients for grants and fellowships appear painstaking and fair. Efforts were far within the boundaries of respectable thought.

Collectively, the directors of the Fund assumed: (1) that Communism was a political conspiracy; (2) that the degree of its domestic infiltration was unknown, though probably exaggerated; (3) that the methods employed to combat that infiltration were often deleterious to civil liberties; (4) that racial segregation was a moral and legal wrong; (5) that civil liberties, the "internal Communist menace," and the situation of minority groups in America were in need of study and widespread discussion. To some these assumptions were radical. But consider again, from 1953, the Fund's five areas of immediate interest:

1 Restrictions and assaults upon academic freedom.
2 Due process and the equal protection of the laws.
3 The protection of the rights of minorities.
4 Censorship, boycotting and blacklisting activities by private groups.
5 The principle and application of guilt by association.

The board's assumptions were in conformity with the corporation's mandate; the mandate was carried out responsibly and, by and large, successfully.

The Fund for the Republic had no control over the work or findings of its grantees, and no evidence suggests that it sought any. Controversy raged over activities representing only a tiny fraction of the corporation's expenditure.

Most of the millions was spent on collecting and distributing facts. What was the condition of the American Indian? How much do the American people think about and understand the Bill of Rights? What happens to a community when Negroes move in? How valid and consistent was the testimony of certain witnesses who appeared repeatedly before certain congressional committees? The answers to these and similar questions were not being sought in equal depth by other sources at the time.

No corporate body during the years of the Fund's first phase even approached its efforts in what Hutchins accurately called "uncharted and dangerous territory." Fear was the great preventative. The most opulent foundations chose to ignore what were, in many ways, the most serious domestic problems of the fifties. No organization went beyond its printed belief in equal opportunities to pour hundreds of thousands of dollars into channels promoting racial equality. None tried as hard as the Fund to keep serious conversation alive. Dr. Hutchins is guilty of a rare understatement by asserting simply that the Fund for the Republic "did as much as any other organization in those years to expand civil liberties."[48] The exact degree of that understatement cannot be known.

Throughout 1957 it was becoming apparent that the nation was moving slowly away from the fear and intolerance so prominent when the Gaither report was written and when some 50 per cent of the American people (according to a Gallup Poll) held a "favorable opinion" of Senator McCarthy. The first civil-rights act of the twentieth century was passed in Congress; a soft-spoken scholar named Martin Luther King, Jr., was getting results in the South; and the United States Supreme Court (the Chief Justice of which privately expressed admiration for the Fund)[49] was reasserting constitutional safeguards ignored by itself and others during the past decade's passion against the wide variety of thoughts, words, and deeds it feared subversive.

In *Watkins v. United States* the Court demanded that legislative inquiries "must be related to and in furtherance of a legislative task of Congress," and declared that "investigations conducted solely for the personal aggrandizement of the investigators or to 'punish' those investigated are indefensible;" in *Sweezy v. New Hampshire* academic freedom was elevated to a full First Amendment status; in two cases it was held that former Communist party membership was insufficient reason in itself to automatically deny an attorney admission to the bar; in a seven-to-one decision the government was ordered to permit a defendant to see evidence used against him contained in the FBI files; and only six years after the Dennis case the Court virtually threw out the Smith Act by voting six to one to distinguish between the permissible advocacy of abstract doctrine and the impermissible "advocacy and teaching of concrete action for the forcible overthrow of the Government." Although the Court would retreat somewhat from its strong positions on civil liberties as a result of pressures by Congress, the Conference of State Chief Justices, and the American Bar Association, it was widely believed by the end of the decade that the Warren Court was most unlikely to return to positions held by the Vinson Court during the McCarthy era.[50]

I. F. Stone sighed warily: "It looks as if the witch hunt is drawing to its close."[51] At a meeting of the Civil Rights Institute in mid-1957, an official of the American Civil Liberties Union said: "Very definitely we're in a state of progress." Roy Wilkins of the National Association for the Advancement of Colored People agreed. Adam Yarmolinsky spoke of "a kind of return to sanity" in America.[52]

It was largely the recognition that the nation was rapidly regaining its composure after its bout with the worst Red scare of its history that caused Robert Hutchins to guide the Fund for the Republic away from the receding battlefront of civil liberties and civil rights toward a broader and deeper examination of the effects on individual freedom of principal institutions in contemporary society. A search for basic values in the theory and practice of self-government, in conjunction with the production of brief, learned, and provocative pieces of literature to stir widespread thought and discussion about individual liberties, might do more than put out occasional fires, and might assist democracy, that least practiced and most fragile form of government, to flourish in an atmosphere of unprecedented change.

The "second phase" of the Fund's history, at least that portion centering on the weekend discussion sessions of the consultants, was, to most observers (and to anyone who has waded through the thick volumes of collected discourses) an expensive and largely futile venture. The often intensely abstract conversations were saturated with displays of personal vanity, pedantry, and dreary quarrelsomeness; evidences of meaningful collective effort, even of reciprocal understanding, are not common. But much of this was due simply to the diverse interests and specialties of the consultants, and it was vital to the endeavor that participants represent a broad variety of viewpoints. Moreover, little harmony and consensus over the full scope of the enormously complex basic issues could be nurtured within a dozen brief meetings. And several ideas of true originality, notably Scott Buchanan's view of the corporation, were encountered, debated, and refined during this period.

Out of the difficulties shared by the consultants came the Center for the Study of Democratic Institutions. The dialogue, the potential of which for clarification and enlightenment had been barely explored in recent centuries, might now be utilized on a continuous and permanent basis. The center's residents would be free, in a literal sense enjoyed by few thinkers in the world, to study, contemplate, and discuss with one another and with scores of celebrated visitors, some of the deepest and most vital matters of the century.

There was, of course, little certainty that the center could succeed in making the kind of fresh and indelible contributions the Fund's president envisioned. But it was hoped that the many publications flowing from the studies of liberty and justice would widen the circles of discussion and stimulate Americans to consider critical questions bearing upon the future of the free society; perhaps center thinkers could provide the nation with clearer ideas and more defensible standards. Robert Hutchins believed the challenge worthy of the Fund for the Republic.

Notes

CHAPTER ONE /

1 William Greenleaf, *From These Beginnings: The Early Philanthropies of Henry and Edsel Ford, 1911–1936* (Detroit, 1964), p. 186.
2 Ibid.
3 See Marion R. Fremont-Smith, *Foundations and Government: State and Federal Law and Supervision* (New York, 1965), pp. 44–50.
4 See Greenleaf, *From These Beginnings*, esp. pp. 1–27.
5 Allan Nevins and Frank Ernest Hill, *Ford Decline and Rebirth, 1933–1962* (New York, 1962), p. 411. Greenleaf's account of this statement charitably omits the last five words. Greenleaf, p. 187. For Henry Ford II's cautious version of the Foundation's origins see U.S. House, *Hearings Before the Select (Cox) Committee To Investigate Tax-Exempt Foundations and Comparable Organizations*, 82d Cong., 2d Sess., Washington, D.C., 1953, p. 222. Hereafter cited as Cox Committee Hearings.
6 The Foundation's tax-valuated (not necessarily actual) assets as of December 31, 1951, were listed as $492,678,254.79. One economist commented: "It would not surprise me if trustees would turn down three-quarters of a billion dollars cold cash for the assets on that balance sheet." Robert Heilbroner, "The Fabulous Ford Foundation," *Harper's Magazine*, December 1951, p. 27.
7 *The New York Times*, April 13, 1950.
8 See Cox Committee Hearings, pp. 219–21.
9 The legal responsibility for the operation of a foundation lies with its trustees. Donor manipulation is common and is tolerated by the Department of Internal Revenue. See Burton Raffel, "Philanthropy and the Legal Mind: An Editorial," *Foundation News*, March 1963, p. 6; U.S. Senate, Committee on Finance, *Treasury Department Report on Private Foundations*, 89th Cong., 1st Sess., Washington, D.C., 1965, pp. 8–9, 54–7.
10 Interview with Robert M. Hutchins, February 27, 1964. Henry's brother, Benson, was also a trustee. See "The Men of the Ford Foundation," *Fortune*, December 1951, pp. 116–17.
11 Ford Foundation, *Report of the Study for the Ford Foundation on Policy and Program* (Detroit, 1949), pp. 9–10. For more on Gaither's friendship with Ford see Bruce L. R. Smith, *The Rand Corporation: Case Study of a Nonprofit Advisory Corporation* (Cambridge, Mass., 1966), pp. 67–72.
12 *Report of the Study for the Ford Foundation*, p. 10.
13 Ibid., p. 11.
14 Ibid., p. 62.
15 Ibid., p. 66.
16 Ibid., p. 67.
17 For early commentary of unusual perception see Henry Steele Commager, "Who Is Loyal to America?" *Harper's Magazine*, September 1947, pp. 195–6;

American Civil Liberties Union, *Our Uncertain Civil Liberties: U.S. Liberties, 1947–48* (New York, 1948).

18 See Robert K. Carr, *The House Committee on Un-American Activities, 1945–50* (Ithaca,, 1952), passim.

19 See Robert H. Bremner, *American Philanthropy* (2d edn., Chicago, 1962), pp. 174–5.

20 Dwight Macdonald, *The Ford Foundation: The Men and the Millions* (New York, 1956), p. 141. Prior to the announcement of its new programs, the Foundation had given away about $32,000,000. *The New York Times,* October 1, 1950.

21 Ibid., September 24, 1950.

22 From "Honorary Doctor of Humanics," given by Hillsdale College, Hillsdale, Michigan (1942), to Yale's LL.D. in 1950. [Viola Pedersen], "Biographical Sketch," April 28, 1953, Hoffman papers. The best profile of Hoffman is in the *London Observer,* December 27, 1959.

23 *The New York Times,* September 26, 1950. Similar editorial praise appeared in the *Times* on November 8, 1950.
   There is much of Hoffman in the following excerpt from a 1953 speech: Under the new Administration, which has just taken office, the voice of business is being listened to attentively for the first time in many, many years. Let us see to it that this voice speaks not in the interest of business alone. We must make absolutely certain that, when business speaks, it is in the interest of all the people. . . . If we do, if we dedicate ourselves anew to making in America a demonstration of a free, just and unafraid society at work, we can show all the world that a government of the people and by the people can do more for the people than any other kind of government on earth.
   "Voluntaryism—The Strength of America," delivered to the Minneapolis Junior Chamber of Commerce, February 16, 1953, Hoffman papers.

24 *The New York Times,* November 7, 1950.

25 Interview with Hallock Hoffman (Paul's son, and until July 1969 a staff member of the Fund for the Republic), March 16, 1964; Nevins and Hill, *Ford Decline and Rebirth,* pp. 415–16.

26 *The New York Times,* September 27, 1950.

27 Heilbroner, "The Fabulous Ford Foundation," p. 26.

28 A. H. Raskin, in *The New York Times,* October 1, 1950.

29 Interview with Hallock Hoffman, March 16, 1964. This condition was later revealed by Henry Ford II. *The New York Times,* February 5, 1953. Shortly after his appointment was announced, Hoffman left for Pasadena to "become acquainted with my grandchildren and reacquainted with my children." Ibid., November 7, 1950.

30 Interview with Hallock Hoffman, March 16, 1964.

31 See Hutchins's autobiographical sketch in Robert M. Hutchins, *Education for Freedom* (New York: Grove Press; 1963), pp. 1–18. No biography of Hutchins has yet been written, but see Ernest Kirschten, "Mind of Bob Hutchins: No Radical but True Conservative," St. Louis *Post-Dispatch,* December 2, 1956; Irwin Ross, "Robert M. Hutchins: A Post Portrait," New York *Post,* February 20–4, 1956; Maxine Greene, "Robert Maynard Hutchins, Crusading Metaphysician," *School and Society,* May 12, 1956, pp. 162–6; Arthur A. Cohen, "Robert Maynard Hutchins: The Educator as Moralist," in Arthur A. Cohen, ed., *Humanistic Education and Western Civilization: Essays for Robert M. Hutchins* (New York, 1964), pp. 3–17.

32 Hutchins, *Education for Freedom,* p. 26.

33 See Herman Kogan, *The Great EB, The story of the Encyclopaedia Britannica* (Chicago, 1958), pp. 249–65.

34 In 1958 it was revealed that Hutchins had had more than four hundred speeches published in over six hundred periodicals and ten books during a fifteen-year period. George Dell, "Robert Hutchins: The Rhetoric of a Rationalist in Higher Education." Unpublished paper delivered at the national convention of the Speech Association of America, December 30, 1958, personal files of Robert M. Hutchins.

    Congressman B. C. Reece of Tennessee, no lover of controversy or universities, would summarize Hutchins's two decades at Chicago thus: "The University of Chicago, under Hutchins' administration, had distinguished itself as the only institution of higher learning in America which has been investigated five times for immoral or subversive activities." *Congressional Record*, 83rd Cong., 1st Sess., Washington, D.C., 1953, 99, 10195.

35 In Selig Greenberg, "Guiding Hand Continually Rubs Fur the Wrong Way," the Providence (R.I.) *Evening Bulletin*, December 21, 1955. Hutchins's wit caused him to be known widely for such statements as "No Chicago faculty member can ever be fired except for rape or murder committed in broad daylight before three witnesses." "Chicago Loses Its Boy Wonder," *Life*, February 19, 1951, p. 49.

36 Robert M. Hutchins, *Freedom, Education and the Fund: Essays and Addresses, 1946–1956* (New York, 1956), pp. 195–6.

37 Interview with Hallock Hoffman, March 16, 1964. From 1943 the two had also served together on the board of directors of Encyclopaedia Britannica, Inc. Kogan, *The Great EB*, p. 261.

38 See *The New York Times*, December 29, 1950. The responsibilities of the associate directors appear in a confidential "Report to the Board of Trustees;" July 15, 1952, Policy folder, Ford Foundation file (hereafter referred to as F.F. file).

39 *The New York Times*, February 24, 1951.

40 "Report to the Board of Trustees," July 15, 1952, Policy folder, F.F. file.

41 Ibid. *The New York Times*, June 29, 1951.

42 Ibid., January 24, 1951.

43 Ford Foundation "Operations Manual," No. 1, April 24, 1951, Policy folder, F.F. file.

44 Robert Bendiner, "Report on the Ford Foundation," *The New York Times Magazine*, February 1, 1953, pp. 6, 12. Hoffman's secretary, Viola Pedersen, escorted the writer on a personal tour of the former personal and official residences of the Foundation's major figures on August 8, 1964.

45 *The New York Times*, June 3, 1951.

46 Ibid., August 2, 1951.

47 $17,000,000 for the semi-independent funds and new programs, $1,400,000 to the Free University of Berlin, and $5,000,000 for the overseas programs. Ibid., September 26, 1951.

48 Form 990A, filed with the Treasury Department, as prepared by Price Waterhouse and Co., "Report to the Board of Trustees," July 15, 1952, Policy folder, F.F. file.

49 *The New York Times*, December 12, 1952.

50 Bendiner, "Report on the Ford Foundation," p. 25.

51 Paul G. Hoffman's appointment book for 1953, p. 34, at his personal office in Pasadena, California; *The New York Times*, February 5, 6, 1953.

52 Ibid., February 5, 1953. Excerpts from the Foundation's official minutes set the exact date at "the previous Monday," which would be January 26. "The Ford

Foundation, Letter Dated March 11, 1954, in Reply to Letter Dated March 2 from the Special Committee to Investigate Tax-Exempt Foundations, House of Representatives, U.S. Congress," Attachment D, F.F. file (hereafter referred to as Reece Committee Report). Hoffman's appointment book reveals for January 29, 1953, p. 29: "Dinner—Henry Ford and Trustees Pierre Hotel [New York] Teakwood Suite."

53 *The New York Times,* February 5, 1953.

54 Ibid., February 6, 1953; interview with Hallock Hoffman, March 26, 1964.

55 Ibid. See *Christian Science Monitor,* March 18, 1953. Hoffman's private secretary supplied the writer with a personal record of her employer's travels which reveals him as one of the world's least stationary citizens.

56 Macdonald, *The Ford Foundation,* p. 25.

57 Washington *Times-Herald,* July 8, 1953.

58 W. H. Ferry to Henry Ford II, January 17, 1952, Henry Ford II folder, F. F. file; interview with W. H. Ferry, March 5, 1964. Cf. Ford's statement to Dwight Macdonald in Macdonald, p. 27.

59 Ibid., p. 148.

60 Gerald J. Lynch to Henry Ford II, April 9, 1952, Henry Ford II folder, F. F. file.

61 Gerald J. Lynch to Henry Ford II, May 1, 1952, ibid.

62 See W. H. Ferry to Robert M. Hutchins, December 17, 1952, Cox Committee folder, ibid. The decision was *Wieman v. Updegraff,* 344 U.S. 183 (1952).

63 See *The New York Times,* November 25, 26, 1952. For Hutchins's appraisal of his appearance before the committee see Robert M. Hutchins to James Laughlin, December 25, 1952, Intercultural Publications, Inc. folder, F. F. file. For other impressions (all affirmative) see Henry M. Wriston to Robert M. Hutchins, January 2, 1953, Cox Committee folder, ibid.; John Cowles to Paul G. Hoffman, December 10, 1952, ibid.; and Thomas R. Carskadon to Robert M. Hutchins, December 10, 1952, ibid.

On the Cox committee see U.S. House, Select Committee To Investigate Foundations, *Final Report of the Select Committee To Investigate Foundations and Other Organizations* 82d Cong., 2d Sess., Washington, D.C., 1953; John Lankford, *Congress and the Foundations in the Twentieth Century* (River Falls, Wisconsin, 1964), pp. 33–53. For Cox's McCarthyite assertions about Owen Lattimore and Hutchins's response see *The New York Times,* December 2, 1952.

64 Interview with Robert M. Hutchins, March 26, 1964.

65 *The New York Times,* March 19, 1952.

66 Ibid.

67 Chester C. Davis, "The Ford Foundation Monthly Letter to the Trustees, Pasadena, April 30, 1952," Trustees folder, F.F. file.

Gaither may have played a role in Ford's discontent. For Gaither's proposals on organization and administration, made to Hoffman early and met with swift approval, see memorandum, H. Rowan Gaither, Jr., to Paul G. Hoffman, November 6, 1951, Paul G. Hoffman folder, ibid.

68 Paul G. Hoffman to the writer, March 9, 1964; Ford Foundation "Staff Meeting Minutes," Vol. 2, No. 4, February 5, 1953, Minutes folder, F.F. file.

69 Macdonald, p. 150.

70 Chester C. Davis, "The Foundation Monthly Letter to the Trustees, Pasadena, May 29, 1952," Trustees folder, F.F. file.

71 Henry Ford II to Paul G. Hoffman, May 22, 1952, Hoffman papers. Ford hastened to add that great strides had been made by the Foundation during

Hoffman's presidency. A week later Hoffman replied: "It is my impression that the departmentalization, which you put into operation, is working very well indeed. I also think that the program for interim visits with the Trustees on the part of the Associate Directors will do much to keep the Trustees better informed." Paul G. Hoffman to Henry Ford II, May 29, 1952, ibid.

72 See Macdonald, pp. 149–50; Nevins and Hill, *Ford Decline and Rebirth,* p. 416; Henry Ford II's preface to *The Ford Foundation Annual Report for 1952* (Detroit, 1952).

73 *Wall Street Journal,* September 22, 1952.

74 Telegram, Henry Ford II to Paul G. Hoffman, September 23, 1952, Hoffman papers. Hutchins's comment on the incident included two of the key words in Ford's telegram: "very untimely." Interview with Robert M. Hutchins, February 27, 1964.

75 Night cable, Paul G. Hoffman to Henry Ford II, September 23, 1952, Hoffman papers.

76 Press release, Ford Motor Company, December 11, 1952, ibid.

77 Ford Foundation, *Report of the Study for the Ford Foundation,* p. 136.

78 For an excerpt of Hoffman's withering schedule of speaking engagements see memorandum, Joseph M. McDaniel to Hoffman, Davis, Gaither, Hutchins, Katz, December 4, 1951, Joseph M. McDaniel folder, F.F. file. See Macdonald, p. 153.

79 Interview with Robert M. Hutchins, February 27, 1964.

80 Macdonald, p. 153. See Bendiner, "Report on the Ford Foundation," p. 25. Years later Hoffman recalled quickly that Ford was "extremely critical of Mr. Hutchins." Paul G. Hoffman to the writer, March 9, 1964.

81 Hoffman reminded the trustees that the Rockefeller Foundation had sustained similar attacks in 1915 when it proposed sweeping changes in the education of physicians. Paul G. Hoffman, "The Ford Foundation Monthly Letter to the Trustees, Pasadena, March 16, 1952," Trustees folder, F.F. file.

82 See Macdonald, pp. 50-7.

CHAPTER TWO /

1 Memorandum, Paul G. Hoffman to the board of trustees, January 29, 1951, Trustees folder, F.F. file.

2 Interview with Robert M. Hutchins, February 27, 1964. See Hutchins, *Freedom, Education, and the Fund,* pp. 57–67.

3 For the Foundation's relations with the commission and its staff see Nimitz Commission folder, F.F. file. See also memoranda, David F. Freeman to Bernard L. Gladieux, June 13, 28, 1951, Bernard L. Gladieux folder, ibid.

4 See Harry S Truman, *Memoirs: Years of Trial and Hope* (Signet edn., New York, 1965), pp. 327–9.

5 Paul G. Hoffman to Russell W. Davenport, May 1, 1951, Bernard L. Gladieux folder, F.F. file.
6 Ford Foundation Staff Meeting Minutes, No. 7, April 23, 1951, Minutes folder, ibid.
7 Robert M. Hutchins to George Kennan, July 9, 1951, George Kennan folder, ibid.
8 Interview with Hallock Hoffman, March 14, 1965.
9 Interview with W. H. Ferry, March 5, 1964. For a highly interpretive biographical sketch of Ferry see Victor S. Navasky, "The Happy Heretic," *Atlantic Monthly,* July 1966, pp. 53–7.
10 Ford Foundation Staff Meeting Minutes, No. 8, April 30, 1951, Minutes folder, F.F. file. "Newsom was against the plan and suggested I show it to Dean Acheson. I did and you can imagine how he reacted. Henry Ford was all for it. I continued throughout the years to drop these kinds of ideas." Interview with W. H. Ferry, June 1, 1965.
11 Interview with W. H. Ferry, March 5, 1964. E.g., James Laughlin to Milton Katz, July 8, 1952, James Laughlin folder, F.F. file.
12 The treatise and the memorandum are in the "Seminar on Freedom" folder, ibid. See also *S* folder, ibid.
13 Unsigned memorandum, September 11, 1951, W. H. Ferry folder, ibid; interview with W. H. Ferry, June 1, 1965.
14 Paul G. Hoffman to Bernard L. Gladieux, October 2, 1951, "Programs and Policies Dec. 14, 1952–" folder, Administration file (hereafter referred to as Admin. file).
15 Hutchins thought of the name in a plane en route to a convocation address at the Free University of Berlin in early August. Interview with Robert M. Hutchins, February 27, 1964.
16 Memorandum, Paul G. Hoffman to the Trustees of the Ford Foundation, October 4, 1951, Paul G. Hoffman folder, F.F. file.
17 The best surveys of the period in the light of civil liberties are: Eric F. Goldman, *The Crucial Decade—and After: America, 1945–1960* (New York, 1960), and Donald J. Kemper, *Decade of Fear: Senator Hennings and Civil Liberties* (Columbia, Missouri, 1965). The outstanding analysis of the post-war Red scare and its observers is M. P. Rogin, *The Intellectuals and McCarthy: the Radical Specter* (Cambridge, Mass., 1967). Particularly impressive and convincing insights on McCarthyism are in Richard H. Rovere, *Senator Joe McCarthy* (New York, 1959), and Richard Hofstadter, *The Paranoid Style in American Politics and Other Essays* (New York, 1965). Important observations on the Republicans and Democratic foreign policy in the early 1950's are in John W. Spanier, *The Truman-MacArthur Controversy and the Korean War* (Cambridge, Mass., 1959), and George H. Mayer, *The Republican Party 1954–1966* (London, 1967), pp. 475–93.
18 See Congressional Quarterly Service, *Congress and the Nation 1945–1964, A Review of Government and Politics in the Post-War Years* (Washington, D.C., 1965), pp. 1650–1, 1654–6.
19 Ibid., pp. 1708–9. The three best books on HUAC (however impassioned) since 1950 are: Telford Taylor, *Grand Inquest* (New York, 1956); Frank J. Donner, *The Un-Americans* (New York, 1961); and Walter Goodman, *The Committee: The Extraordinary Career of the House Committee on Un-American Activities* (New York, 1968).
20 Donner, *The Un-Americans*, pp. 142–6, 157–60.
21 See Joseph H. Schaar, *Loyalty in America* (Berkeley and Los Angeles, 1957), pp. 138–48. Beyond Schaar's first-rate analysis, the best study of the Truman

program is Eleanor Bontecou, *The Federal Loyalty-Security Program* (Ithaca, 1953).

22 Quoted in Robert. S. Herschfield, *The Constitution and the Court: The Development of the Basic Law Through Judicial Interpretation* (New York, 1962), pp. 112–18, an invaluable little volume. See C. Herman Pritchett, *Civil Liberties and the Vinson Court* (Chicago, 1954), pp. 70–9, 244.

23 Paul G. Hoffman to Bernard L. Gladieux, October 2, 1951, "Programs and Policies, Dec. 14, 1952–" folder, F.F. file.

24 Memorandum, Paul G. Hoffman to the Trustees of the Ford Foundation, October 4, 1951, Paul G. Hoffman folder, ibid.

25 Memorandum, Robert M. Hutchins to Hoffman, Davis, Gaither, Katz, Gladieux, McDaniel, Newsom, Ferry, October 15, 1951, "Grant to the Fund" folder, Admin. file.

26 Director [Paul G. Hoffman] to Benson Ford, November 6, 1951, ibid.

27 Ibid.

28 Ford Foundation Staff Meeting Minutes, No. 19, December 14, 1951, Minutes folder, F.F. file.

29 Memorandum, Robert M. Hutchins to Hoffman, Davis, Gaither, Katz, April 4, 1952, Paul G. Hoffman folder, ibid.

30 Henry Ford II to Robert M. Hutchins, May 12, 1952, Henry Ford II folder, ibid.

31 Ford Foundation Staff Meeting Minutes, Nos. 40, 41, May 6, 13, 1952, ibid.

32 Chester C. Davis, "The Ford Foundation Monthly Letter to the Trustees, Pasadena, June 30, 1952," Trustees folder, ibid.

33 Frank W. Abrams to Robert M. Hutchins, July 1, 1952, *A* folder, F.F. file.

34 Memorandum, Robert M. Hutchins to Milton Katz, July 7, 1952, Milton Katz folder, ibid.

35 From the meeting's minutes in "Board Action—Summary of Meeting, July 15–16, 1952" folder, ibid.

36 Interview with Robert M. Hutchins, February 27, 1964. See Hutchins, *Freedom, Education and the Fund*, p. 221.

37 Interview with W. H. Ferry, March 5, 1964. Most of the new directors, however, were Democrats.

38 Robert Strunsky to Robert M. Hutchins, August 8, 1952, Robert Strunsky folder, F.F. file. All but Finnegan appeared in a list of eight submitted by Hoffman within a week of the trustees' July meeeting. Ford Foundation Staff Meeting Minutes, No. 49, July 23, 1952, Minutes folder, ibid.

39 Robert M. Hutchins to Robert Strunsky, August 12, 1952, Robert Strunsky folder, ibid. Several approved candidates, such as publisher Philip Graham, declined the invitation. Ford Foundation Staff Meeting Minutes, No. 54, August 28, 1952, Minutes folder, ibid.

40 Ford Foundation Staff Meeting Minutes, No. 55, September 3, 1952, ibid.

41 Ford Foundation Staff Meeting Minutes, No. 57, September 18, 1952, ibid.

42 Robert M. Hutchins to Robert Strunsky, August 12, 1952, Robert Strunsky folder, ibid. An Alabama paper later accused the board of lacking strong southern representatives. Montgomery *Journal*, May 30, 1956. When asked why the board had so few Southerners, Texan Jubal Parten said: "We tried to get others. We tried." Interview with Jubal R. Parten, February 9, 1966.

43 See Andrews, *Philanthropic Foundations*, pp. 63–91.

44 The unsigned, undated biographical survey is in the James D. Zellerbach folder, Personnel file.

45 Paraphrased in Orm W. Ketcham to David F. Freeman, July 8, 1953, Orm Ketcham folder, Admin. file.

46 The letters and telegrams appear in each of the appropriate folders within the Personnel file.

47 Izaak M. Stickler, also from the Foundation, was made treasurer. Each director, it was agreed, was to receive $3,000 a year plus "reasonable expenses incurred in connection with the performance of his duties." This reimbursement was in harmony with the tradition of the Ford Foundation. Minutes, Fund for the Republic (hereafter referred to as Minutes), December 10, 1952.

48 Whitney Seymour to Robert M. Hutchins, July 1, 1952, S folder, F.F. file.

49 Minutes, December 11, 1952. The entire sum was turned over to the Special Committee within the next three weeks via the tax-exempt American Bar Foundation. See Ford Foundation Staff Meeting Minutes, No. 67, December 12, 1952, Minutes folder, F.F. file; memorandum, David Freeman to board of directors, undated, Board of Directors' Work Papers file (hereafter referred to as B.D.W.P. file).

50 *The New York Times*, December 14, 1952.

51 Robert M. Hutchins to Grenville Clark, December 16, 1952, Grenville Clark folder, F.F. file. Of the board as a whole, Hutchins commented privately: "It is a pretty good group, worried about civil liberties, and also worried about its respectability. I do not know which worry will win." Robert M. Hutchins to James Laughlin, December 24, 1952, Intercultural Publications, Inc., folder, ibid.

52 Fresno *Bee*, December 15, 1952; Terre Haute *Star*, December 14, 1952.

53 *Christian Science Monitor*, December 16, 1952.

54 Grand Junction *Sentinel*, December 26, 1952.

55 Radio Reports, Inc., "Fund for the Republic: Eric Sevareid and the News at 7:30 P.M. over the CBS Radio Network," March 2, 1953, Public Documents file (hereafter referred to as Pub. Docs. file). Unless otherwise noted, the Radio Reports, Inc., broadcast reproductions are all from the Pub. Docs. file.

56 St. Louis *Post-Dispatch*, December 13, 1952.

57 Interview with Robert Hutchins, March 26, 1964. Chester Davis to Malcolm Bryan, September 23 and December 17, 1952, Malcolm Bryan folder, Personnel file.

58 Minutes, December 10, 11, 1952. Malcolm Bryan to David F. Freeman, December 17, 1952, Malcolm Bryan folder, Personnel file.

59 "Notes on interviews in Atlanta, Georgia, February 16–18, 1954," by F. S. Loescher, undated, F. S. Loescher folder, Admin. file. Hutchins had never met Bryan before the December 10 board meeting. Interview with Robert M. Hutchins, March 26, 1964.

60 Chester Davis to Malcolm Bryan, September 23, 1952, Malcolm Bryan folder, Personnel file.

61 Goldman, *The Crucial Decade—and After*, p. 113.

CHAPTER THREE

1 W. H. Joyce, Jr., to David Freeman, January 14, 1953, B.D.W.P. file.
2 Memorandum, David Freeman to Members of the Planning Committee, January 15, 1953, Hoffman papers.
3 Unsigned memorandum, January 16, 1953, "The Fund for the Republic: Officers of the Fund" folder, Admin. file.
4 O. W. Ketcham, "Draft Outline of Program," January 19, 1953, "Program and Policies: December 14, 1952–" folder, ibid.
5 Minutes, January 29, 1953.
6 Hoffman's version of the incident was simple and consistent. For example: "In March of 1953, after I had resigned from the Ford Foundation, I was elected Chairman of the Board of the Fund for the Republic." Paul G. Hoffman, "Address to the Willard Straight Post of the American Legion," May 17, 1956, press release, Fund for the Republic, May 18, 1956, Public Relations file. Unless otherwise stated, all Fund press releases are from the Public Relations file.
7 Minutes, January 29, 1953.
8 "I do not recall precisely when the suggestion was made to me in reference to the chairmanship of the Fund for the Republic. I am sure, however, that the Board was aware on January 29 that I was resigning my post as President of the Foundation." Paul G. Hoffman to the writer, April 14, 1964. Two original directors, Jubal R. Parten and W. H. Joyce, Jr., have confirmed this recollection to the writer.
9 In Reece Committee Report, Attachment D.
10 Paul G. Hoffman, "The Ford Foundation Monthly Letter to the Trustees, Pasadena, January 29, 1953," Trustees folder, F.F. file.
11 Reece Committee Report, Attachment D.
12 "The Fund for the Republic, A Prospectus," unsigned and undated, Hoffman papers.
13 Robert M. Hutchins to Erwin Griswold, February 26, 1953: "I want you to know that in my opinion you single-handed and alone got fifteen million dollars for the Fund for the Republic." G folder, F.F. file.
14 An account of the meeting is in "The Ford Foundation: A Michigan Non-Profit Corporation. Special Meeting of the Board of Trustees, February 23–26, 1953," "Trustees Meeting—February 1953" folder, F.F. file. The date of the confrontation came from the Fund for the Republic, Inc., to H. Rowan Gaither, Jr., January 21, 1954, "Grant to the Fund" folder, Admin. file. The statement of Henry Ford's motion and a general impression of Griswold's speech came from J. R. Parten in an interview of February 9, 1966.

    The method of payment utilized by the Foundation was thought wise in order to protect its own tax exemption from question. Under Section 3814 of the Treasury Department's regulations there is risk in granting more than 10 per cent of a foundation's annual expenditures to a nonexempt organization. The Fund applied for tax exemption, of course, after the grant was made. See unsigned "Memorandum re Effect upon the Tax-Exempt Status of the Ford Foundation of a Lump-Sum Grant to the Fund for the Republic,"

January 28, 1952, "Grant to the Fund" folder, Admin. file; Bethuel M. Webster to Commissioner of Internal Revenue, March 20, 1953, ibid.

15 See Andrews, *Philanthropic Foundations*, pp. 44, 278, 296–8. The major exception to the statement in the text was the grant by the Rockefeller Foundation in the late 1940's to the Cornell University studies on civil liberties, which produced important books by Walter Gellhorn, Edward L. Barrett, Jr., Robert K. Carr, Eleanor Bontecou, and others. For an elaborate survey prepared for the Ford Foundation in 1951 on projects and agencies dealing with civil rights and civil liberties see memorandum, Bernard L. Gladieux to Joseph M. McDaniel, Jr., September 26, 1951, Bernard L. Gladieux folder, F.F. file.

16 For more on this broad issue see Richard Eells, *Corporation Giving in a Free Society* (New York, 1956), esp. pp. 47, 113, 116–23, 146–9, 166–7.

17 The press release of February 26 stressed most heavily the Fund's proposed studies of American Communism. For typical reactions see: Texarkana (Arkansas) *News-Digest*, February 26, 1953; Minneapolis *Morning Tribune*, February 27, 1953; Natchez (Mississippi) *Times*, February 27, 1953; St. Louis *Post-Dispatch*, March 1, 1953. Said the latter: "Fortunately Paul G. Hoffman . . . is continuing as chairman of the board to administer the Fund for the Republic. This is fortunate because pressures of many sorts will be brought against a full inventory of our civil rights. It will take a Paul Hoffman to stand up against these influences."

18 Washington *Times-Herald*, March 3, 1953.

19 Telegram, Paul G. Hoffman to Jubal R. Parten, February 25, 1953, personal files of Jubal R. Parten.

20 O'Brian was elected a director, subject to his acceptance, on February 18. Minutes, April 9, 1953.

21 Memorandum, Orm Ketcham, March 6, 1953, Ketcham Memoranda folder, Admin. file. The omission is mine.

22 Memorandum, Orm Ketcham, March 23, 1953, ibid. Californian William H. Joyce, Jr., approached Earl Warren on March 24. W. H. Joyce, Jr., to David Freeman, March 25, 1953, William H. Joyce, Jr., folder, Personnel file.

23 See Andrews, pp. 59–61.

24 Bethuel M. Webster to Commissioner of Internal Revenue, March 20, 1953, "Grant to the Fund" folder, Admin. file; Bethuel Webster to Erwin Griswold, April 2, 1953, ibid; R. S. Gayton to the Fund for the Republic, Inc., March 27, 1953, "Clifford Case general" folder, Personnel file; Bethuel Webster to Clifford Case, September 29, 1953, "Clifford Case Biography and Publicity" folder, ibid.

25 On April 9 the board voted to request the full remainder of the grant, supporting the view of Hoffman and Webster that the temporary certificate was adequate and was indeed foretold in the February meeting at Pasadena. See Minutes, April 9, May 18, 1953. An official audit of the Fund, several months later, declared: "The Fund is the recipient of a grant from The Ford Foundation of $15,000,000 of which $3,000,000 has been paid up to September 30, 1953. The balance of $12,000,000 will be payable after the Treasury Department has issued a second confirmatory tax-exempt ruling following the usual waiting period of one full year's operation." Lybrand, Ross Brothers and Montgomery, official audit, October 13, 1953, Hoffman papers.

26 Oliver May to the Fund for the Republic, Inc., March 17, 1953, "Grant to the Fund" folder, Admin. file.

27 "Memorandum on 101 (6) ruling prepared by Webster, Sheffield and Chrystie," undated, B.D.W.P. file.

28 The editorial in *The New York Times* for February 27 read in part:
    Research is not enough: consider the excellent work done by the President's
    Committee on Civil Rights, which six years ago rendered a brilliant and
    now half-forgotten report. Have those six years seen any notable increase
    in respect for the basic liberties? There must be constant education, and this
    we have not had. Meanwhile intolerance has brought forth its prophets,
    ignorance has paraded under the guise of patriotism and fear has para-
    lyzed countless members of the meek but well-intentioned.

29 Joseph R. McCarthy to Paul G. Hoffman, March 31, 1953, Hoffman papers.
    Hoffman replied, in part: "In view of the fact that both the executive staff
    and the program of the Fund are still in the process of organization, there
    is little information beyond that contained in this letter which could be
    given you. I would, of course, be glad to meet with you and the members
    of your Committee, but cannot do so in the immediate future as I will be
    out of the country on a trip which I am taking for the Studebaker Corpora-
    tion." He referred to Mr. Webster. Paul G. Hoffman to Joseph
    McCarthy, April 9, 1953, ibid. Hutchins, in Paris in the spring, wrote home:
    "McCarthy gets an incredible amount of publicity over here. Something will
    have to be done about him, too." Robert M. Hutchins to James Laughlin,
    April 21, 1953, James Laughlin folder, F.F. file.
        On May 1, McCarthy asked for a complete list of the Fund's personnel.
    Hoffman complied by letter on May 7. By May 20, however, McCarthy in-
    sisted that he had not received the requested list. David Freeman had a copy
    of Hoffman's reply delivered by messenger to McCarthy's office on May 25.
    Later, McCarthy would issue a press release stating: "The Hennings Com-
    mittee is being used as a 'front' for left wing organizations such as the
    Fund for the Republic and the ADA, whose principal objective is to torpedo
    any effective security program. . . . the National Democrat [*sic*] leadership
    is as soft as ever on the Communist issue." Joseph McCarthy to Paul G. Hoff-
    man, May 1, 1953; Paul G. Hoffman to Joseph McCarthy, May 7, 1953;
    Joseph McCarthy to Paul G. Hoffman, May 20, 1953; David Freeman to
    Joseph McCarthy, May 25, 1953; press release, Joseph McCarthy, November
    25, 1955, Hoffman papers. The correspondence is also in the Senator Joseph
    R. McCarthy folder, Admin. file.

30 Boston *Post*, March 18, 1953. A denial and a rebuke came promptly from
    Gaither, who felt obliged to point out that "the foundation is entirely in-
    dependent of the Ford Motor Company." Los Angeles *Mirror News*, March
    20, 1953.

31 *ALERT: A Journal of Facts and Ideas To Fight for Freedom*, March, 1953,
    p. 34, Hoffman papers.

32 Memorandum, Martin Quigley to H. Rowan Gaither, Jr., April 13, 1953,
    Martin Quigley folder, F.F. file.
        A district sales manager of the Ford Motor Company in Indiana wearily
    informed his corporate superiors of a speaker in Indianapolis with close con-
    nections in the American Legion who warned the local Sons of the American
    Revolution about a fifteen-million-dollar grant the Ford Foundation made to
    subsidize directly the American Civil Liberties Union. He "also referred to
    the fact that ten of the fifteen members of the Civil Liberties Union are what
    the American Legion terms 'fellow travelers' or worse. Mr. Harris . . . also
    made the statement that five were outright Communists, and distinct in-
    ference was given to the people attending the meeting that there was a
    Communist on the Ford Foundation Board." The speaker warned his audi-
    ence of the implications of buying Ford products. A complaint soon arrived

at the Ford Motor Company from a lady who felt "that this civil liberties group is attempting to hamper the work of the groups investigating Communism." Such mail received much attention at the company and copies of several similar complaints were sent to the Fund. See A. F. Bauerbach to L. W. Smead, March 4, 1953, Hoffman papers; memorandum, the New York Office to Clifford Case, David Freeman, Orm W. Ketcham, July 17, 1953, "Administration—Weekly Reports" folder, Admin. file.

33 Paul G. Hoffman to Richard M. Nixon, March 24, 1953, Hoffman papers.

34 See "Committee report—Communist Menace," undated and unsigned, B.D.W.P. file.

35 Prior to the board meeting, the Actors' Equity council had endorsed the Fund in a letter to Hoffman in which the council offered "full cooperation to the end that blacklisting, censorship and guilt by association, practices which have grown up in the entertainment industry without knowledge of the public, endangering the livelihood of artists in ways hidden from them and the public, might be banished from the entertainment industry." *Variety*, April 15, 1953.

36 Minutes, April 9, 1953.

37 David Freeman to Clifford Case, April 22, 1953, "Clifford Case general" folder, Personnel file. Freeman had supported Case in his bid for the gubernatorial race. Clifford Case to David Freeman, February 25, 1953, ibid.

38 Charles W. Cole to David Freeman, May 5, 1953, "Administrative Research" folder, Admin. file.

39 Memorandum, O. W. Ketcham to Paul Hoffman, May 7, 1953, "Programs and Policies, Dec. 14, 1952–" folder, ibid.

40 David Freeman to James Zellerbach, May 12, 1953, James Zellerbach folder, Personnel file.

41 Freeman submitted his resignation "as a member, a director, and president to take effect upon Mr. Case's acceptance of an invitation to serve in these capacities." He would become the Fund's secretary. Minutes, May 18, 1953. Shortly, Freeman informed James Brownlee (who resigned from the board on May 18 to become a trustee of the Ford Foundation): "As Mr. Hoffman may have told you, the Board's reactions to Mr. Case were generally favorable. If the candidate can survive a meeting with Dean Griswold and a discussion with a nominating committee this Saturday, it may be that we will have a president in short order." David Freeman to James Brownlee, May 20, 1953, James Brownlee folder, Personnel file.

42 Telegram, David Freeman to Paul G. Hoffman, May 25, 1953, Hoffman papers; *The New York Times*, May 27, 1953.

43 Washington *Times-Herald*, July 8, 1953. Cf. a generous evaluation of Case, noting his "fine record as a forward-looking liberal," by the New York *Herald Tribune*, May 28, 1953.

44 For the committee report see "Program for the Study of the Legacy of American Liberty," May 8, 1953, B.D.W.P. file.

45 Minutes, May 18, 1953.

46 Stouffer and Sutherland and their committees were to receive only half of their funds if their "blue prints" were not acceptable to the board. Minutes, June 16, 1953.

47 "It was the sense of the meeting that the proposed grant would not establish a precedent, since it was in effect a recognition of a moral commitment to continue a program initiated with Ford Foundation financing. It was stressed that the American Friends Service Committee was in a some-

what different position from other potential grantees in the race-relations field because of its tax exempt status." Ibid.

48 Memorandum, the New York Office to Clifford Case, David F. Freeman, Orm W. Ketcham, July 17, 1953, "Administration—Weekly Reports" folder, Admin. file.

49 Memorandum, the New York Office to Clifford Case, David F. Freeman, Orm W. Ketcham, July 29, 1953, ibid. E.g., "Two communications about employment arrived—one from an FBI agent making preliminary approaches."

50 I. M. Stickler to Clifford Case, July 27, 1953, Hoffman papers. Stickler's resignation was first to be effective on July 31, but he was persuaded to remain until August 15, whereupon Freeman became acting treasurer. Minutes, August 4, 1953.

51 Press release, August 1, 1953, "Clifford P. Case biography and publicity" folder, Personnel file.

52 *Congressional Record*, 83rd Cong., 1st Sess., 1953, 99, No. 141, 10196. The vote was 209 for and 163 against, with 59, including Case, not voting. Democrats voted almost two to one against it; Republicans, almost three to one for it.

53 C. P. Trussell, "House Votes To Renew Private Funds Inquiry," *The New York Times*, July 28, 1953.

Elmer Davis, on his ABC radio network program for July 28, commented: "In other words, like so much else that has been going on in Congress this winter, this is an attack on liberalism disguised as an attack on communism. But it's the Ford Foundation that is Reece's chief target, and especially its Fund for the Republic, set up to work for the removal of restrictions on the freedom of thought, inquiry and expression, freedoms guaranteed by the Constitution but now obviously in considerable danger." Radio Reports, Inc., "Elmer Davis Discusses New Committee To Probe Tax-Free Foundations, Elmer Davis at 7:15 P.M. over WABC (N.Y.) and the ABC Network," July 28, 1953.

Hoffman wrote to an Iowa editor: "What Mr. Reece's real purpose is at the present time, I don't know. I haven't seen him in years but have been told that he holds me responsible for having busted up his 'procurement' of Southern delegates for Mr. Taft, and, as a consequence, he proposes to teach me a good lesson. Ray Tucker, in a recent column, said Reece's real object is the smearing of the whole liberal wing of the Republican party as a preparatory step toward the Old Guard's taking over once Eisenhower steps out of the picture." Paul G. Hoffman to Earl Hall, September 2, 1953, Hoffman papers.

54 Huntington Cairns to Paul G. Hoffman, July 31, 1953; Clifford Case to Huntington Cairns, August 5, 1953, Huntington Cairns folder, Personnel file; interview with Robert M. Hutchins, March 26, 1964.

55 Minutes, August 4, 1953. The amount of Case's annual salary ($40,000) somehow leaked out to the press. E.g., Newark *News*, November 10, 1953.

56 Minutes, September 10, 1953.

57 This was evidently to Case's liking. Concerning the grant to the Bicentennial Committee: "Mr. Case recommends that the Fund make no request for special publicity of its grant or sponsorship." Memorandum, Orm W. Ketcham to the Board of Directors, July 30, 1953, B.D.W.P. file.

58 Lybrand, Ross Brothers and Montgomery, official audit, October 13, 1953, Hoffman papers.

59 Bethuel Webster to Clifford Case, September 29, 1953, ibid.
60 "Eisenhower Tries To Block Investigation of Communist-Aiding Tax-Exempt Foundations," *Williams Intelligence Summary*, September, 1953, Hoffman papers.
61 Joseph P. Kamp, "Ford Company and Bar Association Join Plot Against McCarthyism," *Headlines*, November 1, 1953, ibid.
62 Martin Quigley to Waldemar Nielson, October 20, 1953, Martin Quigley folder, F.F. file.
63 Robert M. Hutchins to J. R. Parten, November 3, 1953, *P* folder, ibid.
64 The Summer Committee consisted of Stanley Pargellis of the Newberry Library, McGeorge Bundy of Harvard, Ralph Gabriel of Yale, Arthur Murphy of the University of Washington, and Clinton Rossiter of Cornell. Its report is sometimes referred to as the Pargellis Report. Minutes, November 18, 1953. The first project relating to the work of this committee was a grant (not to exceed $6,500) for a study entitled "Analysis of the Meaning of Citizenship," to be undertaken by H. Mark Roelofs and Rossiter. The funds were later channeled through a grant to Cornell University. See Pargellis folder, Admin. file. Roelofs published *An Essay on Citizenship* in January, 1956.
65 Minutes, November 18, 1953. The board vetoed Case's suggestion for "the organization of a small group of consultants to make a short but intensive study looking toward the formulation of concrete program objectives." The directors preferred "to engage consultants to advise on particular problems or programs, or to arrange special *ad hoc* meetings of consultants for particular problems."
66 The four were: the American Bar Foundation, American Friends Service Committee, Columbia University, and the Voluntary Defenders. "Statement of Receipts, Grants and Expenses for the period from December 9, 1952, the date of incorporation thru December 8, 1953," appended to Exemption Application (draft), December 19, 1953, "Clifford Case general" folder, Personnel file.
67 Elmo Roper to Robert Hutchins, December 3, 1953, *R* folder, F.F. file.

CHAPTER FOUR /

1 Works of extraordinary usefulness on matters touched in this survey (beyond those previously cited) are: John W. Caughey, *In Clear and Present Danger: The Crucial State of Our Freedoms* (Chicago, 1958); Robert M. MacIver, *Academic Freedom in Our Time* (New York, 1955); G. Bromley Oxnam, *I Protest* (New York, 1955); Ralph Lord Roy, *Communism and the Churches* (New York, 1960); and James A. Wechsler, *The Age of Suspicion* (New York, 1953). Special issues of *The Progressive* (April 1954) and the *Bulletin of the Atomic Scientists* (April 1955) are of great value.
2 Memorandum, Clifford P. Case to the Members of the Board, January 22, 1954, "Tax Exemption Granted" folder, B.D.W.P. file.
3 Memorandum, Charles B. Marshall to Clifford Case, January 14, 1954,

Charles B. Marshall folder, Admin. file. Marshall was employed as a regular
member of the staff on or about December 15. Eric Hodgins was hired in the
same capacity in late November. See Eric Hodgins folder, ibid.

4 Consultants and their fields were: Harold C. Hunt (of Harvard's School of
Education), education; Joseph Volpe (a Washington attorney with experi-
ence on the Atomic Energy Commission), loyalty-security problems; Frank
Loescher (former head of the AFSC Community Relations Department), in-
tergroup relations. Memorandum, Clifford Case to the Members of the Board,
January 22, 1954, "Tax Exemption Granted" folder, B.D.W.P. file.

5 The staff also investigated the Houston *Post* series and decided against mass
distribution. "In reaching this conclusion the staff has in mind that our
projected study of extremist groups will include an examination of the
Minute Women far more thorough than a journalistic report can be." Ibid.

6 Memorandum, Charles B. Marshall to Clifford Case, January 25, 1954,
Charles B. Marshall folder, Admin. file. Reinhold Niebuhr later told Marshall
much the same thing. Memorandum, Charles B. Marshall to Clifford Case,
February 23, 1954, ibid.

7 Minutes, January 28, 1954.

8 René A. Wormser to Clifford P. Case, January 18, 1954, Reece Committee
file.

9 Clifford Case to Norman Dodd, February 2, 1954, ibid. The Ford Foundation created a thorough and official answer to the committee's questions, dated
March 11, 1954.

10 Ibid.

11 Clifford Case to René A. Wormser, March 10, 1954, ibid.

12 Night letter, Paul G. Hoffman to Board Members, March 4, 1954, Hoffman
papers.

13 Minutes, March 16, 1954. See Earl Mazo, *Richard Nixon: A Political and
Personal Portrait* (New York, 1960), p. 153.

14 Clifford Case to Robert Hutchins, June 14, 1954, "Admin. Annual Report"
folder, Admin. file.

15 Macdonald, *The Ford Foundation*, pp. 72–3.

16 Minutes, March 16, 1954. See Fund for the Republic, *The Fund for the Republic, A Report on Three Years' Work, May 31, 1956* (New York, 1956),
pp. 34–5. This important work will be referred to hereafter as *Three Years'
Report*.

17 Minutes, April 1, 1954. See *The New York Times*, April 11, 1954; Henry
Lesesne, "For Better Race Relations: Southern Regional Council Works to
This End," Baltimore *Evening Sun*, May 14, 1954.

18 Both Loescher and Freeman had worked in interracial relations for the Ford
Foundation.

19 On Case's later attacks on McCarthy, see Earl Mazo, "Case Pledges Fight
To Bar McCarthy from Inquiries," New York *Herald Tribune*, December 15
1954; Rovere, *Senator Joe McCarthy*, p. 234.

20 On February 17, 1954. Clifford P. Case to H. Rowan Gaither, February 19,
1954, "Grant to the Fund" folder, F.F. file.

21 Macdonald, *The Ford Foundation*, p. 72.

22 I. F. Stone, *The Haunted Fifties* (New York, 1963), p. 68. Stone's statement
was first published on March 15, 1954.

CHAPTER FIVE

1 For examples see Dyke Brown folder, F.F. file.
2 E.g., Robert M. Hutchins to John Cowles, August 28, 1953, *C* folder, ibid; Robert M. Hutchins to Charles Wyzanski, January 20, 1954, *W* folder, ibid.
3 E.g., Robert M. Hutchins to Henry Ford II, February 3, 1953; telegram, Henry Ford II to Robert M. Hutchins, February 6, 1953, Henry Ford II folder, ibid.
4 Charles Wyzanski to Robert M. Hutchins, December 24, 1953, *W* folder, F.F. file.
5 See Grenville Clark folder, ibid.
6 Grenville Clark to Robert M. Hutchins, March 15, 1954, ibid.
7 Interview with Robert M. Hutchins, August 16, 1965:
We looked widely. I visited Earl Warren in Sacramento, and we talked for over three hours. He was excited about the challenge, but said that he had heard rumors of an even bigger appointment for him. He was right, of course. At the next board meeting I talked hard for Hutchins. He was just sitting in Pasadena, and it was a very awkward position. There was opposition on the Fund's board.
Interview with William H. Joyce, Jr., May 6, 1966:
We sought a dynamic leader for a job badly in need of doing, and we turned to Hutchins, who had thought of the Fund. Some exchange with trustees of the Ford Foundation was made in advance about a possible Hutchins appointment. They were not wild about the idea but there was no veto.
Interview with Erwin Griswold, August 31, 1967.
8 Memorandum draft, Robert M. Hutchins to Paul G. Hoffman, December 13, 1955, Hoffman papers.
9 Hutchins, *Freedom, Education, and the Fund*, pp. 20–1.
10 Editorials from the most respected newspapers were overwhelmingly opposed to the character and slant of the hearings during their progression. E.g., *The New York Times*, May 13, 1954; New York *Herald Tribune*, May 15, 1954. For particularly relevant commentary, see Roscoe Drummond, "What the Reece Committee Is After," ibid., May 26, 1954, and Charles Bartlett, "Reece Foundations Probe Gathers Steam, Interest," Chattanooga *Times*, May 23, 1954. Cf. the view of the New York *Daily News*, May 12, 1954: "Complaints are often heard that a lot of this money is dished out to Reds, Pinks and other subversives. Where there is so much smoke, there is almost certainly some fire." John O'Donnell wrote in the *Daily News* (May 25) of "big foundation dough . . . secretly backing socialists, starry-eyed crypto-Commies and New Deal pinkos."
11 Robert M. Hutchins, "Are Our Teachers Afraid To Teach?" *Look*, March 9, 1954, p. 14.
This article was severely criticized before the Reece committee on June 3 by an assistant staff research director, Thomas McNiece. Committee member Wayne Hays, not at all sympathetic to the hearings, discovered through cross-examination that McNiece's training had been almost entirely in engineering and cost accounting, and that he believed Social Security, unemployment in-

surance, and old-age pensions to be "collectivist concepts." House of Representatives, Special Committee To Investigate Tax-Exempt Foundations and Comparable Organizations, *Hearings*, 83rd Cong., 2d Sess., 1954, pp. 493–520.

The Reece committee hearings ended in uproar on June 17, having heard only witnesses hostile to foundations and modern education. It continued its studies and released a final report on December 20, 1954, to be discussed below. The committee's activities pertaining to the Fund were confined to the making of inquiries, due to the corporation's early difficulties—by all evidence an unintentional circumstance. "There was a certain hangover from the Reece Committee by the time I became the Fund's president. But I doubt that it made much of an impression on the board." Interview with Robert M. Hutchins, August 16, 1965.

12 Minutes, April 15, 1954.
13 *The New York Times*, May 25, 1954.
14 Interview with Robert M. Hutchins, August 16, 1965.
15 Ferry later recalled:
    The main reason for my reluctance was fear of boredom. Most of the people I had encountered who were advocates of civil liberties were bores —one-eyed fanatics; not nuts but unusual. I had visions of scores of these people lining up asking for money. I decided to accept the position for only a year.
    Interview with W. H. Ferry, August 26, 1965. Ferry remained with the Fund until July 1969.
16 *The New York Times*, February 26, 1953.
17 The general idea of a commission on security had been presented to the board as early as April 1 by Case consultant Joseph Volpe. Memorandum, David Freeman to the Members of the Board of Directors, June 21, 1954, B.D.W.P. file. Plans for a study of extremism were based on a resolution of the board of November 18, 1953, recommending research into the matter. Both $25,000 appropriations, then, were responses to ideas explored under the presidency of Clifford Case.
18 The officers had investigated the results of the first grant to the committee (June 16, 1953) and concluded that, in general, they "have been successful and should be continued." Memorandum, David Freeman to the members of the Board of Directors, June 21, 1954, ibid.
    The "officers" frequently referred to the president and his staff, more often simply to the president. The legal definition of an officer is:
    The officers of the Corporation shall be a Chairman of the Board of Directors, an Honorary Chairman, a President, one or more Vice Presidents, a Secretary, and a Treasurer, each of whom shall be elected annually by the Board of Directors at its annual meeting and shall hold office for one year and until his successor is elected.
    The Fund for the Republic, Inc. (By-Laws) (n.p., n.d.), pp. 11–12.
19 This was a new venture for the Fund, though the Ford Foundation had contributed $225,000 to the council since 1950. Paul Hoffman and George Shuster were on the council's board of directors. Memorandum, David Freeman to the Members of the Board of Directors, June 21, 1954, B.D.W.P. file.
20 Minutes, June 30, 1954.
21 E.g., the Fund for the Republic awards: "The basic conception here is that which Plato stated: 'What is honored in a country will be cultivated there.' The Fund has the means of honoring conscientious non-conformity." Memorandum, David Freeman to the Members of the Board of Directors, June

21, 1954, B.D.W.P. file. Hutchins wrote much of the Fund's docket, and reviewed and passed final judgment on all of it. Interview with Hallock Hoffman, August 27, 1965.

22 The exception was over continuing grants to the Catholic Interracial Council of Chicago. The board was more cautious than the president and his staff in this matter and emphasized "that support of such local activities by the Fund was experimental in nature and that the local group should be encouraged to become self-supporting." Minutes, June 30, 1954.

23 Interview with Robert M. Hutchins, August 16, 1965.

24 H. Rowan Gaither, Jr., in a second lengthy reply to charges against the Foundation by the committee, expressed pride in the Fund, and said of this grant: "Such a study is appropriate, it is needed, and I hope the Trustees of the Fund take the necessary action to see the need is filled." "The Ford Foundation, Statement of H. Rowan Gaither, Jr., President and Trustee, to the Special Committee To Investigate Tax-Exempt Foundations, House of Representatives, 83rd Congress," Supplement B, July 16, 1954, Reece Committee file.

The Reece committee continued a stream of specific questions throughout the summer. In late August the Ford Foundation received a frantic letter from committee investigator René A. Wormser which was forwarded to Ferry:

I would appreciate a prompt answer to certain questions regarding a Dr. Thomas B. Pettingill, who is reported to have been employed by or associated with the Ford Foundation. . . .

* * *

3 Is it true that he had previously been a member of the faculty of the People's Educational Center, an allegedly Communist School in southern California? . . .

* * *

5 It is alleged that Dr. Pettingill, shortly after his connection with the Foundation, espoused an investigation in the "civil liberties" area, with particular emphasis on the techniques employed by legislative committees on un-American activities. Is this true? If so, is he the "father" of the Fund for the Republic concept? I would appreciate details. If Dr. Pettingill did not initially support, propose or promote the idea, who did?

See Reece Committee file for letters between the Fund and various committee investigators. For a clear and valuable insight into the vocabulary and outlook of the Fund's most extreme antagonists see René A. Wormser, *Foundations: Their Power and Influence* (New York, 1958), pp. 270–87.

25 Paul G. Hoffman, "House of Representatives Special Committee To Investigate Tax-Exempt Foundations (House Resolution 217), Statement of Paul G. Hoffman, Chairman of the Board, The Fund for the Republic, Inc.," July 22, 1954, Reece Committee file.

26 Memorandum, Walter Millis, "Proposals for a Citizens' Commission on the Federal Security Program," August 23, 1954, B.D.W.P. file.

27 See Donner, *The Un-Americans,* pp. 165–6.

28 Ibid., pp. 122, 173–4.

29 On the broad extent of McCarthyism's popularity see Rogin, *The Intellectuals and McCarthy,* pp. 216–60 and passim. See also Seymour Martin Lipset, "Three Decades of the Radical Right: Coughlinites, McCarthyites, and Birchers," in Daniel Bell, ed., *The Radical Right* (New York, Anchor Books edn., 1965), pp. 392–3, 420–1.

30 *The New York Times,* August 16, 1954.

31 At the time, Rossiter was writing his famous *Conservatism in America* (New York, 1955). For his own view of the Radical Right see esp. pp. 183–6. For a fascinating analysis of Rossiter's personal brand of conservatism see Edward Cain, *They'd Rather Be Right: Youth and the Conservative Movement* (New York, 1963), pp. 120–9.

32 "Status of Grants Already Approved," September 1, 1954, B.D.W.P. file.

33 "Recommendations for Board Action," September 1, 1954, ibid.

34 Requests for board approval were often estimated with less than precision, and this appropriation to the Sutherland committee is a case in point. A financial statement compiled by the most important committee staff member, and dated August 26, estimated the need for an additional $3,600. A few days later, Sutherland added: "Because of pessimism over all estimates, I suggest that if the Fund is willing, they earmark an appropriation of $5,000 for the completion of the project." The letter was passed on to Ferry, who wrote at the bottom: "Why not $5,000? If you agree please prepare an additional item for the Board. . . ." On September 13, Freeman wrote to the directors: "Although Professor Sutherland originally requested an additional appropriation of $5,000, our examination of his estimated expenses for the next two months, and his indication that several of the estimates are, of necessity, largely guesses, persuades us that an appropriation of up to $7,500 would be more realistic." The board agreed at its next meeting. See "Comm. Menace, Short Term Proj. to Nov. 23, 1954" folder, Project Correspondence file. The latter will be referred to hereafter as Proj. Corres. file.

35 "Program development." This category covered the expenses of officers and staff members in the act of exploring possibilities for future recommendations. "To put these costs under administrative expenses would have been inaccurate and bad for public relations." Interview with Hallock Hoffman, September 1, 1965.

36 Public-relations executive Carl Ruff was hired on October 6. He was also to assist in the publicity for the forthcoming study on the Communist record. See Carl Ruff folder, Admin. file.

37 Minutes, September 14, 1954.

38 W. H. Ferry to John Cogley, September 16, 1954, "Blacklist Project" folder, Proj. Corres. file.

39 "Harrington needed a job; he was eating at the *Catholic Worker.* He was very bright, he knew more about the Communist Party than I did; he knew his way around in this ideological world better than I." Interview with John Cogley, July 18, 1966.

> Harrington calls himself "a Socialist in the Marxist tradition":
>
> My job with Cogley was, in a sense, as a personal assistant. I worked with John on practically every one of the interviews. I did various writing jobs, various first drafts, and John and I were the only two people who worked on both the East and West coast on the project. . . . John was the director and I was the only other person involved in the over-all execution of the project.

Interview with Michael Harrington, March 1, 1964.

40 See Andrews, *Philanthropic Foundations,* pp. 329–33.

41 Memorandum, Thomas W. Chrystie, "Addendum to the Tax Memorandum of December 17, 1953," October 1, 1954, B.D.W.P. file.

42 See "Consultants—General Correspondence" folder, Admin. file, for further background and detail.

43 Philip Woodyat to David Freeman, October 22, 1954, Philip Woodyat folder, ibid.
44 "Progress Report," November 4, 1954, B.D.W.P. file.
45 Press release, Fund for the Republic, December 20, 1954.
46 A request would come to the Fund, go to Hutchins, he would assign it to a staff member he felt would best handle it, and the measure would be discussed at meetings of the executive staff. If a consensus appeared, a recommendation was prepared for the board. Hutchins often disliked measures sent to the directors. The Catt discussion program was one. Interview with John Cogley, July 18, 1966.
47 "Proposals for a Study of Race and Housing and the Establishment of a Commission," October 21, 1954, Appendix B, Minutes, November 18, 1954.
48 "Recommendations to the Board," November 4, 1954, B.D.W.P. file.
49 Hofstadter, *The Paranoid Style*, p. 71.
50 A few months later Hutchins gave a stinging address to the American Society of Newspaper Editors on the subject, including: "Of course we have a one-party press in this country, and we shall have one as long as the press is big business, and as long as people with money continue to feel safer on the Republican side." See Hutchins, *Freedom, Education, and the Fund*, pp. 57–67.
51 "Recommendations to the Board," November 4, 1954, B.D.W.P. file.
52 "It was the sense of the meeting that the Fund should not seek publicity for this type of activity but that the Officers should find and assist people of mature judgment who were doing or were qualified to do constructive work in areas of the Fund's interest." Minutes, November 18, 1954.
53 Ibid. The Fund's first grant to the bureau supported a "trial study" of right-wing extremist groups in Hastings-on-Hudson, New York, which the officers found unsatisfactory. The bureau received a second grant for a "study design" which resulted in proposals estimated to cost as much as $650,000. Leo Rosten of *Look* magazine (who had been Hutchins's second choice, after Bosley Crowther of *The New York Times*, for the position given to Cogley) agreed to direct whatever study the Fund approved.
54 See *Three Years' Report*, "Financial Statements," and Macdonald, *The Ford Foundation*, pp. 72–3.

CHAPTER SIX

1 Other committee members were: Charles Fairman, professor of constitutional law and political science, Washington University, St. Louis, Missouri; Rev. Joseph M. Snee, S.J., professor of law, Georgetown University, Washington, D.C.; Clinton Rossiter, professor of government, Cornell University, Ithaca, New York.
   Depositories were: Library of Congress, University of California at Berkeley, the University of Chicago, Harvard University, New York Public Library, Cornell University Library, University of Texas at Austin, University

of Washington, Florida State University at Tallahassee. Copies were also available at the Fund's New York office. Press release, Fund for the Republic, November 23, 1954.

2 Publicity consultant Carl Ruff wanted to publish photographs of microfilm presentations to the Attorney General, J. Edgar Hoover, and others. The idea was vetoed by Professor Sutherland: "I am sorry thus to drape a damp blanket over what I know is an experiment noble in motive. It stems from a constitutional allergy to publicity stunts, and from a conviction that the only thing our books and films can accomplish is to provide a means by which, over a long period of time, sober study of American Communism can be made." Arthur Sutherland to M. S. Bradley, November 15, 1954, "Comm. Menace, Short Term Proj. to Nov. 23, 1954" folder, Proj. Corres. file.

3 Even before the censure, in mid-November, Paul Hoffman contended that the nation was "somewhere past the middle" of the "complex fear." "Unquestionably, a big factor has been the clear and outspoken position taken by the President." Paul G. Hoffman, "To Insure the End of Our Hysteria," *The New York Times Magazine*, November 14, 1954, pp. 9, 62–3.

4 See Kemper, *Decade of Fear*, pp. 94–6; editorial in *The New York Times*, January 4, 1955; *I. F. Stone's Weekly*, January 24, 1955, passim.

5 See especially Arthur M. Schlesinger, Jr., "The Oppenheimer Case," *Atlantic Monthly*, October 1954, pp. 29–36; Charles P. Curtis, *The Oppenheimer Case* (New York, 1955).

6 The Board of Directors of the American Association for the Advancement of Science, "Strengthening the Basis of National Security," *Science*, December 10, 1954, pp. 957–9.

7 Peter Kihss, "City Bar To Study Loyalty Reviews," *The New York Times*, December 22, 1954.

8 Yarmolinsky had been recommended to Hutchins by Charles E. Corker. David Freeman had known the Fund's future secretary in law school. Charles E. Corker to Robert M. Hutchins, August 30, 1954; David Freeman to W. H. Ferry, August 31, 1954; Robert Hutchins to Charles E. Corker, September 10, 1954, "Comm. Menace, Short Term Proj. to Nov. 23, 1954" folder, Proj. Corres. file.

9 Memorandum, Walter Millis, November 30, 1954, B.D.W.P. file.

10 "Single-spaced typewritten instructions for interviewers were 24 pages long. When needed, interviewers who spoke Italian, Spanish and Yiddish were employed." Fact sheet, unsigned and undated, ibid.

11 Fund director John Lord O'Brian soon said of this fact:

> This does not mean that Americans are indifferent to the issues of Communism or civil liberties. It does mean that the Communist danger is no longer directly felt as a personal threat by Americans and that relatively few citizens have experienced any sense of threat to their freedom from that source. . . . In short, and contrary to widespread belief, the country is not now in the grip of hysteria or of emotional fear of Communism.
>
> Assuming that these results are typical of the American people generally, they certainly indicate that the general public today is far less disturbed than are the politicians, so many of whom exploit the Communist issues sensationally and for selfish purposes.

John Lord O'Brian, *National Security and Individual Freedom* (Cambridge, Mass., 1955), p. 54.

Cf. "One must recall that the public merely reported their intolerant *opinions* and did not always act them out, and this implies that a climate of intolerance requires stimulation and mobilization in order to work its social effects." Herbert H. Hyman, "England and America: Climates of Tolerance and Intolerance," in Bell, ed., *The Radical Right,* p. 271. On American intolerance see Seymour Martin Lipset, "The Sources of the Radical Right," ibid., pp. 316–21. For valuable data and reflection on public disinterest in noneconomic issues see Seymour Martin Lipset, *Political Man: The Social Bases of Politics* (Anchor Books edn., New York, 1963), pp. 87–126.

12   See fascinating interviews of the man-on-the-street in "What Is a Communist?" Madison (Wisconsin) *Capitol Times,* February 26, 1953. One housewife replied: "I really don't know what a Communist is. I think they should throw them out of the White House."

13   Gordon N. Allport, "Our National Symptoms," *Saturday Review,* May 14, 1955, pp. 14–15.

14   E.g., Samuel A. Stouffer, "What Are We Worried About?" *Look,* March 22, 1955, pp. 25–7; Stouffer, "How the People Feel About Communism and Civil Liberties," ibid., March 29, 1955, pp. 62, 65–7, 69; "The Businessman and Civil Liberties," *Fortune,* May 1955, pp. 114–15, 165.

15   Hutchins, *Freedom, Education, and the Fund,* p. 34. Cf. Robert M. Hutchins to Allen Wallis, June 2, 1955, *W* folder, F.F. file.

      The idea of having Clifford Case write an introduction to the book came from Hutchins, who scribbled the suggestion at the bottom of a letter by Ken McCormick, editor in chief of Doubleday, to W. H. Ferry, November 12, 1954, "Stouffer Project" folder, Proj. Corres. file. Case assented to the request when posed by David Freeman. Memorandum, David Freeman to W. H. Ferry, December 7, 1954, ibid.

16   Samuel A. Stouffer, *Communism, Conformity, and Civil Liberties* (New York, 1955), p. 220.

17   See Press release, Fund for the Republic, January 10, 1955, and memorandum, M. S. Bradley to W. H. Ferry, October 20, 1954, "Comm. Menace, Short Term Proj. to Nov. 23, 1954" folder, Proj. Corres. file. Charles E. Corker was again in charge of the staff that assembled the material.

18   Hutchins later wrote:

      An enormous amount of popular, and hence effective (or it would not be popular), political argument runs this way: I am very frightened of Communism; you are not as frightened as I am; therefore, you are not as patriotic as I am. . . . At a large meeting at which I spoke recently it was suggested that the address . . . would be much improved if it said that the Fund for the Republic was set up to fight Communism by defending and advancing the principles of the Declaration of Independence, the Constitution, and the Bill of Rights. This would mean that if there were no Communists in the world, there would be no need for the Fund, and presumably no need for the Bill of Rights when it was adopted.

      Hutchins, *Freedom, Education, and the Fund,* p. 22.

19   Minutes, December 9, 1954, and accompanying Note.

20   Chicago *Daily News,* January 10, 1955.

21   See U.S. House, Special (Reece) Committee To Investigate Tax-Exempt Foundations and Comparable Organizations, *Report.* 83rd Cong., 2d Sess., House Report 2681, Washington, D.C., 1954. An admirable summary is in Andrews, *Philanthropic Foundations,* pp. 345–7. For significant reflections on the committee and its effects see Waldemar A. Neilsen, "How Solid Are the Foundations?" *The New York Times Magazine,* October 21, 1962, p. 27; Ralph Henry Gabriel, *The Course of American Democratic Thought* (2d edn., New York, 1956), pp. 458–60. See also David Riesman and Nathan Glazer,

"The Intellectuals and the Discontented Classes," in Bell, ed., *The Radical Right*, p. 131 f.

22 *The New York Times*, December 23, 1954.

23 "Remarks of Robert M. Hutchins, President of the Fund for the Republic, before the National Press Club, Washington, D.C., January 26, 1955," Robert M. Hutchins folder, Personnel file. The entire speech, slightly rewritten, is in Hutchins, *Freedom, Education, and the Fund*, pp. 201–12.
   "When Dr. Hutchins finished . . . Reece walked up to him and offered his hand. He said he had been in politics 34 years and had learned not to be disturbed by what people said about him. Later, however, Reece accused Dr. Hutchins of being at heart a 'book burner.'" Edward T. Folliard, "Reece Hears Hutchins Blast His Report on Foundations as Scandalous Fraud," Washington *Post and Times-Herald*, January 27, 1955. See the complimentary editorial of the same day in the *Post*.

24 " . . . he [Pegler] spent considerable time at the Foundation last week. Some of his conversation there . . . involved the Fund. I leave to your imagination the flattering words he used to describe Hutchins, you and to a lesser extent the Vice President of this organization.
   He indicated . . . that he saw something of sinister significance in the fact that you and I were both identified with the Fund."
   W. H. Ferry to Paul G. Hoffman, December 21, 1954, Hoffman papers.

25 See American Book Publishers Council *Bulletin*, December 28, 1954, passim. Cf. Marjorie Fiske, *Book Selection and Censorship: A Study of School and Public Libraries in California* (Berkeley and Los Angeles, 1959), passim.

26 Hallock Hoffman first broached the idea for the award at the November 18, 1954, board meeting. No action was taken pending an "on-the-spot" investigation by West Coast directors. Paul Hoffman and William H. Joyce, Jr., visited the YWCA in Los Angeles and Joyce recommended either a grant or an award. Paul Hoffman opposed either until "such time as some machinery and criteria had been established within the Fund to select organizations for this type of award." The 8–6 vote sustained Joyce, and the resolution furthermore failed to incorporate Hoffman's additional suggestion that the Fund first inform the chancellor of UCLA and the national board of the YWCA of its intentions. This is but one of many examples of the caution and restraint urged upon the Fund by Hoffman. Minutes, February 17, 1955.
   "This YWCA, considering the regulations enforced by the University of California at the time, was the only place even near the campus where one could say anything he wished." Interview with Hallock Hoffman, September 3, 1965.

27 Before authorizing the commission, the Fund spent $850 for a preliminary report on the first privately built housing development for interracial occupancy, in Trevose, Pennsylvania. Each director received a copy of the report before the February meeting. See Eunice and George Grier, "Interim Summary Report, Concord Park: A Pioneer Attempt at Privately-Built Sales Housing for Interracial Occupancy," January 1955; memorandum, Frank S. Loescher to Members of the Board of Directors, January 19, 1965, B.D.W.P. file.

28 The board was informed that the survey into intellectual freedom would be conducted first at the college-university level and then among high-school teachers and administrators. Recommendations to the Board, February 2, 1955, ibid. As expenses soared the study was limited to interviews with 2,500 college teachers.

29 The Fund also circulated without cost a one-hour film of the interview. By February 2,550 requests had been received. Local American Legion leaders attempted to pressure the board of education of Pleasantville, New York, into prohibiting a showing of the film in the city's junior high school. *The New York Times,* March 23, 24, 1955; Progress Report, February 2, 1955, B.D.W.P. file.

30 Directors were always reasonably informed of the officers' intentions. Requests for general authority in matters such as the purchase and distribution of literature usually contained an outline of proposed actions. E.g.:

The Officers have in mind seeing to a wide distribution of such material as a recent article by Richard Hofstadter, "The Pseudo-Conservative Revolt," published in the Winter edition of the American Scholar and a book by Alan Barth, "Government by Investigation," that will be published in April. They are also exploring the possibility of providing wide distribution for the forthcoming special issue of the Bulletin of the Atomic Scientists on security problems. They would consider under such a general authorization additional suggestions such as that from Freedom House for publication of the proceedings of its recent meeting on "Security and Progress in the Atomic Age," and a proposal to make available recordings of the recent series of lectures on civil liberties at the New School for Social Research.

"Recommendations to the Board," February 2, 1955, ibid.

31 Ibid.

32 Chicago *Daily News,* January 10, 1955. Hutchins himself joined the Illinois post in 1954.

33 The Fund failed to cope successfully with the American legacy project, and $19,727 reverted to the general funds of the corporation. The $8,000 contingency appropriation for the Columbia University Bicentennial Committee also reverted. Minutes, February 17, 1955.

34 See Hofstadter, *Anti-Intellectualism in American Life* (Vintage edn., New York, (1966), esp. pp. 1–7, 12–13, 221–7; Lipset, *Political Man,* pp. 363–71.

35 Press release, "Remarks of Carroll Reece, National Press Club Luncheon," February 23, 1955, Reece Committee file.

Two days later Reece wrote a bitter reply to Hutchins on charges against his committee appearing in Erwin Griswold's *The Fifth Amendment Today.* He requested that copies of his letter be mailed "to anyone who has received through you a copy of Dean Griswold's booklet, in order that the canard, for which he is responsible, be exposed." Hutchins replied that he regretted the Fund could not comply. B. C. Reece to Robert M. Hutchins, February 25, 1955; W. H. Ferry to Robert M. Hutchins, February 28, 1955; Robert M. Hutchins to B. C. Reece, March 2, 1955, ibid.

Hutchins spoke out against the Reece committee again on April 2 in the course of a speech before the American Academy of Political and Social Science. He failed to mention the Fund. See "Remarks of Robert M. Hutchins, President of the Fund for the Republic, before the American Academy of Political and Social Science, Philadelphia, Pennsylvania, April 2, 1955," ibid.

36 John O'Donnell, "Capitol Stuff," New York *Daily News,* February 24, 1955. Cf. William Stringer, "The Fund for the Republic," *Christian Science Monitor,* March 21, 1955.

37 The committee for 1955 consisted of Paul Hoffman, Robert Hutchins, Erwin Griswold, Elmo Roper, and George Shuster. The committee often took up matters on its own, as it had the right to do. But on major recommendations it was felt wise to seek the full board's consent. Minutes, November 18, 1954.

38 Before the appropriation, Mr. Segal's fee and expenses were charged to "pro-

gram development" to reduce the total of the Fund's administrative expenses. Minutes, April 7, 1955.

39 The carefully balanced seventeen, recruited by Hutchins, were: Gordon W. Allport, professor of psychology, Harvard University; Elliott V. Bell, chairman, executive committee and director, McGraw-Hill Publishing Company, and editor and publisher of *Business Week*; Laird Bell, Chicago attorney; Rev. John J. Cavanaugh, C.S.C., director of the University of Notre Dame Foundation, Notre Dame, Indiana; Peter Grimm, chairman of the board and director, William A. White and Sons, New York; Charles S. Johnson, president, Fisk University; Charles Keller, Jr., president, Keller Construction Corporation, New Orleans; Clark Kerr, chancellor, University of California at Berkeley; Philip M. Klutznick, chairman of the board, American Community Builders, Inc., Park Forest, Illinois; Henry R. Luce, editor in chief, *Time, Life, Fortune, Sports Illustrated, Architectural Forum,* and *House and Home*; Stanley Marcus, president, Neiman-Marcus, Dallas; J. C. McClellan, president, Old Colony Paint and Chemical Company, Los Angeles; Ward Melville, president, Melville Shoe Corporation, New York; Francis T. P. Plimpton, New York attorney; R. Stewart Rauch, Jr., president, the Philadelphia Savings Fund Society; Earl B. Schwulst, president, the Bowery Savings Bank, New York; and Robert R. Taylor, executive director of the Illinois Federal Savings and Loan Association. Press release, Fund for the Republic, May 20, 1955.

"We had an extremely difficult time getting good people—businessmen and bankers especially—to sit on the Commission." Interview with Hallock Hoffman, June 29, 1965.

40 The total audience through March was estimated at 36,297. "Another 25 prints, in the permanent possession of universities and foundations, have accounted for approximately 400 showings in addition to those reported by the Fund's own distributor, Association Films." Press release, Fund for the Republic, May 11, 1955.

41 The articles were by Vannevar Bush, Paul G. Hoffman, Richard Hofstadter, Richard Rovere, Paul Willin, and from the Denver *Post*, and the *Bulletin of Atomic Scientists*. The speech was by former Republican senator Harry P. Cain (of which more will be said below). Authors of the books were Alan Barth, Erwin Griswold, May Sarton, and Telford Taylor. Also distributed were 2,000 copies of "Banned Books," a bibliography of book censorship over the centuries. "Progress Report," May 5, 1955.

42 "Blacklist Probe: Meaning to Admen," *Sponsor*, May 2, 1955, p. 43.

43 Ibid. One staff member, a veteran of *Time* magazine, wrote of her interviews:
There was not a single instance . . . of concern over the rights, over the justice involved in the blacklisting activity. There were instances of scoffing over the pressure groups which came into play over a possible controversial personality, but no show of resistance, no thought of resistance, to what they consider foolish—foolish, but not unjust.
O tempores! O mores!
[Margaret] Peggy Bushong to John Cogley, February 24, 1955, "Blacklist Project" folder, Proj. Corres. file. See George Sokolsky, "Quarantine," Washington *Post and Times-Herald*, January 4, 1955.

44 The Writers' Guild of America, East and West, actively supported the competition. Press release, Fund for the Republic, April 26, 1955.

45 This review was adapted from the "Progress Report," May 5, 1955.

46 *Three Years' Report*, p. 46.

47 Press release, Fund for the Republic, March 30, 1955.

48 The executive committee terminated Capp's services on April 7, providing a small grant to cover additional expenses. The total cost to the Fund was $20,781.49. Minutes, April 7, 1955.

CHAPTER SEVEN

1 Finnegan died on May 6, 1955, of a heart attack. Memorandum, W. H. Ferry to Members of the Board, May 10, 1955, Richard J. Finnegan folder, Personnel file. Hutchins later told a would-be biographer that "Mr. Finnegan had the only mind in Chicago journalism that was at once independent and flexible. He was the only man who saw that we had a new society and a new world and that we had to do something about them." Robert M. Hutchins to W. Cameron Meyers, June 30, 1958, ibid.

2 Dean was selected for nomination by Paul Hoffman, who had appreciated his support of the Marshall Plan against various conservative critics. Interview with Hallock Hoffman, March 11, 1964.

3 This commission grew out of the earlier idea of a commission on the right to read. J. Russell Wiggins, managing editor of the Washington *Post and Times-Herald,* sent a memorandum to each director on April 14 referring to recent efforts in censorship. The board had not been eager to comply with Hutchins's earlier wishes, but, said the recommendation: "The Officers continue to believe that the Fund should encourage the establishment of such a group, and should assist in its formation to the extent that it seems desirable to do so. Mr. Wiggins and others like him should take the initiative." "Recommendations to the Board," May 5, 1955, B.D.W.P. file.

4 On Herblock see Caughey, *In Clear and Present Danger,* pp. 168–9.

5 Under the direction of Hallock Hoffman, the Fund had produced twenty-three such film clips. Average audience per clip was about 1.5 million viewers. Typical of the film clips were "excerpts from Chief Justice Warren's speech at St. Louis on the present state of American freedom, an ex-Hearst editorial writer protesting the Post Office Department confiscation of his subscription to the Russian Literary Gazette, statements by representative lawyers on disbarment for invocation of the Fifth Amendment." "Recommendations to the Board," May 5, 1955, B.D.W.P. file.

6 Actually, as one Fund staff member summarized the newspaper clippings to Hutchins, "Specific references to your suggestion of a study commission on the press have been meagre." The three editorials favoring it were from the Boston *Herald,* the Chattanooga *Times,* and the Adirondack (N.Y.) *Daily Enterprise.* Memorandum, Edward Reed to Robert Hutchins, May 16, 1955, "Commission on the Mass Media" folder, Proj. Corres. file.

7 The Fund, as noted earlier, had distributed Richard H. Rovere's powerful "The Kept Witnesses," *Harper's Magazine,* May 1955, pp. 25 f. See Harvey Matusow, *False Witness* (New York, 1955).

8 "Recommendations to the Board," May 5, 1955, Appendix C, B.D.W.P. file. Several writers, including the Alsops, had begun such studies, but not on the scale envisioned by Millis and the officers.

9 An appropriation of $100,000 was authorized on May 19 to be expended by the committee "in honoring and rewarding the conduct of men, organizations and institutions that exemplify the liberties this Fund was established to support." It was agreed that awards were to be received by the directors at their quarterly meetings for approval, "but that where the time factor was important, in the judgment of the Committee, it would have the power to act without prior consultation." Minutes, May 19, 1955.

10 See Civil Liberties Committee of the Philadelphia Yearly Meeting of the Religious Society of Friends, *The Plymouth Meeting Controversy* (Philadelphia, 1957); Henry M. Christman, "Mary Knowles and the Quakers: Why Friends Meetings Support a Persecuted Librarian," *The Churchman*, May 1, 1957, pp. 6–8; and Herbert A. Philbrick, "Story of a Boston 'School' and a Librarian," New York *Herald Tribune*, August 21, 1955.

11 E.g., Maureen Black to Richard Bennett, May 9, 1955; Maureen Black to Harry E. Sprogell, May 9, 1955, "Plymouth Awards" folder, Awards file; *The Plymouth Meeting Controversy*, p. 15.

12 Minutes, May 19, 1955.

13 Press release, Fund for the Republic, June 23, 1955.

14 Ibid., July 6, 1955.

15 Gordon Carroll, ed., Booton Herndon, *Praised and Damned: The Story of Fulton Lewis, Jr.* (New York, 1954), pp. 106–7. This little biography, the product of a major publishing house (Duell, Sloan, and Pearce), must be ranked among the truly humorous books of the decade. The author's thesis may be conveyed succinctly: "Lewis has one bias—his patriotism. He loves America, believes in America." See also H. W. Oliphant, "Fulton Lewis, Jr.: Man of Distinction," *Harper's Magazine*, March 1949, p. 76.

16 Los Angeles *Mirror*, June 15, 1955. Cf. " 'The honest American of liberal political bent, says Lewis, 'even a former Communist who has seen the light and is willing to admit it, has nothing to fear in the way of persecution from any Congressional investigating committee, including that of my friend, Joe McCarthy.' " Herndon, *Praised and Damned*, p. 118.

17 Los Angeles *Mirror*, June 17, 1955.

18 Memorandum, David Freeman to W. H. Ferry, undated, "Public Relations—General" folder, Public Relations file, hereafter referred to as Pub. Rel. file.

19 Harold Lord Varney, "Are the Foundations Untouchable?" *American Legion Magazine*, June 1955, pp. 18–19.

20 J. B. Matthews, "Hutchins To Investigate Communism?" *American Mercury*, June 1955, pp. 71–81.

21 See comments by Representative Frank Thompson of New Jersey in *Congressional Record*, 84th Cong., 1st Sess., 1955, 101, A4812–13.

22 Memorandum, Joseph Lyford to Adam Yarmolinsky, July 11, 1955, "Public Relations—General" folder, Pub. Rel. file.

23 The Conshohocken (Pennsylvania) *Record*, August 4, 1955.

24 See the Fund for the Republic, *Report of the Fund for the Republic, May 31, 1955* (New York, 1955).

25 For a view from 1943 on Communism see Robert M. Hutchins, *Education for Freedom* (1st Evergreen Edn., New York, 1963), pp. 41–2. Hutchins's much-misinterpreted testimony before an Illinois subversive activities committee in 1949 is presented and analyzed in E. Houston Harsha, "Illinois: The Broyles Commission," in Walter Gellhorn, ed., *The States and Subversion* (Ithaca, New York, 1952), pp. 95–109. Mr. Harsha notes that the official version of the testimony suffers from distortion and is unreliable. The account contained in his own article comes from notes taken by a private stenographer during

the hearings. For more recent commentary on Communism in America, see memorandum, Robert M. Hutchins to H. Rowan Gaither and Dyke Brown, April 13, 1953. H. Rowan Gaither, Jr., folder, F.F. file; Robert M. Hutchins to Howard L. Chernoff, October 3, 1955, Hoffman papers; Hutchins, *Freedom, Education, and the Fund*, pp. 158–9, 226–7. These citations were chosen for their typification of Hutchins's thoughts on the matter and are by no means exhaustive.

26 Interview with Robert M. Hutchins, February 27, 1964.

27 Hutchins, *Freedom, Education, and the Fund*, pp. 22–3.

28 Fulton Lewis, Jr., *The Fulton Lewis Jr. Report on the Fund for the Republic* (Washington, D.C., 1956), p. 2. This is a collection of the author's radio broadcasts from August 22 through October 27, 1955.

29 When Lewis was informed of the error, and this process occurred several times, he obligingly recanted on a subsequent broadcast.

30 The heated twenty-minute exchange was taken down by staff employee Winifred Meskus, much to Lewis's irritation. See memorandum, Winifred G. Meskus to Files, August 26, 1955, "Public Relations—General" folder, Pub. Rel. file. It was Miss Meskus who discovered Lewis searching the files. Interview with W. H. Ferry, August 2, 1964.

W. H. Ferry's elderly mother asked her son, on a visit to the family home in Detroit: "How is it that Mr. Lewis can be right about so many things and wrong about you?" Ibid.

31 New York *Herald Tribune*, August 23, 1955.

32 Radio Reports, Inc., "Advocates Taxes for All, Tom Duggan at 11:00 P.M. over WBKB-TV (Chicago)," August 26, 1955.

33 Ibid., "Harvey Calls Fund for the Republic Project a Smear Job, Paul Harvey at 6:15 P.M. over WABC (N.Y.) and ABC Network," August 28, 1955.

34 Don O'conner, "Mich. Rep. Hits Republic Fund," Detroit *Times*, August 31, 1955.

35 See Rowland Watts, *The Draftee and Internal Security: A Study of the Army Military Personnel Security Program* (New York, 1955), I, 95–6. This study was reproduced in limited numbers by photo-offset rather than printed. The Fund assisted Watts through the grants-in-aid program.

The work was presented to the Secretary of the Army by Norman Thomas on the very day that Eugene William Landy was refused a commission in the Naval Reserve because his mother was a former Communist.

36 Adam Yarmolinsky, *Case Studies in Personnel Security* (Washington, D.C., 1955), pp. 154–5.

37 See *The New York Times*, August 6, 16, 1955.

38 *The Tablet*, August 20, 1955.

39 Minutes, September 1, 1955.

40 Lewis, *The Fulton Lewis Jr. Report*, p. 43. See also pp. 95–6. The plan to assist the subcommittee was later blocked by Senator John Bricker.

41 Supplemental recommendations at the meeting made the actual total requested $1,707,600.

42 Recommendations to the Board, September 1, 1955, B.D.W.P. file.

43 Radio Reports, Inc., "Dr. Hutchins Discusses the Fund for the Republic, Bill Leonard, This Is New York, at 11:30 P.M. over WCBS (N.Y.)," September 13, 1955. He went on to say: "At the rate at which we are now going we're spending about $4,000,000 a year."

44 Sources of Mr. Lewis's confidential information on this and other matters were never discovered. "We set several traps for him," Ferry recalls. Interview with W. H. Ferry, September 17, 1965. Ferry and staff member Ed Reed

narrowed one lead to a Missouri congressman. See W. H. Ferry to Hon. Thomas B. Curtis, August 19, 1955, "Admin. Annual Report" folder, Admin. file.

45 Lewis, p. 28.

46 Ibid., p. 41. Hutchins labeled Collins's statement "misleading and libelous" and asked the national adjutant of the Legion by telegram for the ". . . NAMES AND ADDRESSES OF LEGION'S 17,000 LOCAL POST COMMANDERS SO THAT WE MAY SEND THEM ANNUAL REPORT OF FUND." Press release, Fund for the Republic, September 13, 1955. The names were not forwarded.

47 "Dean Clarence E. Manion, Weekly Broadcast No. 50, The Fifth Amendment," September 11, 1955, "Publicity—September 1955" folder, Pub. Rel. file.

48 Lerner also noted: "There are all kinds of hints that unless the Fund for the Republic mends its ways the whole Ford Foundation will get far harsher shrift from Congress than the incredible Reece Committee gave it last year." Max Lerner, "Rich Men's Money," New York *Post*, September 14, 1955.

CHAPTER EIGHT /

1 The statement ("From the beginning the Board has held that the major factor affecting civil liberties today is the menace of communism and communist influence in this country, etc.") was placed as a full-page advertisement in the December issue of the *American Legion Magazine.*

2 This oft-noticed feature is most persuasively examined by Seymour Martin Lipset in his "Three Decades of the Radical Right," in Bell, ed., *The Radical Right*, pp. 440–6. See also Talcott Parsons, "Social Strains in America," ibid., pp. 226–7.

3 The budget reports and forecasts included in the recommendations for this meeting were the most extensive ever presented to the board, the explanations the most lucid and elaborate. Always eager, and even more so now, to drop names and statistics into the recommendations, the officers pointed out that the chairman of the Christian Life Commission was Congressman Brooks Hays of Arkansas. The Methodist Church was "the largest Protestant denomination in America with more than 8,000,000 members." Its executive director of the Board of Social and Economic Relations was "A. Dudley Ward, who was director of 'A Study of Ethics and Economic Life,' financed by the Rockefeller Foundation with others for the National Council of Churches."

4 Norman Isaacs, managing editor of the Louisville *Times*, wrote a letter, placed in the docket, explaining the proposal in greater detail. Roscoe Drummond and others had expressed their approval to Hutchins.

5 Tabled for other reasons was an astonishingly silly scheme (to have cost $37,700) involving a "Liberty 1776" telephone contest based on the Bill of Rights. No action was taken on a $25,000 provision for aid to Georgia teachers, no doubt because it was vaguely worded and because it was partly covered by an award to the NAACP's Legal Defense and Educational Fund.

See "Recommendations to the Board," September 1, 1955, B.D.W.P. file; Minutes, September 15, 1955.

6   Press release, Fund for the Republic, September 19, 1955. Radio commentator Cecil Brown said of this address before the American College of Hospital Administrators: "Dr. Robert Maynard Hutchins is a man made for controversy—and dedicated to it." Radio Reports, Inc., "Cecil Brown Quotes Robert Hutchins, Fund For Republic Head, Cecil Brown, at 5:55 P.M. over KFRC (San Francisco) and the Mutual Broadcasting System," September 20, 1955.

7   Lewis, *The Fulton Lewis Jr. Report*, p. 49. Lewis professed to oppose the award to the Quaker Monthly Meeting solely on the ground that Mrs. Knowles might still be a Communist. "And if Mrs. Knowles has reformed, really, and no longer is a communist, all well and good." Ibid., p. 47.

8   Later there was confusion about whether Mr. Dean received the Progress Report and recommendations for the May 19 meeting. Even if he had, his knowledge of the award to the Quaker Meeting, for example, would have been scant, as the Committee on Special Awards first outlined the proposal at a May 19 meeting that Dean did not attend. Memorandum, David Freeman to W. H. Ferry, November 10, 1955, Arthur Dean folder, Personnel file.

9   Lewis, p. 49.

10 Ibid., p. 37.

11 Statement by J. E. Wallace Sterling, President, Stanford University, September 16, 1955, Pub. Docs. file.

12 Lewis, p. 54.

13 Press release, "From the Office of Senator Joe McCarthy, P.M.'s Thursday, September 22, 1955," September 21, 1955, Pub. Docs. file.

14 See the editorial "Fund For What Republic?" New York *Daily News*, September 18, 1955.

15 One newspaper in Henry Ford's area of the country wrote four articles on the issue. E.g., Will Muller, "Ford Fund Stirs Storm in Battle on Civil Liberties," Detroit *News*, September 20, 1955. See also Richard L. Strout, "Legion Ranks Split Over Foreign Policy" and Godfrey Sparling, Jr., "Americanism Issue Racks Illinois Legion," *Christian Science Monitor*, September 19, 1955.

16 David Freeman to Arthur H. Dean, August 19, 1955, Arthur Dean folder, Personnel file.

17 Arthur H. Dean to Robert Hutchins, September 20, 1955, ibid.

18 Arthur H. Dean to Paul Hoffman, September 27, 1955, ibid.

19 Robert Hutchins to Arthur H. Dean, September 29, 1955, ibid.

20 Lewis, p. 58.

21 Radio Reports, Inc., "Wonders Why American Legion Is Singled Out by Fund for the Republic? Walter Winchell at 6:00 P.M. over WOR (N.Y.) and the MBS Radio Network," September 25, 1955.

22 Memorandum, David F. Freeman to Robert M. Hutchins, September 26, 1955, "Grant to the Fund" folder, Admin. file.

23 Quoted in Radio Reports, Inc., "Shares Lewis Sentiments on Fund for the Republic, Hubert Kregoloh, at 7:15 P.M. over WSPR (Springfield, Mass.)," September 30, 1955.

24 Press release, Federal Bureau of Investigation, "Address of Mr. J. Edgar Hoover, Director, Federal Bureau of Investigation, delivered at the 62nd Annual Meeting of the International Association of Chiefs of Police, in Philadelphia, Pennsylvania, at 12:00 Noon (EDT) on October 3, 1955," Pub. Docs. file. For surveys of Hoover's rendezvous with McCarthyism see Alan Barth, *The Loyalty of Free Men* (New York, 1951), pp. 147–76, and

Fred J. Cook, *The FBI Nobody Knows* (New York, 1964), esp. pp. 272–6, 362, 421–3. Cook is tempered slightly by Joseph Kraft in his *Profiles in Power: A Washington Insight* (New York, 1966), pp. 131–8.

25 Press release, "Address by Honorable William F. Tomkins, Assistant Attorney General of the United States, Prepared for Delivery Before the International Association of Chiefs of Police, Benjamin Franklin Hotel, Philadelphia, Pennsylvania, Monday, October 3, 1955," Pub. Docs. file.

26 Press release, Harvard University, "Text of an address by President Nathan W. Pusey of Harvard University at the John Marshall Bicentennial Dinner, given in Memorial Hall on Saturday night, September 24, by the Harvard Law School," September 24, 1955, B.D.W.P. file.

27 "The Ford Foundation: The Fund for the Republic," October 1, 1955, ibid.

28 Washington *Post and Times-Herald*, September 25, 1955.

29 Fulton Lewis, Jr., spent five broadcasts on the issue, which actually involved (as Lewis well knew) a 1952 grant by the Ford Foundation to the University of Chicago for a study of the American jury entitled "Behavioral Science and the Law." Said Lewis: "That 'Behavioral Sciences' business gets under my skin, anyway. . . . did you ever hear such a lot of hogwash!" His broadcasts sparked a congressional investigation into the matter. Lewis, p. 72.

30 Ibid., p. 73. See the editorial in *The New York Times*, October 6, 1955.

31 Lewis, pp. 52–3. *Time* magazine described Herblock more accurately as "a Fair Deal Democrat whose best target is the Republican right wing." "Herblocked," *Time*, October 24, 1955, p. 72.

32 Press release, Fund for the Republic, October 13, 1955.

33 The award to Stiles Hall, the YMCA at the Berkeley campus of the University of California, was left intact. It was far less likely to evoke wrath— and the director of the YMCA branch was an old friend of Paul Hoffman's.

34 Minutes, September 15, 1955.

35 Ibid., October 6, 1955. Directors present at this meeting, along with Paul Hoffman and Dr. Hutchins, were Erwin Griswold, Elmo Roper, Russell Dearmont, John Lord O'Brian, Robert E. Sherwood, and Eleanor B. Stevenson. Of course, the executive committee (Hoffman, Hutchins, Griswold, and Roper), officially took the actions described above.

36 Memorandum, Robert M. Hutchins to Members of the Board of Directors, October 19, 1955, Hoffman papers.

37 E.g., *Closer Up*, October 21, 1955, Pub. Docs. file. To the editors of this weird and grotesque sheet the Southern Regional Council was a "notorious communist front organization"; Mortimer Adler was a "Yid."

38 Radio Reports, Inc., "Says Ford Sponsored Fund Has Tried To Put America To Sleep, Earl Godwin at 6:15 P.M. over WRC (Washington)," October 7, 1955.

39 *The New York Times*, October 10, 1955. The Los Angeles County Democratic Central Committee promptly defended the Fund. Los Angeles *Mirror News*, October 12, 1955.

40 This report was not submitted to the convention delegates, and the executive committee members heard only a summary of the report read by its author, James F. O'Neil, publisher of the *American Legion Magazine*. *Labor*, October 22, 1955. See Memorandum, Walter Millis to W. H. Ferry entitled "The Miami Convention of the American Legion, Oct. 10–13, 1955," undated, B.D.W.P. file.

41 Landman, employed in the Fund's public-relations office, had been identified as having been a Communist by Winston Burdett, Columbia Broadcasting System commentator, who confessed on June 30 to being a former Soviet

spy. After Landman's appearances before the Senate Internal Security Sub-committee in July he was fired as publicity director for the National Municipal League. "Landman needed a job and Ferry felt it was the Fund's duty to help victims of this kind of persecution." Interview with Edward Reed, September 28, 1965. For more on Landman see Leon Racht, "Landman Got Job After He Took 5th," New York *Journal-American,* October 13, 1955; Memorandum, Joseph Lyford to Frank Kelly, May 1, 1957, "Public Relations General, May 1957" folder, Pub. Rel. file.

42 Detroit *Free Press,* October 18, 1955.
43 Arthur H. Dean to Paul G. Hoffman, October 18, 1955, Arthur Dean folder, Personnel file.
44 New York *Herald Tribune,* October 27, 1955.
45 Ibid.
46 Washington *Post and Times-Herald,* October 20, 1955. See Frank Kelly to Elmo Roper, May 2, 1957, "Pub. Relations General, May 1957" folder, Pub. Rel. file.
47 Seattle *Post-Intelligencer,* October 24, 1955.
48 See Jack Steele, "Ford Fund Project Hires Ex-Red Boss Browder," New York *World-Telegram and Sun,* October 19, 1955.
49 Hartford *Times,* October 20, 1955.
50 Milwaukee *Sentinel,* October 20, 1955.
51 "Remarks by Abe Fortas, American Veterans' Committee Dinner, Washington, D.C., October 7, 1955," F folder, Pub. Docs. file. Said the future Supreme Court Justice: "The future belongs to men like Robert Hutchins, who dares to fight for the freedom of the mind." Dr. Hutchins spoke at the same dinner; for his remarks see the Fund's press release of October 7, 1955.
52 E.g., Radio Reports, Inc., "Hutchins Defends Fund for the Republic, Edward P. Morgan at 10:00 P.M. over WABC (N.Y.) and the ABC Network," October 7, 1955.
53 Washington *Post and Times-Herald,* October 19, 1955.
54 On occasion Dr. Hutchins warned violent correspondents to watch their language. E.g.: "As a lawyer I must warn you that your post card received here today is libelous and the gentlemen you have libeled cannot be expected to submit to continued accusations of this type." Robert Hutchins to Mrs. C. Joseph Nowak, October 21, 1955, "Publicity General from October 1, 1955" folder, Pub. Rel. file. Fulton Lewis, Jr., read an abridged version of the response on his broadcast shortly. Memorandum, W. H. Ferry to Winifred Meskus, October 26, 1955, ibid.
55 Memorandum, Maureen Black to Joseph Lyford, October 24, 1955, ibid.
56 Memorandum, Robert Hutchins to Members of the Board of Directors, October 19, 1955, p. 3, Hoffman papers.
57 Ibid., pp. 1–2. The comment on the blacklisting study was changed in the November 3 version of the memorandum sent to the board to read: "Since we do not know what the final report will be, we cannot predict the response it will receive. It seems unlikely that it will be welcomed enthusiastically by the media affected." The last two quoted sentences were dropped altogether.
58 Ibid., p. 4. This sentence was dropped from the November 3 memorandum.
59 Ibid., p. 6.
60 Ibid., p. 7.
61 Ibid., pp. 7–8. This was softened in the November 3 version to read "by a special committee or by the full Board."

62 Ibid., p. 8.
63 Ibid., p. 10. This was dropped from the November 3 memorandum.
64 These words were also eliminated from the version sent to the directors.
65 Ibid., p. 11. This was diluted by November 3 to read: "I believe that if we stand firm we shall look back on this period as one in which the Fund achieved recognition as a powerful and beneficent force in American life."
66 Los Angeles *Mirror News,* October 25, 1955.
67 Frederick Woltman, "Ford Fund Guide on Reds Criticized," New York *World Telegram and Sun,* October 28, 1955; *The New York Times,* October 29, 1955. See Taft's letter of apology in ibid., November 2, 1955.
68 John A. Sessions, "A Misleading Guide to U.S. Communism," *New Leader,* October 31, 1955, pp. 25–7. Dr. Sessions was at the time preparing a history of the League of American Writers for the Fund's study of Communist influences in major segments of U.S. society, under the direction of Clinton Rossiter. Professor Sessions failed to check the bibliography's appendix, overlooking extended references to Eastman and Wolfe. Dr. Sutherland caught this error and passed it along to the directors, with excerpts of the highly complimentary reviews of the bibliography. See memorandum, Maureen Black to the Officers, November 4, 1955, B.D.W.P. file.
69 Memorandum, Robert Hutchins to the Board of Directors, November 3, 1955, ibid. The president assured the board:

> I know of no way in which the Fund could have exercised effective control or could have determined whether or not the bibliography was adequate. The Fund must seek out competent people to conduct studies in which it is interested and then rely on them. The Committee of Directors who recommended the project was satisfied that Mr. Sutherland was competent.

70 New York *Herald Tribune,* October 39, 1955.
71 Woltman, "Ford Fund Guide on Reds Criticized," New York *World Telegram and Sun,* October 28, 1955.
72 Press release, Fund for the Republic, November 7, 1955.
73 Lewis, p. 108.
74 Joseph M. Snee, S.J., to Bethuel M. Webster, November 2, 1955, B.D.W.P. file.
75 In Woltman, "Ford Fund Guide on Reds Criticized."
76 Joseph Lyford to William Clancy [editor of *Newsweek*], November 3, 1955, "Publicity—General, November 1955" folder, Pub. Rel. file.
77 Harold G. Stearns to Paul G. Hoffman, October 3, 1955, "Publicity-Response to Bd. Statement (Hoffman)" folder, ibid. "The thing that amazes me most about the results of the [Fulton Lewis, Jr.] broadcasts is the limited number of letters I have received from his listeners. With some fifty broadcasts, the record is six up to the present time. Bob Hutchins has, I understand, received about twice that number. This is just a trickle compared to the letters I got when I was engaged in the hassle with Senator McCarthy." Paul G. Hoffman to Elmo H. Conley, November 9, 1955, Hoffman papers.
78 Memorandum, Adam Yarmolinsky to Robert Hutchins and W. H. Ferry, November 2, 1955, "Publicity General, November 1955" folder, Pub. Rel. file.
79 In Radio Reports, Inc., "San Franciscan Reports Favorably on Fund for Republic Award, Jim Grady, This Is San Francisco, at 7:15 A.M. over KGBS (San Francisco)," November 8, 1955.
80 For these documents plus excerpts from the extremely flattering acceptance speech by the executive secretary of the University YMCA see B.D.W.P. file.

81 Elmont Waite, "Fight for Civil Liberties: Hoffman Answers Critics of Ford Group," San Francisco *Chronicle,* November 5, 1955.

82 E.g., Macdonald, *The Ford Foundation,* p. 78.

83 Peter Kihss, "Hutchins Condemns Red Party But Would Give Job to Member," *The New York Times,* November 8, 1955; attendance sheet, "11/7 Press Conference RMH," "Publicity General, November 1955" folder, Pub. Rel. file.

84 Interview with Walter Millis, September 21, 1965.

85 See Robert M. Hutchins, "The Freedom of the University," *Bulletin* of the American Association of University Professors, Summer 1951, pp. 238–52.

I regard indoctrination in Republicanism just as revolting as indoctrination in Communism. Therefore if a man was a Communist and attempted to indoctrinate, I would say he was not suitable. But if a man is a sound scholar on any subject and at the same time a Communist, I can't see any objection to him.

Interview with Robert M. Hutchins, February 27, 1964.

86 Joseph Lyford passed a note toward Hutchins requesting that he elaborate upon this sensitive issue. It got as far as Ferry, who opened it, read it, and tossed it away. This incident was observed by several staff members, including John Cogley and Edward Reed.

87 New York *Herald Tribune,* November 8, 1955. The New York *Daily News* ran the headline (November 8, 1955): "HUTCHINS OFFERS AN AYE FOR RED HE CAN WATCH." See "The Controversial Man," *Newsweek,* November 7, 1955, pp. 65–6.

NBC-TV took films of the press conference but decided against their use. Memorandum, Joseph Lyford to W. H. Ferry, November 9, 1955, "Publicity General, November 1955" folder, Pub. Rel. file.

88 Memorandum, Adam Yarmolinsky to Robert M. Hutchins and W. H. Ferry, November 9, 1955, "Grant to the Fund" folder, Admin. file.

89 Washington *Post and Times-Herald,* November 11, 1955; "What Makes a Foundation Tax-Exempt?" *Congressional Quarterly Weekly Report,* November 11, 1955, p. 1198.

90 Undated and unsigned statement. "The preceding statement was issued by a spokesman for the Fund in New York City in response to a query from the Washington *Post,* November 10, 1955, 4:30 P.M.," "Publicity—General, November 1955" folder, Pub. Rel. file.

91 Radio Reports, Inc., "Paul Hoffman Defends Fund for the Republic, Paul Harvey at 12:15 P.M. Over KABC (Los Angeles) and ABC Network," November 10, 1955.

92 Memorandum, W. H. Ferry to Joseph Lyford, November 11, 1955, "Publicity General, November 1955" folder, Pub. Rel. file.

93 Memorandum, Hallock Hoffman to Joseph Lyford, November 11, 1955, ibid.

94 Memorandum, Joseph Lyford to Robert Hutchins and W. H. Ferry, November 15, 1955, ibid.

95 Memorandum, Joseph Lyford to W. H. Ferry, November 14, 1955, ibid.

96 Memorandum [the Officers] to the Board of Directors, November 14, 1955, B.D.W.P. file.

97 See Leon Racht, "Name 21 Pro-Reds on Board of Dixie Race Study Council," New York *Journal-American,* November 7, 1955.

98 See the editorial in *The New York Times,* November 8, 1955.

99 "Freedom Agenda Conference," November 15, 1955, B.D.W.P. file.

100 C. P. Trussell, "12 Chosen for U.S. Panel To Study Loyalty Program," *The New York Times*, November 11, 1955.

101 Hutchins shortly thereafter summarized this brand of optimism in a sentence: "I would remind you of the words variously attributed to William the Silent and Charles the Bold: I have quoted them over and over: 'It is not necessary to hope in order to undertake, nor to succeed in order to perservere.'" Hutchins, *Freedom, Education, and the Fund*, p. 15.

102 "Progress Report," November 9, 1955, B.D.W.P. file.

103 "The Fund for the Republic, Inc., Part II," *The American Legion Firing Line*, November 15, 1955, p. 1.

CHAPTER NINE

1 Interview with Elmo Roper, October 29, 1965; interview with William H. Joyce, Jr., May 6, 1965. See George N. Shuster to Paul G. Hoffman, November 3, 1955; M. Albert Linton to Robert M. Hutchins, November 7, 1955. Hoffman papers.

2 ". . . Mr. Dean's letter will certainly come to the attention of any investigating committee or officials and for that practical reason I think it essential that the views of the Board should be set straight on the record and not be left in the position of seeming to acquiesce in the strictures suggested in the Dean letter." John Lord O'Brian to Paul G. Hoffman, November 2, 1955, ibid. See also John Lord O'Brian to Erwin Griswold, October 28, 1955, ibid.

3 Paul G. Hoffman to Arthur Dean, November 17, 1955, Arthur Dean folder, Personnel file.

4 New York *Mirror*, November 18, 1955.

5 Henry Ford II to Paul G. Hoffman, October 27, 1955; Paul G. Hoffman to Henry Ford II, November 1, 1955, B.D.W.P. file.

6 Paul G. Hoffman to Henry Ford II, November 17, 1955, ibid.

7 Minutes, November 17, 1955.

8 David Sentner, "Fund for Republic Quiz Held Certain," New York *Journal-American*, November 19, 1955.

9 Radio Reports, Inc., "Discuss Ford Foundation & Fund for the Republic, Barry Gray at 12:00 Midnight over WMCA (N.Y.)," November 19–20, 1955.

10 Memorandum, W. H. Ferry to Robert M. Hutchins and Joseph Lyford, November 11, 1955, "Pub.—Meet the Press with RMH. Nov. 1955" folder, Pub. Rel. file. For an echo of Ferry's sentiment see John Crosby, "That's Not Journalism, Man, That's Bearbaiting," Washington *Post and Times-Herald*, February 11, 1956.

11 Los Angeles *Times*, November 21, 1955.

12 Irwin Ross, "Robert M. Hutchins, Article 1," New York *Post*, February 20, 1956.

13 Interview with Harry Ashmore, August 1, 1966.

14 Roger D. Lapham to Paul G. Hoffman, November 30, 1955, Hoffman papers.

15 Mrs. Roger D. Lapham to Paul G. Hoffman, November 21, 1955, ibid.

16 Paul G. Hoffman to Helen [Mrs. Roger D.] Lapham, November 23, 1955, ibid.

17 "It was a sort of incredible sort of total suicide, the explosion of a myth about a man, and the explosion left the man a rather sadly defunct individual." Radio Reports, Inc., "Full Text, Fulton Lewis, Jr., at 7:00 P.M. over WOR (N.Y.) and the MBS Network," November 21, 1955.

18 Martin Quigley to Robert M. Hutchins, November 21, 1955, "Pub.—Meet the Press with RMH. Nov. 1955" folder, Pub. Rel. file. Even the sympathetic Denver *Post* felt obliged to write: "Unfortunately, the Fund for the Republic officials, like their critics, and like many public officials, are inclined to slip and make indiscreet statements that foster bad publicity and distort public attitudes." Denver *Post*, December 29, 1955. The Fund refused requests for transcripts of the program.

Dr. Hutchins told several staff members that before the program he had taken a medication that had dulled his wits. The story was met with much skepticism.

19 Senator James Eastland's Senate Internal Security Subcommittee was also working on some form of inquiry. *The New York Times*, November 24, 1955.

20 Donner, *The Un-Americans*, p. 163.

21 Quoted in John B. Stone, "The Anti-Liberal Career Of Witch-Hunter Francis Walter—3," York (Pennsylvania) *Gazette and Daily*, September 26, 1956.

22 See the memorandum "Mr. Scott McLeod," December 1, 1955, B.D.W.P. file.

23 The Meeting consisted of 115 adult members. Under the rules of the Quaker group, a unanimous vote was required for acceptance. At the Monthly Meeting in September it was decided to let the money remain in escrow until the Meeting "can in unity agree to its deposition." See *The Plymouth Meeting Controversy*, pp. 17–18, and the memorandum "Plymouth Monthly Meeting and Status of Fund's Award," October 6, 1955, B.D.W.P. file.

24 A committee budget, it was decided, beyond the fees and expenses of an advisory consultant, would have to be submitted to the full board, along with a proposed program. Minutes, December 2, 1955.

25 The conference was held as scheduled, though little was achieved. See day letter, Paul G. Hoffman to Bethuel Webster, December 8, 1955, Hoffman papers; Roger D. Lapham to Paul G. Hoffman, January 30, 1956, ibid.

26 New York *Herald Tribune*, December 8, 1955.

27 Interview with Elmo Roper, October 29, 1965.

28 *The New York Times*, November 1, 1955, and February 20, 1956.

29 The Fund's "activities have seriously frightened Ford dealers in this region, which may be unfair but nevertheless is a demonstrable fact." Thomas R. Waring [editor, Charleston *News and Courier*] to Walter Millis, July 20, 1956, "Publicity—General, June 1956" folder, Pub. Rel. file. "Ford was most deeply upset, as I recall, by the letters from southern dealers." Interview with Paul G. Hoffman, August 29, 1967.

30 William F. Buckley, Jr., "A Letter to Mr. Henry Ford," *National Review*, December 14, 1955, p. 5.

31 New York *World Telegram and Sun*, December 8, 1955. See "The American Legion's Position on the Fund for the Republic," *American Legion Magazine*, December, 1955, p. 45—across from the Fund's full-page advertisement.

32 New York *Herald Tribune*, December 8, 1955.

33 "The Ethics of Controversy," *Bulletin*, American Committee for Cultural Freedom, July, 1954, p. 1.

34 Quoted in Earl Latham, *The Communist Controversy in Washington: From the New Deal to McCarthy* (Cambridge, Mass., 1966), pp. 286–7. Professor

Latham's analysis of *The New Leader*'s editorial position during the Tydings committee hearings is penetrating and judicious, as well as indicative of the tone and temper of later views expressed by the journal.

35 See Dwight Macdonald, "Foundation II—How To Spend Henry's Money," *New Yorker*, December 3, 1955, p. 95; Arnold Beichman, "Robert Hutchins Meets the Press," *The New Leader*, November 21, 1955, pp. 18–20. Beichman's disposition was similar to Fulton Lewis, Jr.'s: "The Fund for the Republic has reached the climactic moment in its five-year [*sic*] existence. Its Board of Directors must now decide whether it wants to be a tax-exempt foundation, dedicated to performing good works, or wants to be the $15 million propaganda vehicle of its president, Robert Maynard Hutchins, for the dissemination of his personal views."

36 Kihss, "Hutchins Condemns Red Party But Would Give Job to Member," *The New York Times*, November 8, 1955.

37 The correspondence is in "Comm. Menace, Comprehensive History (Am. Comm. Cult. Freedom)" folder; "GIA Loyalty—American Committee for Cultural Freedom—Govt. Loy. Sec. Program—Affects of" folder; "GIA Censorship—American Committee for Cultural Freedom—Study of Unions in Theatres and Arts" folder; "GIA Communist Menace—American Committee for Cultural Freedom—1956 'Party Line Project' " folder; and "GIA Loyalty —American Veterans Committee—Reject" folder, Grants Reject file. Two of the ACCF requests cited above were made orally.

38 See Michael Harrington, "The Committee for Cultural Freedom," *Dissent*, Spring, 1955, pp. 115–6.

39 "John Dewey and I once participated in a debate at which my opening sentence was: 'Judging from what Mr. Dewey has just stated, either I cannot write or he cannot read.' Hook was furious. I had assailed God." Interview with Robert M. Hutchins, May 20, 1966. For a bit more depth on the matter, see Sidney Hook, *Education for Modern Man* (New York, 1946), pp. 18–27, 34–5, 70, 81–3, 159–71, 197–229.

40 See Sidney Hook, *Heresy, Yes—Conspiracy, No* (New York, 1953), passim, and his *Political Power and Personal Freedom: Critical Studies in Democracy, Communism, and Civil Rights* (New York, 1959), esp. pp. 105–321. Hook may have been writing autobiographically at one point within the latter volume:

> The former Communist knows, as no other can, that the Communist Party means business, deadly business, especially when it puts on a smiling visage for innocents and dupes. His most frustrating experience is to encounter incredulity, and sometimes abuse, when he warns the intended victims or tools of Communist intrigue that they are being used for purposes which in the end will encompass their destruction.

Ibid., p. 219. See also Frank A. Warren III, *Liberals and Communism: The 'Red Decade' Revisited* (Bloomington, Indiana, 1966), pp. 182–5, 228–34, and Vernon Countryman, *Un-American Activities in the State of Washington* (Ithaca, 1951), pp. 381–6.

41 See memorandum, Paul Jacobs to Robert M. Hutchins, December 11, 1955, "American Committee for Cultural Freedom" folder, "Correspondence with Organizations" file. For an account of the meeting (incorrectly dated) see Paul Jacobs, *Is Curly Jewish?* (New York, 1965), pp. 222–4.

42 See Irwin Ross, "Robert M. Hutchins, Article V," New York *Post*, February 24, 1956. For the correspondence surrounding Ferry's remark see "GIA, Communist Menace—American Committee for Cultural Freedom—1956, 'Party Line Project' " folder, Grants Reject file. In a brief exchange on April 27,

1966, Dr. Hook's first complaint against the Fund was its distribution of literature policy. He cited Ferry's comment in the Ross article as evidence of the officers' unfairness to him personally.

43 Sidney Hook, "Six Fallacies of Robert Hutchins," *The New Leader*, March 19, 1956, pp. 18–28. A decade later, Hook's animosity had not faltered. See his letter to the editor in the Santa Barbara (California) *News-Press*, February 27, 1966. He is an advocate of the revocation of the Fund's tax exemption.

44 Edward Reed to Mrs. Diana Trilling, May 11, 1956; Norman Jacobs to Edward Reed, May 15, 1956, "GIA, Communist Menace—American Committee for Cultural Freedom—1956, 'Party Line Project' " folder, Grants Reject file.

45 Robert M. Hutchins to Paul G. Hoffman, December 13, 1955, Hoffman papers.

46 William O. Douglas to the writer, February 18, 1966.

47 *The New York Times*, December 15, 1955.

48 Erwin N. Griswold to David F. Freeman, December 16, 1955, Hoffman papers.

49 Selig Greenburg, "Fund for Republic Criticism Leads to Directors' Inquiry," Providence *Sunday Journal*, December 18, 1955. Greenburg was the first reporter to have access to Arthur Dean's letter of resignation, and throughout several articles on the Fund, displayed an unprecedented public knowledge of the corporation. "The stories by Greenburg came from Griswold. I reproved him at a board meeting for them, but to little effect." Interview with Robert M. Hutchins, November 4, 1965.

50 Selig Greenburg, "Directors Make Reappraisal of Policies, Employes," Providence *Evening Bulletin*, December 23, 1956.

51 Erwin N. Griswold to Paul G. Hoffman, December 19, 1955, Hoffman papers.

52 M. Albert Linton to Paul G. Hoffman, December 19, 1955; John Lord O'Brian to Paul G. Hoffman, December 23, 1955; James D. Zellerbach to Paul G. Hoffman, December 29, 1955, ibid. Linton was clearly the least enthusiastic of the three.

53 Ibid. Zellerbach stressed the importance of including Ferry in the change.

54 Paul G. Hoffman to John Lord O'Brian, December 30, 1955, ibid.

55 Los Angeles *Times*, January 4, 1956.

56 William O. Douglas to Louis M. Rabinowitz, December 11, 1955, B.D.W.P. file.

57 "Minutes of Special Meeting American Section Committee for Rights of Conscience Program Held December 12, 1955, Philadelphia, Pennsylvania," ibid.

58 Interview with Elmo Roper, October 29, 1965. Jubal Parten's comment on this quotation: "Elmo is exactly right." Interview with Jubal R. Parten, February 9, 1966.

59 The five allocations were: $10,000 to Loyola University of New Orleans to finance an education project involving the proposed integration of the parochial schools in the diocese of New Orleans; $7,500 to the Anti-Defamation League of B'nai B'rith to strengthen its participation in the freedom agenda program; $5,255 to the American Veterans of World War II (AM-VETS) to enable them to participate in the freedom agenda program; $19,300 to the Jesuit-operated Institute of Social Order for a college essay contest on the Bill of Rights; and $750 to the Department of Racial and Cultural Relations of the National Council of Churches to finance a conference of agencies interested in assisting southern citizens suffering economic reprisals for their support of school integration. The fact that four of the five recipients were

religious groups and the fifth a veterans' organization could hardly escape the attention of future inquirers. Also approved as recommended was a list of materials to be distributed and an appropriation of $30,000 to continue the distribution program. Minutes, January 6, 1956.

The phrase in the November 16 minutes stating that "No publications by political figures are to be distributed" was rescinded.

60 Robert M. Hutchins to the Editor of *Time*, November 25, 1955, "Publicity General, November 1955" folder, Pub. Rel. file. The letter appeared, skillfully edited, in *Time*'s December 12 issue.

61 Robert M. Hutchins, "Memorandum to the Board of Directors," December 21, 1955, B.D.W.P. file.

62 Minutes, January 6, 1956.

63 *The New York Times*, January 10, 1956. See memorandum, Joseph P. Lyford to Elmo Roper, January 9, 1956, "Publicity—General, January 1956" folder, Pub. Rel. file.

64 Irwin Ross, "Hutchins Reelected Quietly as Fund Head," New York *Post*, January 9, 1956.

65 New York *Journal-American*, January 11, 1956.

CHAPTER TEN

1 Paul G. Hoffman to Roger D. Lapham, January 3, 1956, Hoffman papers.

2 Memorandum, David F. Freeman to Members of the Board of Directors, January 16, 1956, B.D.W.P. file. See Latham, *The Communist Controversy in Washington*, pp. 344–6.

3 Memorandum, Maureen Black to W. H. Ferry, January 18, 1956, "Publicity— General, January 1956" folder, Pub. Rel. file. See Paul G. Hoffman to Robert M. Hutchins, February 9, 1956, Paul G. Hoffman folder, Personnel file.

4 Victor Riesel, "Leave Security to Professionals," Boston *Record*, January 18, 1956.

5 *The New York Times*, January 22, 1956.

6 Victor Riesel, "Why Pick an Expert with Leftist Tendencies?", New York *Mirror*, January 23, 1956. Hutchins responded to the suspicious executive committee of the ACCF:

> . . . of the nine jurors, four are representatives of the various communica-tion media, and five, a majority, represent the general public. For the four places reserved for jurors with a professional interest in the television field, we chose a theatrical producer, a theatre critic, a publisher and a TV sta-tion executive. . . . Mr. Bloomgarden was selected because of his recog-nized eminence in the theatrical profession. We did not inquire about Mr. Bloomgarden's previous associations in an earlier decade, nor into those of the other jurors.

Robert M. Hutchins to James T. Farrell, February 17, 1956, B.D.W.P. file.

7 See Norman E. Isaacs, "Says Press Study Not Inspired by Hutchins," *Editor and Publisher*, December 10, 1955; *The New York Times*, January 27, 1956; editorial in New York *Post*, February 5, 1956.

8 Philip Warden, "Propose New Rules for Tax-Exempt Units," Chicago *Daily Tribune*, February 2, 1956.
9 Memorandum, W. H. Ferry to the Members of the Board, December 1, 1955, B.D.W.P. file.
10 Memorandum, Joseph P. Lyford to W. H. Ferry, November 14, 1955, "Publicity—Reaction to Bd. Statement and PGH letter of Sept. 1955" folder, Pub. Rel. file.
11 Don Irwin, "Danger Is Not Yet Over, House Red Probe Says," New York *Herald Tribune*, January 18, 1956.
12 *The New York Times*, February 2, 1956.
13 W. H. Ferry to Earl Newsom, January 23, 1956, "Blacklist Project" folder, Proj. Corres. file.
14 "An automotive outfit that pours a vast amount of money into TV advertising has again reminded the agencies that there will be no relaxing of policy against putting alleged subversives on its programs." Danton Walker, "Broadway Beat," New York *Daily News*, February 1, 1956.
15 Earl Newsom to W. H. Ferry, January 30, 1956, "Blacklist Project" folder, Proj. Corres. file.
16 See Josephine Ripley, "The League of Women Voters, 'Doers . . . with a bump of curiosity,'" *Christian Science Monitor*, February 9, 1956, and Malvina Lindsay, "Defending the Right To Discuss Freedom," Washington *Post and Times-Herald*, November 21, 1955.
17 Minutes, February 15, 1956.
18 Memorandum, Walter Millis to W. H. Ferry, undated (stamped received on January 16, 1956), "Publicity General, January 1956" folder, Pub. Rel. file. Herbert Philbrick called the handbook "definitive." Herbert A. Philbrick, "What Individuals Can Do About Communism," New York *Herald Tribune*, March 4, 1956. For the New York *Daily News*'s reaction to the Fund's refusal, see its editorial, March 19, 1956.
19 Memorandum, DJC to BMW [Bethuel Webster] and FRV, February 13, 1956, B.D.W.P. file.
20 Don Ross, "Legion Head Would 'Deter' Hutchins from Spending Ford Fund Principal," New York *Herald Tribune*, February 19, 1956.
21 Francis E. Walter to Bethuel M. Webster, March 5, 1956; Bethuel M. Webster to Francis E. Walter, March 7, 1956, B.D.W.P. file.
22 Memorandum, Robert M. Hutchins to the Members of the Board of Directors, March 12, 1956, ibid.
23 Interview with Frank K. Kelly, September 30, 1965. "Kelly said to me a few weeks after his hiring: 'I feel like I've been hired by Amalgamated Lepers of America to make them popular.'" Interview with John Cogley, July 18, 1966.
24 Memorandum, Robert M. Hutchins to the Members of the Board of Directors, March 22, 1956, B.D.W.P. file.
25 It was understood, however, that "All officers will . . . be expected to be informed on all aspects of the work of the Fund. . . . In view of the large volume of work and the small size of the organization, it is desirable that flexibility be retained." Ibid.
26 Interview with Frank K. Kelly, June 25, 1965.
27 Minutes, March 22, 1956; interview with John Cogley, July 18, 1966.
28 Minutes, March 22, 1956.
29 New York *Daily News*, May 10, 1956.
    The board chose not to distribute *"Cross-Currents*, a book by Arnold Forster and Benjamin R. Epstein. . . . A 400-page 'report' sponsored by the Anti-

Defamation League of B'nai B'rith on the spread of anti-Semitism and 'professional intolerance' during the last half-decade and the relation of this 'hate movement' to the area of civil liberties." "Recommendations to the Board," March 9, 1956, B.D.W.P. file.

30 Paul G. Hoffman to Henry Ford II, March 26, 1956, Hoffman papers. The board was presented with a draft of this letter at its March 22 meeting.

31 Henry Ford II to Paul G. Hoffman, April 11, 1956, B.D.W.P. file.

32 "Letters re Fund to Ford Motor Company," May 15–16, 1956, ibid.; memorandum, Joseph P. Lyford to Frank K. Kelly, May 11, 1956, "Publicity—General, May 1956" folder, Pub. Rel. file.

33 Interview with Frank K. Kelly, September 30, 1965. Ford inaccurately referred to the letters as "public correspondence which we have received expressing disapproval of the Fund for the Republic." Henry Ford II to Paul G. Hoffman, September 5, 1956, "Ford Letters 1956" folder, Pub. Rel. file.

34 Frank K. Kelly to Forest Murden, May 18, 1956; Frank K. Kelly to Henry Ford II, June 20, 1956; Henry Ford II to Paul G. Hoffman, September 5, 1956, ibid.

For a letter by Henry Ford II to southern Ford dealers virtually repudiating actions by the Fund *and* the Ford Foundation (under attack for a grant to the NAACP), and assuring the businessmen that "it is not Ford Motor Company policy to attempt, directly or indirectly, to influence the personal affairs of Southerners . . ." see memorandum, W. H. Ferry to Frank K. Kelly, Joseph P. Lyford, Robert M. Hutchins, and David F. Freeman, May 20, 1957, F folder, Basic Issues General file (hereafter referred to as B.I. General file).

35 The officers withdrew a recommendation for $125,000 to advance the cost of preparing a screenplay for a new version of "The Birth of a Nation" after discussion with the executive committee. Minutes, May 15, 1956.

36 "Supplemental Recommendation," May 14, 1956, B.D.W.P. file. The executive committee on the 15th appropriated $38,000 for five more issues at 100,000 copies each. Minutes, May 15, 1956.

37 *Congressional Record*, 84th Cong., 2d Sess., 1956, 102, A3718.

38 HUAC was after the Fund's complete minutes. See memorandum, DJC to BMW [Bethuel Webster], May 7, 1956, "Publicity—General, May 1956" folder, Pub. Rel. file.

39 Philadelphia *Inquirer*, May 1, 1956.

40 Two photo-stories, one on the freedom agenda activities in the Chicago area, and the other on the Concord Park project in Philadelphia, wrere already completed from funds appropriated March 22. "Proposed Public Information Program," May 2, 1956, B.D.W.P. file.

41 This resulted officially from a recommendation by Frank Kelly, a former employee, who disclaimed any financial interest in the agency and went on to cite Mr. Fitzgerald's "deep interest" in and "background of knowledge" of the Fund's work. Minutes, May 16, 1956. "The board thought it would add stature to our name by having an established public-relations agency working for us." Interview with Joseph P. Lyford, February 4, 1966.

42 Memorandum, Robert M. Hutchins to Members of the Board of Directors, May 4, 1956, "B.I. General" folder, Basic Issues file (hereafter referred to as B.I. file).

43 On the easing of tensions, see American Civil Liberties Union, *36th Annual Report of the American Civil Liberties Union, July 1, 1955, to June 30, 1956* (New York, 1956), passim; L. Brent Bozell, "National Trends," *National Review*, November 19, 1955, p. 12; a speech by Elmer Davis, *The New York Times*, December 17, 1955. For specific examples see Anthony Lewis, "Army

Eases Code in Security Cases," ibid., April 28, 1956; Anthony Lewis, "A.E.C. Eases 'Risk' Rules; Will Question Informants," ibid., May 10, 1956. On the Coast Guard's revision of its security-screening regulations, see San Francisco *Chronicle*, April 26, 1956.

44 Murray Marder, "U.S. Has Moved Far from Loyalty Hysteria of '54," Washington *Post and Times-Herald*, February 12, 1956.

45 Paul Hoffman later appointed George Shuster, Meyer Kestnbaum, and Howard Marshall to serve on the *ad hoc* committee. Shuster was its chairman. Minutes, May 16, 1956.

CHAPTER ELEVEN /

1 "Address by Paul G. Hoffman, Bernard M. Baruch School of Business and Public Administration, The City College Baruch Lecture, New York, New York, May 15, 1956," B.D.W.P. file.

2 Once Hoffman wrote to the Attorney General of the United States, an old friend, urging him to read a speech Lewis had publicly misinterpreted. Paul G. Hoffman to Herbert Brownell, May 22, 1956, Paul G. Hoffman folder, Personnel file.

3 Lewis was desperate: "It might be mentioned also that Mr. Paul Hoffman was head of the ECA, as President Truman's appointee, from 1948 to 1950, the foreign economic aid giveaway program, and left that organization in such shape that it finally had to be abolished." Radio Reports, Inc., "Lewis Enlarges on Hoffman's Connection with Fund and Ford Foundation, Fulton Lewis, Jr., at 7:00 P.M. over WOR (N.Y.) and the MBS Network," May 3, 1956.

4 Ibid, "Discusses Possible Hoffman Appointment to U.N., Fulton Lewis, Jr., at 7:00 P.M. over WOR (N.Y.) and the MBS Network," June 4, 1956.

5 Cf. Alistair Cooke, *A Generation on Trial: U.S.A. v. Alger Hiss* (New York, 1952), passim.

6 Goldman, *The Crucial Decade—and After*, p. 293.

7 Radio Reports, Inc., "Styles Bridge Protests Hoffman Appointment to U.N., Fulton Lewis, Jr., at 7:00 P.M. over WOR (N.Y.) and the MBS Network," May 23, 1956.

8 *Congressional Record*, 84th Cong., 2d Sess., 1956, 9552–5.

9 Radio Reports, Inc., "Lewis Attacks Possible Wyzanski Appointment to U.N., Fulton Lewis, Jr., at 7:00 P.M. over WOR (N.Y.) and the MBS Network," June 11, 1956.

10 Anthony Lewis, "Investigation of Fund for Republic Announced by House Committee," *The New York Times*, June 11, 1956. Walter had mailed a letter to Hutchins informing him of the hearings, but sent it to Pasadena and it did not catch up with the intended recipient until after the story appeared. Robert M. Hutchins to Francis E. Walter, June 15, 1956, B.D.W.P. file.

11 Press release, Committee on Un-American Activities, June 7, 1956, "Publicity—General, June 1956" folder, Pub. Rel. file.

12 New York *Journal American*, June 12, 1956.
13 Washington *Post and Times-Herald*, June 22, 1956.
14 Lewis, "Investigation of Fund for Republic," *The New York Times*, June 11, 1956.
15 Chicago *Sun-Times*, June 12, 1956.
16 Frank K. Kelly, "The Press and the Fund for the Republic," *Nieman Reports*, January, 1957, p. 8. The handbook may in part explain the hearings. It was discussed on March 5 when, after a three-and-a-half-month wait, Bethuel Webster had an interview with a perturbed Francis Walter. Even before that, on January 19, an officer of the American Legion inquired about a rumor of a $250,000 grant for a "comprehensive study of existing immigration laws." Hutchins replied correctly that an appropriation, not to exceed $20,000, had been authorized "to assist in the publication and distribution of a proposed handbook on immigration law," but that the handbook was still in the discussion stage. Lee R. Pennington to Robert M. Hutchins, January 19, 1956; Robert M. Hutchins to Lee R. Pennington, January 30, 1956, B.D.W.P. file; Fund for the Republic, *Bulletin*, "Congressman Walter Investigates," September 1956 (hereafter referred to as *Bulletin*).
17 See Donner, *The Un-Americans*, pp. 50–3.
18 Ibid., p. 65. See the editorial "Off to a Fast News Leak," New York *Herald Tribune*, June 20, 1957.
19 Arens promised to supply the names of committee witnesses in advance and declared that cross-examination would not be permitted. By the 15th, when Hutchins replied to Walter, no names had been furnished. *Bulletin*. They never were.
20 Robert M. Hutchins to Francis E. Walter, June 15, 1956, B.D.W.P. file.
21 Interview with Frank K. Kelly, November 22, 1965. For comments by a participant, see Frederic W. Collins, "Fund for Republic Operations Make It Target for Red Hunters," Providence *Journal*, June 24, 1956.
22 Walter "said preliminary staff work had gone slower than expected. No pressure has been exerted on him to call off the investigation, he added." *The New York Times*, June 21, 1956. House Speaker Sam Rayburn implied to his old friend Jubal R. Parten that he had caused the postponement after hearing from an aide of Congressman Walter's plans to deny the Fund a hearing. At Rayburn's insistence, Walter granted Parten an interview, did most of the talking, and left after ten minutes. Rayburn expressed confidence that the Fund would be allowed to present its case before the committee. Interview with Jubal R. Parten, February 9, 1966. See comments by Arens in Washington *Post and Times-Herald*, June 22, 1956. See also Willard Edwards, "Insists Fund for Republic To Be Probed," Chicago *Daily Tribune*, June 23, 1956. Edwards reported that J. Addington Wagner had declined to testify before HUAC and contended that this was a major cause of the postponement.
23 A reporter from the hostile New York *Daily News* mixed the dates slightly and asserted that the postponement of the hearings "was announced shortly after advance copies of the Fund report were circulated in Washington." John Desmond, "Fund for Republic Tells Work, Aims," New York *Daily News*, June 22, 1956. This error was corrected in the Washington *Post and Times-Herald*, June 22, 1956.
24 The introduction was unsigned but was obviously written by Hutchins, and was so identified by *The New York Times*. See Russell Porter, "Hutchins Reports on Fund's 3 Years," *The New York Times*, June 22, 1956.
25 *Three Years' Report*, p. 11.

26 Richard F. Shepard, "3 TV Shows Win Sherwood Prizes," *The New York Times*, June 23, 1956.

27 Radio Reports, Inc., "Calls Hoffman Part of 'Third State Department,' Fulton Lewis, Jr., at 7:00 P.M. over WOR (N.Y.) and the MBS Network," June 21, 1956.

28 Boston *Post*, August 12, 1956.

29 *The New York Times*, June 22, 1956.

30 *Bulletin.*

31 Also approved for distribution (subject to approval by counsel) were two books on race relations—*Success Story*, by David Loth and Harold Fleming, and *The Negro Potential*, by Eli Ginzburg—an address by Dag Hammarskjold on the Bill of Rights, and a half-hour television film on integration by San Francisco's Council for Civic Unity, entitled "Barrier." Minutes, June 22, 1956.

32 Robert Williams, "Radio Humorist Sues for $1½ Million over AWARE 'Blacklist,' " New York *Post*, June 18, 1956. For the complete story see John Henry Faulk, *Fear on Trial* (New York, 1964), passim.

33 Will Lissner, "Actor Blacklist Found Powerful," *The New York Times*, June 25, 1956. Cf. Sidney Hook, "Wanted, an Ethics of Employment for Our Time," New York *Herald Tribune*, July 22, 1956.

34 Cf. Jack Gould, "Report on Blacklisting," *The New York Times*, July 1, 1956.

35 John Cogley, *Report on Blacklisting I. Movies* (New York, 1956), pp. 196–233. For a moving account of HUAC's first successful assault in the motion-picture industry in 1947–8 see Murray Kempton, *Part of Our Time* (New York, 1955), pp. 184–210.

36 New York *World-Telegram and Sun*, June 25, 1956.

37 *Congressional Record*, 84th Cong., 2d Sess., 1956, 10910; *The New York Times*, June 26, 1956.

38 New York *Journal American*, June 27, 1956.

39 Kelly, "The Press and the Fund for the Republic," pp. 12–13; Frank K. Kelly to Seymour Berkson, June 28, 1956, "Blacklist Project" folder, Proj. Corres. file.

40 *The New York Times*, July 2, 1956.

41 New York *Herald Tribune*, June 29, 1956; Kelly, "The Press and the Fund for the Republic," p. 9.

42 Press release, Fund for the Republic, June 28, 1956. In the foreward Paul Hoffman had written that while Cogley "accepts responsibility for this report as its director and author, the Board of the Fund for the Republic wishes to state its full confidence in the calm deliberation which he has given to its preparation. We believe he has done a thorough job in a very difficult field." Cogley, *Report on Blacklisting I. Movies*, pp. ix–x.

43 Press release, Fund for the Republic, June 28, 1956.

44 Frank K. Kelly to Jubal R. Parten, July 2, 1956, "Blacklist Project" folder, Proj. Corres. file.

45 Frederick Woltman, "Hutchins Hides Identity of 'Blacklist' Informant," New York *World-Telegram and Sun*, June 29, 1956. See John Cogley, *Report on Blacklisting II. Radio-Television* (New York, 1956), pp. 89–90, 116.

46 Lewis had the story a day before the United Press. Radio Reports, Inc., "Commentator Continues Series on TV-Blacklist Study, Fulton Lewis, Jr., at 7:00 P.M. over WOR (N.Y.) MBS Network," July 6, 1956; *The New York Times*, July 8, 1956.

47 Radio Reports, Inc., "John Cogley To Be First Witness Before House Committee, Fulton Lewis, Jr., at 7:00 P.M. over WOR (N.Y.) MBS Network," July 9, 1956.

48 Jacobs, *Is Curly Jewish?*, p. 230.
49 See Kemper, *Decade of Fear*, pp. 138–9.
50 Anthony Lewis, "Warren Assailed by Two Senators," *The New York Times*, June 27, 1956.
51 See the extensive coverage of the report and the editorial in *The New York Times*, July 9, 1956.
The study's disclaimer was extraordinarily protuberant:
> In accepting the generous grant for the expenses of the study from the Fund for the Republic, Inc., our Association's customary understanding was clearly expressed in writing—that the Committee was to work with complete independence. This understanding has been scrupulously regarded. No official or representative of the Fund has in any way sought to suggest or advise as to the appointments to the Committee, nor has the Fund in any way interfered with the choice of our research staff or sought to influence our findings or conclusions.

Report of the Special Committee on the Federal Loyalty-Security Program of the Association of the Bar of the City of New York (New York, 1956), p. xi.
52 Interview with Michael Harrington, March 1, 1964.
53 House Committee on Un-American Activities, *Investigation of So-Called "Blacklisting" in Entertainment Industry—Report of the Fund for the Republic, Inc.*, 84th Cong., 2d Sess., 1956, Part I, 5222 (hereafter referred to as *Blacklist Hearings*). See Gwen Gibson, "Bares Pinko Tint in Fund Report," New York *Daily News*, July 11, 1956; Jacobs, pp. 17–21.
54 *Blacklist Hearings*, Part I, 5180.
55 Quoted in Carl Beck, *Contempt of Congress: A Study of the Prosecutions Initiated by the Committee on Un-American Activities, 1945–1957* (New Orleans, 1959), p. 141. Notes Beck: "If this is the recognized sole or major purpose of an investigation the committee ceases to have any legislative function. Indeed, it assumes the characteristics of a star chamber proceeding."
56 *Blacklist Hearings*, Part I, 5221. "When Walter said this I almost jumped out of my chair. At this point I knew that the committee had defeated itself." Interview with Joseph P. Lyford, December 6, 1965. Over nine years later Lyford still knew the quotation verbatim from memory.
57 *The New York Times*, July 11, 1956.
58 Press release, Fund for the Republic, July 11, 1956.
59 See *Blacklist Hearings*, Part I, 5228–30.
60 Ibid., pp. 5235–6.
61 Ibid., p. 5253.
62 Ibid., pp. 5243, 5253.
63 Ibid., p. 5243. Miss Poe replied: "It is interesting to note that Mr. Woltman, even hiding behind Congressional immunity, doesn't say I am a Communist. This is because he knows I have never been one." *The New York Times*, July 12, 1956. For Cogley's telegram to the *Times* on the employment of Miss Poe see ibid., July 13, 1956.
64 *Blacklist Hearings*, Part I, 5254. Walter commented at the conclusion of the testimony (p. 5256): "Mr. Woltman, I want to take this opportunity to tell you publicly that you have made a great contribution in this fight for freedom and liberty."
65 Ibid., 5281. See Cogley, *Report on Blacklisting II. Radio-Television*, pp. 110–14.
66 *Blacklist Hearings*, Part I, 5257.
67 Ibid., p. 5285.

68 Ibid., 5283. For the report's findings and analysis of this procedure see especially Vol. I, pp. 126–60.
69 *Blacklist Hearings,* Part I, 5267.
70 Ibid., p. 5288. For the Cogley report's findings on Sokolsky see Vol. I, pp. 128–31, 168–9; and Vol. II, pp. 60–1, 112–4.
71 See ibid., Vol. II, pp. 92–9.
72 *Blacklist Hearings,* Part II, 5296, 5310.
73 Ibid., p. 5297.
74 Ibid., p. 5294.
75 Ibid., p. 5300.
76 Ibid., p. 5293.
77 Robert S. Morgan, "Is Ad Alley Still with a 'Blacklist'?" New York *World-Telegram and Sun,* November 7, 1958. "This comes as a surprise to Madison Ave. observers of his operation, since it was always left to appear that Mr. Hartnett was doing this more out of conviction than for profit." The Cogley Report (Vol. II, pp. 93–4) stated: "Certainly Hartnett has not grown rich on his profits, and he is a hard-working, thoroughgoing researcher."
78 *Blacklist Hearings,* Part II, 5318.
79 Ibid., p. 5316. Earlier, Brewer told a radio audience that "the previous activities of the Fund for the Republic have generally convinced the American people that they are not genuinely concerned about the Communist problem as such. They are more concerned about fighting people who fight communists." Radio Reports, Inc., "Film Head Criticizes Fund's Blacklist Study, Barry Gray at 12:00 Midnight over WMCA (N.Y.)," June 29–30, 1956.
80 *Blacklist Hearings,* Part II, 5326–7. See Jacobs, pp. 199–200.
81 Radio Reports, Inc., "Lewis Suggests His Reportorial Work on Fund Is Bearing Fruit, Fulton Lewis, Jr., at 7:00 P.M. over WOR (N.Y.) and the MBS Network," July 12, 1956.
    That same evening Mr. Walter told a Philadelphia VFW gathering: "It is peculiar that the report deals at great length with the rights of Communists but never with the rights of loyal patriotic citizens." *Congressional Record,* 84th Cong., 2d Sess., 1956, 12767.
82 See Cogley, *Report on Blacklisting II. Radio-Television,* pp. 129–42 and passim.
83 *Blacklist Hearings,* Part II, 5330.
84 Ibid., p. 5332.
85 Ibid., p. 5340.
86 Ibid., p. 5331.
87 Ibid., p. 5334.
88 Ibid., pp. 5355, 5360.
89 Ibid., p. 5365.
90 Ibid., p. 5355.
91 See ibid., pp. 5368–88. See Cogley, *Report on Blacklist II. Radio-Television,* pp. 1–21 and passim.
92 *Blacklist Hearings,* Part II, 5367–8. "Mr. Hutchins and the directors of the Fund for the Republic shrewdly disclaimed all responsibility for the 'facts' in Mr. Cogley's book on the entertainment industry. So do I."
93 Robert M. Hutchins to Francis E. Walter, July 13, 1956, B.D.W.P. file. On July 17, Hutchins sent a memorandum to each grantee asking them "to complete the record before the Committee, by submitting statements de-

scribing their experiences with the Fund. We think that it would also be useful to have such statements released to the press, so that a public record can be made on the Fund's activities." Memorandum, Robert M. Hutchins to All Grantees, July 17, 1956, ibid. Several complied.

94 *Blacklist Hearings*, Part I, 5236. See also Part II, 5343–4. "The examination of witnesses by a Congressional Committee has always been the exclusive prerogative of the Committee and its counsel." Francis E. Walter to Robert M. Hutchins, July 20, 1956, B.D.W.P. file.

95 *Congressional Record*, 84th Cong., 2d Sess., 1956, 12292. See Rovere, *Senator Joe McCarthy*, pp. 238–40.

96 *The New York Times*, July 13, 1956. This was inserted into the *Congressional Record* by New York Senator Herbert Lehman, a future Fund director. *Congressional Record*, 84th Cong., 2d Sess., 1956, 12787.

97 Washington *Post and Times-Herald*, July 13, 1956.

98 "Report on a Report," *Commonweal*, July 13, 1956, pp. 359–60. This also was placed into the *Congressional Record* by Senator Lehman. *Congressional Record*, 84th Cong., 2d Sess., 1956, 12472–3.

99 Patrick O'Donovan, "Probers of Fund's Probe Seeking Rich Red Vein," Toronto *Globe and Mail*, July 18, 1956. O'Donovan was covering the hearings for the *London Observer*.

100 *Christian Century*, July 25, 1956, pp. 867–8.

101 New York *Herald Tribune*, July 18, 1956. See Cogley, *Report on Blacklisting I. Movies*, pp. 80, 162–3.

On June 27, Walter was quoted as being " 'unalterably' opposed to what he called the kind of blacklisting aimed [by the Philadelphia Council of the American Legion] at keeping Gale Sondergaard from appearing in a play here." *The New York Times*, June 28, 1956.

102 William G. Weart, "Quaker's Discord on Award Aired," ibid., July 19, 1956.

103 House Committee on Un-American Activities, *Investigation of the Award by the Fund for the Republic, Inc.* (Plymouth Meeting, Pa.), 84th Cong., 2d Sess., July 18, 1956, p. 5457 (hereafter referred to as *Plymouth Hearings*).

104 Harry E. Sprogell [attorney for the library committee] to Francis E. Walter, July 12, 1956, B.D.W.P. file; New York *Post*, July 16, 1956.

105 Interview with Mrs. Eleanor B. Stevenson, May 9, 1966.

106 Press release, Fund for the Republic, July 17, 1956.

107 Draft, "To be signed by all Directors or by the Executive Committee in their behalf," to Francis E. Walter, undated, unsigned, "Plymouth Meeting" folder, Awards file. This draft was written in mid-August by Joseph Lyford, who attended the hearings and noted Walter's exclamation (edited out of the official record). Interview with Joseph P. Lyford, December 3, 1965. See *Plymouth Hearings*, p. 5458.

108 Press release, Fund for the Republic, July 18, 1956.

109 Radio Reports, Inc., "Fund's Awards Committee Chairman Not Given Opportunity To Testify, Night Beat at 11:20 P.M. over WIP (Philadelphia, Pa.)," July 18, 1956.

On August 21, Arens telephoned Mrs. Stevenson, inviting her to testify eight days later. Through counsel she refused, "on the grounds that her appearance to testify on a single action of the Fund could serve no useful purpose, and that it would not satisfy the repeated requests of the Fund's Directors and Officers for a full and impartial hearing before your Committee." Bethuel M. Webster to Francis E. Walter, August 22, 1956, B.D.W.P. file. .

110 "The most recent petition calling for Mrs. Knowles' dismissal contained 66 signatures of Quakers, but only 30 signers are members of Plymouth Monthly Meeting." "Plymouth Monthly Meeting," July 17, 1956, B.D.W.P. file.
111 *Plymouth Hearings,* p. 5508.
112 Ibid., pp. 5499, 5510.
113 Ibid., pp. 5481–2, 5522–4.
114 Ibid., p. 5464.
115 Ibid., p. 5478. Dr. Hutchins wrote to the Philadelphia *Inquirer,* July 23, 1956: "The directors and officers relied on Mrs. Ogden's report to satisfy themselves that the decision to retain Mrs. Knowles was taken with deliberation and on conscientious grounds. The directors did not attempt to make an independent judgment of Mrs. Knowles' qualifications, or of her loyalty."
116 Conshohocken (Pennsylvania) *Recorder,* July 26, 1956.
117 Ibid. In the same issue was a letter from Mrs. Philip Corson. Writing for the Citizens for Philbrick, she summarized their case: "The Jeanes Library committee claims this librarian should be retained because she is efficient. Alger Hiss was an efficient State Department employee. Robert Oppenheimer was an efficient Atomic Scientist. Communists make a specialty of being efficient."
118 Ibid.
119 Easton (Pennsylvania) *Express,* August 3, 1956.

CHAPTER TWELVE

1 *National Review* editor William F. Buckley, Jr., sent postcards to his subscribers apologizing for the "clerical accident." Frank K. Kelly to Paul G. Hoffman, July 31, 1956, Hoffman papers.
2 Senate opposition consisted of sixteen Republicans, five southern Democrats, and Senator Frear of Delaware; it was by and large the very heart of the McCarthyite claque in the Upper House, including such later seekers of Republican greatness as Everett Dirkson and Barry Goldwater. Debate on the nomination is in *Congressional Record,* 84th Cong., 2d Sess., 1956, 13513–23, 13638–42, 13648–9. A major plank in the opposition's case was the false contention that Hoffman supported entrance by Communist China into the United Nations. Senator Jenner included Hoffman's association with the Fund in his objections. The Fund was, he said, "engaged in propaganda to soften American public opinion in the direction of further appeasement."
3 Ibid., pp. 14328–9.
4 Ibid., p. 13459. Congressman Henry S. Reuss of Wisconsin inserted portions of the *Three Years' Report.* Ibid., pp. A5912–13.
5 Ibid., p. A6295.
6 *The New York Times,* July 31, 1956.
7 Frank K. Kelly to Paul G. Hoffman, July 31, 1956, Hoffman papers.
8 Frank K. Kelly to R. P. Brandt, July 31, 1956, ibid.
9 Frank K. Kelly to Paul G. Hoffman, July 31, 1956, ibid.
10 *The New York Times,* August 4, 1956.
11 Frank K. Kelly to Paul G. Hoffman, August 6, 1956, Hoffman papers.

Public-relations staff member Joseph P. Lyford traveled often throughout this period, visiting newspaper editors and talking about the Fund. Interview with Joseph P. Lyford, December 6, 1965.

12 The American Civil Liberties Union also distributed widely a letter to *The New York Times* by its executive director, criticizing HUAC and its recent encounter with the Fund. Alan Reitman to W. H. Ferry, August 3, 1956, "Publicity—General, August 1956" folder, Pub. Rel. file.

13 *Congressional Record,* 84th Cong., 2d Sess., 1956, 15030. Stennis also called upon the Treasury Department to reconsider the tax exemption of the Educational and Scholarship Fund, Inc., of the NAACP.

14 *The New York Times,* August 7, 1956.

15 Radio Reports, Inc., "Lewis Supports Stennis Attack on Fund, Fulton Lewis, Jr., at 7:00 P.M. over WOR (N.Y.) and MBS Network," August 6, 1956.

16 Bethuel M. Webster to Robert M. Hutchins, July 26, 1956, B.D.W.P. file.

17 Telegram, Bethuel Webster to Francis E. Walter, August 7, 1956, "Blacklist Project" folder, Proj. Corres. file.

18 Robert M. Hutchins to Sam Rayburn, August 7, 1956, ibid.

19 *The New York Times,* August 10, 1956.

20 See *The Plymouth Meeting Controversy,* pp. 11–12, 33–5, and Appendix 4. See also Joseph P. Lyford, "Un-Americanism Among the Quakers," *New Republic,* August 27, 1956, pp. 13–16.

21 *The New York Times,* August 15, 1956. See George Shuster's letter to the *Times,* ibid., August 17, 1956.

22 E.g., "I hope you will continue to give me the benefit of your criticism. I find as I get older that it is increasingly difficult for me to be an effective critic of myself." Robert M. Hutchins to Erwin Griswold, March 1, 1956, Erwin Griswold folder, Personnel file.

23 E.g., Pensacola (Florida) *Journal,* August 14, 1956.

24 Minutes, August 14, 1956.

25 Bethuel Webster to Robert M. Hutchins, July 26, 1956, B.D.W.P. file.

26 St. Louis *Post-Dispatch,* August 31, 1956. Fund bulletins for May, June, and September 1956 were mailed in quantities of 100,000 each. Four issues of leaflets entitled "Fund Facts" each received printings of 100,000 as well. "Progress Report," August 30, 1956, B.D.W.P. file.

27 Hartford *Courant,* August 31, 1956.

28 *The New York Times,* August 30, 1956.

29 Gladwin Hill, "Legion Criticizes U.S. on Benefits," ibid., September 5, 1956. Earlier, resolutions attacking the Fund were passed by Illinois and Maryland legionnaires, who requested removal of its tax exemption. Chicago *Daily News,* August 2, 1956; Baltimore *Sun,* August 24, 1956.

  Wagner's successor, W. C. "Dan" Daniel of Virginia, was soon telling a television network audience that the Fund was "Very definitely" soft on Communism. "I think it promotes the Communist conspiracy in this country." Radio Reports, Inc., "Legion Commander Calls Fund Evil, Reporter's Roundup at 4:30 P.M. over the Mutual Television Network," September 23, 1956. Nine months later an all-Negro chapter of the American Legion unanimously passed a resolution demanding Daniel's resignation for allegedly making racist remarks before the Georgia House of Representatives. Los Angeles *Herald-Dispatch,* June 27, 1957.

30 *The New York Times,* September 7, 1956.

31 W. R. Hearst, Jr., to Paul G. Hoffman, September 12, 1956, Paul G. Hoffman folder, Personnel file.

32 E.g., Stephen Fitzgerald to Paul G. Hoffman, September 26, 1956, ibid.; Paul G. Hoffman to W. R. Hearst, Jr., October 1, 1956, Hoffman papers.

33 In addition, the sum of $20,000 was added to the popular education project approved on May 15, and an interest-free loan of $10,000 was made to the Theatre of Life, Inc., to complete a film on Navajo Indians. Minutes, September 13, 1956.

34 Basil L. Walters, "Gadfly Hutchins Needs a Mirror," Chicago *Daily News,* September 24, 1956.

35 Hutchins, *Freedom, Education, and the Fund,* pp. 219–20.

36 E.g., John Oakes, "A Non-Conformist Conscience," *The New York Times,* October 14, 1956; Mary Bingham, "Robert Hutchins as the Goad of Apathy," Louisville *Courier-Journal,* October 30, 1956; Kirschten, "Mind of Bob Hutchins," St. Louis *Post-Dispatch,* December 2, 1956. Neither the Hearst nor Scripps-Howard newspapers reviewed the book.

37 Robert M. Hutchins, *Education for Freedom* (New York, 1943), p. 91.

38 The details of this paragraph are documented within the following folders of the F.F. file: "Fund for Advancement of Education (C. Faust)," "Adler, Mortimer S.," "Hoffman, Paul G.," "The Institute for Philosophical Research," and "London Conference—May 4–8, 1953 (Fund for the Advancement of Education)." The best statement of Hutchins's desires is in memorandum, Robert M. Hutchins to Clarence Faust, November 7, 1951, "Fund for Advancement of Education (C. Faust)" folder, ibid.

39 "I was made a member of the staff on January 2, 1956. Before then I was on contract. After about three months I went to Hutchins to resign. Foundation life just wasn't cut out for me—reading long requests for money and so on. Hutchins said: 'If you're bored there must be a reason. I'm bored too. If we're both bored we must do something about it. Facts are boresome.'" At that point Hutchins first broached the idea of the academy to Cogley. Interview with John Cogley, July 18, 1966.

40 Memorandum, Robert M. Hutchins to Members of the Board of Directors, May 4, 1956, B.D.W.P. file.

41 Hutchins attributes the original idea of the center to Shuster. Interview with Robert M. Hutchins, January 5, 1966. See Robert M. Hutchins to George N. Shuster, March 28, 1956, George N. Shuster folder, Personnel file.

42 Kestnbaum was the only one of the three to attend a session. He was present on one day of a two-day session. Memorandum, Robert M. Hutchins to the Board of Directors, September 6, 1956.

43 "There was little discord among any of those with whom we discussed the idea. I visited [Robert S.] McNamara [Vice-President of the Ford Motor Company] at his home. He was aware of the hot winds blowing between Ford and the Fund and was pleasantly noncommittal. He wanted to know more." Interview with W. H. Ferry, December 20, 1965.

John Cogley, who attended each of the sessions and conducted interviews, was later of the opinion that "Hutchins couldn't care less what these people thought about the idea. He wanted to go before the board and drop important names." Interview with John Cogley, July 18, 1966.

44 Memorandum, Robert M. Hutchins to the Board of Directors, September 6, 1956, B.D.W.P. file.

45 Memorandum, Robert M. Hutchins to the Board of Directors, October 15, 1956, B.D.W.P. file. In two appendixes the memorandum outlined the apparatus of the Council on Foreign Relations and the Committee for Economic

Development. The letter organization featured two Fund board members among its executive committee: J. D. Zellerbach and Meyer Kestnbaum.

46 Minutes, November 15, 1956. Wealthy industrialist Zellerbach had been greatly upset by the House committee hearings, and returned his last three quarterly paychecks in November to the Fund. He was soon met with opposition when nominated to succeed Clare Booth Luce as United States ambassador to Italy. Several American Legion leaders cited his connections with "leftist" organizations like the United World Federalists and the Fund for the Republic. Fulton Lewis, Jr., asked: "If Mr. Paul Hoffman is able to successfully plant James D. Zellerbach as Ambassador to Rome [*sic*] . . . then why isn't Mr. Hoffman able to plant some of his screwball protégés in the State Department positions that are going to decide on the disposition of these economic aid funds under the Eisenhower doctrine?" He felt obliged to add that under Hoffman's leadership, "projects which the Ford Foundation made grants for in this very part of the world—the Arab countries and the Middle East—were enough to curl the hair of even an American Indian." Radio Reports, Inc., "Lewis Raps Hoffman's Service with Ford Foundation and Fund for Republic, Fulton Lewis, Jr., at 7:00 P.M. over WOR (N.Y.) and the MBS Network," January 24, 1957.

47 Roger D. Lapham to Paul G. Hoffman, October 26, 1956, Hoffman papers.

48 Memorandum, David F. Freeman and Adam Yarmolinsky, "Memorandum on the President's Recommendation of October 15," October 31, 1956, B.D.W.P. file.

49 "Freeman and I felt it our obligation to our employers—the directors—to disagree with Hutchins's proposal. We were not challenging his authority, but Hutchins was outraged by what he considered insubordination." Interview with Adam Yarmolinsky, August 31, 1967.

50 The first action pertained to Walter's nemesis, the study of policies and procedures in passport matters, approved by the board at its last annual meeting. The grant was transferred to the Association of the Bar of the City of New York Fund, Inc., due to the inability of the original grantee, the District of Columbia Bar Association, to undertake the proposed study. Minutes, November 15, 1956.

51 See New York *Herald Tribune*, November 21, 1956. Roper believes that this announcement was a critical turning point in the Fund's troubles. "The very act of Hoffman stepping down took some of the heat off the Fund. Lewis and others had been aiming at him. I was a little harder target to attack. I had had no feud with Henry Ford [II] and had given no aid to those 'damn Europeans.' I was more obscure. My election was a sign of the Fund's creeping respectability." Interview with Elmo Roper, October 29, 1965.

52 Directors Joyce and Marshall opposed the resolution on the ground that "the matter should be handled in February, in view of the large proposals for studies of basic issues which might be made at this time." Minutes, November 15, 1956.

53 William Joyce, a member of the NPA's Advisory Committee, opposed the recommendation because it "did not need financing by the Fund." Zellerbach and Roper were on the Association's board of trustees and voted for the measure. Ibid.

54 Memorandum, Joseph P. Lyford to Robert M. Hutchins and Frank K. Kelly, December 18, 1956, "Publicity—General, December 1956" folder, Pub. Rel. file.

Supreme Court Justice William O. Douglas spoke out publicly in favor of the Fund and its president in mid-December. The story, not carried widely, quoted Douglas as saying that Hutchins was "undoubtedly one of the great men of this century," a "great educator steeped in the American traditions and philosophies of academic freedom, freedom of conscience and freedom of mind." This testimony went unused by the Fund's public-relations staff, possibly because Douglas prefaced his remarks with a confession that he knew nothing of the Fund's work, "nor anything about any criticism." Arthur B. Dunbar, Jr., "Justice Douglas Hails Fund for the Republic," Providence *Journal*, December 25, 1956. "The reporter came up to me and asked what I thought. To my recollection, there was nothing prearranged about the interview." Interview with William O. Douglas, December 16, 1965.

55 "Elmo Roper . . . said the fund has asked Mr. Millis to analyze recent shifts in the party line because Communist activities 'always create problems for advocates of civil liberties.' " *The New York Times,* December 10, 1956.

56 New York *Herald Tribune,* December 10, 1956; *The New York Times,* December 10, 1956.

57 Symbolic of the harmony among the directors by this time was a letter by Erwin Griswold to Jubal R. Parten, lated December 7, which said, in part:

There have been problems on the Board of the Fund for the Republic, of course. Nevertheless, I do not believe that I have ever worked with a finer or abler group, nor with persons more dedicated to a common and important objective. The differences are as to means, but even there the differences are not really very great, looking at the matter from a broad point of view. These are all differences which can be worked out satisfactorily, I think, if we give them sufficient time and thought.

Personal files of Jubal R. Parten.

58 Radio Reports, Inc., "Finds Quaker Stand in Knowles Case Untenable, Fulton Lewis, Jr., at 7:00 P.M. over WOR (N.Y.) and the MBS Network," January 25, 1957.

The conviction was later reversed by the United States Court of Appeals. *The New York Times,* June 19, 1960.

59 Robert Crater, "House Prober Blasts Republic Fund Backer," New York *World Telegram,* January 26, 1957; New York *Herald Tribune,* January 28, 1957.

60 Minutes, February 20, 1957.

61 Memorandum, Robert M. Hutchins, "Recommendations on Basic Issues," February 6, 1957, B.D.W.P. file.

62 Minutes, February 21, 1957.

63 Walter added: "Some of those people down in Philadelphia are burned up at me because I've helped expise some of their connections with this ungodly conspiracy which is menacing our way of life." Charles R. Allen, Jr., "Blocker for Dixiecrats," *Nation,* February 16, 1957, pp. 140–1.

64 Interview with Frank K. Kelly, September 30, 1965.

65 Address by Elmo Roper, American Traditions Dinner, February 21, 1957, Pub. Docs. file.

66 Bruce Catton, "The American Tradition," ibid.

67 Interview with Frank K. Kelly, June 25, 1965.

68 For many of these responses, see Hoffman folder, "Distribution Project" file. By November requests had exhausted the supply of 10,000 booklets.

James Real to George Shuster, November 4, 1957, James Real folder, Pub. Rel. file.

69 *Congressional Record,* 85th Cong., 1st Sess., 1957, A1762–4.
70 *Christian Science Monitor,* March 11, 1957.
71 New York *Herald Tribune,* March 10, 1957. The Very Reverend Francis J. Lally also issued a statement to his local newspaper in praise of the Fund. Boston *Herald,* March 8, 1957.
72 "The Missourian said Mr. Walter had not discussed with him the possibility of further public hearings this year on some of the Fund's activities." New York *Herald Tribune,* March 10, 1957.
73 Ibid. The anonymous "reporter" was Frank Kelly, permitted by the *Herald Tribune* to write the Fund's praises. Interview with Frank K. Kelly, September 30, 1965.
74 Alone among reviewers, Hook, Eastman, and Thomas, former members of the now-defunct American Committee for Cultural Freedom, failed to mention the Fund for the Republic.
75 "By a strange coincidence (yeah?), on the very day the Draper book was published the U.S. Communist Party made public its new constitution, in which it claims to have cut itself loose from the Kremlin. That is complete hooey, as J. Edgar Hoover promptly pointed out." New York *Daily News,* March 17, 1957. Cf. Robert Friedman, "Theodore Draper Writes About 'Roots of American Communism,'" *Daily Worker,* March 13, 1957.
76 Francis E. Walter to Bethuel M. Webster, March 29, 1957, B.D.W.P. file.
77 Bethuel M. Webster to Francis E. Walter, April 12, 1957, ibid.
78 Clyde Doyle to Bethuel M. Webster, April 19, 1957, ibid.
79 Bethuel M. Webster to Clyde Doyle, April 24, 1957, ibid.
80 Clyde Doyle to Bethuel M. Webster, April 26, 1957, ibid.
   A month earlier a HUAC subcommittee, chaired by Doyle, drew a formal protest to Congress by the California State Bar. Among the charges was one that Arens had referred to a lawyer accused by a witness as being a Communist as "Comrade." See Gladwin Hill, "California's Bar Protests Inquiry," *The New York Times,* March 28, 1957.
81 John Cogley to Francis E. Walter, May 3, 1957, B.D.W.P. file. Walter replied, in part: "The investigation that the Committee staff has made since your appearance before the Committee convinces me that you are not entitled to withhold the requested information from the Committee." Francis E. Walter to John Cogley, May 7, 1957, ibid.

CHAPTER THIRTEEN

1 Memorandum, "The Individual and the Trade Union," undated and unsigned, B.D.W.P. file.
2 Minutes, May 16, 1957.
3 Ibid.

4   Memorandum, Robert M. Hutchins to the Board of Directors, September 4, 1957, B.D.W.P. file; Washington *Post and Times-Herald,* September 20, 1957; Minutes, September 18, 1957. On September 18, Hallock Hoffman was elected secretary and treasurer of the corporation. Ibid.

5   The project on the mass media received an appropriation of $245,000; the study of the contemporary American political process received $113,850. See Minutes, November 21, 1957.

6   The Fund for the Republic, Inc., *Two-Year Report, May 31, 1958* (New York, 1958), p. 9.

7   *The New York Times,* July 19, 1957. Frank Kelly, Paul Hoffman, Jubal Parten, and Elmo Roper sent reproductions of the overwhelmingly favorable editorials on the basic-issues announcement to influential friends, along with personal letters. Dozens of prominent Americans responded favorably. Senator J. William Fulbright, for example, wrote to Elmo Roper: "I certainly concur with your view that there has been a much better understanding of the Fund and its objectives in recent months. Of course, I have never felt any doubt about your purposes, and when Carroll Reece or Joe McCarthy attacked you it only confirmed my confidence that you would render a worthwhile service." J. W. Fulbright to Elmo Roper, July 26, 1957, B.D.W.P. file.

8   W. H. Ferry to Mrs. Eleanor B. Stevenson, August 12, 1957, Eleanor B. Stevenson folder, Personnel file.

9   George Sokolsky, "Fund for Republic Tackles U. S. Issues," New York *Journal-American,* October 12, 1957.

10 Bethuel M. Webster to Francis E. Walter, July 2, 1957, B.D.W.P. file.

11 John Cogley, "Return Engagement," *Commonweal,* June 7, 1957, pp. 251–4.

12 Frank Kelly, form letter, May 27, 1957, "Blacklist Project" folder, Proj. Corres. file.

13 Salt Lake *Tribune,* June 6, 1957.

14 *Wall Street Journal,* June 11, 1957.

15 *Editor and Publisher,* June 1, 1957.

16 Minneapolis *Star,* June 30, 1957.

17 Gene Arneel, " 'Blacklisting' Report Still Reverberates," *Variety,* June 12, 1957.

18 *Congressional Record,* 85th Cong., 1st Sess., 1957, A6547. Humphrey inserted into the *Record* seven newspaper editorials praising the Fund for its basic-issues program. See also remarks and insertions by Senator Ralph W. Yarborough, a close friend of Jubal Parten's, in ibid, pp. A7200–2.

19 See Jack Steele, "Report Urges Fund for Republic Be Stripped of Tax-Exempt Status," Washington *News,* February 3, 1958. A spokesman for the Internal Revenue Service replied: "I don't know if anything has been done in this case." New York *Herald Tribune,* March 30, 1958.

20 Robert M. Hutchins to Francis E. Walter, February 13, 1958, B.D.W.P file.

21 Fulton Lewis, Jr., "Report May Knock FFR Out of Business," New York *Mirror,* February 26, 1958.

22 New York *Herald Tribune,* March 30, 1958; Washington *Post and Times-Herald,* March 30, 1958.

23 Ibid., May 5, 1958.

24 Interview with Jubal R. Parten, February 9, 1966.

25 Memorandum, W. H. Ferry to Robert M. Hutchins and Hallock Hoffman, August 21, 1959, "Inter-Office Correspondence, April 1958" folder, Admin. file.

26 St. Paul (Minn.) *Dispatch,* August 26, 1959.

27 Charles Bolte to W. H. Ferry, July 1, 1957, "Admin. Basic Issues (IV), From 7/1/57–8/31/57" folder, B.I. file.
28 Center for the Study of Democratic Institutions, *Report of the President, 1958–59* (Santa Barbara, 1959), p. 2.
29 "Unlike many of the Fund for the Republic's fuzzy-minded and/or subtly pro-Red publications, this booklet of Berle's strikes us as a constructive contribution to economic thinking, and we recommend it with considerable enthusiasm." New York *Daily News*, January 27, 1958.
30 Memorandum (draft), Harry S. Ashmore to the Board of Directors, November 17, 1958, B.D.W.P. file.
31 See William Haddad, "Eaton Subpoenaed, Hennings Wants Walter To Call FBI's Hoover, Too," New York *Post*, May 20, 1958; *The New York Times*, May 5, 20, 21, 30, July 1, 1958; New York *Post*, May 8, 19, 20, 22, 1958; Washington *Post and Times-Herald*, May 22, 24, 1958; "General E" folder, B.I. file.
32 Press release, Fund for the Republic, "Can a Free Society Survive? An address by Robert M. Hutchins to the Cleveland City Club, Cleveland, Ohio, March 22, 1958."
33 Elmo Roper to Robert M. Hutchins, July 9, 1957, "Admin. Basic Issues (IV), From 7/1/57–10/31/57" folder, ibid.
34 Mortimer Adler to Robert M. Hutchins, October 9, 1957, "Adm. Basic Issues, Greenbriar Meeting of 9/8–9/13" folder, ibid.
   Adler's Institute for Philosophical Research was hired to do evaluations of each of the consultants' meetings. One of Adler's staff members wrote Hutchins:

> The worst phases of the *Auseinandersetzungen* were those where the speakers felt quite free to follow the association of ideas, waited politely to bring in their own nifties, often oblivious to the importance of what they were interrupting. The result is an almost painful discontinuity, marked by brilliant insights not developed, leads not followed up, sharp discrimination of trends not exploited.

V. J. McGill to Robert M. Hutchins, October 28, 1957, ibid.
35 Memorandum, W. H. Ferry to Robert M. Hutchins, October 15, 1957; memorandum, Hallock Hoffman to Robert M. Hutchins, October 15, 1957, ibid.
36 Robert M. Hutchins to Mortimer Adler, October 16, 1957, ibid.
37 Scott Buchanan to Robert M. Hutchins, January 2, 1958, "Adm. Basic Issues (V), From 11/1/57–" folder, ibid.
38 Hallock Hoffman to Robert M. Hutchins, March 28, 1958, ibid.
39 Robert M. Hutchins to Adolf A. Berle, Jr., May 7, 1958, ibid.
40 Memorandum, Robert M. Hutchins, "Reports and Recommendations To the Board, May 6, 1958," B.D.W.P. file.
41 Minutes, May 21, 1958. Erwin Griswold finally resigned on November 19, 1958, stating that he "had wanted to do so only in such a way and at such a time that his resignation could not be subject to unfavorable inference by persons outside the Fund." Minutes, November 19, 1958.
42 *The New York Times*, October 17, 1958.
43 See correspondence between the two in "Adm. Basic Issues (V), From 11/1/57—" folder, B.I. file. Douglas became a consultant, though no announcement of his membership was made public. He accepted no money, attended but one meeting, and contributed little.
44 Memorandum, Robert M. Hutchins, "Report and Recommendations to the Board," May 7, 1959, B.D.W.P. file.

45 Minutes, May 20, 1959. The Fund began investing large sums of its remaining resources in May 1958. A few months later the corporation announced
its probable demise in 1961, in the vain hope of attracting foundation support. See John G. Rogers, "Fund for Republic May End in '61, Money
Gone," New York *Herald Tribune*, July 21, 1958.

46 Robert M. Hutchins to Bertrand de Jouvenel, August 13, 1959, Bertrand
de Jouvenel folder, Basic Issues General file; Santa Barbara *News-Press*, June
4, 5, 1959.

47 *The New York Times*, September 22, 1959.

48 Scott Buchanan was the exception; he moved to Santa Barbara and became
a permanent resident at the Center.

49 Memorandum, W. H. Ferry to Robert M. Hutchins, September 24, 1959,
General folder, Basic Issues General file.

50 W. H. Ferry to Stuart Chase, October 20, 1959, Stuart Crase folder, ibid.

51 Edward Reed to Lindsay Rogers, December 2, 1959, "General Pub. Dist.
1959 to 1960" folder, Distribution file.

52 *Report of the President 1958–59*, p. 5.

53 The Fund for the Republic, *Bulletin*, November 1959.

CHAPTER FOURTEEN /

1 See New York *Post*, November 26, 1956.

2 See *The New York Times*, January 10, 1956.

3 See Harry Kalven, Jr.'s, review in *Journal of Legal Education*, 10 (1957),
141–6. See also Macdonald, *The Ford Foundation*, p. 72.

4 Radio Reports, Inc., "All About Men, at 2:00 P.M. over WRCA-TV (N.Y.),"
August 9, 1956.

5 Kalven in *Journal of Legal Education*, p. 145.

6 Interview with Scott Buchanan, January 3, 1966.

7 See, for example, Thomas C. Reeves, "Foundations in Blinders: The Cool
Billions," *Nation*, April 4, 1966, pp. 381–5.

8 Memorandum, Paul Jacobs to Robert M. Hutchins, December 9, 1955, "Publicity—General, December 1955" folder, Pub. Rel. file.

9 *Report of the President, 1958–59*, Appendix. The Fund's president lamented
in early 1956:

It does cost a good deal of money to give away money intelligently and
one of the most distressing parts of it all is that it costs about as much
money to give away $25,000 intelligently as it does to give away $5,000,000
or $1,000,000 intelligently. In this field where you may not seek to in-
fluence legislation, where you may not conduct propaganda, where you've
got to be absolutely sure that you are engaging the most competent people
to do the most careful job, it takes a good deal of money to give away
the funds that the Fund for the Republic has. I don't see any way out of it.
Radio Reports, Inc., "Interviews Dr. Robert Hutchins of Fund for the Re-

public, Tex and Jinx McCrary at 10:35 P.M. over WRCA (N.Y.)," January 30, 1956.

Particularly relevant to the percentage figure in the text are directors' salaries, the time spent in setting up the Fund, a large legal fee paid Bethuel Webster's legal firm at the insistence of certain board members, the amount paid the Stephen Fitzgerald agency, an extraordinarily high annual office rental in New York City, the expenses of cross-continent trips, and healthy salaries for both officers and staff members. For a valuable discussion of foundation expenses see Wright Patman, "The Free-Wheeling Foundations," *The Progressive,* June 1967, p. 28.

10 Warren Unna, "The Fund's Out To Assay Freedom," Washington *Post and Times-Herald,* December 29, 1957.

11 Memorandum, Walter Millis to Robert M. Hutchins, "Publicity—General, December 1955" folder, Pub. Rel. file.

12 For a penetrating summary and critique of the major explanations of McCarthyism see Latham, *The Communist Controversy in Washington from the New Deal to McCarthy,* pp. 408–23.

13 Note the lineup of opposition to the Hennings committee in Kemper, *Decade of Fear: Senator Hennings and Civil Liberties,* p. 129. Hennings "dismissed this type of opposition as inevitable." The Fund could not so easily ignore these same critics.

14 "There is . . . a dynamic of dissent in America today [1954]. Representing no more than a modest fraction of the electorate, it is not so powerful as the liberal dissent of the New Deal era, but it is powerful enough to set the tone of our political life and to establish throughout the country a kind of punitive reaction." Hofstadter, *The Paranoid Style in American Politics and Other Essays,* p. 43. See Hans Morgenthau, *The Purpose of American Politics* (New York, 1960), pp. 144–5.

15 Interview with Robert M. Hutchins, January 5, 1966.

16 From a promotional page in Roy, *Communism and the Churches.* The other five were: *The Roots of American Communism,* by Theodore Draper; *The Communists and the Schools,* by Robert W. Iversen; *The Decline of American Communism,* by David A. Shannon; *American Communism and Soviet Power,* by Theodore Draper; and *Marxism: The View from America,* by Clinton Rossiter.

17 The total appropriation for studies of American Communism and the revision of the bibliography was $462,500. *Two-Year Report May 31, 1958,* p. 27.

18 "Address by Paul G. Hoffman Before the Overseas Press Club of America, New York, New York, September 6, 1956," Pub. Docs. file.

19 E.g., *The New York Times,* July 9, August 24, 1956; Washington *Post and Times-Herald,* August 6, 1956; *Labor's Daily,* November 21, 1956. See Alan F. Westin, "The Security Issue: Progress Since 1952," *The New Leader,* October 8, 1956, pp. 3–6.

20 See the editorial "School Segregation Here!" *The New York Times,* November 8, 1955.

21 Unna, "The Fund's Out To Assay Freedom," Washington *Post and Times-Herald,* December 29, 1957.

22 Ibid.; "Address by Elmo Roper, Chairman of the Board of the Fund for the Republic at the Ninth Annual Conference of the Commissions Against Discrimination, Riversea Inn, Old Saybrook, Conn., June 11, 1957," Pub. Docs. file.

23 Faulk, *Fear on Trial,* p. 53. See Elizabeth Poe, "Blacklisting and Censorship

in Motion Pictures," *Mass Media*, July, 1959, pp. 14–18; Frank P. Model, "Robert Hutchins' New TV Crusade," *Television Magazine*, September, 1959, p. 55; Murray Schumach, *The Face on the Cutting Room Floor* (New York, 1964), pp. 120–9.

24 E.g., Joseph H. Baird, "Regional Council Aids South's Test," *Christian Science Monitor*, July 18, 1956; *The New York Times*, August 11, 1957; "Recommendations to the Board," May 1, 1957, B.D.W.P. file. See Chase C. Mooney, *Civil Rights: Retrospect and Prospects* (New York, 1961), pp. 13–14. For reactions of other foundations to the Southern Regional Council, see Philip M. Stern, "An Open Letter to the Ford Foundation," *Harper's Magazine*, January 1966, p. 84. The Ford Foundation, within a few weeks of this article's appearance, granted $300,000 to the Council.

25 W. W. Keeler to the writer, June 15, 1967.

26 E.g., *Labor's Daily*, April 10, 1957.

27 See Davis McEntire, *Residence and Race* (Berkeley and Los Angeles, 1960), passim.

28 *The New York Times*, February 26, 1956; "Recommendations to the Board," May 1, 1957, B.D.W.P. file.

29 *Three Years' Report*, p. 81; John M. Harrison, "How Toledo Bar Spent $10,000 Given in '55 by Fund for Republic," *Toledo Blade*, August 5, 1956.

30 "Progress Report," August 30, 1956, B.D.W.P. file; Milt Fishman [assistant news director, American Broadcasting Company] to the Fund for the Republic, Inc., August 20, 1956; Roger E. Sprague [manager, central news desk, National Broadcasting Company, Pacific Division] to George Martin, Jr., September 17, 1956; Charles Collingwood [Columbia Broadcasting System News] to George Martin, Jr., October 5, 1956, ibid.

31 "Recommendations to the Board," October 31, 1956, ibid.; *Three Years' Report*, pp. 48–9. For more on the Fund's efforts with churches, see James R. Harkins, "Education and Freedom," *The Living Church*, March 3, 1957, pp. 14–16.

32 St. Louis *Post-Dispatch*, October 26, 27, 1956; April 28, 1957. See Charles Menees, "Television Town Meeting in St. Louis," ibid., February 24, 1957.

33 See Alfred H. Kelly, ed., *Foundations of Freedom in the American Constitution* (New York, 1958), passim; Russell Turner, "The Ladies and the Pamphleteers," *American Legion Magazine*, June 1956, pp. 14–15, 57–9; *Christian Science Monitor*, May 16, 1956.

34 *Three Years' Report*, pp. 38–9.

35 Out of the 800 scripts submitted, only 35 were from professionals. The fund hired an agent to sell the winners. Jay Nelson Tuck, "On the Air," New York *Post*, March 14, 1957; *The New York Times*, June 16, 1957. See Leo Rosten, "Wanted: Men" *Harper's Magazine*, October 1957, pp. 16–18, 20.

36 Helen Dudar, "TV Won't Buy 'Controversy,' Fund for Republic Reports," New York *Post*, June 22, 1956.

37 Tuck, "On the Air," ibid., March 14, 1957. Several prints were shown on educational television. "Progress Report," February 7, 1957, B.D.W.P. file.

38 Val Adams, "$55,000 TV Prizes Awarded by Fund," *The New York Times*, June 20, 1957. By May 1958 the total appropriation for the Awards was $218,062. "General Work in Television and Radio" totaled $248,318. *Two-Year Report, May 31, 1958*, pp. 27–8.

39 "Recommendations to the Board," May 1, 1957, B.D.W.P. file.

40 Dudar, "TV Won't Buy 'Controversy'," New York *Post*, June 22, 1956.

41 Interview with Joseph P. Lyford, December 6, 1965. See Richard F. Shepard, "Men with a Script," *The New York Times*, February 24, 1957.

For a brilliant analysis of the implications of advertising as an American institution on dissent and controversy, see David M. Potter, *People of Plenty: Economic Abundance and the American Character* (Chicago, 1960), pp. 166–88.

42 *Three Years' Report*, p. 43.

43 E.g., George Tackman, "Clickin' the Channels," Richmond (California) *Independent*, February 28, 1956.

44 Jack Shanley, "TV: Documentary on Bias," *The New York Times*, June 17, 1957. The film was shown widely in the South, much to the surprise of the American Broadcasting Company. New York *Post*, June 7, 1957. For examples of the Fund's successful distribution of radio materials, see *Three Years' Report*, pp. 40–2, 44; "Progress Report," February 7, 1957, B.D.W.P. file.

45 *Two-Year Report, May 31, 1958*, p. 18.

46 Donner, *The Un-Americans*, p. 3.

47 "The Fund distributed Mr. Griswold's book because it is an outstanding, dispassionate appraisal of a much-discussed article of the Bill of Rights. The volume, it might be noted, was cited by the U.S. Supreme Court majority in the case of Slochower v. New York City Board of Education." Joseph P. Lyford to Editor, Chicago *Tribune*, May 17, 1956, "Publicity—General, May 1956" folder, Pub. Rel. file. Griswold's book would again be cited by the Court in a unanimous decision of 1957. See James Reston, "High Court Decries Assumption of Guilt in Pleading of Fifth," *The New York Times*, May 31, 1957.

   Two views of the Fifth Amendment at variance with Griswold's were also distributed by the Fund, though in lesser numbers. See *Three Years' Report*, p. 56.

48 Dial Torgerson, "Funds Gone—But Not Dr. Hutchins," Santa Barbara *News-Press*, June 1, 1964.

49 See untitled, unsigned memorandum, January 15, 1957, B.D.W.P. file; Henry M. Christman to The Honorable Earl Warren, June 13, 1958. "General C" folder, B.I. file; Frank Kelly to Chief Justice Earl Warren, June 4, 1959, ibid.

50 See Milton R. Konvitz, *Expanding Liberties: Freedom's Gains in Postwar America* (New York, 1966), pp. 91–5, 109–67; Kemper, *Decade of Fear: Senator Hennings and Civil Liberties*, pp. 142–88; American Civil Liberties Union, *Justice for All "Nor Speak With Double Tongue," 37th Annual Report of the American Civil Liberties Union, July 1, 1956 to June 30, 1957* (New York, 1957), pp. 5–13.

51 Stone, *The Haunted Fifties*, p. 199.

52 Tom Gavin, "Experts Cite Progress in Civil Liberties Field," *Rocky Mountain News*, July 6, 1957.

Index

A Note About the Author

Thomas C. Reeves was born in Tacoma, Washington, in 1936. Since receiving his doctorate in 1966 at the University of California at Santa Barbara, Mr. Reeves has been assistant professor of history at the University of Colorado. His major interests are political and constitutional questions of twentieth-century America. He is currently engaged in a full-scale study of McCarthyism. Mr. Reeves is married, has three daughters, and lives in Colorado Springs, Colorado.

A Note on the Type

The text of this book was set in Granjon, a type named in compliment to Robert Granjon, type cutter and printer—in Antwerp, Lyons, Rome, Paris—active from 1523 to 1590. The boldest and most original designer of his time, he was one of the first to practice the trade of type founder apart from that of printer.

This type face was designed by George W. Jones, who based his drawings on a type used by Claude Garamond (1510-61) in his beautiful French books, and it more closely resembles Garamond's own type than do any of the various modern types that bear his name.

Composed, printed, and bound by
The Haddon Craftsmen, Inc., Scranton, Pa.
Typography and binding design by Bonnie Spiegel